# Making Sense of Mass Education

*Making Sense of Mass Education* provides a comprehensive analysis of the field of mass education. The book presents new assessment of traditional issues associated with education – such as class, race, gender, discrimination and equity – to dispel myths and assumptions about the classroom. It employs governmental forms of analysis to better understand the role played by mass education in the management of populations; it examines the complex relationship between the media, popular culture and schooling; and it places the expectations surrounding the modern teacher within ethical, legal and historical contexts.

The book seeks to blur some of the disciplinary boundaries within the field of education, drawing upon sociology, cultural studies, history, philosophy, ethics and jurisprudence to provide stronger and more convincing analyses. Additional resources are available at www.cambridge.edu.au/academic/masseducation to aid readers' understanding of the book's content.

*Making Sense of Mass Education* reframes the sociology of education as a complex mosaic of cultural practices, forces and innovations. Accessible, engaging and contemporary, this book is an invaluable resource for pre-service teacher education students, and anyone interested in a better understanding of mass education.

**Gordon Tait** is Associate Professor in the School of Cultural and Language Studies in Education at the Queensland University of Technology.

# Making Sense of Mass Education

Gordon Tait

CAMBRIDGE UNIVERSITY PRESS
Cambridge, New York, Melbourne, Madrid, Cape Town,
Singapore, São Paulo, Delhi, Mexico City

Cambridge University Press
477 Williamstown Road, Port Melbourne, VIC 3207 Australia

Published in the United States of America by Cambridge University Press, New York

www.cambridge.org
Information on this title: www.cambridge.org/9781107660632

First published 2013
Reprinted 2013 (twice)

Cover and text design by Tanya De Silva-McKay
Typeset by Newgen Publishing and Data Services
Printed in Australia by Ligare Pty Ltd

*A catalogue record for this publication is available from the British Library*

*A Cataloguing-in-Publication entry is available from the catalogue
of the National Library of Australia at* www.nla.gov.au

ISBN 978-1-107-66063-2 Paperback

Additional resources for this publication at www.cambridge.edu.au/academic/masseducation

This book has been printed on paper certified by
the Programme for the Endorsement of Forest
Certification (PEFC). PEFC is committed to
sustainable forest management through third party
forest certification of responsibly managed forests.
For more info: www.pefc.org

For all the students I've laughed
with over the last 30 years.

# Contents

# Contents

# Contents

# Contents

# Acknowledgements

I would like to thank Cambridge University Press for giving me the opportunity to write this book, for allowing me to shape it pretty much as I wished, and for not badgering me when the scheduling started to slip. In particular, I would like to thank Nina Sharpe for guiding me through the process with patience and good humour.

I would like to thank all of the anonymous reviewers who appraised each section of the book in turn, and whose positive comments gave me the confidence to stay on the same track. I was given some excellent advice, which I tried to incorporate as best I could, in the time and space available.

I would like to thank my colleagues at Queensland University of Technology, especially my Dean, Professor Wendy Patton, and my Head of School, Professor Annette Patterson, for giving me the professional latitude to complete the book. Thanks also to my other colleagues for sharing their company, and their ideas, with me over the years, and for keeping my spirits up while putting this book together.

Finally, I would like to thank my generous partner, Professor Belinda Carpenter, an excellent editor, who has taken the time to read and comment upon every word of this book – while at the same time writing her own book, which I did not read or comment upon.

# Introduction

## Making sense of mass education

One of the many exasperating things about our education system is that it keeps changing: how we think it works, what we think it seeks to accomplish, and what we think its consequences are. It certainly isn't like the study of human anatomy, where a book from the 1920s will still give a pretty accurate account of how the human body works, and what goes where. A book on education from the same era is unlikely to make any mention of many of the issues we now consider to be of importance. Take, for example, Sechrist's (1920) *Education and the General Welfare*. With chapters on 'School Attendance' and 'Why Children are Dull', the focus was firmly on the pragmatics of how to make a school function effectively.

By the 1950s however, new ways of thinking about schools had emerged. Concerns did not necessarily begin and end with educational efficiency, but also sought to address the relationship between schools and society. The influential theorist Parsons, in his book *The Social System* (1951), regarded education as a vital component within a complex machine, and this was a machine that needed 'dull children' to do dull work. This wasn't a seen as problem; this was part of the design. Society was a finely tuned instrument, and education helped its cogs turn.

The average book on education soon changed its focus again. Henry et al.'s (1988) *Understanding Schooling* was far more interested in the relationship between education and social power – as in the myth of our 'meritocratic' education system, and in the way class, gender and race directly correlated with schooling success – than it was on society as a 'finely tuned instrument'. Finely tuned for whom? There was nothing in this book about 'why children are dull', rather the emphasis was on why our system seems to confuse 'dull' with 'disadvantaged'.

What about today? Do any of these approaches to education still have currency? After all, some children probably *are* dull; society *is* complex; and the notion of a genuine 'meritocracy' *is* rather dubious. What kind of approach ought we to take, and what issues should be covered? In the second decade of the twenty-first century, what should a general book on education look like?

Hopefully, it should look rather like this one.

## Changing contexts of education

The world serviced by our contemporary education system is very different from the one written about by Sechrist in 1920; consequently, the anxieties we now have about how our schools work – and who gets to benefit – are also very different. Certainly, we are no longer concerned about education for racial or national efficiency, or for the glory of the British Empire, as we were a hundred years ago. We now have a variety of other concerns, as evidenced by a series of debates about the state and direction of Australian education. There are now debates over levels of funding for public education, and the ongoing flight of the middle classes into the private school system. There are concerns over standardisation, and the relentless imperative to collect data and rank schools. Some newspapers continually tell us that our schools have lost their way, and that we should return to traditional educational techniques and philosophies, ones based upon tried and trusted truths of yesterday. There are also worries about the levels of difference – physical, intellectual and even cultural – that schools should be required to accommodate. Should we return to the logic of the special school?

These debates raise a number of questions, but one is particularly important: How do we approach such dilemmas conceptually? Or to put it another way: Is there a single theoretical model that can help us make sense of these problems, or do we have to address them on an issue-by-issue, case-by-case basis? This question has wider implications, not just about understanding specific changes and tensions within the institutions of mass schooling, such as the ones outlined above, but also about how to make sense of contemporary education in the broadest of ways.

Arguably, almost every general work dealing with the sociology and philosophy of education has attempted to answer this question, and this book will add to that tradition. However, this is not intended as just an updated repetition of previous approaches, which have tended to take one of three forms: first, some have taken a single approach, for example critical theory as in Henry et al.'s book. This is fine if that approach is stated explicitly, right upfront (which it was). Otherwise, the book is in danger of passing off a particular perspective as the singular, unequivocal and uncontested truth of the matter – which isn't very honest. Second, some books have appeared to take no specific approach at all, in which case they are either kidding themselves, or their readers. All sociological analyses – and for that matter, all histories and all philosophies, in fact, probably all forms of knowledge – come from a particular perspective; the trick is to know what it is, and again, to be honest about it. Finally, others still employ a mishmash of theories, either because they don't realise it, because they hope no one will notice it, or because they are trying to be all things for everyone.

This book adopts none of these forms, instead presenting a number of different approaches, which are placed in relation to each other, and which are shown to offer specific kinds of advantages (and disadvantages), to answer questions in particular kinds of ways, and to be useful in addressing given kinds of problems. As such, the intention has not been simply to produce an updated version of previous books on Australian education, it has been to offer something new altogether, and hopefully, to keep moving the analysis onwards.

# Some problems with modernist sociologies

But what exactly is *onwards*? One of the wonderful things about modernism was that we used to be able to answer that question without hesitation; now it's nowhere near as straightforward. If anyone needs reminding, modernity is generally regarded as beginning in the final years of the eighteenth century, at the end of the Enlightenment. Lasting some 200 years, this was an era characterised by the underpinning belief that through the use of reason, it would be possible to solve humanity's problems. With its mantra of truth, objectivity and progress, and under the banner of its greatest exemplar – science – society now was to be free of the superstitions and dogmas that had previously decided our fates; humanity had come of age.

Unfortunately, towards the end of the twentieth century an increasing number of voices pointed to some significant problems with this optimistic narrative. It was suggested that the modernist project had failed, and that we had entered a new era, the era after modernity: that of postmodernity. By rejecting the grand narratives of modernism, postmodernists such as Lyotard (1984) and Baudrillard (1993) seek to describe a world characterised not by truth and progress, but by many different truths, and by the belief that history is not synonymous with progress, such that all we could really make claim to was 'change'. Other writers, most notably Giddens (1990, 1991), while reluctant to call time on modernity altogether, argue instead that we have simply entered a period of late modernity (an era still largely modernist, but now characterised by continual crisis, and a greater scepticism toward the power of reason). These writers still seek to question the belief that we are making 'progress' in any manageable way.

And therein lies part of the problem with the notion of onwards. Though we aren't necessarily convinced that we are making theoretical progress in any real sense, certainly approaches to education have largely mirrored the broader move from modernism to postmodernism. Therefore, if 'moving the analysis onwards' means anything, in the context of this book, it means precisely that.

Most books on education revolve around explanatory features characteristic of modernist sociologies – most notably class, gender and race. The idea here is that these three elements represent objective 'facts' about how our society is structured, and its populations ranked and organised. This logic suggests that when we understand how these three social axes work, we will be able to account for their effects and solve the problem. This book will take a somewhat different approach.

# Beyond modernist sociologies of education

This book will begin by addressing these three familiar conceptual axes, but then extend the analysis into a more postmodern interpretation of each of the same generalised notions. For example, when discussing issues of the relationship between schooling and gender, modernist accounts have stressed the role played by patriarchy – the global system of male domination – in the ongoing educational subordination of women. Such second-wave feminist accounts have now been replaced by more nuanced, less deterministic explanations of the same generalised area, and those will be discussed here.

This is not the only way of altering the focus on education, of moving the analysis onwards. There is an alternative tradition of analysis that largely avoids the modern/postmodern dichotomy, one based around Foucault's work on governance. Rather than concentrating on issues of power and inequality, this paradigm focuses instead upon the techniques and practices by which we are shaped as particular types of individual, and by which we have our conduct regulated. From the early nineteenth century onwards, the school has had a central role to play in producing a disciplined and docile population, in producing the categories of difference necessary to permit effective, targeted social management, and latterly, even providing the primary site for the governance of students' subjective experience.

This book will not only address the broadest issues within education, it will also attempt to understand education's place within a complex and changing society, and supply the conceptual tools for providing non-reductionist accounts of a number of contemporary cultural forms. Whether addressing the effects of the news media, or of popular culture, or how digital technologies are reshaping both the classroom and the capacities of the people in them, arguably many previous attempts to describe the relationship between these issues and our education system have relied upon modernist binaries to provide their foundation. This book will not do so.

The overall intention here is to provide the best possible tools for making sense of mass education, however the tools available within sociology and cultural studies are not the only ones on offer. If we are to understand the ideas that have animated education over the last 2500 years – or more importantly, if we are to recognise which of these ideas still have currency within contemporary mass education and how those ideas are operationalised – then the discipline of philosophy is required. Arguably, philosophy's utility also extends beyond these issues, into assessments of schooling, ethics and the law, as well as understanding the educational legacy of Australia's status as a former British colony.

# The structure of the book

This book is organised in a somewhat unusual way, both in the way the chapters are located within four distinct parts (each with a different focus and theoretical alignment), and in terms of the structure of the chapters. All 12 chapters are organised in the same way: they are based around a number of familiar myths common to popular discourses on the topic in question. For example, Chapter 1 on social class is based around three myths: 'Australia is a society characterised by equality', 'Schooling success is only about individual ability', and 'Social class is all about money'. In the process of debunking these statements, it is also possible to ascertain what each different approach to understanding mass education can offer us.

Part 1 is entitled *Re-assessing the Three Pillars: Modern and Postmodern Sociologies of Education*. This sets out the dominant framework for the study of mass education. The familiar axes of class, race, and gender, and the resulting forms of disadvantage that emerge from them, are assessed and, in many ways, found wanting in the light of the broader changes associated with contemporary educational thought. The challenge then becomes to determine how these categories and concerns can now best be utilised.

Chapter 1 *Social class* addresses the logic of meritocracy, and examine the viability of oppositional conceptions of social class. It will be concluded that the way forward within educational research lies with more nuanced understandings of social distinctions, based around the notion of habitus, and the specifics of language use. Chapter 2 *Gender* assesses the contributions made to educational debates by first-, second- and third-wave feminist logics. Remaining inequities within the schooling system will be analysed, as will the role played by education in the formation of gendered identities. This latter concept will be used as a device for reworking the notion of 'hegemonic masculinity', and illustrating the complex ways in which schools shape 'acceptable' boys and girls. Finally, having debunked longstanding, yet persistent, biological arguments concerning race, Chapter 3 *Race/ethnicity* will examine the cultural construction of racial difference, address indigenous perspectives on educational issues, and unpack 'white privilege' theory. The central goal of the chapter is to assess what remains – at a practical level – of a concept that appears to have lost almost all of its intellectual purchase. This chapter will also address the central logic of discrimination, focusing on the notion of 'othering', as well as the rise of cultural discrimination.

Part 2 is called *The Foundations of an Alternative Approach: Education and Governance*. This part outlines the possibility of an alternative approach to the social analysis of education – based around the work of writers such as Foucault, Hunter and Rose – which can augment, or arguably even replace, even the more sophisticated application of modernist sociology outlined in Part 1.

Chapter 4 *Governance* details the historical circumstances that gave rise to the phenomenon of mass schooling. Working as a history of the present, the intention here is to explain not only how the familiar, central features of modern educational institutions came about – timetables, record-keeping, surveillance – but also how these came to constitute fundamental foundations of our broader society. This chapter will also address the importance of various forms of liberalism in shaping the logic of the modern school. Chapter 5 *Subjectivity* will extend the analysis beyond the 'objective' regulation of schools described in Chapter 4, to the governance of the 'subjective' experiences of students. It will be argued here that the rise of psychology in schools has resulted in the steady pathologisation of student behaviour, and that rather than simply uncovering and explaining student differences, the discipline of psychology is now instrumental in their production and distribution. That is, using examples such as the rise of ADHD, it can be shown that students are increasingly regulated via 'categories of abnormality'. Chapter 6 *Pre-adulthood* examines the rise of the persona of the child, and its most recent variant, youth. As a rebuttal to naturalist understandings of children, this chapter will seek to explain constructs such as the child and youth, not as simple stages of life, but rather as the products of various forms of government, constructed in a range of different sites, and by a multiplicity of practices of self-making.

Part 3 is called *Cultural Contexts of Contemporary Education*. Theoretical foundations and interpretations of education aside, it is important to locate modern mass schooling within some important cultural, political and technical contexts. This part raises questions about the relationship between school knowledge and popular culture, the effects of public discourse on educational debates, and the rise and rise of digital technologies within the classroom.

Chapter 7 *The media* examines the way in which educational debates, perceptions, and policies are shaped by public discourse. While arguing against simplistic understandings of the hegemonic power of the mass media, the focus will fall upon a nuanced account of the frequent moral panics associated with issues such as 'illegal immigrants' and the teaching of literacy, as well as the recurrent scapegoating of teachers for their 'failure' in various aspects of broader social governance. Chapter 8 *Popular culture* attempts to go beyond the neo-Leavisite view that popular culture has nothing of value to offer the modern classroom, while at the same time recognising that organising content around the simple maintenance of student interest is an insufficient rationale for a valid education. At which point, the question becomes a philosophical one: what constitutes a valid education? Chapter 9 *Technology* attempts to avoid the speculation and crystal-ball gazing common to writing on the subject. It will be argued here that the issue is not whether digital technologies constitute a bright new dawn of virtually limitless educational possibility, nor whether they simply represent new possibilities of student disadvantage and professional redundancy. Rather, the central issue should be more about the role teachers will have to play in articulating the distinction between information and knowledge.

Part 4 *Philosophy and Mass Education* examines some of the many ways that philosophy can help us better understand our schooling system. That is, philosophy is not just some abstract university knowledge system doomed to fail the most basic tests of utility. The mass school is a site of great ethical and epistemological complexity, and philosophy can help us make sense of it in ways that other discipline can't.

Chapter 10 *Philosophy* argues the importance of philosophy as a subject in the school curriculum, not just in terms of clarity of thought, but also for improving student sensitivity to social and ethical issues. In addition, it allows us to better understand why our education system has taken its current form, and it provides a vocabulary of ways for teachers to organise their own professional practice. Chapter 11 *Ethics and the law* sets out to unpack the relationship between ethics, education and the law. The chapter addresses the three great normative systems of Virtue Ethics, Consequentialism and Kantian ethics, and in particular the institutional pressures to adopt consequentialist ethical decision-making practices. It is also argued that teachers are now subject to a dense patchwork of legal interventions that structure their professional conduct and environment, and that there are still a number of important ethical and legal debates occurring within mass education, debates in which teacher need to be able to make their voices heard. Chapter 12 *Truth and postcolonialism* addresses the continuing legacy of colonialism within the classroom. It will examine the ways in which particular sets of truth become prioritised within the curriculum, and how different forces shape not only what counts as knowledge, but also how that knowledge is approached, organised and deployed. It will also address the homogenisation of knowledge within an increasingly globalised society.

In summary, and in keeping with all good social analysis, this book will attempt to address the central myths and domain assumptions surrounding the institutions of mass education. After all, the meritocratic belief that schooling is a fair race – there to be won by the best and brightest – is as prevalent now as it was at the beginning of the last century. This book will also provide a contemporary assessment of some of the ideas that have traditionally dominated education research, asking: to what extent do notions such as 'social class', 'childhood' and 'hegemonic masculinity' still have purchase within current debates, and do any viable conceptual alternatives exist? Finally, this book will seek to blur some of the disciplinary boundaries within the field of education. It will draw not only upon traditional sociology, but also cultural studies, history, philosophy, ethics, and jurisprudence – and hopefully, the resulting analyses will be stronger, more comprehensive, and more convincing as a result.

# Part 1

## Re-assessing the Three Pillars: Modern and Postmodern Sociologies of Education

Open any book on sociology, whether it is about education or not, and you can almost guarantee that there will be chapters on social class, gender and race. There are also likely to be other common themes – the family, ageing, deviance and so on – but none of them are regarded as quite as foundational as the three familiar pillars of social structure. That is, not everyone has a family, or is old, or deviant, but everyone is deemed to have a social class, a gender and a race/ethnicity, and more often than not, where you stand in relation to these categories correlates fairly directly with access to power, resources … and education. This part will examine these three social axes and draw some conclusions about how they structure our society, and how they affect the probability of success within our schools.

Though these conclusions may still be interesting and informative, sociological analysis has moved on somewhat from the belief that there are three straightforward categories that shape the structure of our society, categories that have an objective reality that we can come to know – i.e. the singular 'truth' of social class, gender and race/ethnicity. While this modernist understanding has had some interesting things to tell us, it has largely been superseded by more postmodern approaches to the same issues. These approaches attempt to avoid the sweeping generalisations, and the either/or logic, of previous work in the area. As such – while staying on the same terrain as social class, gender and race/ethnicity – this part will also examine how these three solidly nineteenth- and twentiety-century concepts can be best understood in the more nuanced sociological environment of the twenty-first century.

Chapter 1 *Social class* examines the relationship between the first of the three pillars and our education system. It begins by questioning the common assertion that Australia is an extraordinary equal society; it also questions the belief that how well we do in school is determined by our intellect, and not our social backgrounds; and finally, it challenges the assumption that social class is determined solely by how rich you are.

Chapter 2 *Gender* investigates the second of the three pillars and its relationship to mass education. It questions the common view that gender is simply a function of sex; that while gender differences certainly exist, schools play no part in their construction; and that for all the fuss about girls, it's actually boys who are on the receiving end of social injustice.

Chapter 3 *Race/ethnicity* addresses the final pillar of social structure and our education system. It questions the belief that race has any validity as a concept at all; that racial discrimination has all but disappeared in Australia; that race/ethnicity has virtually no role to play in determining how well we do in school; and that there is a serious and intractable 'Indigenous problem' within Australian education.

There is a temptation to look at modernist sociologies of education and dismiss them out of hand: 'They gloss over important differences'; 'They are overly deterministic'; and 'They create structures where none actually exist'. There is then a temptation to disparage everything they have told us about important aspects of how our society works. Although these criticisms have significant merit, the answers you get to questions are only ever as good as the questions you ask. We started out by asking some simple questions about our society (and in the context of this book, about our education system), from within a relatively simple modernist conceptual framework, and we got some simple answers. We are now asking some more complex questions, from within a more nuanced and flexible postmodern conceptual framework, and the answers we are getting reflect this shift.

# Chapter 1

# Social class

This chapter argues that understanding social class isn't a straightforward matter. First, it is a subject that many feel uncomfortable discussing, let alone applying to themselves or anyone else. Second, there is only tenuous agreement about exactly what it is, exactly how it organises the life opportunities of our citizens, and how best to study it.

In attempting to better understand the relationship between social class and education in Australia, this chapter will address three familiar myths. In doing so, it will trace important changes in the way that the social sciences have tried to explain this phenomenon. Most notably, these changes involve a shift away from a focus on economic and structural aspects of social class, to a greater emphasis on issues of cultural practice.

## Myth #1 Australia is a society characterised by equality

*It is often suggested that Australia isn't beset with the social or economic distinctions that characterise many other countries.*

Success in Australia is deemed to be based upon merit. However, contrary to this belief, the evidence suggests that there is an inequitable distribution of wealth in Australia, one that is no different to other industrialised countries. Furthermore, this inequality extends to gaining access to well-resourced schools.

## Myth #2 Schooling success is only about individual ability

*Given we all sit the same exams, it seems perfectly appropriate to claim that education is a fair race, and that hence the winners deserve their victory.*

Research into schooling success presents a more complex picture. The dominant model – that of Critical Theory – points to the vital role that schooling plays in the processes of social reproduction. According to this reasoning, wealth buys educational success, that success guarantees more wealth, which then buys the next generation's educational success. Individual ability is only one small part of this cycle.

## Myth #3 Social class is all about money

*Many supposedly working–class people earn very good wages, therefore claims about middle-class advantage must be false.*

More contemporary theoretical approaches to social class point to a variety of forms of capital, not just economic. It is these forms of capital – cultural, social, symbolic – which help shape how people live, how they organise their relations with one another, and how much access they have to resources. It is these factors that most likely constitute our best understandings of social class.

# Introduction

## The trouble with social class

It's difficult to say why social class is such a difficult, and often uncomfortable, subject. Social stratification, in all its forms, is a feature common to all societies and cultures – whether we admit it or not – and yet it's a topic that is widely regarded as failing the polite conversation test, alongside the traditional no-go areas of politics and religion. Most of us would be cautious about asking someone we had only just met what class they come from, just as we would about informing them of our own: 'Hi. I'm Gordon, and I'm upper-middle class.'

Interestingly, we can look at other cultures and societies and easily point to their various types of stratification, internal systems of ranking, and forms of social differentiation, and we can develop assorted explanatory mechanisms as we go, accurate or otherwise. We can scratch our heads at the seeming unfairness of the Hindu caste system, one that categorises some citizens 'untouchable' from the moment of birth, and wonder why it is still tolerated when so many suffer through its existence. We can puzzle at the British obsession with social class and its covert boundaries shaped by accent, manners and education – less formal than a caste system perhaps, but just as pervasive. Arguably, most of us would find both these topics to be perfectly appropriate for after-dinner conversation, presumably as long as we're not in London or New Delhi.

So why can we talk about other countries' social class systems, and yet cringe at the thought of discussing our own? Campbell (2010) rightly points to a couple of factors at play here. First, given that social class correlates directly with access to resources, power and status, most of us would be justifiably wary of admitting we are at the bottom of the social pile (or alternatively, reluctant to whinge about it), just as good manners prohibits us from pointing out that same lack of power and status in others. Second, it is normally regarded as inappropriate to talk openly about our own wealth and success, lest we are seen to be gloating, and no-one likes a gloater.

So the circumstances at both ends of the social class spectrum make any discussion of its existence, or its consequences, quite problematic. However, this doesn't mean that it therefore somehow magically ceases to exist. The evidence has long shown that all cultures have one form of stratification or another, and most have many (Reissman 1973). But even accepting this fact doesn't mean the field is clear for an unproblematic explanation of just what's going on. Social class is a complex, murky and highly contested issue, as this chapter will demonstrate, particularly as it applies to education.

## Some conceptual problems
### What exactly is social class?

In a terminological sense, it is an umbrella phrase that covers a lot of ground, most frequently all the ground covered by the very similar notion of *socioeconomic status*, and then a little bit more. For the purposes of this book, we'll stick with 'social class', as it lends itself to an analysis not solely focused on the more material aspects of stratification.

Semantics issues aside, what about the conceptual aspects of social class? Early functionalist explanations, such as those of Durkheim (1964), regarded society as some sort of smoothly operating clock, where each of the cogs – us – has a clearly defined role to play, some of them important, others less so. The more valued the role, the higher the status attached to it, and hence the higher the social class of the cog. This model of society, one based around consensus, has been the subject of considerable criticism over the years, and no-one really does 'functionalist' research any more, at least not if they want to get a job at a university. Criticisms of this position are many, but are mostly based around the notion that somehow we all have neatly defined 'functions'. It has also been argued that this model can't adequately account for rapid social change; after all, how do the various cogs of a grandfather clock suddenly transform themselves into the components of a digital watch?

An alternative set of explanations, generally referred to as conflict theory, see social class as a side effect of a competition for power. In a kind of zero-sum game, society is divided into those who have power and those who lack it, with the two sides locked in an ongoing struggle. This model contends that the more power you are able to mobilise, then the higher your social class. More subtle variants on this approach, mostly notably in the form of critical theory, have dominated social and educational research until relatively recently. However, just as Functionalist explanations of social class fell to the logic of conflict theory, as will be argued in more detail later in this chapter, so has conflict theory begun to flounder in the face of a concerted onslaught from various forms of postmodernism; that is, a type of reasoning that seeks to reject singular explanations of otherwise complex social phenomena.

### What kind of social and cultural effect does social class have?

So, even though there remain marked differences of opinion over what lies at its core, surely we are capable of reaching agreement over this question. Apparently not: some researchers consider that social class pretty much determines an individual's chances in life: how they'll do at school, what kind of job they'll get, who they'll marry, how and where they'll be able to live. Others researchers consider that such outcomes can't simply be read off from a person's background – that relevant factors are too complex and the causal chains too long – and at most, your social class gently whispers life suggestions to you, rather than bellows instructions. Others still, most frequently within the psychology-based disciplines, look towards individual ability as the greatest determinant of success, playing down the importance of pre-existing social factors. While there will be more on that particular belief later, it's obvious from these different perspectives that this represents a complex and contested field.

## How do we go about researching social class?

Once again, there are different views as to the most effective way to make social class an object of knowledge. The first, and arguably dominant, approach to research has been that of quantitative analysis, which seeks to amass statistical data that can answer the 'how many?' type of questions: How many people are in each social class, as a percentage? How many upper-class kids drop out of school? How many working-class kids get to university? Answers to these questions help with a *structural* analysis of our society, and help us with our understanding of who has what.

The second main approach is that of qualitative analysis, which engages in research that attempts to answer the 'why?' type of questions: Why do we feel uncomfortable talking about social class? Why do some upper-class kids drop out of school? Why do middle-class kids feel more comfortable in schools than those from the working-class? These answers constitute an *interpretive* analysis of our society, and add depth and texture to our understanding of the lived experience of particular social classes.

Neither of these approaches represents the right way to study Australian society. Indeed, the best research most likely tries to employ both, given that this form of *methodological triangulation* promises to paint a richer, and more balanced, portrait of our social reality. In this manner, the arguments developed in this chapter are constructed from the evidence produced through both kinds of analysis. Unfortunately however, it should be pointed out that academic researchers tend to have expertise in one of these methodologies, and they often don't like the other much at all. That is, quantitative research is often characterised by its critics as the mindless assembly of vast columns of numbers, none of which bear any relation to the real life of anyone. Alternatively, qualitative research is lampooned as merely the collected transcriptions of barely interesting chit-chats, none of which bear any relation to proper research data. There are probably elements of truth in both these assertions.

All of these basic questions about social class will be addressed here, not just in relation to its impact on the social fabric of our nation, but more specifically about its effects on our education system. The most straightforward route into this analysis is to address three common beliefs about social class within the Australian context. As discussed in the introduction to this book, those employed in the business of researching and explaining issues of social stratification – sociologists, philosophers, historians, cultural studies academics, criminologists, anthropologists – are confronted by commonsense assertions and mythologies about this issue on a daily basis. Consequently, addressing some of these myths serves the dual purposes of:

1 assessing whether they have any truth to them at all, or whether they are simply part of the background noise of a society that isn't great at admitting it has some significant faults; and

2 acting as a vehicle for an effective analysis of the complex relationship between social class and mass education.

The three myths are:

**Myth #1** – Australia is a society characterised by equality

**Myth #2** – Schooling success is only about individual ability

**Myth #3** – Social class is all about money

# Myth #1 Australia is a society characterised by equality

As Donald Horne (1968) pointed out, we live in 'the lucky country'. We generally take this to mean that Australia, and therefore its inhabitants, have it all: the beautiful weather, the abundant natural resources, the fact that other countries don't appear to hate us or want to annex our land, and the fact that we appear to have escaped the rigid hierarchies that characterise the old world, into a new dawn of social and economic egalitarianism. Australians are lucky because we're all equal down here – no landed gentry tooting fox horns and slurping Pimms, no grinding urban poverty and social decay, and no invisible social barriers blocking the way of those who wish to change their stars.

It is these latter beliefs about Australian society – a variant of liberalism, which will be discussed in detail in Chapter 4 – that form the foundation of some of our most important cultural narratives. After all, not only do they tell us what we are, they separate us from what we're not. Our accents are pretty much the same, we wear similar kinds of clothes, and none of us lay claim to the hereditary superiority of aristocracy. Case closed then for an egalitarian country. Unfortunately, from a philosophical point of view, just thinking something is the case, or wishing it to be the case, doesn't make it the case.

So, we may unpack the social inferences that can be drawn from notions of the 'lucky country' a little more. This can be understood in two ways: first, that we don't have the social and economic disparities that characterise the European countries from which most of us came; and second, that we don't have much of a rich/poor gap.

# The comparison with other countries

Popular discourse here would suggest that we set an example to other countries in terms of our economic equality. That is, Australia is not a country that tolerates the existence of a European-style greedy nobility, hogging all the wealth, nor an American-style conspicuous consumption where motorised mini-Cadillacs are bought for wealthy children, while more than 40 million of the population live in abject poverty (US Census Bureau 2010). However, we're also not a culture that needs economic equality forced upon us, like Cuba, China or North Korea. Rather, our equity emerges from the wellspring of our own natural egalitarianism.

Fortunately, there are international statistical instruments available to test the truth of this belief. Economists employ a mathematical device called the Gini Coefficient, which enables the ranking of nations based upon their equality of income. The index goes from 0 (the hypothetical result if everyone is paid the same income) to 100 (the hypothetical result if all the income was paid to one person). Australia's position on the Gini Index rankings is shown in Table 1.1 below.

**Table 1.1** *In terms of income equality, where does Australia stand?*

| RANK | COUNTRY | INCOME EQUALITY (GINI INDEX) |
| --- | --- | --- |
| 1 | Sweden | 23.0 |
| 2 | Hungary | 24.7 |
| 3 | Norway | 25.0 |
| 4 | Austria | 26.0 |
| 5 | Czech Republic | 26.0 |
| 6 | Malta | 26.0 |
| 7 | Luxembourg | 26.0 |
| 8 | Serbia | 26.0 |
| 9 | Slovakia | 26.0 |
| 10 | Kazakhstan | 26.7 |
| 27 | Australia | 30.5 |

Source: Central Intelligence Agency 2011

As can be seen, we don't even make the top 25 in terms of income equality. Certainly, we're not like the USA (bad), or Namibia (the worst), but just the same we don't stand out from the pack. Actually, we're probably pretty average for a Western, industrial country – so much for the belief that Australia sets the international benchmark for equality. Ranking 27th is hardly the stuff of a utopian, egalitarian mythology.

## The rich/poor gap in Australia

That isn't the end of the myth though. After all, even if we're no different to every other middling first-world country, this doesn't mean that we're still not quite an equal country in terms of wealth distribution, as maybe the disparity in wealth in all these countries is actually relatively small. Maybe the gap between what the rich and poor own still merits a belief in a national, level economic playing field.

Figure 1.1 below tells a different story. The statistical evidence suggests that almost half the wealth of Australia is concentrated in the hands of only 10% of the population. In fact, the wealthiest 5% are shown to own 31% of the nation's wealth. Worryingly, for those invested in the myth of equality, the concentration of wealth in the hands of the few also appears to be in the process of increasing (Headley, Warren & Wooden 2008, 15). Once again, it is probably worth making a comparison with other countries. The top 10% of our population owning 44.9% of our wealth puts us square in line with a large number of Western, industrial countries – Ireland (42.3%), Germany (44.4%), South Korea (43.1%), Finland (42.3%) (Davies et al. 2009) – so once again, nothing outstandingly egalitarian there

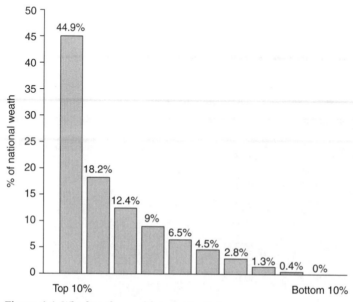

**Figure 1.1** *Who has the wealth in Australia?*
*Source: Headley, Warren & Wooden 2008.*

In the light of all this comparative, quantitative evidence, it seems apparent that Australia is not a society overly characterised by economic equality. However, two other familiar sub-myths often follow on from the initial myth. The first is that, though we may not have economic equality in Australia, we do have a sort of *cultural* equality. Our cultural practices tend not to vary according to social class, marking a stark contrast to countries like England, where an individual's social background gets stamped into accent and manners from the very beginning. This assertion forms the basis for the third part of this chapter, and so will be dealt with then – but without wishing to give the game away, it doesn't look particularly good for that myth either.

The second sub-myth is that, once again, though we may not have economic equality in Australia, it doesn't really matter that much. We all get stuck in together, regardless of our backgrounds. We all do the same things, we play sport, go to the beach, have barbeques, and we sit the same school exams. There is a kind of national path to being Australian that we all share. Leaving aside the issues of gender, and race/ethnicity for later chapters (as well as various other important factors), the issue of us all sitting the same school exams warrants further mention, particularly since this is a book on mass education.

Hopefully, it will be demonstrated that understanding the relationship between social class and education can act as the perfect case study for understanding social class in a more general way. After all, we may well all sit for the same school exams (for those who make it through to the final year of schooling, itself a classed issue), but our route to those exams is often very different. As Figure 1.2 shows, our social class plays a large role in determining what kind of school we're able to go to. Clearly, quantitative research shows that, far from all getting stuck in together, wealthier families tend to cluster in fee-paying schools. Why?

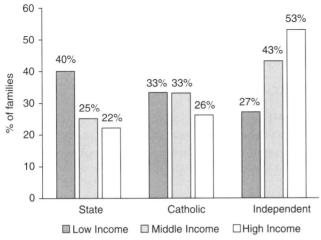

**Figure 1.2** *Who attends which type of school in Australia?*
*Source: Preston 2007*

And let's not think that this graph tells the whole story. Within each of these categories of school, there is a continuum of wealth and resourcing. Some state schools, generally those in high socioeconomic status areas, quite closely resemble independent schools in terms of ethos and expectation, and as such, the effects of social class background are all the more systemically pervasive.

The next myth deals with the question: if there is this kind of class-based difference within Australian education, does it actually make any difference? So far, debunking the first myth has simply involved the presentation of various sets of statistical data. Myth #2 will involve a much greater degree of social analysis and interpretation.

# Myth #2 Schooling success is only about individual ability

It's simple. Schools reward those with ability, which makes the system work. Those students who come out on top are the smart, the diligent and the determined. Those students who do poorly, do so because they lack these fundamental qualities, and as a consequence, the blame for their failure is all their own – sorry, but bad luck.

In a very important sense, this myth provides the central logic for our schooling system. Indeed, addressing this assertion has formed one of the foundational pillars of modernist approaches to the study of education. There wouldn't be much point in taking part in a sporting competition if the result was fixed before hand, and equally we wouldn't be overly happy if we were told that the results of the final year school assessment had been decided before the children even got into the exam room. This is the foundational logic of a meritocracy – a system of rules based upon the principle that success, and the power that comes with it, should go to those with the ability, rather than be given by birthright, or to those who can simply take it by force (Young 1958). With his tongue firmly in his cheek, Young organised the logic of meritocracy as an equation:

$$\text{Success} = \text{IQ} + \text{Effort}$$

If only it were that straightforward.

Henry (2000) addresses this issue in her assessment of how best to approach the issue of social class within the education system. She cited the one phrase she has heard more often than any other during her time as a university lecturer:

*'Yeah, but in the end, it all comes down to the individual – it's all up to the individual, isn't it.'* If I could have a dollar from every time I've heard that phrase – *it's all up to the individual* – I'd be a rich person now. It seems one of the defining ideas of our society. Yet it is a flawed idea … it is simplistic because it does not take sufficient account of the way society is structured. (Henry 2000, 47)

If we are to accept the claim that our education system is a genuine meritocracy, then we have to accept, as a fact, that the students who come out on top are unequivocally our smartest and most worthy. Unfortunately, that also means that we must accept that our smartest and most worthy students disproportionately attend the most elite of our private schools. The evidence for this statement can be seen in Figure 1.3 below. Any number of different data sets could have been used to make this point: disproportionate percentage of tertiary offers made to independent school students; disproportionate percentage going to university; disproportionate percentage in the more prestigious university faculties.

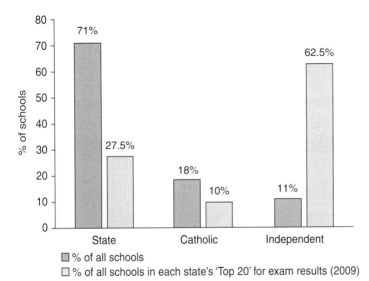

**Figure 1.3** *Which types of school win the 'Educational Race'?*
*Compiled from Australian Bureau of Statistics 2010a and Better Education 2011.*

To put it another way, if we are to accept that our education system is a genuine meritocracy, then we also have to accept that out most privileged students are also our best. That would be quite a coincidence. Let's assume then, if the whole system isn't fixed in some ludicrous, conspiratorial way – which it isn't – that something else must be going on. There must be some other, more subtle, way that social class advantages manifest themselves in terms of educational success. What are they, and how have social and educational researchers attempted to explain them?

The dominant explanatory model has belonged to critical theory, an offshoot of Marxist theory. Both are premised on the contention that economic factors play the greatest role in explaining how social class works. Originally, Marxist ideas sought to divide the social world into two halves: those who owned the machinery of economic production, and those who worked on those machines. These two different statuses represented two opposing social classes, and everything else – political power, culture, knowledge, education – became a function of this fundamental division. Revolutionary ideas at the time, literally.

This early, clumsy model evolved into a more subtle form of analysis. That is, though founded on the same logic, critical theory went on to provide a far more nuanced account of how the world works. Gone are the two opposing classes, locked in economic war, replaced instead by a range of social classes, operating within a far more complex industrial environment. What has *not* gone, however, is the understanding that the right to exercise of power is something to be struggled over, and that in the final analysis, it is still determined by economic factors. Importantly, within this logic, education is deemed to have a very special role to play in these processes.

## Some of the logic of critical theory

In order to best understand the relationship between social class and education, according to the reasoning of critical theory, the work of a number of writers needs to be briefly addressed. These writers don't tell the complete story, because there's no 'complete story' to tell, but their work provides some of the central landmarks of the position, and offers a generalised flavour of how social class has been understood within educational research from the 1960s onwards. So who should we look at?

## Althusser

Althusser (1971) attempts to explain how society works by adopting the basic Marxist model of an economic base acting as the foundation for a social superstructure (that is, all the legal, political and cultural systems that define a society). Within this superstructure, Althusser delineates the 'repressive State apparatus', which includes the police, the courts, the army, i.e. all the machinery necessary to exert control by force if necessary, and of importance to us, the 'ideological State apparatus' – all those mechanisms which exert control through the use of ideas. He argues that the ruling class (the bourgeoisie) uses the education system, more than any other part of the ideological State apparatus, for maintaining its power.

> What the bourgeoisie has installed as its number-one, i.e. as its dominant ideological State apparatus, is the educational apparatus, which has in fact replaced in its functions the previously dominant ideological State apparatus, the Church. (Althusser 1971, 103–104)

Yes, the wealthy may send their children to different schools to the poor, but according to Althusser, that's only one small part of how social class and education interact. He argues that the schooling system acts as a sophisticated filter, both ideologically and practically, one which spits out the working classes at an early stage with the belief system necessary to do what's asked of them. Likewise, the ruling classes stay on longer in school, and learn very different lessons, about life and about the exercise of power.

## Bowles and Gintis

Extending these arguments, Bowles and Gintis (1976) address in particular the myth of meritocracy within modern society. They argue that the schooling system is the main site for the propagation of the false belief that success in our system is based upon your intrinsic merit. Once this belief is installed in the population – largely through the usual tactics of school hierarchies, continual assessment and an overtly ideological curriculum – it legitimates the same beliefs within the wider society, in that disparities in wealth and power become explained almost exclusively in terms of personal factors, rather than any underlying social inequalities.

To put this argument more simply: once we come to believe what we've been told in school – that the reason we've done poorly is because we're stupid – it makes perfect sense to tell ourselves that the reason we've also done poorly in life is because we're talentless. All of this then is nobody's fault but our own, and from this point on, we'll no longer complain about our lot. We'll become good little workers, and good little consumers, all of which allows the system to continue to tick over, generation after generation. Of course, the 'we' referred to here is not uniform across all strata of society; rather there are 'specific forms of consciousness distributed across a differentiated class structure' (Ladwig 1996, 23). That is, social elites are taught to see themselves, and the world, very differently.

## Apple

This writer examines the way the system 'keeps ticking over' in great detail. Apple's (1979) work on education and social reproduction challenges another of the great myths of the schooling system: that mass education is a positive force for social change, and that an educated population is a population equipped to question its inequalities, particularly those relating to social class. Apple contends instead that schools have exactly the opposite effect; that they act to maintain the status quo, and to keep power in the hands of the lucky few.

Apple's arguments are far more sophisticated than simply pointing to the fact that wealthy and powerful parents send their kids to private schools, who then do well themselves, become wealthy and powerful, and send their kids to private school, and so on. He focuses instead upon the role that the curriculum plays in social reproduction, arguing that ideology – beliefs systems organised according to vested interests – get passed off as objective school knowledge. Internalising this 'knowledge' during their years at school renders students (and teachers) unable to meaningfully question the social order. For example, we are taught from kindergarten onwards that teacher always knows best, that it is inappropriate to question those in authority, and that truth emanates from the front of the classroom. This probably constitutes the most foundational of all school knowledge, and obviously, this mind-set doesn't exactly make for a political active citizenry.

## Giroux

Giroux examines all those other things we learn in school without necessarily realising it. This involves not the formal curriculum of the three Rs, but the *hidden curriculum*, a curriculum comprised of all those other things we learn in school on the way through. He defines this as:

> those unstated norms, values, and beliefs embedded in and transmitted to students through the underlying rules that structure the routines and social relationships in school and classroom life.
> (Giroux and Purpel 1983, 47)

After all, not questioning authority isn't the only covert lesson that school teaches us. There is ongoing deference to that authority, in being quiet when the teacher speaks, and standing up when they enter the room. There's learning how to be punctual, how to work hard now if we want to succeed in the future, and how to be a good, moral citizen. All in all, it involves learning how to get ahead by learning how to fit in, and since fitting in normally means not rocking the boat, the hidden curriculum constitutes an important part of how society, or more specifically, the society's class system, replicates itself.

## So what can we conclude from critical theory?

With each of these writers, there is considerable overlap in their ideas, and the decision as to which parts of their work to include could have been made very differently. In spite of this limitation, some specific conclusions can be drawn about critical theory, what it says about social class and education, and the insights it brings to the analysis of some of our most pervasive inequalities. Conclusions can also be drawn about the paradigm's shortcomings, and about why other approaches come to be regarded as more convincing.

First, all of these writers, and in fact, anybody who has ever studied education in a coherent way, would argue that the assertion: 'Schooling success is only about individual ability', is way off the mark. Next time you find yourself saying: 'It's all up to the individual, isn't it', pause for a moment, and have a think about exactly what that statement implies.

Second, all of these writers found their theories upon the possibility of social and educational equality. They contend that through political action at all levels – challenging some of the structures of our society, addressing educational policy and focusing on the professional actions of committed teachers – it's possible to mount a resistance to the inevitability of the classing process. Schools don't have to simply provide the rubber stamps, the credentialing, that cements your place within a particular social class. Schools can be about change.

Third, it's obvious from these writers that the nexus between social class and education remains a complex one. Educational outcomes can't be simply 'read off' from a knowledge of the social class of the student, a class determined by the school they went to, and how much money their parents earn. There's much more going on, and critical theory has pointed to issues such as the filtering effects of education, the myth of meritocracy, the role of schooling ideologies in social reproduction and the effects of the hidden curriculum.

It should be pointed out here that all of these remain astute observations, give or take a centimetre or two, and just because Critical Theory may have been challenged by more nuanced theoretical models, it doesn't suddenly make these observations wrong, or irrelevant. However, Critical Theory has certainly been challenged, and it has struggled in the face of approaches that have sought to frame the problem in a number of different ways, and according to some very different assumptions. To avoid the risk of needless detail, only two of those assumptions need be addressed here.

First, this approach seems to be premised upon the belief that there is a solution to the 'social class problem' within education. That is, with the right social structures in place, and the right education policies operating, we can turn schools into genuine meritocracies. The unspoken subtext to this presumption is a *teleology* – a belief that history is heading in a specific direction – which implies that the current class crisis in education is but a bump in the road on the way to an education system, indeed a society, free of the curse of social class.

Disagreeing with this optimistic presupposition isn't therefore to say that working within a social justice agenda is a waste of time; far from it. It is just that there's little evidence for a singular 'truth' of social class, one waiting to be found and cured, based on the modernist belief that every problem has a solution if only you look hard enough. As discussed in the introduction to this book, Giddens (1990) argues that our society is characterised by continual crisis. A longstanding, endemic lack of educational equity is just one of them. And as will be discussed in Chapter 4, another fundamental characteristic of our society is the continual failure of government to solve its problems.

Second is the contention that critical theory represents a reductionist and homogenising approach to social class, or to put it in simpler terms, it oversimplifies what is actually a very complex phenomenon. Just as Marxism reduced society down to two ever-warring classes, in the final analysis, so too does its more sophisticated descendant, except the focus is now on a slightly different issue: power – who has it, who gets to keep it, and how. This differential access to power results in a class-based social structure, one that is real, tangible, and objectively knowable – the 'truth' of social class.

It is assertions such as the one above that prove to be critical theory's downfall. Ultimately, critical theory presents itself as a *master discourse*, a singular explanation that seeks to place all aspects of the social world within its explanatory range. The trouble is, no-one really accepts master discourses any more. The world is just too complex. In which case, where do we go from here? Perhaps the last myth will be able to offer an answer to that question.

# Myth #3 Social class is all about money

Blue-collar workers, like miners, plumbers and bricklayers, earn a lot more than white-collar professionals, such as teachers, physiotherapists and accountants. Therefore, since social class is all about money, bricklayers must be upper-class, and teachers must be working-class – or to put it another way, all this class stuff is rubbish.

This assertion is normally used as supporting evidence for the claim that there's no social class in Australia. After all, if we accept the proposition that social class is determined by how much money you have – and therefore what school you can afford to send your child to – it becomes very easy to start charting who earns what, and rightly observe that this doesn't necessarily follow the accepted relationship between wealth and traditional, occupationally determined notions of social class.

The truth is, most people's experiences of class differences don't relate directly to how much money they have in relation to others. Whatever social class is, there's a lot more to it than simply taking a student and measuring the size of their parents' wallets. We all know it's far more complex than that. As discussed at the beginning of this chapter, it's not really part of polite conversation to ask people about their social class background, or to inform people of yours. So how is it then that we are all able to make an educated guess about someone's class background after just the briefest of chats? We already know the answer to this: it's because social class is manifest in a wide variety of ways, and it is these that we pick up on. These ways might include how they dress, how they speak, the language they use, what they talk about, what they enjoy doing, where they live, how they live, and so on. All of these are cultural issues, and this means it can be argued that most of 'the stuff' of social class exists in this domain, rather than in the realm of the purely economic.

This isn't a new revelation. Previous modernist sociologies, including some operating under the broad umbrella of Critical Theory, have long pointed to issues of culture when addressing social class. This can be exemplified by two of Connell's earlier books. The first book, *Ruling Class, Ruling Culture* (1977), examines Australian society during the 1970s, which is, in part, used as a case study to explore the notion of *hegemony* – Gramsci's (1971) idea that the ideas of the socially dominant eventually become the dominant ideas. In this way, social control doesn't have to occur through any kind of force, but rather it works through the shaping of the culture in ways which suit the interests of the powerful, and often most effectively, through the use of the media and the school. Indeed, much is made in the book of the role of teachers in the transmission of dominant values, but also, on a more optimistic note, in the role they can play in social change.

The second of Connell's books, *Making the Difference* (1982, with Ashenden, Kessler & Dowsett), focuses specifically on cultures of schooling. It examines the way that the 'hegemonic curriculum' sorts students on the basis of social class, even though it is portrayed as a neutral body of information. The curriculum does this by drawing a distinction between academic knowledge and practical knowledge, valuing the former and marginalising the latter. Moreover, the various cultural skills that the higher social classes bring to the school – more complex language use, greater skill at organising argument, a wider knowledge of high culture, and so on – become crucial to that educational success. That is, while it would be an oversimplification to state that these pre-existing cultural practices are the same as academic ability, or are mistaken for it, they are certainly the fabric from which the construct 'academic ability' is cut.

Even though both of these books stress the importance of culture in the analysis of social class, they still operate according to the assumption that class-based cultures are somehow an expression of a more fundamental organisational reality – i.e. how much money you have – and that this primary core of class division somehow lies beneath culture. However, in contrast to this, there is a body of work premised upon the assumption that, rather than class-based cultures being a direct function of underlying economic differences, such cultures constitute a relatively autonomous sphere of life. These ideas are generally associated with the French writer Bourdieu.

## Bourdieu and his four types of capital

So far, when analysing social class, and more specifically the relationship between social class and education, the spotlight has fallen squarely on questions of money. As previously discussed, the bedrock of social class has always been regarded as the realm of the economic – who's got the cash, who works for pay, and who takes the profit. This has constituted the essential, modernist 'truth' of a society characterised by economic classes and ideologies. Bourdieu (1986) sees it somewhat differently, and he bases his ideas around four different types of capital.

## Economic capital

This has already been discussed at length in this chapter, and represents wealth in its broadest and most familiar sense. It can include money, property, shares, readily convertible possessions and investments. There's no real need to discuss this any further.

## Cultural capital

Bourdieu argues that there are other types of non-economic wealth that can still be spent, and that have massive implication for educational success. He points to all the practices that higher social class kids bring with them to the school, just as did Connell, and notes that they form a type of *habitus,* a term he borrowed from Mauss

(1973), meaning a set of socially acquired dispositions, skills and forms of conduct. At a mundane level, these might include such practices as how to walk, talk, hold the body, shake hands, particular types of gesture, dress and even haircut. All of these help mark out an individual as having a given class background, and as previously mentioned, most of us are pretty good at reading these cues, and drawing appropriate conclusions from them.

At an institutional level, schools are no different. They can also spot various types of habitus, such as those associated with the middle classes, and they 'read off' this habitus as academic ability. As such, particular embodied cultural skills (for example, linguistic dexterity, bodily self-discipline, good manners) actually have a value, a practical worth. They constitute a form of capital. Bourdieu contends that this form of cultural wealth comes in three types: embodied cultural capital, objectified cultural capital and institutionalised cultural capital.

*Embodied cultural capital* consists not only of the kinds of physical practices described above, but also of the forms of conduct associated with a given social group. This might include going to the theatre for the higher social classes, and going to the footy for the lower. Neither of these cultural practices is intrinsically better than the other, however knowledge of the former is far more likely to be of use within fields such as the academic curriculum. That is, this knowledge can be 'spent', and hence can be regarded as capital. These forms of capital are usually inherited from our families, and take a long time to acquire. Likewise, we pass them on to our own children as a form of tangible inheritance, one they can also 'spend' – long before they get the leftover cash we haven't spent ourselves.

An important subset here is *linguistic capital*, in that the effective use of language is one of the most crucial criteria for determining educational success. It is argued that a student's linguistic sophistication acts as important capital within the school, and that this sophistication often correlates directly with social class background (Bourdieu & Passeron 1990). This idea is also evident in the work of Bernstein (1990), who has worked on linguistic codes. He argues that *restricted codes* (forms of communication relying on shared and taken-for-granted knowledge) are more common among working-class students, whereas *elaborated codes* (forms of communication where all necessary information is included in the statement), as well as restricted codes, are commonly used by middle-class students. For example, the statement: 'I blew it – left my stuff in the back', is a restricted code, only making sense to someone with a significant amount of shared knowledge. An elaborated version of this might read: 'I've done very badly in the open-book exam. I left all the notes I needed in the back seat of the car.' Bernstein is not saying that the elaborated codes of the middle class are any better than the restricted codes of the working class, but he is saying that the ability to use elaborated codes is significantly more useful within the field of education. Consequently, middle classes can convert this ability into linguistic cultural capital, a currency readily accepted by the school.

*Objectified cultural capital* incorporates physical objects that give the owner status. These might include objects such as paintings, musical instruments, particular kinds of cars, and so on. While these can be sold, thereby converting them into economic capital, they have value in their own right as cultural capital, in that they can speak about the owner. Owning a grand piano arguably brings with it more cultural capital than owning a piano accordion. Likewise, owning a Bugatti Veyron brings with it more cultural capital than owning a Kingswood, at least to all but the most deranged of Holden fans. Of course, there's more than a significant price differential between these cars, so the issue of the Veyron's associated cultural capital spills all too readily into economic capital. Perhaps then a comparison between a child being dropped off at school in a vintage MG, rather than an old Mitsubishi Magna, is more appropriate.

*Institutionalised cultural capital* includes the recognition associated with institutional qualifications. This often converts to economic capital directly through the labour market. After all, there are reasons of both cultural and economic capital that mean a university qualification in education is of greater value than the qualifications necessary to be a McBurger flipper, second class.

Although the notion of cultural capital is probably Bourdieu's most significant contribution to an understanding of social class that extends beyond the purely economic, he delineated two other forms of capital which also add to the complexity of the issue.

## Social capital

This includes all the relationships, mutual acquaintances and memberships that an individual can call upon. Often a person has social power, not simply because of who they are, but because of all the people they know that they can call upon, and the influence they can wield accordingly. Old boy/old girl networks – the old school tie – are not simply clichés about how attendance at elite schools provides a benefit long after leaving the institution itself, they represent an appropriate example of what Bourdieu means by social capital. The more people you know, and the more powerful they are, the more capital you have to spend yourself.

> The volume of the social capital possessed by a given agent thus depends on the size of the network of connections he can effectively mobilise and on the volume of capital (economic, cultural and symbolic) possessed in his own right by each of those to whom he is connected. (Bourdieu 1986, 247)

Therefore, an individual may have little economic capital, but if they have a large number of influential friends, then this constitutes an important form of capital, one that can be converted to more useable forms when necessary.

## Symbolic capital

This incorporates issues such as status, prestige and honour. Though perhaps less tangible than other forms of capital, it is just as significant. The right to be listened to is often determined by the many forms of ranking, both overt and covert, that exist within social groupings. In the context of the school, captains of sporting teams are frequently accorded greater status, and can wield greater power, due to the prestige of their position. This prestige can often still be spent, years after leaving the school itself. Likewise, attendance at a particularly elite school, such as Eton in England, while bringing with it obvious social capital, contains an important component of symbolic capital as well.

To summarise the discussion of myth #3: it would appear to be a gross over-simplification to claim that social class is all about money. There appears to be a far greater component of social class that is about culture. The central question here is whether class-based cultures are somehow, ultimately, a direct function of underlying economic issues – money – as more traditional, modernist sociologies tend to assert. Alternatively, are such cultures relatively independent social formations that have their own histories and momentum, with the economic constituting only one element? The work of Bourdieu leads towards the latter conclusion, take it or leave it.

# Conclusion

Upon closer scrutiny, three of the most common assertions about education can't be supported. First, the available evidence suggests that Australia is not a place fundamentally characterised by equality – at least, no more than any other industrial, Western country. Second, schooling success does not appear to be only about individual ability. Instead, the various resources children bring to the school play a huge role in how well they do when they get there. The education system appears to act as a giant social filter, one filtering not solely on individual ability – whatever that means – but rather on how far through the filter the individual's parents got. Third, social class is not simply about money. Arguably the more convincing theorising on the subject suggests that if you want to understand how social class works, particularly in relation to education, the best place to start looking is within the realm of culture.

Clearly then, whatever social class is, there are a number of common misconceptions about how prevalent it is, how it works, and where its boundaries lie. It seems apparent from the arguments set out here, that not only does social class have a significant role to play in structuring opportunity, access and reward within Australian life, it affects our education system in very similar ways.

With regards to understanding the connection between social class and education, this chapter has discussed how earlier attempts to explain this relationship largely resulted in reductionist, teleological models promising a 'solution' to the problem of class. These models have located class as one of the three fundamental pillars of human social existence, along with sex/gender and race/ethnicity, as the next two chapters will attest. This chapter has gone on to suggest that perhaps a more sophisticated approach to social class now focuses on its existence as sets of cultural practices, and sets of lived relations, elements which in turn have significant implications for all aspects of education.

Ultimately then, rather than these practices and relations reflecting some underlying truth about a unified and objective notion of social class, perhaps these diverse and often unconnected components are all there is to the matter – all there is to the thorny issue of social class. Furthermore, if one of the central intentions of a socially just approach to education is to try and give students from the lowest of social class background a decent shot at doing well, perhaps the best way forward is to focus, not upon the large-scale, seemingly immutable, economic inequalities that characterise Australian society, but rather upon the smaller scale, more manageable, issue of fostering cultures of learning.

# Chapter 2

# Gender

Gender is far from a settled issue. There are still some significant debates occurring around the different educational practices, expectations and outcomes experienced by boys and girls. Important wider questions also still attract attention: just what is gender, and why bother talking about it – after all, aren't we all equal now? Isn't biology about to explain all of this stuff anyway? And what is the best theoretical framework for approaching gender? Do we still have to go down the 'men are to blame for everything' route?

This chapter will unpack the complex and changing relationship between gender and education. In order to accomplish this, the chapter will link each of the most common myths in the area with one of the three waves of feminism that characterised the twentieth century. As with the arguments surrounding social class, it will ultimately be suggested that explanations relying upon a master discourse – not 'the economy' again, but rather it this case 'patriarchy: a unified system of male-domination' – have had their day.

## Myth #1 Sex and gender are really the same thing

*Girls are girls, and boys are boys, because nature made them that way. Masculinity is a function of being a man, and men run society because biology determined they would be better at it.*

First-wave feminism rightly challenged this biological determinism, contending instead that our genders are the flexible product of a range of cultural and historical factors. We have a choice in what we become.

## Myth #2 Schools are passive spectators to existing gender differences and inequalities

*While it's true that our parents, friends, and popular culture might shape our genders, schools are simply about getting an education.*

Second-wave feminism pointed to the role played by schools in the reproduction of unequal power relations. Significant issues still exist regarding the production of very particular models of masculinity and femininity, models which do not always operate in women's best interests.

## Myth #3 Boys are the latest victims of the schooling system

*Feminists have whined for so long about the plight of girls that nobody noticed it's the boys who are now on the receiving end of educational inequality.*

Third-wave feminism challenges this notion in a number of ways: the simplistic notion of victimhood, questions regarding *which* boys, more nuanced understandings of gender identity. This approach no longer locates the two genders at opposite ends of a battlefield.

# Introduction

## Gender as a topic of educational concern

Of all the debates over education currently being played out in the media, those with a gendered theme consistently have the highest profile. Even those not specifically about gender often find a way of veering in that direction at the slightest opportunity. For example, recent concerns over the fairness of the National Assessment Program – Literacy and Numeracy (NAPLAN) testing have often quickly become part of the 'What about the boys?' debate. An article in the *Herald Sun* (McArthur & McMahon 2011) addressed the effects of a number of factors within the NAPLAN results – non-English speaking background, geographic location, ethnicity, state – but also gender, which seemed to be the only issue readers were interested in commenting upon. The article concluded that girls had scored better than boys in 19 of the 20 categories measured by the tests. The responses were informative:

> TF – 'I don't know about other boys, but when I had to do these tests when I was at school and I found out they didn't mean anything, my male friends and I no longer tried or cared'
>
> Shanna – 'This is also because the education system has been hijacked by man-hating feminazis and it favours girls far above boys'
>
> Batts – 'All those smarts won't count for much when you're baking cakes and doing the washing'

The incensed readers' responses can be placed into a number of groups:

1  Who cares, men get the better jobs anyway (true).
2  NAPLAN is a load of rubbish (partly true, but for different reasons).
3  The tests are all rigged by angry feminists (highly unlikely).
4  The entire education system is now one big feminist plot (really?).

Adherents to this final claim often support their argument with data from another of the gendered debates about education: the declining numbers of male within the teaching profession. It has been pointed out that in South Australia, the number of male teachers has dropped from 37% in 1993, to only 31% in 2009 (Australian Bureau of Statistics 2010b). Clearly, 'man-hating feminazis' are driving them out.

Other gendered debates include ongoing concerns over the ethics, desirability and outcomes of single-sex education; issues of differential subject selection for boys and girls; divergent approaches to discipline, dress codes and resourcing; concerns surrounding text choice; overall attitudes to schooling, and so on. These issues will be dealt with in greater depth later in the chapter, but they illustrate here the ongoing nature of the concerns we have over the 'right' way to school boys and girls.

One final topic that keeps cropping up in the newspapers concerns supposedly 'natural' differences between the brains of boys and girls. The argument here is that boys will always be better at maths than girls because their brains are wired differently. This question will be addressed at length when discussing myth #1, however it raises the preliminary question: just what is the link between sex and gender?

## So what is sex, and what is gender?

More often than not, these terms are used synonymously. People often use the term 'gender' because it seems less loaded than 'sex', which brings with it some uncomfortable baggage. Obviously, given this chapter is attempting to understand some of the complexities associated with the relationship between sex and gender, blurring the two into one is simply unsatisfactory.

More generally, the two terms are deemed to be part of a binary, the opposite sides of the same coin, mutually exclusive and yet somehow linked. *Sex* is generally understood as a biological categorisation, dependent upon the possession of particular sexual organs, chromosomes, and hormones. More often than not, the human species is divided into two groupings according to their sex: male and female.

Different to this is *gender*. This is not a measure of whether or not you have breasts and a womb, but is rather an assessment of social factors: how you dress, how you conduct yourself, the roles you occupy, the identity you adopt. These are not inherited through our genetics, they are given to us by culture and history. Once again, more often than not, we divide ourselves into the gendered categories of man and women, although in this instance, how this can be accomplished stretches to far more than the two choices associated with 'sex'. After all, there are many possible femininities available to a women, just as there are masculinities for men, although as will be discussed when addressing myth #2, they are not all ranked equally.

As such, sex and gender form a pigeon pair, separate and yet linked, linked because specific genders are normally attached to an associated sex. The central question within the social sciences has been: what is the nature of this association? Certainly, it has proved fruitful to distinguish the two concepts, in that it provided the initial artillery in the battle against the sociobiological contention that sex causes gender – more of that in myth #1.

## Why still bother with gender?

All this aside, the assertion is often made that the most important struggles over gender are now over. Aren't we all equal now? Surely no-one really thinks that women are less able than men – maybe the odd dinosaur – but the rest of us live in the twenty-first century. This equality is even enshrined in law, and women's rights are now protected by the *Sex Discrimination Act 1984*.

So are women equal? The evidence suggests there may be a long way to go. That is, women are now in a position to apply for almost any job they want, but that doesn't mean they're going to get it. They can legitimately aspire to any career they choose, but will they do as well as equivalent men? Taking the law, for example, research suggests that in Victoria, over 60% of law graduates are women, but only 14% make it to become a partner in a law firm (McLeod 2008). Of the 48 judges who have sat on Australia's High Court, only four have been women. Currently, only 16% of the Federal Court Bench are women. In business, women are paid an average of 17% less than men. Only 3% of CEOs are women in the ASX 200 listed companies (i.e. the big ones), and only 8% of their board directors are women (EOWA 2010). In federal parliament in the House of Representatives, it's a bit better, but still only one in four members are women – a poor effort, for what is the seat of our democracy.

What about education? We all know that this is a female-dominated profession, so surely this means that women get a fair go when it comes to being a school-teacher. The latest census statistics put the overall number of female teachers at 68% (Australian Bureau of Statistics 2007). More specifically, to quote the *Staff in Australia Schools 2007* report:

> **Teachers:** Teaching has a high proportion of females (79% of primary teachers, and 56% of secondary, are female). The proportion of females has increased slightly in recent years.

> **Leaders:** Females hold 57% of the leadership positions in primary schools, while males hold 59% of leadership posts in secondary schools. The proportions of females holding leadership positions are much lower than the proportions of female teachers. Females comprise higher proportions of Deputy Principal than Principal posts. (McKenzie et al. 2008)

Figure 2.1 sets out this information in graphic form. To put it simply, women may dominate education in terms of total number of teachers, but this dominance disappears when it comes to an assessment of who is actually running the show.

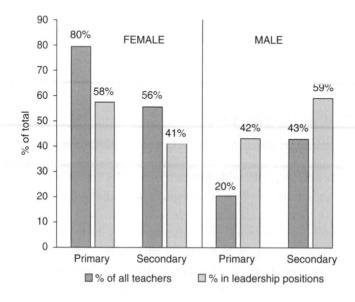

**Figure 2.1** *Which sex runs our schools?*
*Source: McKenzie et al. 2008*

So it would appear that the entire matter of gender and education is a long way from being settled in a satisfactory and equitable manner. Furthermore, this issue is of interest to far more people than disappointed female applicants for principal's positions, and education academics with nothing better to do. Those who continue to contribute to this debate include policy designers, curriculum specialists, mainstream teachers, concerned parents, educational administrators, politicians, and writers, researchers and activists on gender issues, to name but a few.

## Theories of gender: three waves

Regarding this final group, the history of women gaining full social and political rights is normally broken down into three stages, or three 'waves', each characterised by different concerns, sets of underpinning ideas and types of action and response. Although each of these will be discussed in greater detail shortly, to summarise:

> **First-wave feminism**: during the late nineteenth and early twentieth centuries, sought the right for women to become full citizens, principally through the right to vote.

> **Second-wave feminism**: from the early 1960s to the late 1970s, attempted to address a broad range of sex-based issues and inequalities, including reproductive rights, the family, in the workplace, and also within education.

> **Third-wave feminism:** of the 1990s onwards, has sought to approach gender from a less fixed and deterministic standpoint – i.e. it's not all simply about men oppressing women – accepting that complex issues arise from the relations created between a variety of masculinities and femininities.

Probably more than any other area within the social sciences, commonsense assumptions about gender are often based upon everything from subtle biases, half-truths and dodgy extrapolations, right through to convenient fabrications, out-right falsehoods and good old-fashioned chauvinist drivel. When it comes to gender, finding out which arguments and concepts are actually valid is not always as straightforward as it ought to be. There are some strange players in this game (as we'll see when we discuss sociobiology), some powerful vested interests, and several thousand years of gendered history to contend with. Any number of myths about gender could have been addressed here, but the following three should prove to be the most fruitful:

> **Myth #1** – Sex and gender are really the same thing

> **Myth #2** – Schools are passive spectators to existing gender differences and inequalities

> **Myth #3** – Boys are the latest victims of the schooling system

Conveniently, unpacking these three statements can best be done in tandem with a discussion of the three waves of feminism outlined above, as each bears directly on the logic supporting the myth.

# Myth #1 Sex and gender are really the same thing

We all know there are two sexes – male and female. Then there's this thing called 'gender', which is supposed to be shaped by culture. We have masculinity and femininity, which social scientists claim develop according to how we are brought up, according to the expectations of the society we live in. Rubbish. Gender is just a function of sex. Our sex creates our gender. As men, we naturally do 'manly' things. After all, in the final analysis modern men are just cavemen with suits on. They are hunters, conquerors and rulers. Men spread their seed and are good at long division. Of course, women are naturally different. They are gentle, docile, nurturing and subservient. They can't wait to have children, hang out in the kitchen and/ or become teachers. It's in the genes. All the various manifestations of culture are therefore simply an expression of this basic fact: sex causes gender.

## Sociobiological explanations of gender

This is a popular point of view. So far, the *Men Are from Mars, Women Are from Venus* collection of books have sold over 40 million copies. The primary assumption supporting these texts is that somehow our biological sex inevitably makes us socially different. Likewise, *Why Men Don't Listen and Women Can't Read Maps* (Pease & Pease 1999), with 12 million sales to its credit, also looks for biological answers to social differences, such as 'why men focus on one thing at a time' and 'why women can speak, listen and write simultaneously'. Based upon what it refers to as 'detailed scientific research', it contends that male and female brains are hardwired differently, and as a consequence of these innate, immutable neurological differences, men can't take advice and women can't parallel park.

This isn't a new explanation of the differences between men and women; far from it. Looking back at Victorian England, the reasoning is the same, only the examples are different. The central concern then appeared to be that women were thought not to be 'naturally' cut out for thinking. Mosedale (1978) details a range of wonderful nineteenth-century examples of the scientific logic used to prove women's relative stupidity. The eminent scientist George Romanes started out by correlating the smaller size of women's brains with their obviously diminished intellectual powers, and ended up by suggesting that because women are physically weaker, they clearly can't sustain the effort of prolonged brain action. An equally eminent Harvard professor of medicine, Edward Clarke, seriously contended that educating adolescent girls was dangerous because it could divert important energy from their ovaries to their brains, rendering them sterile. However, probably the most straightforward argument for the intellectual inferiority of women belonged to a certain Miss Hardaker, published in *The Popular Science Monthly* in 1882:

> The sum total of food converted into thought by women can never equal the sum total of food
> converted into thought by men. It follows, therefore, that *men will always think more than women.*

It was sociobiological arguments like these that provided much of the justification for continuing to limit the rights granted to women, principally the right to property and the right to vote. Consequently, first-wave feminists had a significant vested interest in debunking the validity of this particular line of reasoning. First-wave feminism is most frequently understood in terms of the suffrage movement of the late nineteenth and early twentieth centuries. Arguably, its initial impetus came from the earlier publication of such books as Mary Wollstonecraft's *Vindication of the Rights of Women* (1792), but it was through campaigns of public education and civil disobedience that they finally managed to turn the tide of public opinion and change the law in their favour. Women were given the vote in Australia in 1902, but not until 1918 in the UK, and 1920 in the USA.

Importantly, it was not just the suffragette movement that found fault with the objective scientific evidence that supported their natural intellectual inferiority. A significant number of early-twentieth-century writers, and even scientists, seemed well aware that age-old stereotypical opinions about women had simply been translated into scientifically proven facts by simple sleight of hand.

> Those who espouse a scientific superstition are still more formidable than those by whom it was
> created. The dogma of the inferiority of woman is so deeply rooted in the mentality of our times that
> the idea of attempting to dislodge it almost borders upon insanity. This is the reason that the majority
> of scientists appear among the most ardent advocates of the theory of the inferiority of woman. (Finot
> 1913, 122)

Clearly, these kinds of arguments are no longer taken seriously, hopefully by anyone. But that doesn't mean that new, more sophisticated versions haven't taken their place. That is, no contemporary scientist would give any credence to the contention that men are smarter than women, but a limited number of scientists – generally called *sociobiologists* – who argue that other kinds of social difference have their origins in the natural differences deemed to exist between males and females.

For example, there exists a body of literature that explains boys' better results in maths as a direct function of differences hard-wired into the human brain. A number of articles point to differences between males and females in their corpus callosums, the set of nerves that connect the left and right cerebral hemispheres of the brain, in that it was said to be significantly wider in women (Gorman 1992). The outcome, it is argued, is a naturally greater level of intuition in women, and an impaired level of spatial awareness and mathematical ability. The implication here is that boys do better at maths, not because they are relentlessly pushed towards the hard sciences, both overtly and covertly (and also away from the 'girly' humanities subjects), all for heavily gendered cultural reasons, but because of a few extra bits of wiring in the brain.

## Some problems with the 'boy-brain vs girl-brain' argument

There are, however, problems with almost every element of this argument. First, there are no longer any significant differences between boys and girls in their maths results (Hyde et al. 2008), so the entire argument is built upon a fallacy. And yet, the stereotype of the natural superiority of boys at maths persists, even though in the USA as many girls as boys take advanced high school maths, and 48% of all undergraduate maths degrees go to women.

Second, the assertion that the corpus callosum is larger in females appears to be false. Recent research has shown that the initial measurements, upon which the entire argument is based, haven't been replicated within later studies. The part of the brain that has supposedly doomed females to be rubbish at maths is actually the same size as in males (Bishop & Wahlsten 1997).

Third, and of greatest importance, since it has implications across a range of sociobiological arguments, is the observation that *even if* there were differences between adult male and female brains in the size of the corpus callosum, there have never been shown to be any differences in infants (Fausto-Sterling 2000). Why is this so important? It is important because if brain differences do exist, whether in the corpus callosum or anywhere, they are the *product* of gender, not the other way around. That is, if you treat a male differently to a female for their entire lives, it wouldn't be remotely surprising if you found their brains to be dissimilar – indeed, it would be surprising if they weren't. The research suggests that from the earliest ages, boys and girls are talked to differently, played with differently, disciplined differently, encouraged differently, touched differently and presented with completely different models of what they ought to be (Gilbert & Gilbert 1998).

Fine (2010) argues that the issues raised by Finot in 1913 still apply to contemporary sociobiological 'brain' research. Countering what she calls 'neurosexism', she argues that the brain is not hard-wired from birth, as the sociobiologists would have us believe; rather the wiring is 'flexible, malleable and changeable'. Some boys develop better spatial skills because they are expected to throw and catch balls more often, reflecting dominant models of masculinity. Likewise, girls are expected to be more expressive and emotional, and hence emphasis is placed on their verbal skills. These are not innate differences; they are the product of how we raise our children, and what we expect of them. Female babies grow into young girls as the result of a 'pernicious pinkification', not because of the shape of their brains, or their genes, or their chemistry.

Importantly, if such factors are deemed to influence us at all, then that influence is very small. After all, if boys and girls are naturally different, then those differences could be seen globally, across all cultures – they can't; those differences should also be historically fixed – they aren't; and those differences should result in a rigid binary between men and women – they don't.

In truth, sociobiological arguments are not widely held, either by medical or social scientists – indeed, they are regarded as rather weird, and a bit of a throwback – but one place they do appear to have currency is in the popular media, which in turn gives them currency within popular discourse. Consequently, anyone trying to address the possibilities of change in the field of gender is confronted by the constant presupposition that, 'in the final analysis, boys and girls are just naturally different, aren't they'. But as Roland Barthes (1972) famously wrote: 'What is sickening in myth is its resort to a false nature.'

In summary then, gender can't just be read off from sex as a causal relationship – far from it. Culture intervenes at every stage of the gender-forming process. Nicholson (1994) uses the metaphor of sex as simply a 'coat-rack' upon which gender is constructed. That is, each society superimposes a gender on an existing male or female sexed body – the coat-rack – in a manner that suits their own needs, culture and history. The coat-rack has next to no say in the cut of the gender coat that gets hung from it. So, when attempting to understand the relationship between gender and education, rather than spending all this effort focusing on any tiny natural differences that might exist between the brains of males and females, perhaps concentrating on the vast amount we have in common might prove to be more productive.

# Myth #2 Schools are passive spectators to existing gender differences and inequalities

Fortunately, education has always managed to stay immune to the effects of a male-dominated society. Fair enough, other areas of society may favour men, to some extent, but education is a fair race, with the best and the most worthy gaining the greatest success; and if that happens to be men, so be it. The school itself is a gender-neutral institution. Children of both sexes appear in grade 1, they get an education, and they leave between grade 10 and grade 12. The fact that they acquire a gender in the meantime has nothing to do with the school. Indeed, schools explicitly don't privilege one sex over the other in any way. Yes, gender differences and inequalities may exist in the wider society, but our education system is a non-combatant in the gender wars.

After the first battles over voting and property rights were won by the suffragettes, for a while 'the sex problem' appeared to be resolved, and it wasn't until after World War II that new issues started to arise. While the men were away fighting, women had successfully occupied a wide variety of roles previously thought to be beyond their capabilities, forever reshaping what women could be, and what they might aspire to. However, when the men returned from war, women were pushed back into the home, with a vengeance, and for the next 20 years, the dominant model of femininity centred on their supporting role within the nuclear family. However, the genie was now out of the bottle.

Consequently, from the start of the 1960s through to the end of the 1970s, a new group – the second-wave feminists – sought to question what they saw as, not only the tired old arguments about the 'natural' role of women, but also the power structures that kept women in their place. Informed by such texts as Simone de Beauvoir's *The Second Sex* (1960) and Betty Friedan's *The Feminine Mystique* (1963), they set out to challenge the entire system of male domination: the system of *patriarchy*. They noted that men called the shots in almost every avenue of life: the workplace, the home, public office, relationships, religion, the judiciary. Second-wave feminists attempted not only to raise awareness of this power imbalance, but also to do something about it.

The question now is: does this male domination extend to our education system? After all, surely if the rest of our society plays a role in the production of masculinity and femininity, as well as the power relations between them, why should schooling be any different? Answer: it isn't.

## Schooling as a gender regime

Taylor (2004) contends that, contrary to the myth of neutrality, the school is indeed a heavily gendered site.

> … gender discourses shape our behaviour, attitudes and expectations in profound and pervasive ways. It is therefore not surprising that they influence school and classroom practices in various ways as well. Schooling, as a disciplinary institution … is a key site for re-producing gender relations, but it is also a key site where change can occur. (Taylor 2004, 91)

Taylor refers to the school as constituting a *gender regime*. This regime extends from the most direct and obvious of strategies for the production of different genders, to the subtle and the indirect. While even the most ardent of second-wave feminists wouldn't suggest that each of these factors represents an attempt to disempower women, they would likely contend that the overall effect is consistent with the logic of a patriarchal society. There are 10 gendered differences outlined below (with many more for those with the time and energy to think of them).

## 1   Single-sex schools

First and foremost, the sex of our children is considered so important, and the processes by which they become gendered so different, that we have set up completely separate schools for them. The most recent available data shows that over 43% of non-government secondary schools are single-sex institutions (ABS 1997).

Various arguments are used to justify this division, but the primary rationale is that males and females gain a better education, and more comfortably engage with the process of growing into acceptable men and women, in the absence of the other. While this may or may not be true, what this separation also does is reinforce the fundamental significance of the differences between the sexes. That is, society signals in the clearest possible manner that men and women, masculinity and femininity, are not the same.

## 2   School ethos

Arguably, the point of single-sex schools is not simply to separate the males from the females, but to engage in different processes within those schools. Even a casual glance at an all-boys private school would generally reveal a very specific type of operating ethos, a gendered philosophy, underpinning life there. While many commonalities exist between boys' and girls' schools – likely to include valuing learning, respect, community, and so on – the dissimilarities are especially notable.

The ethos at many boys' schools is specifically about learning a given type of masculinity. School mottos are particularly informative in this regard (Synott & Symes 1995). *Viriliter Age* (Act Courageously), *Virtus Ubique Vincet* (Courage Conquers All), *Vincit Qui Se Vincit* (He Conquers Who Conquers Self), are mottos which all suggest a very particular understanding of what it is to be a man. Indeed, the parents of one boys' school objected to attempts to make it co-educational, on the grounds that the value of 'strength', as endorsed by their school motto, would be diluted by the presence of girls.

A different ethos appears to operate at girls' schools, as made manifest by mottos such as, *In Love Serve One Another*, *Fide et Amore* (In Faith And Love), *In Strength and Sweetness*. Given the lack of words such as 'courageous' and 'conquer', it seems fair to assume that these institutions are out to foster very different learning environments, and very different types of student, to the boys' schools. These are institutions where 'conquest' isn't necessarily on the agenda.

It has been suggested that the ethos existing within boys' schools are one mechanism whereby a particular type of masculinity is constructed: *hegemonic masculinity*. This concept, most frequently associated with the work of Connell (2005), describes a version of masculinity that dominates the other possible options, a masculinity based upon strength, self-confidence, assertiveness and ambition; more on this shortly.

## 3   Subject enrolment

Whether we are at a single-sex or a co-educational school, we are all viscerally aware that certain subjects seem to be gendered from the very start. As a result of this, by the time students arrive at grade 12, these largely covert cultural messages have been translated into increasingly clear gendered demarcations, as measured by enrolment percentages (see Figure 2.2).

These numbers are relatively predictable. Some subjects are considered 'hard' sciences, or subjects directly appropriate for dominant models of masculinity, such as physical education, and these are dominated by boys. Others are 'soft' sciences, or subjects tied to stereotypical models of femininity, such as the humanities and languages, and these are dominated by girls. Importantly, these subject choices spill over into the trajectories students take into post-compulsory education and future employment, constituting a very clear example of the social reproduction of gender.

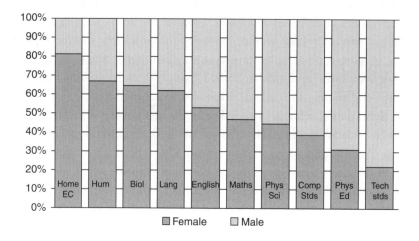

**Figure 2.2** *Subject enrolment by sex*
*Source: Fullarton & Ainley 2000*

It should also be pointed out that these figures are simply the result of boys and girls making choices for themselves about what subjects to take. At many single-sex schools, subjects deemed 'gender-inappropriate' (read 'home economics' for boys, and 'technical studies' for girls) are not even offered as part of the curriculum.

## 4 Subject preference

Even before students get around to making formal choices as to the subjects they will continue with and those they will drop, subjects are allocated roles to play in the formation of gender, whether they like it or not, and students respond to this accordingly.

For example, English is often marked out as a feminised subject, and male students can struggle to accommodate any enthusiasm for it, while at the same time attempting to shape a masculine identity acceptable to their peers. Indeed, belittling the study of English, and those boys who enjoy it, can form a significant component of heterosexual masculinity, as the following quote from a grade 10 boy demonstrates:

> This subject is the biggest load of utter bullshit I have ever done. Therefore I don't particularly like this subject. I hope you are not offended by this, but most guys who like English are faggots.
> (Martino 2000)

Of course, other subjects can play exactly the opposite role in the construction of masculinity. Physical education has long played a role in the shaping of men, allowing them to demonstrate physical strength, speed, courage and confidence – the very definition of hegemonic masculinity – and is hence a very popular subject with boys. Incorporating these crucial components within their identities not only marks them out as superior to other, less dominant, forms of masculinity, but also superior to girls, an attitude that can carry over into the wider world. As one male competitor said, during a strike protesting women's participation in the famous Acapulco cliff-diving championship: 'This is a death-defying activity – men are taking a great gamble to prove their courage. What would be the point if everyone saw that women could do the same' (Bryson 1990).

## 5   Discipline

Research has consistently shown that school discipline is not simply a straightforward and impartial framework that it portrays itself to be, one that allows schools to function effectively, while also producing organised and respectful citizens. The evidence suggest that social class, race and gender all play a significant role in who gets punished, how often, and for what (Wallace et al. 2008).

With specific respect to gender, this body of research points to the same two conclusions; first, boys are subject to greater disciplinary intervention than girls. That is, they engage far more frequently in behaviours that result in punishment: admonishment, detention, suspension and expulsion. Second, and far more interestingly, boys and girls are disciplined differently, often based upon pre-existing beliefs about what is 'natural' behaviour for each sex (i.e. back to some good, old-fashioned, subliminal sociobiology). Boys are often not disciplined for noisy, boisterous and unruly behaviour, because teachers regard this as part of some intrinsic masculinity. Girls, however, will often be punished for the same conduct, as this is deemed to run counter to the way they 'ought' to behave. As such, school discipline becomes part of a regime of moral judgement, one that succeeds in reinforcing dominant understandings of gender: confidence and assertion in boys, passivity and obedience in girls (Robinson 1992; Hart 2000; Ryan & Cooper 2010).

## 6   Time with teacher

Exactly who gets the teacher's attention follows a very similar logic to that of discipline, and in one way, boys often receive more teacher time simply because their behaviour demands it. However, more generally, boys are given more teacher time than girls, both positive and negative, are called by their names more often, have their questions answered more frequently, and are asked more complex questions (Sadker 2000, 2002). One well-known study on this issue found that boys take up about two-thirds of teacher time, and if this percentage is reduced, 'they feel they are being discriminated against' (Spender 1982, 57).

The outcome of this disparity is a further reinforcement of existing gender expectations. For example, when boys call out in class (up to eight times more often than girls) they are often responded to directly, while girls are more likely to be told to raise their hands if they want an answer. Once again, such interactions succeed in cementing the notion that boys are active and forceful, while girls are placid and compliant – notions that, after years spent interacting with teachers, become part of the way children both understand themselves, and their gender (Frawley 2005).

## 7 Dress codes

As within the wider cultural contexts, the ways in which boys and girls are encouraged, or required, to dress at school reinforces a range of dominant understandings of gender. Traditionally, boys' uniforms have been practical, durable and plain, precisely the outfit you'd want for boisterous playground activity. Conversely, girls' uniforms are generally more aesthetic and much less amenable to any kind of physical activity, either through choice of colours, or the fact that many are required to wear a skirt – the natural enemy of all things athletic.

Most co-educational schools now offer unisex clothing options, but the not-so-subtle social pressures of schooling life often make this option a difficult one. Probably needless to say, even though girls are allowed to wear traditional boys attire, the reverse is normally forbidden, as it does not 'reflect community standards' (Hoffman 2009). Such expectations are not limited to clothing, but also encompass hairstyles, jewellery, and the use of make-up. Once again, with their short hair and make-up and earring-free faces, boys are ready for activity; girls, not so much. In the area of physical appearance, the school is not a passive spectator to existing gender differences and inequalities; it's a showcase for them.

## 8 Access to resources

Not all playing fields are level, and even though resources such as computers are readily available in most schools, this doesn't mean that everyone gains access to them equally. As will be discussed in greater detail in Chapter 9, there are various types of digital divide – differences in the ability to access and use digital technologies – one example of which involves gender. Blackmore et al. (2003) note that not only are girls under-represented in ICT clubs and the use of ICTs outside school, they can struggle to gain access to computers in co-educational classrooms. Furthermore, when they get on the computers, they are likely to face greater levels of criticism from boys, who buy into, and hence reinforce, the dominant assumption that when it comes to ICTs, they are simply better (Cooper 2006).

This isn't the only example of resourcing issues. Provision of funding for male, as opposed to female sport, has long been a matter of contention. It is, however, one of the most important ones. After all, arguing that the boys have greater access to computers at school is of significantly greater importance than observing that the boys might also monopolise the crayons. ICTs now form a crucial component of most young people's social, educational and future professional life-worlds. Somehow carving this out as a male domain has massive equity implications. That said, times are changing very quickly in this area. Perhaps the next research to emerge in this area will paint a rosier picture.

## 9   Classroom texts

Even the materials schools use to teach students have been criticised for presenting a very particular gendered take on the world, one which has traditionally foregrounded men, and presented gender abilities and relations in predictably stereotypical ways. As Ryan and Cooper note:

> Textbooks, other reading materials, and educational software, despite attempts at improvement by publishers and authors, often still portray females as more helpless than males. Although sexism has decreased in many texts … researchers argue that examples of gender stereotyping, tokenism, and omission still occur in reference to girls and women (2010, 88).

A recent study by McCabe et al. (2011) of over 5600 children's books from throughout the twentieth century have shown that boys are represented twice as often in titles of books, and over one and a half times as often as central characters, than are girls. The animals in the books are also predominantly male, with over two and half times as many portrayed as female. It doesn't take much to see how being a girl has come to be understood as 'marginalised other' in so many ways. Even the storybook puppies are boys.

## 10   Employment for teachers

There is little need to pursue this final issue further, as it was discussed in the introduction to this chapter. Schools display all the same gender inequities of the wider world of employment. Not only are males disproportionately represented in all the leadership positions, and females find themselves clustered in those parts of the system that educate younger children (they need more 'caring'), and the 'fluffier' subject areas (i.e. those that involve reading), they are also far more likely to put their careers on hold by staying at home with a young family, than any of their male teaching counterparts. None of this goes unnoticed by students.

### Some problems with this approach

So, contrary to myth #2, schools appear to have a huge role to play in the reinforcement of gender differences. While they don't necessarily overtly work for the continuation of gendered inequalities, schools do play a significant role in the social reproduction of roles, practices and identities that often appear to work against women's best interests. That, however, is far from the end of the matter.

The foundation upon which these observations stand has been subject to no little amount of criticism, which doesn't mean the facts themselves are suddenly suspect, but it does mean they may need to be interpreted in a somewhat different way. The central problem here revolves around the underpinning notion of patriarchy, i.e. the belief that society is organised around the fundamental principle of male domination. Within the logic of second-wave feminism, the 10 examples of the non gender-neutrality of schools act as proof that we live in a patriarchy. That is, each in turn adds another evidentiary pillar holding the concept off the ground.

The trouble is, the notion of patriarchy appears to have had its day. This approach to gender has been criticised for a number of reasons, the following being only some of them.

## It's dichotomising

The notion of patriarchy divides the world into two neat halves. There are the men, who have the power, who dominate, and for whom everything is rosy. Then there are the women, who lack power, who are subject to male domination, and for whom life is rubbish. As discussed in the introduction to this book, this form of binary reasoning is common within modernist forms of thought: mind vs body, culture vs nature, and so on. Masculinity vs femininity fits right in.

## It's reductionist

The notion of patriarchy necessitates boiling all the complexity of social relations down to a simple power relation. Girls wear dresses? Patriarchy. Girls don't do technical studies? Patriarchy. Girls find it harder to become head of school? Patriarchy. It's a one-stop shop for all questions relating to gender. It makes asking those questions kind of redundant.

## It's homogenising

The notion of patriarchy assumes that all women are somehow the same. As such, all men are somehow inherently more powerful than all women. It doesn't matter if you are a high court judge, or a hillbilly living in a shack – if you are a man, you possess some innate authority that sets you above women. Predictably, it might come as a surprise to the female members of Australia's High Court, that the above-mentioned male toothless shack-dweller is somehow on the winning end of life's power equation, just because he's a man.

## It's disempowering

The notion of patriarchy means that given male domination appears to be everywhere, chipping away at one small part of it is simply delaying the inevitable. Who cares if we finally manage to remove all traces of gender bias from our textbooks, or make sure boys get asked to put their hands up in class, just like girls are? What's the point if there's still this huge slant to the playing field that affects every other component of their lives? It makes the struggle against gender inequality all but pointless. Women are victims, end of story.

It was primarily feminists themselves who articulated these criticisms (along with a few disgruntled men), thereby seeking a way to keep the debates around gender equity moving forward. Arguably, addressing the final myth offers a solution to some of these problems, by way of third-wave feminism.

# Myth #3 Boys are the latest victims of the schooling system

Yes, girls might have once had cause for complaint, but that was quite a long time ago now. The pendulum hasn't just swung back towards the middle, it's gone so far it's in danger of hitting the side of the clock. Boys are now being actively victimised within an education system dominated by vengeful feminists. The curriculum is biased towards girls; the teaching methods are biased towards girls; and boys aren't even allowed to be real boys any more.

This belief has significant currency, and can be found in the most surprising of places. However, if we were seeking expertise on gender equity issues, would we really consult with the headmaster of the world's most elite private boys' school?

**Boys failed by education system, says Eton headmaster**

Boys are being failed by the British education system because it has become too focused on girls, the headmaster of Eton has warned. Tony Little said that the different sexes required different teaching methods to bring out students' potential and that GCSEs favour girls more than boys. He also blamed teachers for failing to realise that boys are 'more emotional' than girls, despite the fact that girls 'turn on the works'. (Roberts 2010)

Significantly, the initial concerns over the performance of boys in school have been taken up by two sets of commentators. The first, often referred to as 'the backlash', has been described as a counterattack against the ideas of second-wave feminists. Describing this phenomenon, Faludi (1992) noted how the gains made by the women's movement of the 1960s and 1970s prompted near-hysterical responses suggesting that, having gained equality, women were now taking over the whole show. Indeed, it has been widely argued that most of the 'What about the boys?' debate is part of this hysteria.

The second response to this debate came from the third-wave feminists. Third-wave feminism is a little harder to pigeonhole than its two predecessors. Prompted by books such as Naomi Wolf's *The Beauty Myth* (1991), this new approach also sought to challenge second-wave feminism, to the extent that, for a while, such writers were deemed part of 'post-feminism'. Their concerns, though complex and varied, largely centred upon the homogenising aspects of the notion of patriarchy. They rightly concluded that second-wave feminism had at its heart an understanding of 'woman' that was essentially white and middle class – the unspoken essence of the female. Third-wave feminists pointed out that no such essence exists, and they focus instead upon the various ways in which gendered identities produce, and are produced by, our complex social and cultural relations. That is, women do not constitute a stable, coherent group of people, sharing common interests, any more than men do. Consequently, the notion of a 'global sisterhood', so central to second-wave feminism, is simply a fable. White women are just as capable of oppressing black women as white men.

This new approach has implications for myth #3 in three separate ways.

## Which boys?

In no longer seeming to 'blame men', third-wave feminism has been more receptive to the recent discourses over the 'What about the boys' debate. However, they note that it appears to be based upon the same faulty premise that animated earlier forms of feminism. Just as the notion of the archetypal 'girl' – forever oppressed within a patriarchal schooling system – doesn't hold water, so too the notion of the universal 'boy' is equally flawed. When we say that the modern schooling system is now slanted in favour of girls, and that boys are consequently failing, do we mean all boys? Even at first glance, this does seem like another example of a modernist binary in operation. If we begin by stating that '*some* girls' are now doing better in school, this quickly becomes 'girls', and in binary-thinking land, this must mean that the other half of this self-created binary, 'boys', must be doing correspondingly badly. That's the way that the maths works. Except that it isn't.

Vickers (2010, 227) contends: 'the proposition that boys are uniformly failing and girls are uniformly winning is seriously misguided'. She uses both national and international data to show that the most appropriate response to the question, 'What about the boys?' is: 'Which boys are you talking about?' To summarise: there appear to be relatively small differences in the results gained by boys and girls in testing, with girls going very slightly better in literacy, and boys doing very slightly better in numeracy. However, these results are dwarfed by the differences between social classes. For example, in the Year 3 NAPLAN results (2008), the girls' mean is 408.2 points, as opposed to 393.1 points for boys – a gap of only 15.1 points. The reading scores for the children of highly educated parents (which correlates directly to social class) is 436.0, as opposed to 358.7 for the least educated parents – a 77.3 point gap. To put it another way, when it comes to doing well in school, whether you are a boy or a girl is relatively unimportant in comparison to which social class you come from.

Of course, the problem really arises when you combine both of these factors – i.e. being a male, *and* from the working class – in which case, the big question should really be: 'What about the *working-class* boys?' After all, what the advocates of the 'schools are conspiring against boys' position never seem to get around to mentioning, is that boys still do better than girls when it comes to getting the very best grades. For example, in the 2010 Queensland grade 12 results, boys still took out more of the top results (OP 1s and 2s) (Chilcott & Tin 2010). The truth is: boys dominate both ends of the normal curve.

Finally, Vickers (2010) also notes that a further argument in favour of the educational bias against boys – that they drop out of school in greater number than girls – may be something of a furphy. From the early 1990s onwards, approximately 10% more girls complete grade 12 than boys (about 80%, as opposed to 70%). While this has been held up as further proof of how unsuited the current schooling system is for boys, a more plausible explanation notes that poorly performing boys can drop out of school and look for a job with some confidence (via the male-orientated apprenticeship system). Equivalent girls have much more limited options, and therefore often decide to stay on.

## Must we have 'victims'?

Foster, Kimmel and Skelton (2001, 4) address the issue of 'the problem of boys' and conclude that within a number of educational discourses, 'boys are positioned as "victim", specifically of: single (fatherless) families; female-dominated primary schooling; and feminism, which has enabled girls' success'. Interestingly, one of the central features of third-wave feminism has been its rejection of the 'victim' status accorded to women by second-wave feminism. The all-encompassing notion of patriarchy meant that, no matter how women tried or what avenue of life they embarked upon, they were always destined to be on the losing end of male power. However, the 1990s saw the rise of a new way of understanding femininity, with a whole new range of female role models – Madonna, Xena, Buffy – all of whom managed to combine confidence, assertiveness and power with a sexiness for which they didn't feel they had to apologise.

> … the new girl hero doesn't need a man to define her – she has staked her own claim to the privileges of both masculinity *and* femininity. She is not the overly emotional victimised heroine – she does her own hunting, fighting and monster-slaying. (Hopkins 2002, 3)

The issue here is that power is no longer necessarily regarded as a zero-sum game. Just because one group can exercise power within a given context, or according to a particular logic, doesn't therefore mean that someone else is automatically suffering. Besides, if this new approach teaches us anything, it's that gender domination can't just be 'read off' from social structure. Certainly, gendered issues and inequalities still exist, but it's much more complicated than that. Genders come in all shapes, sizes, colours, classes, ages, sexualities, cultures and opinions. Exactly who is dominating whom? And is domination even the right word?

Also, it must be said that women haven't rightly abandoned the rhetoric of victimhood, whether in the workplace, relationships, or the school, just to see it picked up and wielded by men. Men still get the best grades and the best jobs, so it seems somewhat disingenuous to extrapolate the educational struggles of one cohort of boys into some global war on masculinity, which men are deemed to be losing.

## And when we say 'boys' ...

One of the central themes of third-wave feminism has been to address the structuring of gender identities. Part of the problem has always been that just as males and females were placed within a binary – 'the opposite sexes' – so too were genders. Masculinity and femininity are depicted as opposites: if men are strong, women have to be weak; if men are smart, women have to be stupid (and now vice-versa). Third-wave feminism rejects this either/or approach.

Most writers and researchers who consider themselves third-wave feminists have now aligned themselves to far broader programs of gender studies. These programs don't only seek to understand the multiple, and often contradictory, ways in which feminine identities are shaped; they regard masculinity as an equally fertile ground for study. Understanding how a modern 'boy' constructs his identity, and has that identity constructed, involves far more than a grasp of the notion of 'hegemonic masculinity'. Indeed, this important concept has itself been challenged as an over-simplification of what is actually a fluid cluster of behaviours and statuses.

Therefore, just as the question 'What about the boys?' proved inadequate to the task due to its lack of social-class specification, so too is it inadequate due to its presumption that all boys somehow struggle for the same reasons within the school, and that masculinity is a coherent entity. They don't, it isn't, and sophisticated contemporary forms of gender research can help unpack the problem far more clearly.

In summary, the idea that boys are somehow the latest victims of the schooling system requires considerable qualification. Certainly, there are some cohorts of boys, most notably working-class boys, who are struggling – and are therefore worthy subjects of specific policy interventions. However, to extrapolate that to all boys, and hence make it some kind of gender war issue, borders on the ridiculous. The discourse of 'victimhood' should no longer have a place within education for boys or for girls. Much more interesting research is being conducted into how we become one of a large range of different types of men and women, and the role that our schools play in that process.

# Conclusion

Upon closer scrutiny, the first two common assertions about gender and education don't hold up to scrutiny, and the third needs significant qualification. First, gender is not unrelated to sex, but neither is it simply a function of it. Sociobiological arguments about the educational effects of brain differences or hormones weren't convincing in the late nineteenth century, and they're not convincing now. We become men and women through complex life-long processes given to us by our social background, our culture and our history. The same is true for how we learn.

Second, schools are not simply spectators to the process for gendering, quite the contrary. Educational institutions have a comprehensive role to play in the transmission of gender, both masculine and feminine. Everything from school ethos, uniforms and discipline, to resourcing, curriculum and employment structure affects the types of boys and girls we produce. While the evidence suggests that, historically, the school hasn't exactly been a force for gender equity, neither can it realistically be depicted as some kind of 'tool of patriarchy' by which females were kept in their place.

Finally, more recent approaches to gender in the school have stressed the compound ways in which schools both fail, and succeed for, their students (boys and girls), the possibilities opened up by more nuanced and contingent understandings of gender, the continuum of gendered identities, and the need for teacher to understand them.

All of which makes the ongoing focus on the topic by academics, policy makers, educational administrators and teachers both appropriate and important. In spite of what some dominant discourses within the area might assert, this particular social issue is still a long way from a satisfactory resolution. One of the many great things about being a teacher is that they have a significant role in shaping the future, and once we abandon the notion that our genders are given to us by nature, or that one gender necessarily dominates the other, this leaves teachers in a better position to help create strong, confident and thoughtful citizens of both sexes.

# Chapter 3

# Race/ethnicity

The issue of race is both complex and emotive, as it is for its somewhat less problematic cousin, ethnicity – and that's before they are discussed in relation to education. Of all the ways humans have chosen to divide themselves, none has a history as arbitrary, as spurious and as terrible as the concept of race. A range of terms are used in this area of study, but probably the most important is 'othering' – i.e. the process of deciding who's in, who's out, and why. Arguably, two of the most pernicious examples of this are racism, and ethnic discrimination.

## Myth #1 Humanity is naturally divided into races

*Just as there are different breeds of dog, or species of beetle, so too are there different races of people. It's just part of nature: yellow people are naturally clever, black people are naturally good at sport, and white people are naturally good at being in charge.*

None of this is true. Race is a relatively recent invention; one that has found a way of blaming nature for a series of socially constructed forms of discrimination. Unfortunately, though this concept is without foundation, it still has real effects.

## Myth #2 We no longer discriminate on the basis of race or ethnicity

*Sure, people who aren't white once had a rough time in Australia, but now most of us have friends with every skin colour imaginable. No-one cares anymore.*

While hopefully there's some truth in these statements, the evidence suggests that discrimination extends beyond the simple and the overt, and is often at its most pervasive in its institutional and cultural forms.

## Myth #3 Educational outcomes are unaffected by race or ethnicity

*Maybe there's still some discrimination around, but the education system educates all kids equally. In the end, it just matters how smart you are.*

Whether by deliberate discrimination or otherwise, some racial and ethnic minorities often still find themselves at the losing end of the education system. In particular, the evidence suggests refugees are in an especially vulnerable position.

## Myth #4 There is an 'Indigenous problem' in education

*Indigenous Australians lack what it takes to do well in school. Whatever their problem is, there's no ready solution.*

The fact that Indigenous students can struggle at school is not an 'Indigenous problem', it is an issue that all Australian need to take responsibility for. Setting up the binary of 'us' vs 'them', homogenising their culture, and employing a deficit model, is not a good start. A better approach might begin with greater consultation with local Indigenous communities, and more effective embedding of Indigenous perspectives in the curriculum.

# Introduction

As discussed in Chapter 1, we appear to be somewhat touchy about the issue of social class, but race is in another league of sensitivity altogether. The probable reasons for this are twofold: the first lies in the way we go about constructing our identities. Whereas we may well recognise that we fit the criteria for membership of a particular social class, this doesn't necessarily mean that this classification becomes a central component of how we understand ourselves. Certainly, an 'untouchable' in India, or one of the British aristocracy, may be constantly and acutely aware of this status, and may therefore regard this as one of the most important things about themselves. In contrast however, it is unlikely that the identity of 'middle-class person' is of sufficient importance to Australians that it plays any role in shaping any kind of 'inner identity' – whatever that means.

Generally, the same can't be said for issues of racial and ethnic identity. If you ask an Indigenous Australian, or a Vietnamese or Lebanese Australian, whether this 'racial' or 'ethnic' identity was of greater significance to them than any class-based identity, then the answer would almost certainly be 'yes'. This is an interesting issue, all the more interesting when compared to the likely answer given by an Anglo-Celtic (white) Australian to the same question, which would generally be that 'they don't have a race'. This will be discussed in greater length when addressing myth #4.

The second reason for sensitivity over this issue involves a long history of the terrible consequences that could arise from being deemed to belong to a given race. Up until the American Civil War, black Americans had to carry papers to prove they were free, otherwise the mere colour of their skin would make them slaves. Just over half a century ago, six million people were exterminated for being part of the 'Jewish race'. In Australia, Indigenous Australians weren't even allowed to vote until 1967, and it was only in 1973 that the last vestiges of the White Australia policy were removed. It took until 1975 before it became unlawful to discriminate against someone on the basis of their race.

So this is serious stuff, and while coming from the wrong social class can mean you don't get access to a good education, or don't get invited to the rich kids' parties, coming from the wrong race could get you hung from a tree (Elder 2003). And let's not kid ourselves, even in the twenty-first century, in many places around the world, it still can.

## Getting our terms straight

Before having a reasoned discussion of the role of race and ethnicity in Australian education, it is probably useful to explain some of the common terms. There appears to be a lot of terminological slippage when addressing these issues, i.e. using the same word to mean different things, or different words to mean the same thing. If there's one thing we need here, it's a bit of clarity. Even though each of these terms will be expanded upon later, not only will it be useful to provide a preliminary sketch of their meanings, it will also help to show the links between them; how one concept often leads on to the next, like falling dominoes.

## Othering

This term is based upon a very simple premise: that we largely determine the membership of our own social groups, and its boundaries, by deciding who we are not. That is, a necessary part of figuring out who is the same us, and why, is deciding who isn't. The term was first popularised through Edward Said's (1979) work on colonialism (more on this in Chapter 12), describing who 'we' were, and contrasting that construction with the lesser grouping of 'them' – the other, the native peoples.

Importantly, othering isn't just about peoples deemed to be of a different race, ethnicity, culture, religion or nationality, although when it came to colonialism, they were the ones that probably counted the most. Othering is the core of most unequal power relations, and can be seen every day in schools, workplaces and in the street. You can be othered for almost any reason, not just the colour of your skin, or the god you worship. You can be othered because you are disabled (us = able bodied, other = people in wheelchairs), because of your sexual preference (us = heterosexual, other = homosexual/lesbian), or even because of the colour of your hair (us = everyone except, other = rangas). Othering is all about deciding who's in, who's out, and why. No-one is immune to possible othering, and it forms the foundation of most of what is to follow.

## Ethnocentrism

Having sorted out the boundaries of our own social grouping – who is one of us, and who isn't – the next step appears to be to assume that *we* are somehow better than *them*. Ethnocentrism is the practice of placing your own group on an unrealistically high pedestal, and then looking down on all those who are not part of that group. Once again, this isn't just about the big-ticket issues of race and ethnicity, it can be about anything.

Take rugby league, for instance. In New South Wales, those from the city look down on the country-dwellers (straw-sucking yokels) – and vice versa (stuck-up slickers) – right up until the team is selected for the State of Origin. Then, the now-united New South Waleans(?) can now all look down on Queenslanders as somehow inferior (banana-bending yokels) – and vice-versa (stuck-up slickers) – right up until the test team is chosen to play the English. And so on. Insert your own 'Pommy bastard' stereotype here.

The point is: part of belonging to a group often seems to be thinking that your group is better than all the other groups. We're great, and they're not. That's ethnocentrism, and its boundaries can slide around all over the place, depending upon who 'we' are at any given moment.

## Prejudice

Arguably, it is the notion of ethnocentrism that forms the foundation of prejudice. Having decided that 'we' are better than you, we can start mentally finding fault with you, because, let's be honest, you are useless. Prejudice is best understood as a hostile attitude towards a person from another group, based solely upon membership of that group. Most of us probably carry around some prejudices, rational or otherwise, whether they involve the members of political organisations we really don't like (e.g. neo-Nazis – perfectly rational), or the players in sporting teams we can't stand (e.g. Manchester United – probably not so rational). However, for prejudice to work effectively as a concept, it needs to be teamed with another idea, one that produces a coherent target for that prejudice to focus on: stereotyping.

## Stereotyping

There's not much point in having a prejudice against a group of people, if we then admit that the group is actually just a diverse collection of individuals with one feature in common: their membership of that group. Instead, the entire group becomes characterised without regard for individual difference – and usually negatively. Staying away from our own offensive ethnic labelling for a while, in the United States, 'Mexicans' have long been the subject of derogatory stereotyping. So, in spite of the fact that the term refers to a single characteristic (someone from Mexico, or at a stretch, someone of Hispanic origin), and in spite of the fact that 'Mexicans' do much of the truly back-breaking labour in America, they are often stereotyped as lazy and shiftless. Such stereotyping occurs when an image is formed of a 'typical' member of a group, and the assumption is made that this applies to all members of a group. These stereotypes are almost entirely context-bound, as 'Mexicans' may be 'lazy and shiftless' in the United States, but in Australia, not so. After all, Speedy Gonzales is a Mexican, therefore all Mexicans etc., etc.

Arguably, the end result of the process outlined so far is twofold: *scapegoating* and *discrimination*. An example of how this all works might be useful at this stage. Let's take an issue which currently appears to have traction in many places around the world, but in particular in the United States, Great Britain and Australia: that is, illegal immigration.

We start with othering. There's 'us' who were born here, or at least came here legally; and then there is 'them', who weren't or didn't. In terms of ethnocentrism, clearly we're better than them, as we have homes, jobs, a stable political system, and we don't have to beg others for help. And when it comes to prejudice, easily done; we didn't ask them to come here, we don't want them, and we don't like them. And not wishing to stereotype, but one lot blew up the World Trade Center, didn't they? All of which leads to: scapegoating.

## Scapegoating

We now have a group of people we can blame for all our problems. Not many jobs around? The illegal immigrants have taken them all. There are lots of drugs on the street? Gangs of illegal immigrants sell them. You live in a high-crime area? Bet the illegal immigrants take everything. Are you unhappy with your life? Illegal immigrants.

Scapegoating also goes hand in hand, not only with stereotyping, but also with victim blaming. Back to the Mexicans. Illegal or otherwise, Mexican-Americans occupy some of the lowest rungs of American society, as most avenues of social mobility have traditionally been closed off to them. As a consequence, they take many of the hardest, and lowest paid, jobs around – jobs that nobody else wants. So when the question is asked: why are so many Mexican-Americans living in poverty? the answer is generally not: 'because they are badly disadvantaged from the get-go'; rather the answer is, 'because they are lazy and shiftless … and take our jobs'. The victims of the system are blamed for the problems within it.

## Discrimination

The second outcome of the above process is discrimination. This is the process whereby members of particular groups are denied equal treatment, based solely upon their membership of that group. For example, if you are an Indigenous Australian and you apply for a job, and you don't get it because someone else was better, we call that the 'economic marketplace'. If you are an Indigenous Australian and apply for a job, and in spite of being the best candidate, you don't get it simply because you are Indigenous, we call that 'racial discrimination'. Quite rightly, it's against the law.

Discrimination comes in a number of forms – individual, institutional, cultural – all of which will be dealt with when addressing myth #2. It can also cover a range of areas – such as sex, age, religion, sexual preferences and so on – which will be a discussed in greater detail in Chapter 11. The only two examples of discrimination relevant to this chapter are race and ethnicity

## Race

The term race is used with confusing levels of flexibility, perhaps as a reflection of its origins as a term that simply sought to differentiate disparate social groupings, e.g. the 'English race', as opposed to the 'Irish race'. However, from the eighteenth century onwards, its meaning began to solidify as referring specifically to observable physical differences, and the notion of race came to presume that all people can be classified into one of several distinct, biological groups on the basis of their physical characteristics. However, this understanding has continued to evolve, and as will be discussed when addressing myth #1, the purely biological definition has been blurred into an explanation that involves significant social components.

If 'race' can be defined at all today, it is a contradictory complex of vestiges of earlier 'natural' definitions that are merged uneasily with assumptions of ethniclike traits drawn from the common experiences of groups. (Doane 2003, 9)

## Ethnicity

While ethnicity is often used as a synonym for race, it is built around an entirely different logic, in that there are no necessary biological components to ethnicity, as there are with race. Certainly, different ethnic groups may vary in appearance, but this not the pivotal issue. Ethnic classifications are based upon social factors such as nationality, culture, religion and language.

For example, most people would be unable to tell the difference between an Irishman and an Englishman, unless they were holding some kind of cultural clue, like a cricket bat, or a pint of Guinness (speaking of stereotypes). That is, there are limited grounds to accept that they belong to different races, even if we were to accept that such a concept had any validity. However, they would clearly consider themselves to have different ethnicities, certainly in terms of the elements of nationality, culture, religion and language mentioned above. After all, the notion of ethnicity does not have to refer to something exotic; some non-Anglo-Celtic 'other'. The term ethnicity is applicable to any group that shares an identity and a past.

Arguably, ethnicity is also dependent upon how tightly you focus the lens. On the lowest possible magnification, there is an Australian ethnicity. When we are compared to Americans or the British, we have a different nationality, a different shared culture and history, and a different past. Increase the magnification again and we have a range of ethnicities within Australia. As previously mentioned, along with Anglo-Celtic Australians, we have Indigenous Australians, Vietnamese Australians, Lebanese Australians, and so on into the hundreds, each rightly claiming a coherent ethnic identity. Tighten the focus further still, on the Lebanese Australians for example, and you would find Druze, Copts, Catholics, Muslims, once again, each with a shared history and identity. Like Russian dolls, each ethnicity can form one component of a larger construct. It seems that ethnicity is often about who you are comparing yourself with.

## Racism

This is a term used in a number of different ways. The first is the most specific. It involves the belief that humanity can be organised in various groups – races – and that these groups can be ranked according to achievement, and worth. Poplin (1978, 280) defines it as 'the belief that some groups are inherently – biologically – inferior to other groups'.

The second usage is somewhat more general. It involves a generalised dislike of those perceived to be from a different racial grouping, whether manifest in terms of simple prejudice or actual discrimination. This dislike is most focused upon the colour of a person's skin (the central signifier of race), although as will be discussed in myth #2, this is often now expressed in cultural terms. Such dislike is not necessarily founded upon any underlying belief in biological inferiority.

The final definition is the most general, and is the one used within Australia's racial vilification legislation. Racial hatred extends not only to a person's perceived race, but also to their colour, nationality and ethnic origin. Therefore, it would be considered racist for an Anglo-Australian to call out offensive comments to someone from an Irish or Serbian background, even though they may appear to be from the same 'race'.

Now that we have framed a basic language for approaching this area, we can tackle some of the central myths that seem to keep cropping up when looking at race/ethnicity and education. These are:

**Myth #1** – Humanity is naturally divided into races

**Myth #2** – We no longer discriminate on the basis of race or ethnicity

**Myth #3** – Educational outcomes are unaffected by race or ethnicity

**Myth #4** – There is an 'Indigenous problem' in education

# Myth #1 Humanity is naturally divided into races

Humanity is divided into different groups. Those groups – races – can be relatively easily delineated because they don't look the same. There are Caucasians, Negroids, Orientals, Asiatics and Mongoloids … er, or is it Malaysiatics and Indigenoids …? It gets a bit confusing. Anyway, the separate groups are clearly defined in nature, and not only do they look different, they have different qualities, characteristics and abilities. History suggest that Caucasians, i.e. white people, are the best since they invented civilisation, and came to run everything. Nothing much you can do about that really, it's just the way it is. It's a scientific fact.

It's hard to know where to start with this myth really. It would be hard to think of anything else that was so 'obviously' true for so long – nearly 500 years – yet turned out to be such utter rubbish. In the meantime, it caused untold damage and suffering, and yet, even when we found out it was nonsense, it still refused to go away and die. It would be laughable, if it wasn't so tragic. Probably the best way to approach the issue of race is to examine it in two parts: first, how the concept developed, and how it became a scientific fact; and second, how that fact came to be questioned, and ultimately debunked.

## The history of race

It's impossible to understand the invention of the notion of race without, at the same time, examining the history of slavery. If we say that the concept of race, as we understand it, began to take shape around 1500, we can also say that the phenomenon of human slavery is much older, probably as old as humanity itself. The ancient Greeks certainly took slaves, but this had nothing to do with the colour of their skin, or any perceptions that they had less intrinsic worth as people. People normally became slaves simply as a result of military conquest, or having the wrong religion.

So how did we get to the position, not only where slaves were considered to be fundamentally different, but were also considered to come from a lower rung of some natural hierarchy? Writers such as Banton (1998) and Jackson and Weidman (2004) point to a number of historical issues, each of which was crucial to the final emergence of the notion of race.

## Slavery on the Iberian Peninsula

Between 711 and 1492, Muslims dominated what is now Spain and Portugal, and like most other cultures of the time, they took slaves – black and white. Importantly, the white slaves were worth more, as they could be more readily ransomed back to the Christians, with whom they were constantly at war. This difference in value often meant that white slaves were given less onerous labour, usually domestic, while the black slaves worked outside in the heat, or down the mines. Eventually, this division became naturalised – of course whites are better at more civilised activities, and of course blacks are more suited to the brute work. Consequently, out of this division developed the first two prerequisites of a theory of race:

1  Outer physical attributes somehow reflect inner moral worth; and.

2  Physically different groups belong in a hierarchy, with white at the top.

## European exploration

From 1500 onwards, the great European powers started to expand beyond continental Europe. The underlying rationale behind this expansion, though initially military, quickly became economic. For the first time, slaves were taken not as a result of conflict, but simply to provide labour; and the largest source of this labour was Africa. In a very short time, the third prerequisite fell into place:

3   Blackness equals slavery, and slavery equals blackness.

Although the Bible was deemed to contribute a vital argument in favour of slavery – 'bringing the heathens to God' – it also contributed a second important piece of the jigsaw. At this time, the biblical belief in *monogenesis* provided the dominant model of human origins (i.e. we all come from the same starting point: Adam and Eve), therefore all physical differences between peoples must have developed later, most likely as a result of climate. Curiously though, even though North and South American Indians were more naturally suited to their environments, they died in droves soon after the Europeans turned up. As they had no understanding of smallpox or influenza, the visitors took this to mean:

4   Europeans are superior to indigenous Americans, as well as blacks; and

5   The difference is some natural, internal quality of the body.

## The rise of science

The Enlightenment of the eighteenth century is credited with stimulating a number of notable social changes: the decline of the absolute power of the monarch; scientific explanations replacing those based upon tradition or theology; the belief in a notion of progress, that human civilisation would make things 'better'. Given the self-evident progress made by European civilisation, as opposed to other peoples, Europeans were clearly superior. After all, their new-found system of knowledge – science – could be employed to explain everything, and just as science divided the natural world up into phylum, genus and species, so too could humanity be placed in convenient packages. A number of early scientists developed typologies for human difference; lists of different races, always in a hierarchy, always with white European at the top. Much of this work was premised upon the heretical logic of *polygenesis*: the belief in multiple creations. This is important because it meant that white and non-white races were not necessarily related in any fundamentally binding way.

6   Different races are like different species.

## Theories of evolution

Darwin's theory of evolution didn't just pop into the world, fully formed and uncontested by the scientific community; it had to fend off some similar, but rival, ideas first. Although Darwin's ideas immediately seemed to offer a viable explanation of how we got here, they didn't just offend some religious sensibilities, they also offended the new scientists of 'race', since Darwin was clearly a monogenesist (in that we all developed from the same, first organism … not Adam and Eve). This didn't sit well with those polygenesists now convinced the different races had fundamentally different points of origin. The solution to this problem was to construct an early version of evolution that borrowed a bit from both camps. That is, that when it came to humans:

7   The evolutionary 'struggle for survival' is between races, not individuals.

## The politics of race

Races were now deemed to be naturally at war with each other. This war manifested itself in a number of ways. First, a number of concerns were raised about waves of immigrants from different races 'flooding' into countries where the numerically and socially dominant race was white. Clearly, since whites were the superior race, the genetic result of this mass-immigration of inferiors could only be negative.

8    The better races can be contaminated by less worthy ones.

At this point, the political and the scientific merged within the new discipline of *eugenics*: the science of improving the genetic composition of the population. We no longer had to be passive spectators to the slow destruction of the white race by less worthy ones; we could intervene to keep our race strong. This intervention could take any number of forms: sterilisation of the 'feebleminded', immigration laws, marriage laws (Montagu 1974).

9    Actions can be taken to protect the purity of races.

And we know what number 10 would be, given the progression of this logic. In retro-spect, it almost seems inevitable that, under the right political circumstances, some-one would decide to 'remove' lesser races from the equation altogether – even though Jews aren't a race by anything other than the most deranged formulation.

## Debunking race

So there we have it; the progression of logic that led to the invention of race. In many ways, it is the perfect example of othering: decide who *we* are, create an *other,* and then blame nature for it. And yet, in spite of its apparent scientific validation, fairly soon after the end of World War II the entire edifice of race started to collapse; not all at once, and not in its entirety, but collapse it did. There isn't enough space here to detail all the shortcomings of race as a theory, however it failed as an idea across three separate areas.

## The logical failure of race

First and foremost, it is almost impossible to construct a coherent racial grouping. All the evidence suggests that there are far, far greater differences *among* races, than there are *between* them. Take any given racial trait – height, shape of nose, colour of hair – and compare within any grouping deemed to be a race. The differences are enormous. For example, when it comes to height of the 'black race', what about the lanky Sudanese, the medium-sized Bantu, the stocky west-Africans, and the tiny Bushmen? Or are they all to be deemed separate races now? Even then, there are very tall Sudanese and there are very short Sudanese. The normal curve of a given trait from any race will generally overlap the vast majority of the curve of the same trait of any other race. It just makes no coherent sense.

A second notable failure in the logic of race is its self-evidently flexible boundar-ies, with 'whiteness' being the most flexible of them all. Given that being categorised as white has brought with it many advantages, removing that categorisation can be particularly punitive. Back to Mexicans again. Mexicans had always been regarded as white, right up until 1930. However, a social panic at the time about – you guessed it – immigration, meant that they were re-categorised with the stroke of a pen as 'not white', hence less worthy, and hence much easier to kick out (Hochschild & Weaver 2007). But then, if race is really natural, surely its boundaries can't be moved around at a whim? Quite.

## The scientific failure of race

There are any number of examples of how race has failed the test of modern science. Probably the most telling involves the notion of intelligence. Gould's book *The Mismeasure of Man* (1996) details an array of ways early scientists sought to demonstrate the superior brain-power of the white race over all others. Skull size was one early favourite, as clearly the bigger the brain, the smarter the individual (so goes the logic). By filling skulls with lead shot, their internal size could be measured. Early studies showed the expected results: whites have bigger heads. However, not only have later studies shown this to be completely false – most likely a subconscious fiddling of the results by researchers – but also that brain size doesn't correlate with intelligence anyway (see elephants).

IQ testing was another method that established white superiority with absolute certainty. Tests conducted for the US military around World War I showed that whites were significantly smarter than blacks, confirming everything proponents of race always knew. However, dozens of later studies have shown that IQ (assuming this concept has any validity at all, which it probably doesn't) correlates with social advantage, not racial classification. Middle-class blacks do as well as middle-class whites.

## The political failure of race

This final issue proved catastrophic for advocates of racial theory. There was really nowhere to go after the Nazis. It was widely realised that dividing people into 'natural' races served no worthy social or intellectual purpose. As stated in the preamble to the *International Convention on the Elimination of All Forms of Racial Discrimination*:

> ... any doctrine of superiority based on racial differentiation is scientifically false, morally condemnable, socially unjust and dangerous, and that there is no justification for racial discrimination, in theory or in practice, anywhere ...(UN 1965)

Even though the notion of race is clearly erroneous and no-one really believes it any more, this doesn't mean it can't still affect people, particularly 'non-whites'. Indeed, the ghost of race seems to hang around somewhere at the back of discourses about ethnic difference, never quite going away; the ghost of nature. But we shouldn't be surprised, as just because something isn't real, doesn't mean it can't have social power. Harry Potter isn't real, but he still represents a multibillion-dollar industry. And he never gets made to sit at the back of the bus.

# Myth #2 We no longer discriminate on the basis of race or ethnicity

It may once have been the case that non-whites got a rough time in Australia. People would use a variety of racist terms to describe people who were different to themselves; we all know what they are, so there's no point in listing them here. Those days are long gone, and only the most ignorant and uneducated now discriminate on the basis of race or ethnicity, and given most of these people have next-to-no social or economic power anyway, I think we can say discrimination is a thing of the past. After all, does anyone really say, 'You're black, so you're not getting the job anymore?' I don't think so.

The argument supporting this myth has two elements: first, that discrimination occurs directly, when someone won't let someone else have something – a job, accommodation, entry into a pub – simply because of their racial/ethnic identity. This is a direct, individual-centred form of discrimination. The second element of the myth is that this doesn't really exist anymore; we are better than that now. This section of the chapter will address these two claims, and in doing so, will contend that *individual discrimination* is just one form bigotry, and that *institutional discrimination* and *cultural discrimination* are now significantly more prevalent than this, but they are just harder to spot.

## Individual discrimination

What we're really talking about here is person-to-person discrimination; that moment when someone decides that the individual standing in front of them isn't going to get what they want, simply because of what they are. Myth #2 argues that this is no longer prevalent, and therefore, discrimination is all but a thing of the past. So has it gone away?

Colic-Peisker and Tilbury (2007) draw a number of interesting conclusions from their work on discrimination, but also cite some pertinent, and disturbing, examples of the continued existence of direct individual discrimination, both overt and covert.

## Overt

This is where race/ethnicity is openly and directly used to deny an opportunity to an individual. Under these circumstances, there is no pretence made that any other factors may be in play.

One man, a former electrician supervisor, currently unemployed, described his experience thus:

*One Employer admitted to me during interview that if he employed me he will lose clients due to the feeling [about] people from Middle Eastern appearance after September 11 events.* (Colic-Peisker & Tilbury 2007, 20)

This form of overt racism is by no means limited to the employment sector. Indeed, it spills over into the most direct and unpleasant forms of abuse and vilification.

> An ex-Yugoslav man, a former pilot, described his experience while working as a taxi-driver:
>
> *As a taxi driver I have been exposed to all kinds of racism. On one occasion a customer asked about my name and the spelling and I wrote it down on a piece of paper. I asked her why she [wanted to know] that. She said because she was looking for a name for her new dog … (Colic-Peisker & Tilbury 2007, 19)*

These are two examples of the kind of discrimination that myth #2 is referring to. Perhaps it is on the decline; it would be nice to think so. However, there are other forms of discrimination that aren't so readily visible.

## Covert

Not all individual discrimination is so open and unashamed. Much of it is disguised behind convenient excuses, non-returned phone calls, ignored curricula vitae, and silence:

> A Somali man, a former GP medical researcher, described a similar experience:
>
> *I went to an agency that was looking for someone with qualifications and experience like the ones I had. The receptionist had a hard time in accepting that fact that I was applying for that high position and, after asking me to wait while she talks to her supervisors, she came back to tell me the position was already filled even though the deadline was not until two weeks later. (Colic-Peisker & Tilbury 2007, 18)*

This is still an individual form of discrimination, as it is still operating at a person-to-person level. It is highly unlikely that somehow policies were put in place by that agency to necessarily restrict access by racial/ethnic minorities, however this is often the way it works out. So, as Burnett (2004a) points out, while there is clearly a need to address racism on the individual level, to focus on it too readily is to risk underestimating the pervasive effects of institutional and cultural discrimination.

## Institutional discrimination

At the risk of prejudging the conclusions to be drawn while examining myth #3, if it turns out that that racial/ethnic minorities don't do as well in Australian schools as Anglo-Celtic students, then this leads to one of only two possible conclusions. Either, they are naturally more stupid (and we've disposed of that possibility during myth #1), or there is something about the education system that subtly advances Anglo-Celtic students, while at the same time disadvantaging all the rest.

Of course, there are a number of possible reasons for this, reasons which are not directly about the relationship between racial and ethnic minorities and the education system, but are rather about some of the broader facts of Australian society. After all, in an education system that almost exclusively operates in English, it is obviously more difficult to succeed if this is not your native language. Likewise, given the continuing Anglo-Celtic dominance within Australian cultural and economic life, and given the arguments set out in Chapter 1 about the relationship between social class and educational success, it is hardly surprising that members of ethnic groups that often find themselves on the lower rungs of Australian society consequently perform less well at school.

However, there are also forms of discrimination which directly relate to the way educational institutions operate, and the outcomes for specific racial and ethnic minorities. For example – and perhaps with perfectly well-meaning intentions, or perhaps as a function of the pressure on schools to do well in inter-school academic ranking tables – it has been suggested that young African migrants are often encouraged to apply for apprenticeships, rather than go down the route of university entrance certification (Macdougall 2008). The end result of this is obvious: the education system acts to discriminate against a particular ethnic minority, since they end up with significantly reduced choices in life.

A further example involves the issue of testing. There exists a significant body of literature which shows – once again, in spite of the best of intentions – that the large-scale, centralised examinations which make all education systems tick, exhibit covert and pervasive forms of social bias.

> With the level of cultural diversity in Australia, external tests cannot claim to be fair and just …
> It is difficult to believe that students in a remote Aboriginal school would acquire the social and cultural knowledge in terms of Bourdieu's notions of 'habitus' and 'cultural capital' that students in a middle class suburb in Melbourne would have. It is therefore highly likely that centralised tests are socially and culturally discriminatory, despite the best intentions of the test designers.
> (Meadmore 2004, 33)

Exley (2010) extends this point in her analysis of standardised testing, as applied to children on the Torres Strait island of Tortol. The example given by the *Queensland Comparable Assessment Tasks* (QCATs) involved a written piece about a little girl's lost puppy. Exley shows that at almost every level, the story makes no cultural sense to the islanders: puppies aren't kept as pets at all; puppies aren't fenced in, so the notion of being 'lost' is incomprehensible; and working dogs, not puppies, become companions of boys nearing puberty; and most crucially, young girls simply do not own dogs. So no wonder the islanders struggle on the test.

Of course, similar versions of this argument readily exist for most racial and ethnic minorities within Australian education. There is no 'perfect test' out there that succeeds in including all cultural groups equally. What we end up with is an unspoken, privileging of the white, middle-class majority (see myth #4), and a subtle, and not so subtle, institutional discrimination occurring against all those who do not share this background.

## Cultural discrimination

One final form of discrimination merits a mention. When looking specifically at issues of racial discrimination, whether individual or institutional, the essential point of reference has always been the notion of race itself – obviously. However, the goalposts seem to have moved somewhat, and it is increasingly rare to witness race as constituting the focus of discriminatory discourse. That discrimination now appears to be cut from the fabric of culture instead.

As Burnett (2004a) points out, the familiar phrase, 'I'm not racist, but ...' is no longer generally followed by the individual outlining some spurious argument about why a particular racial grouping is less physically/intellectually/morally worthy than their own, rather it is now almost always followed by some measure of that group's lack of *cultural* worth. That is, those with an interest in doing so no longer point at the colour of someone's skin to explain why they don't fit in here, instead they point to the fact that they still have arranged marriages, or that they cover their heads in a veil.

> What is important is that although race remains the primary signifier of difference, the notion of difference and associated claims of incompatibility are now expressed in cultural and, increasingly, religious terms. (Burnett 2004a, 106)

So of course, we're largely still talking about the same people – pick your minority – it's just that we've found a new rationale to justify our discrimination. Importantly, the issue of discrimination is discussed from a legal perspective in Chapter 11.

# Myth #3 Educational outcomes are unaffected by race or ethnicity

> Haven't we been through this before with the issue of social class in Chapter 1? So maybe there's still some discrimination around, even if the really obvious stuff isn't as common as it used to be, but this doesn't necessarily mean that the education system doesn't do its job and educate all Australian kids equally. In the end, it doesn't matter what your racial or ethnic background is, it just matters how smart you are.

This doesn't need to be a particularly long section. The evidence is out there for those who wish to look. Just as the game appears to be stacked in favour of those from higher social classes, so too does the game favour those from Anglo-Celtic ethnic backgrounds, people who are unequivocally part of the dominant Australian culture. After all, as Welch (2010) rightly observes, the hidden curriculum of the school still succeeds in perpetuating mono-cultural values and practices, which in turn significantly benefits those from that culture.

For the purposes of this chapter, the category of 'non-Anglo-Celtic' can probably be divided into two separate statuses:

1 Those Australians who, as a result of the colour of their skin, or the language they speak at home, or the clothes they wear, or the god they worship, constitute ethnicities somehow different to the perceived norm.

2 Indigenous Australians.

## Ethnicity and educational outcomes

This section requires further subdivision, as there are also two relatively separate issues that warrant discussion and shed light on the circumstances ethnic minorities often find themselves in. The first is the straightforward matter of the relationship between ethnicity and educational success; the second is the effects of being a migrant/refugee upon education outcomes.

## Non-Anglo-Celtic ethnicity

The issue of teaching students of non-Anglo-Celtic ethnic backgrounds is just one of the factors that make the profession complicated yet rewarding. Partington (2001) notes some of the many difficulties teachers face in structuring an equitable and productive classroom for ethnic minority students. This includes organising a welcoming learning environment, fostering important student attributes, providing a viable and fruitful setting for English-language acquisition, developing the full range of literacy skills, all the while keeping a wary eye out for racism and stereotyping.

Assuming teachers are able to do all of this effectively, the evidence still suggests that ethnicity plays a significant part in determining educational outcomes, although its role is not as clear-cut, or one-sided, as might initially be imagined. In his comparative study of students from Anglo-Celtic, Middle-Eastern and Asian ethnic backgrounds, Marjoribanks (2005) points to a complex interrelationship of factors, including social class and gender, contributing to the likelihood of achieving educational aspirations. The results suggest ethnicity does play a role in educational success, but that role is fairly limited in comparison to the effects of social class. Interestingly, the results also show that when it comes to doing badly at school, no-one does it quite as well as white, working-class males.

Some pertinent observations have also been made by Ho (2011) in her analysis of the data from the 'My School' website. She notes that in Sydney, more than half the students at public schools are from language backgrounds other than English, compared with 37% at Catholic schools, and only 22% at independent schools. Ho explains this ethnically based division, in part, by the fact that there has been an ongoing 'flight' to private schools since the mid-1990s. Since many private schools aren't exactly cheap, public schools are often left with those students whose parents simply can't afford to make the switch – i.e. the working classes and migrants.

However, even at the non-elite level, in the less-affluent suburbs of Sydney the public schools 'appear to have been abandoned by Anglo-Australians'. For a country premised upon multiculturalism, the creation of educational 'bubbles of segregation and isolation' should be a cause for concern.

## Immigrants/refugees

The situation is a little different when addressing the issue of migrants and refugees who suddenly find themselves in the Australian education system. Citing the Organisation for Economic Cooperation and Development (OECD) figures, Vickers and McCarthy (2011) make some pertinent observations about the educational fate of immigrants and refugees who arrive here. They note that while a high proportion of the Australian population is born overseas (25%), Australia is one of only four countries (along with Canada, New Zealand and Ireland) where immigrant students perform above the OECD average – a good result.

They also note that the top 25% of immigrants perform better than the top 25% of Australian-born students, while the bottom 25% of immigrants perform significantly worse than the bottom 25% of the Australian-born. This result should not come as a surprise, as there are important divisions hidden within this data, with no distinction being made between those students who came here as voluntary migrants, and those who came here as refugees. As Vickers and McCarthy note, it can probably be assumed that the success at one end, and the failure at the other, is in large part a result of these two separate cohorts. Certainly, the children of high-status, highly educated Chinese migrants have done very well within the schooling system, as have Greek and Jewish students. Other groups of immigrants have not done so well.

Even so, these are generally not the students in the bottom 25%. Refugees from conflict areas, particularly those from Africa, continue to struggle in our education system. Not surprising really, given that many of them have lived in refugee camps for years, have had next to no formal education at all, and have witnessed terrible events that no-one, let alone children, should ever have to witness. The complexity of this issue is compounded by the age at which the refugee enters the schooling system. If they are young, there are reasons to be positive; if they are older, their prognosis within formal education can be bleak.

## Education and Indigenous Australians

The final myth of this chapter will deal explicitly with the relationship between schooling and Indigenous Australians, however almost everything that needs to be said about the claim that educational outcomes are unaffected by race and ethnicity can be summed up in Figure 3.1. Clearly many Indigenous students, by the time they reach the last three years of school, have reached the conclusion that, for whatever reason, staying at school is no longer viable. So what is to be made of this?

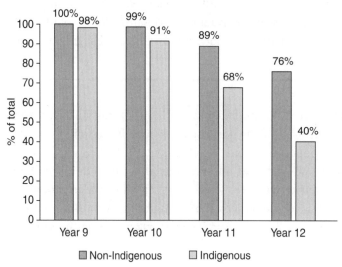

**Figure 3.1** *Who stays on in school?*
*Source: Australian Bureau of Statistics 2006*

# Myth #4 There is an 'Indigenous problem' in education

Indigenous Australians struggle in our education system. We've tried our hardest to solve the 'Indigenous problem', but in the final analysis their culture is just too different from ours. They seem to lack whatever it is that enables ordinary kids to do well in school. There's no solution to this issue.

It's hard to know where to start with this myth. There are so many assumptions, generalisations and misconceptions built into the statement above, that it needs to be unpacked piece by piece in order to find some solid ground to build upon. Unfortunately, it could be argued that a number of existing sociological approaches to Indigenous education contain many of these same errors, errors similar to those we've already seen in the preceding chapters on social class and gender. For example, there is the homogenisation of cultures, the prevalence of simple binaries, a zero-sum understanding of power, and an unshakable belief in their own objectivity. It will be argued here that a more nuanced understanding of Indigenous education can open up a range of new and productive possibilities.

In terms of a very preliminary analysis, there are five issues and presuppositions inherent within the myth outlined above that immediately warrant discussion:

1  the belief that there is a single Indigenous culture whose problems need to be addressed;

2  the understanding that 'they' are somehow outsiders to 'our' education system;

3  the notion that Indigenous children fail in the education system because of some kind of cultural 'deficit';

4  the understanding of the dominant white culture as neutral in the entire process of 'problem' creation; and

5  the belief that this amounts to an intractable problem, one with no ready solution, or even prospect of improvement.

## 1   The complexities of Indigenous identity

There often seems to be some very fixed ideas of what constitutes a proper Indigenous person. That is, within the popular imagination, proper Indigenous Australians have dark skin, come from the bush, and have a spiritual connection with their land; they are good at sport, and can throw things and make them come back; they make amazing dotty paintings, and can produce haunting noises from cylindrical objects.

Needless to say, there are any number of problems that come with this cartoon understanding of what a proper Indigenous Australian ought to be (Phillips 2005). First and foremost is the notion that they form a coherent group, when in fact they only came to be shaped as a singular identity when constructed as the 'other' by the first Western settlers to arrive. Before that time there existed hundreds of different cultures, around 250 different languages, spread throughout the entire continent. Even now, there remain nearly 150 different Indigenous languages spoken in Australia (NILS Report 2005). The only people to regard them as 'the same' were the people who arrived on the boats, in large part because by clearly demarcating 'the other', this helped cement a unified identity for themselves (Kostanski 2009).

Likewise, many of the most familiar symbolic markers of Indigenous culture actually have their origins with some of the desert peoples, and have simply been extrapolated to all Indigenous groups. So, not only is there an incredibly wide variation within Indigenous culture, there is a wide variation in type of terrain occupied, and the way of life organised there; in physique and in skin and hair colour; in kinship structure; and in belief systems. To make matters more complex still, there are now significant variations within the urban/rural divide among the Indigenous, in wealth, education and social status, and most importantly, in the degree to which individuals identify *as* Indigenous. Some choose not to do so for personal reasons; some identify only within certain contexts, and to certain people; for some, being an Indigenous Australian is the cornerstone of their identity, for others not so much.

So, while there has been some political logic in playing along with the creation of a single pan-Indigenous identity – i.e. acquiring voting rights and so on – in general, positioning Indigenous Australians as an homogenous population, with identical cultural practices, and similar senses of identity, is to reduce a diverse cluster of different peoples to a single stereotype. Arguably, if you want to learn more about

'Indigenous culture', the best place to start will be with the specific culture of the peoples in your area. It will be their children you are teaching, and they'd be happy to help you learn.

## 2   Us vs them

Many discussions of the issues surrounding Indigenous education seem to operate from within a familiar modernist binary. First of all there is the unspoken 'us', normally constituted as the white, middle-class owners of the system; the writers of the curriculum, the teachers of the knowledge, the best students in the classroom. Those who consider themselves part of 'us' not only feel at home in the system, they *are* the system. It is this reasoning that validates the statement: 'Indigenous Australians struggle in *our* education system'.

In contrast to this of course, having homogenised all Indigenous Australians into a single grouping, this grouping is then constructed as 'them': the other, social and cultural outsiders, visitors to our sensible system from a different planet. Importantly, much as we may try to integrate 'them' into 'our' classroom – and certainly, they are more than welcome there – this doesn't alter the fundamental fact that 'we' have organised the life-world of the classroom in our own image; they are just visitors to it, and have to make do the best they can. This is a familiar situation that any number of 'othered' groups find themselves in. The problem lies primarily with the notion of *integration*. Within the integrated classroom, students who lie outside the mainstream (whether culturally, physically, sexually or linguistically) are brought inside the big tent, and they are taught how to fit in (Uditsky 1993). We know we have succeeded when they become just like us.

Arguably, a far more preferable approach to dealing with difference involves the notion of *inclusion*. Within the inclusive classroom, the cultures and abilities of all students are valued equally, and the variations they bring with them are incorporated into the fabric of the learning environment (Topping & Maloney 2005). One culture does not exert its hegemony over all the others, such that they can either march in step, or sit at the back of the class – or sit somewhere else altogether (Slee 2011). An inclusive classroom tries very hard to do away with 'us' and 'them', and focus on working towards a 'we'. Given the many covert and subliminal contexts within which the 'we/them' binary operates, this has not proved to be an easy task.

## 3   The deficit model of Indigenous education

Having rolled all Indigenous Australians into a single ball, and labelled it 'them', we quickly note that 'they' aren't doing too well at school. The answer to this is simple: there's something wrong with them. This is a very common argument, and it is normally called the *Deficit Model* of educational failure. The solution to why working-class students don't do as well as their middle-class counterparts is often to look at working-class lifestyles, language and ways of learning, and to contend that they are somehow not as good. The same happens with Indigenous Australians. Once we believe in the objectively neutral character of our education system, those who fail to succeed must shoulder the burden of responsibility for that failure themselves – the Indigenous included. It's a meritocracy, after all.

Actually, this seems like a pretty good example of victim blaming, discussed in the introduction to this chapter. We set up a school with a whole series of subtle cultural biases ingrained within it, and when other cultures fail to do particularly well there, we hold them responsible. That is, we rarely think to examine the various components of the school that might predetermine this failure: an irrelevant curriculum, inappropriate instructional practices, unsuitable disciplinary codes and authority structures, culturally problematic timetabling, out of place organisational arrangements, the list goes on.

The contention that Indigenous cultures – or even Indigenous people themselves, if we really want to head back to the discredited racial theories of myth #1 – lack what it takes to fit into mainstream Australian schools is bunk (Valencia 1997). If some Indigenous students struggle to find a place for themselves within our schooling system, the issue doesn't pivot upon what they 'lack', or what's 'wrong' with them. The debates need to focus around issues of difference, not absence.

## 4   White race privilege

The great thing about the deficit model – at least, the great thing for the non-Indigenous – is that it absolves the rest of us, and the education system we created, from any real responsibility for the 'Indigenous problem'. As discussed, this understanding is based upon an erroneous belief in the cultural neutrality of our schools. Failure is deemed to be, first and last, an individual matter, and if an Indigenous student fails, maybe they should take a good long look in the mirror.

However, the issue of erroneous neutrality extends beyond the boundary of the school, into the very essence of how those members of the dominant, white Australian culture see themselves. There is a significant body of literature concerning white race privilege, which examines 'whiteness', and its place – or rather, its invisibility – within debates over race. For most whites, race is something that other peoples have: black people, yellow people, brown people, red people. To be white is to not have to regard race as an issue (Kendall 2006).

However, there's more to it than that. Not only is whiteness *not* neutral, it also brings with it some very real advantages. McIntosh (1997, 291) contends that being white is like owning 'an invisible weightless knapsack of special provisions, assurances, tools, maps, guides, codebooks, passports, visas, clothes, compass, emergency gear and blank cheques'. As a general rule, white people don't have to worry about their race limiting access to important resources, or whether their race will be depicted positively in the media, or whether their children will face discrimination on the basis of their race.

White people need not wonder, for example, if their achievements (a job, an award, a scholarship) will be seen as happening because of their race; they need not worry that if they fail, their failure will be used to judge their race. Whiteness just is; no white person is seen as representing their race. Indeed, most white people do not even think of themselves as raced subjects. (Anderson 2003, 26)

Proponents of white race privilege suggest that white kids enter schools with a thousand invisible little advantages under their belt, and not just in the big issues concerning curriculum content and dominant teaching styles, but also all the little ones: assumptions about how well they'll do, language codes, shared history, familiarity, and the confidence born of insider status. To somehow suggest that Indigenous Australians are given social or educational advantages, as can often be heard in talk-back radioland and other domains of shared ignorance, is to suffer from one of the most pernicious form of colour blindness: the inability to see what whiteness means to those who have it (Rosenberg 2004).

So, as long as those in the dominant culture continue to regard themselves, and the institutions they create, as simply passive bystanders to the unsatisfactory relationship between the Indigenous and our schools, nothing much is ever really going to change. This isn't about finding someone to blame; it's about finding a way forward.

## 5  Strategies for Indigenous education

Part of the problem with finding solutions to all the issues raised here concerns the paralysis involved in yet another binary: 'we have to change everything' vs 'there's nothing we can do'. Modernist sociologies of race often seem to be based upon the fabrication of utopian solutions, built upon total, and highly improbable, structural change for their viability. Alternatively, popular discourses about the relationship between education and Indigenous Australians often involve the wringing of hands, and the assertion that nothing can be done.

Neither of these approaches is helpful, either at the macro level for organising a society's responsibility to its indigenous citizens, or at the micro level of helping school teachers do a more effective job. In contrast to this inertia, Lampert (2005) suggests four quite practical ways in which Indigenous education might be improved, all beginning with the teacher in the classroom.

## Making a commitment to Indigenous education

If teaching is about making a difference, here is a cohort within our community where a difference is truly needed. This involves more than just putting ideals into practice, although that is certainly an important component. It involves the self-scrutiny necessary to locate and understand one's own values and assumptions, and to recognise how these impact on the teaching process. Or to put it another way, it requires an understanding of whiteness, just as much as it requires an understanding of blackness.

## Engaging with knowledge in the area

That said, effective teaching in this field still requires teachers to do their homework. There is extensive literature on the subject, and those wishing to work effectively in this area needs to become well-versed in it. After all:

> When non-Indigenous teachers teach curriculum from a non-Indigenous worldview (as would most in Australia) they can, to some extent, have confidence that they know what they are talking about. Their white culture matches the white content of their curriculum, their pedagogy and their overall perspective. But if they are teaching as an outsider (for example, when non-Indigenous teachers teach about Indigenous issues), they really must take that responsibility particularly seriously. (Lampert 2005, 94)

## Embedding Indigenous perspectives

Effective and long-lasting change will not come about from offering a scattering of bits and pieces about Indigenous history, and a video of how to do the emu dance. What is required is a serious attempt to embed Indigenous perspectives from the ground up. This is not as radical, or impossible, as it might first appear. Most universities within Australia have by now made concerted attempts to establish such perspectives across the board within their diverse curricula. Of course, how successful this has been to date remains open to question. However, within the boundaries of their own classrooms, teachers can make organised and comprehensive efforts to do the same.

## Consultation

One place to start this process is by consulting local Indigenous communities, and getting them involved as partners in the process. It's not really enough to have a generalised knowledge of Indigenous issues. As has already been discussed, there is no single, satisfactory one-size-fits-all knowledge base that allows teachers to do their job effectively at every school in the country. Therefore, this kind of local consultation can help in tailoring appropriate ways of teaching, the use of particular materials and ideas, and in organising suitable guest speakers. It can also assist in breaking down any perceived divide between the world of the school and the life-worlds of both the broader Indigenous community, and of the young Indigenous students themselves.

# Conclusion

It would appear then that none of the myths outlined here have much basis in fact at all. First, humanity is not naturally divided into separate races. Any divisions we have made between peoples are almost entirely social in origin. Unfortunately, just because we now know race isn't real, doesn't mean that its effects have all gone away. The notion of race somehow still seems to haunt our popular discourse and imagination. That's not good.

Second, racial and ethnic discrimination haven't gone away either. Even though there are some grounds for supposing that the worst elements of individual racism are becoming more of a rarity, institutional and cultural discrimination are still part of the Australian landscape. Unfortunately, these are often significantly more difficult to spot, although being aware of their existence is the first step in the process of doing something about it.

Third, educational outcomes are most certainly affected by racial and ethnic background. Although some ethnic minorities actually do better in school than those from the dominant Anglo-Celtic culture, many also do significantly worse. This is especially the case for those who came here as refugees, and the later they came, the more they will struggle. The statistics also suggest that Indigenous Australian children start to drop out of school in far greater numbers than non-Indigenous children from grade 10 onwards.

Finally, to say there is an 'Indigenous problem' within the Australian education system is to consent to placing blame where it doesn't belong. Indigenous children do not succeed in the same numbers as non-Indigenous children, largely due to the structure of our education system, the way knowledge is organised, the way it is delivered, and the measures that are used to assess success. These reduced rates of success cannot be accounted for by some deficit, either within the Indigenous brain, or within Indigenous culture.

Of the three topics covered in the first part of this book, issues raised by this chapter on race/ethnicity perhaps lend themselves to the greatest degree of optimism. That is, for those invested in a career within the education system, most of us would think that at the heart of racial and ethnic discrimination – and the educational inequalities that flow from it – lies ignorance. And if anyone's in a position to do something about that, it's teachers.

# Part 2

## The Foundations of an Alternative Approach: Education and Governance

Making the move from modern to postmodern forms of social analysis is not the only option open to those unhappy with the shortcomings of the traditional social class/gender/race approach. It is possible to step out of this paradigm, and to address mass education, and society in general, from another direction altogether. Part 2 will explore the possibilities associated with this alternative direction. Not only does this alternative approach ask different questions, it also asks them about largely different elements of the social fabric, and it underpins its ideas within entirely different domain assumptions.

The theories outlined in Part 1 – even those more clearly postmodern in orientation – tend to ask questions about who has what, and who is exercising power over whom, while focusing primarily upon issues of disadvantage and inequality. This model is built upon a coercive understanding of power, one that describes struggles over resources and access, one which notes who wins and who loses, and one which positions mass education as ground zero in the ongoing battles between classes, genders and races,

The approach taken in Part 2 is very different. Largely based upon the work of Foucault, the questions it asks focus more upon the ways in which institutions like the school produce particular kinds of individuals, both as objects of knowledge, and as objects of governance. Power is no longer regarded as necessarily coercive; rather it is usually productive; it brings new ways of understanding, and new identities, into being. As will be discussed in Chapter 4, governance is about how categories of difference are created and managed; it is about the strategies through which particular populations are normalised; it is about 'the conduct of conduct'. According to this logic, mass education is not principally about the social reproduction of advantage and disadvantage; it is about distributing and classifying individuals for the purposes of social administration.

Chapter 4 *Governance* addresses the central premise of the part, that mass education has a crucial role to play in managing the conduct of the population. It questions the commonsense assertions that individuality is the same now as it was 300 years ago; that schools have nothing to do with social administration, being there solely for educational purposes; and that the internal structure of the school – its organisation of space and time – isn't really that relevant.

Chapter 5 *Subjectivity* investigates the rise of psychology, and its role in the governance of subjectivity. It questions the view that psychology is solely about uncovering the mysteries of the human mind; that the human mind remains largely ungoverned; and that the categories of difference we now take for granted – such as ADHD – were simply uncovered by psychology, and the discipline itself had no role in its emergence

Chapter 6 *Pre-adulthood* examines the ways in which various categories of pre-adulthood have been organised, and the role they play in governance. It questions the belief that categories such as 'childhood' and 'youth' exist as natural stages of life; that those categories have nothing to do with contemporary social governance; and that these categories have natural characteristics, such as 'innocence', that determine how those placed in these categories will necessarily behave.

The central point of this approach – certainly in the context of a book on education – is to show that contemporary mechanisms of rule are not really about the authority of 'the State', or the instilling of unquestioning obedience to the law, or figuring out who has power and who does not. Rather, we are ruled (and rule ourselves), in large part, through the techniques of governance made possible through institutions such as the modern school.

# Chapter 4

# Governance

This chapter argues that the modern school isn't just about 'education', but has a big role to play within contemporary governance. It is tempting to think that the process of teaching children has always been pretty much the same, and that mass schooling emerged as a result of greater concern for the wellbeing of the young. The evidence paints a somewhat different picture, wherein mass schooling formed a crucial component of a new form of social regulation, one based upon an increasing focus on individuality, one where the school subtly conforms to the requirements of the state, and one where the disciplinary management of the population is made possible through continual surveillance, and through the close regulation of space, time and conduct.

## Myth #1 Society has always been simply a collection of individuals

*Whether 300 years ago, or in the present day, we have always regarded ourselves as individuals, part of a population, but each of us is different in thousands of ways.*

Modern governance – and indeed individuality itself – really only became thinkable when we changed from being a mob, into a population; a change that came about as a result of new techniques of information gathering, allowing for the construction of endless new categories of difference. Importantly, with each new category, came new possibilities of intervention and regulation.

## Myth #2 Schools are primarily about education, not regulation

*Schools aren't about the exercise of power, or about population control, they are simply about giving children an education.*

With the demise of sovereign power throughout the eighteenth century, liberal forms of governance sought less intrusive ways to regulate the population. One of the most effective strategies was to 'govern at a distance' through relays like the mass school. All the required capacities could be inculcated into the population without the government seeming to be involved.

## Myth #3 The structure of the school isn't really that important to the education process

*It doesn't matter where we educate our students, or how, it's just the knowledge that counts; the organisation of the school is ultimately irrelevant.*

The mass school is an example of a disciplinary society, a society based upon continual surveillance, the close regulation of space and time, and the detailed management of behaviour. This new institutional logic, with its threefold process of individuation, differentiation and normalisation, soon proved so successful that it spilled out of the school ground, and came to organise society in general.

# Introduction

This chapter is, first and foremost, about the history of mass education: what schools used to be like, how the modern school arose, why it emerged at the time it did, and why it took its current familiar, all-pervasive form. However, the interesting issue here isn't really a curiosity concerning how schools once were – fascinating though that might be – rather the central purpose is to better explain why things now are as they are. This approach that has often been referred to as writing a *history of the present* (Foucault 1977, 31), a method that will, in this instance, not only tell us a great deal about how our education system works, it will also go a long way towards explaining some of the most important ways in which our society is governed.

## Two foundational historical myths regarding education

This chapter, like all others in this book, is based around three commonly held myths about a given topic area within education, in this case, the rise of the modern school. Before addressing these myths, two preliminary sub-myths will be addressed in passing here in the introduction. These do not warrant the status of 'full myth', as debunking them doesn't represent much of a challenge; in truth, they operate more at a subliminal level, and a brief trip through virtually any book on the history of education would amply demonstrate their invalidity. Also, the three myths warranting a section each in this chapter will shed a far more valuable light on issues of contemporary social governance.

## 1   A classroom is a classroom, irrespective of when and where

It is frequently assumed that teaching is a relatively unproblematic activity: one person has some knowledge – the teacher – and a small group of generally younger people – the pupils – gather around them to acquire that knowledge. It is also assumed that this process is, with a few minor historical and cultural provisos, pretty much universal. The contemporary school is simply an effective, modernised extension of the same story. Of course we should organise our learning in the way we do, with the emphasis on teacher–pupil interaction, formalised learning spaces, graded broadly based curricula, timetables of activities, various forms of assessment, and a clear hierarchy of authority. These features of the education system merely reflect the fact that this is self-evidently the best system available. After all, how else could education possibly be organised?

The answer to this question is: in many, many different ways. In the centuries leading up to the establishment of the mass education system, what was understood as 'schooling' often operated according to very different systems of reasoning, social purposes, accessibility, spatial arrangements and practices of instruction. For example, there is nothing fixed or inevitable about the desirability of children receiving a broadly based general education; schooling has often only been about religious knowledge, or specific skill training. Equally, most people, for most of Western history, didn't get to go to school at all; access to education was often a direct function of social status.

Likewise, the notion of 'teaching' has had very different meanings in the past to its current connotation. Teachers haven't always sat at the front of the class, keeping an eye on their pupils, indeed in the past much of the actual instruction was done by the older children. Teaching itself wasn't even regarded as a profession until relatively recently. Even as late as the mid-nineteenth century, little was expected of teachers. As Vick (2001, 68) notes, 'there were no formal or mandatory qualifications, no required minimum length of training, no test of knowledge or classroom competence'.

The point here is that there is nothing natural about our education system. There isn't a *teleology* – an inevitable, underlying purpose – that has shaped the way we've chosen to organise our schools. Our system of mass education developed the way it did, not because it unequivocally represents the best way to educate, but because of the historically contingent social, cultural and governmental forces that shaped it, forces that will be discussed at length in this chapter

## 2  Mass schooling and the civilised society

Introductory myth #2 involves probably the most frequently told story charting the rise of mass schooling. This story normally centres around the post-Enlightenment social changes of the late eighteenth and early nineteenth centuries, and details how society slowly became more caring and more humane, and how we all decided that rather than simply being fodder for the mills, all children – including those from the working classes – had the right to an education. The more 'civilised' we became, the more we pushed back the school leaving age, until we eventually developed schools which clearly reflected the values and ambitions of the wider community.

Once again, there is no teleology here; instead it will be argued that our schooling system did not emerge as an inevitable by-product of our increasingly civilised society, rather the structure of the modern school came about due to the possibilities it gave for more effective social governance, with its associated rationales of a ranked and differentiated population, mass literacy and numeracy, and the productive needs of a disciplined national workforce. Indeed, the evidence suggests that far from schools coming to reflect the logic of the wider 'civilised' society, in many ways society came to reflect the logic of the school. That is, the forms of disciplinary organisation that developed inside the new institutions of the early nineteenth century, such as the mass school – timetables, record-keeping, surveillance – spilled out into the general management of the population, such that they now constitute fundamental foundations of our broader society.

This chapter will seek to address these issues by asking the questions: why is schooling organised in the way that it is? Or rather, what were some of the historical circumstances that led to the shaping of what constitutes a 'normal' education? Furthermore, why is the notion of 'discipline' so central to this? We can answer these questions by focusing on how various disciplinary practices came to constitute a central strategy, not only for the running of schools, but also for the government of society itself.

## A different perspective on governance

If we look into the past, it is often easiest to imagine it populated with individuals who understood themselves in pretty much the same way as we do now. While we in the twenty-first century now live longer, have different kinds of houses and clothes, do different jobs, eat different foods, and entertain ourselves differently from our medieval forebears, surely the more crucial elements of individual consciousness have remained constant? This would include how we understand ourselves as autonomous beings, and our relations to, and differences from, other people. Surely they are the same? Well … very probably not.

It has been argued that over the last 200 years, there have been a number of significant changes in the way in which society is governed. These changes have not only affected how schools sought to educate their pupils, but also actually reorganised the way in which people conceptualise who and what they are, as individuals. At the risk of oversimplification, three interrelated issues will be addressed here as being of greatest significance to the formation of contemporary mass schooling.

## The population

The first is the invention of the notion of a 'population'. It will be argued that towards the end of the eighteenth century, the process started whereby the social body was transformed from an undifferentiated 'mob,' into a workable and more readily governable 'population', one comprised of differentiated individuals, each with increasingly discernable capacities and characteristics. Separating people out in this manner radically increased the possibilities of targeted, effective government.

## Liberalism

The second is the rise of liberalism. The Enlightenment signalled the beginning of the end of the absolute power of the monarch, and this triggered a series of debates about the extent of the legitimate power of the State. Liberal philosophy held that the State ought to be involved in issues such as law enforcement and international affairs, but stay out of, for example, the running of the marketplace and the raising of children. It was soon decided that producing the next generation of citizens was far too important to be left to chance, and the State began to involve itself in the process 'at a distance', most notably through the new medium of the mass school.

## The modern institution

The third involves the birth of the modern institution. While schools, prisons and hospitals obviously weren't invented at the end of the eighteenth century, their forms were radically transformed, and all according to the same underpinning reasoning. As such, new school designs meant that pupils could be placed under constant surveillance, and hence their conduct more closely and effectively governed; indeed, the emphasis shifted from governance, to self-governance. Within such institutions, through the threefold processes of individuation, differentiation and normalisation, and through a pervasive regimen of disciplinary management, acceptable citizens could be shaped and regulated.

The taken-for-granted effects of each of these historical changes can be best addressed through an analysis of three commonsense assumptions about the relationship between governance, citizenship and schooling. The three myths are as follows:

**Myth #1** – Society has always been simply a collection of individuals

**Myth #2** – Schools are primarily about education, not regulation

**Myth #3** – The structure of the school isn't really that important to the education process

# Myth #1 Society has always been simply a collection of individuals

People are just people, irrespective of when they were born. There's no real difference between a person from 300 years ago, and someone who lives now. Physically we're the same, mentally we're the same, and in terms of outlook, we probably see the world in pretty much the same way. We may now drive cars, watch TV, and know the world is a sphere, but ultimately we're all simply individuals trying to find out about ourselves.

Most of us know a great deal about the society in which we live – how many of us there are, what part of the country the majority of us inhabit, what kinds of things we do, how long most of us live – and we take that kind of knowledge for granted. Importantly, such knowledge not only informs us about our community, it informs us about ourselves. We know where we stand in relation to others: we know if we are smarter than national averages, or heavier, or wealthier, or drink more.

Such knowledge, however, has not always been available. In Europe, prior to the nineteenth century, the vast majority of the people, including those who ruled, would have known very little about the demographics of their social surroundings, quite simply because the mechanisms did not exist to accumulate the necessary information. We might then legitimately ask: how do you rule a country about which you know next to nothing? This is an interesting historical question, not least because it helps shed light on our past, but also because it goes to the heart of how we have come to govern.

## A new model of rule

The philosopher and historian Foucault (1977) famously begins his book *Discipline and Punish: the birth of the prison,* with a comparison of the horrendously brutal execution of Damiens the Regicide in 1757 (the price for trying to kill King Louis XV), with an example of the exercise of power from only 80 years later – a set of rules from the House for Young Prisoners in Paris, rules structuring daily tasks according to tightly regimented subdivisions of time and conduct. Foucault is making a very clear point here: that within the space of only 80 years, something significant had changed about the way in which we govern.

Damiens' punishment served a very clear purpose. That is, by executing him with such ferocity, in front of thousands of people, the king was symbolically reinforcing his own authority in the clearest possible terms. Public execution had always served this function: *challenge the power of the sovereign, and this is what you get!*

However, with the decline in sovereign power during the eighteenth and nineteenth centuries – along with the advent of a more complex, industrial society (among other reasons) – new ways of governing were sought. It would no longer be enough to simply execute a few people every now and again, to keep the rest of the mob in line; a new approach was needed, one based upon the acquisition of social information (Kay-Shuttleworth 1973). With this realisation came the first use of statistics in social governance; indeed, the word *statistics* comes from the German, meaning 'the science of state'.

This process began with the deployment of relatively modest devices, such as a simple national census, early versions of which enabled disparate organs of government to sketch out a preliminary map of some of the most important contours of community life. These contours included, for example, how many people lived in a particular country, how they were employed, where they lived, and for how long. Then, as the nineteenth century progressed, more and more statistical information was gathered about almost every conceivable aspect of existence, what Hacking (1982) refers to as 'an avalanche of printed numbers'. With this knowledge developed the notion of a population, complete with 'inherent' characteristics, features and categories.

For instance, no longer were there just 'thieves', to be caught and publically punished in the name of the sovereign. Sufficient data were gathered to break this category down into a large number of subcategories, each of which could be addressed and managed in their own way, a process out of which developed the science of criminology. Likewise, the nebulous character of 'the pauper' began to be subdivided, giving way to a series of well-delimited categories based upon perceptions of their relative idleness ('good poor', 'bad poor', 'wilfully idle', 'involuntarily unemployed')

(Foucault 1984). Modern medicine also developed largely as a result of new forms of information gathering, recording and categorisation. New categories of illness were invented, burgeoning throughout the ninteenth century (and which still continue to burgeon), each more specific and targeted than the last.

## The rise and rise of individuality

The important issue here is that people were no longer part of an unknown and unknowable mob. Instead, they had become part of a population, a new and pivotal phenomenon which was soon to replace the wealth of the sovereign as the central *raison d'etre* of government. That is, prior to this time, government – the exercise of state authority – had, in a sense, been its own purpose, operating almost exclusively in the interests of the ruler. It now began to be directed at the population. This occurred both directly and indirectly, not simply in improving its conditions, but also in managing its habits, aspirations and interests. Government would therefore become 'the conduct of conduct' (Gordon 1991, 2).

One of the most significant side effects of the creation of a population, certainly for the purposes of this chapter, was the exponential growth in the notion of individuality. Prior to this time, individuality wasn't really that important. People tended to regard themselves, first and foremost, as members of particular communities. If *individuality* is the number of ways we know we differ from others in that community, prior to the advent of 'the population', people could barely be regarded as individuals at all. As Foucault states:

> For a long time ordinary individuality – the everyday individuality of everybody – remained below the
> threshold of description. To be looked at, observed, described in detail, followed from day to day by an
> uninterrupted writing was a privilege. (1977, 191)

Foucault is making two points here: the first is that only the wealthy and important were deemed worthy of separate, recorded identities. The vast majority of us – the poor and the common – passed under the radar of relevance, remaining simply part of an undifferentiated mass. Second, in comparison to the intensely individuated beings we are today, individuality barely existed. It was only through Hacking's avalanche of printed numbers, the manic counting first begun early in the nineteenth century, that first tens, then hundreds, then thousands of new categories of being were brought into existence. These categories were medical, social, criminological, intellectual, moral, physical; indeed, they covered every human capacity imaginable, and it was from this new palette of difference that individuality first took shape ... and then grew, and grew, and grew.

Returning to the myth at the beginning of this section: the historical evidence would suggest that people aren't the same, irrespective of what era they came from. Prior to the mid-eighteenth century in Europe, people did not regard themselves, above and beyond anything else, as individuals, clearly and endlessly different to others around them. Neither the mechanisms, nor any kind of desire, to measure those differences were in place. It took the widespread use of social statistics to make those differences visible. Significantly, as we will soon find out, it also took the advent of mass schooling to provide suitable sites for much of this measurement to occur.

Of course, most significantly of all, as soon as all this measurement took place, and almost endless new categories of difference were created, each of these new categories could be intervened upon differently. This is the point. The possibilities of government had now been increased exponentially. You can't really govern a mob, but you can most certainly govern a population.

# Myth #2 Schools are primarily about education, not regulation

Schools aren't about the exercise of power, or about somehow producing a manageable population; schools are about giving children an education. We educate our children because we want them to reach their full potential, not because of any grand scheme of social regulation.

## The advent of liberalism

The second significant change to the way we govern involved the effects of an important change in eighteenth- and nineteenth-century society: the advent of liberalism. The Glorious Revolution of 1688, in which James II of England was removed from the throne of England – not by force of arms, but by the will of the people – signalled both the beginning of the Enlightenment, and the beginning of the end of absolute monarchy. This left a clear problem: the monarch had always had total power; since this was no longer to be the case, how should the exercise of power be understood? Absolute rulers could do what they liked, but surely we hadn't replaced one form of despotism with the rule of an equally despotic state? What should the State be allowed to do? Where should its power begin and end? It is questions such as these that form the fundamental foundations of liberalism.

These concerns over how to determine the limits of government were articulated principally within the philosophical writings of John Locke and David Hume, as well as the economic theories of Adam Smith. The publication of Smith's *The Wealth of Nations* resulted in both a change in political and economic thinking, but more importantly, a shift in ideas about how society ought to be governed. Liberalism depends upon a certain distance from matters of state, a state with inherent limitations in its ability to know. It also expresses a scepticism about the ability, or the right, of the State to know perfectly and in all details the reality to be governed (Burchell 1993). This is particularly significant because, as was discussed in the last part, the State now had at its disposal an array of new tools for finding ever-more information out about the population. But could it ever find out everything it needed to know? And should it? All in all then, liberalism has rightly been characterised as:

> a doctrine of limitation and wise restraint, designed to mature and educate government by displaying to it the intrinsic bounds of its power to know. Liberalism undertakes to determine how government is possible, what it can do, and what ambitions it must needs renounce to be able to accomplish what lies within its powers. (Gordon 1991, 15)

To put it more simply, liberalism took as its central problem the demarcation of the governable from the ungovernable, and of those areas of necessary state intervention from those of autonomy. For example, it was argued that while it was still appropriate for the State to organise the defence of the nation, as well as the judgement and punishment of criminal conduct, it should stay out of the economic marketplace, and leave families with the right to raise children as they see fit – an understanding of government that is now, more or less, taken for granted.

This all sounds great. The unlimited power of the monarch has become a thing of the past. The State would only intervene where it was deemed necessary, and it was widely held that children would be none of the State's business. So did this mean that large portions of society were just to be left to their own devices? After all, this had certainly worked in pre-industrial, undifferentiated societies where any kind of close management of the citizenry was impossible, but times had changed. The State now had the potential not only to find out about its population, but also to begin the process of shaping it. But how could this happen, given that the doctrine of liberalism had placed this kind of interference beyond its legitimate powers?

## Government at a distance

The answer to this question: with a great deal of subtlety. Some of those domains where governmental intervention was deemed inappropriate, such as those responsible for the raising of children, were organised by far less direct forms of management – mechanisms of government which 'operate at a distance' (Rose & Miller 1992). That is, the State did not organise the internal conduct of the family based upon such clumsy coercive mechanisms as laws, decrees and regulations. Rather, it administered the raising of children through the expertise associated with disciplines like family guidance, welfare, psychology, community medicine, counselling and pedagogy (Rose 1985). In this way the family could at once be private and autonomous, while at the same time being regulated as one of the most important sites for instilling the capacities, aspirations and habits required of the population (Donzelot 1979). This has often been referred to as the *pedagogic family*.

Significantly, the school also became one of the most important sites where this 'government at a distance' was to occur. The expertise of the teacher became a vital component in the management of an entire segment of the population (Rose

1990). Schools would no longer be places where a few, wealthy children went to acquire the cultural capital necessary to maintain their social status, schools would now be put in place for everyone, regardless of background. Crucially, within these new mass institutions, the population would be shaped, governed, in ways deemed necessary for the common good – with teachers providing both the expertise and the moral guidance to accomplish this government – all the while giving the appearance that the State had nothing to do with it. The school would become a relay, an intermediary device for producing the kind of citizens needed, without seeming to break its own rules of non-intervention.

This is an important issue, particularly in relation to the myth at the beginning of this section. Schools are often regarded simply as places where children learn the knowledge we consider especially important, and to some extent this is true. However, this is not why mass education has become the most important of all our institutions. It is because of the role they play in social regulation. If you want to understand how we govern contemporary societies, the first place to look is the mass school.

## Liberalisms

It should be noted that, although the central principle of liberalism has remained constant – that is, setting limits to government – government itself has experienced a number of important modifications. Rose and Miller (1992) outline two of the most important of these modifications to classic liberalism.

First, they argue that the late nineteenth and early twentieth centuries witnessed an increasing conviction that classic liberalism was failing to produce the kind of society that many desired; there were high levels of poverty and social disadvantage, and very limited social mobility. In response to this dissatisfaction, many Western societies became welfare states. This did not signal the founding of a new form of state altogether; rather, it initiated a new mode of rule. Welfarism attempted to transform the State into a more interventionist entity, one which, while retaining some distance from those domains in need of intervention, still succeeded in their effective management.

The second change involves the rise of neoliberalism from the mid 1970s onward. As with classic liberalism, neoliberalism concerns itself primarily with setting limits to governmental intervention, however it characterises welfarism in terms of a counterproductive expansion of the state. Because the state is deemed to be inherently unable to deal with the marketplace, it should therefore all but leave it alone. Furthermore, the principles of the market should be applied more widely within society, even to the level of the construction of a particular type of subjectivity. That is, within the logic of neoliberalism,

> the rational principle for regulating and limiting governmental activity must be determined by reference to … the free, *entrepreneurial* and *competitive* conduct of economic-rational individuals (Burchell 1993, 271).

So, whereas welfarism attempted to govern through the concept of 'society', neoliberalism governs through managing the choices of individual citizens, within a market governed by 'the rationalities of competition, accountability and consumer demand' (Rose 1993, 285), and a culture 'driven substantially by notions of self-development, personal progression and self-actualisation' (O'Brien & Osbaldiston 2010, 174). Given the ever-increasing levels of individuation discussed in Part 1 of this chapter, this final element of neoliberalism shouldn't come as any surprise: as we have become more and more individualised, liberalism has too.

# Myth #3 The structure of the school isn't really that important to the education process

It doesn't really matter where we educate our students; for us it just happens to be the modern classroom. It's the information, the knowledge, that counts, and even that can be presented in any number of different ways. Likewise, we don't have to keep student records, or our students under continual surveillance, or engage in continual assessment.
It isn't crucial, it's just convenient.

Following the work of Foucault (1977), it will be argued here that the major social institutions that developed into their current forms during the ninteenth century – the school, the prison, the barracks, the hospital, the asylum and the factory – all share a similar structure and logic. These similarities didn't come about by chance. These institutions developed as they did because they enabled the effective management of the individuals contained there, whether they were pupils, inmates, soldiers, patients or workers, and each is organised according to a fundamental underlying principle: *discipline*.

According to O'Farrell (2005), discipline is a mechanism of power which regulates the behaviour of individuals within the social body. It regulates the organisation of space and time, people's activity and behaviour, and is enforced with the aid of complex systems of surveillance. As such, schools are examples of a 'disciplinary society'. That is, rather than the current structures of schools being simply a random convenience – rows of desks, timetabling, a progressive curriculum … all just a quirk of history – those structures are absolutely fundamental, not only to what schools can accomplish, but also to the way we have come to regulate our wider society (Gore 1998).

## Disciplinary societies
This term describes the form that modern institutions, such as the school, came to adopt. Largely following the reasoning of utilitarian philosophers such as Bentham,

it was realised that a series of architectural and organisational changes could result in new sets of possibilities about the role that institutions could play in the modification of human conduct (Symes & Preston 1997). The most crucial components in such 'disciplinary societies' are as follows.

## The panopticon

Arguably, all modern institutions are founded upon the possibility of continual surveillance. The reasoning behind this is simple. While the modern state had already moved social governance far beyond the notion of periodic symbolic execution as the principal method for the exercise of power, the panopticon took the process one stage further, in that the emphasis was to move from governance, to self-governance.

Once again, it was Foucault (1977), in his book on the history of the modern prison, who sought to demonstrate that through the use of architectural devices like the panopticon (where all prisoners were continually visible from a central observation point) it became possible to enlist prisoners in the process of their own reformation. Since the prisoners would never be sure if they were under surveillance, they would have to keep their conduct in check at all times, thus becoming, in essence, their own gaolers. The discipline imposed by this surveillance would become self-discipline, and regulation, self-regulation.

The use of panopticons was not restricted to the prison. Educational institutions quickly adopted this system of organisation, and it soon became the norm for all classrooms. Take a look around any lecture theatre: the speaker will almost certainly present from a single vantage point, from where all students are visible at all times, and thereby one lecturer can regulate the conduct of 500 students. This did not just happen by accident. Likewise, in the school classroom, teachers can continually surveil the conduct of their all pupils, and consequently – so the theory goes – university students and school pupils alike (and prisoners and factory workers) all learn to govern their own behaviour.

The process does not stop there. More often than not, architectural and administrative mechanisms are in place such that the teachers can themselves be surveilled, and just as the pupils are watched by the teachers, so the teachers are watched by the head of department, who is watched by the deputy principal, who is watched by the principal, who is watched by the Department of Education. This is called *hierarchical observation*, and it forms the core of a disciplinary society. However, in addition to this new disciplinary mechanism, is the threefold strategy of individuation, differentiation, and normalisation.

## Individuation

As was discussed in myth #1 in this chapter, the possibilities of effective government increased exponentially with the change in society from an unknowable mob, into a modern population – an entity comprised of distinct individuals, each with their own measurable, and governable, characteristics. While this came about as a result of new methods of counting and analysis, it also came about as a result of the architecture of the new mass institutions. Within these institutions, each prisoner/pupil was now to be allocated their own space. No longer could they be treated as part of a mob, moving around without restriction. Instead they were to be individuated – prisoners were placed in specifically allocated cells, pupils organised into rows and columns in particular classrooms, each knowing their place, and in turn being known. After all, we now take it for granted that a competent head of school could pinpoint the whereabouts of any given student, at any given time, almost to the desk. It is as if each individual is now an identifiable 'case', to be placed on a specific seat with an empty folder attached to it, a folder than can now be filled with an almost endless amount of information about that person.

## Differentiation

The question now is: how do we start the process of filling that folder? The most obvious answer is through continual, systematic, and wide-ranging assessment, a fact most readily observable within the disciplinary society of the school. Through such testing, it is now possible to identify particular characteristics, skills, capacities, and weaknesses of any pupil – and thereby to *differentiate* them from their peers. That is, the results from each of these tests can be used to construct tens of thousands of normal curves, against which each individual result can be compared.

Add to this testing the effective keeping of records, and new identities started to emerge, identities with far greater depth, texture and permanence than was previously possible or even thinkable. Students are now intimately known and documented as part of what is considered to be good practice in education. Of course, now that the folder on each chair is now brimming with information, and places on the normal curve allocated, it is now possible to begin the process of intervention and correction.

## Normalisation

Probably the most significant aspect of this process was that it has now become possible to normalise the population in ways that were previously inconceivable. By divining ever-increasing numbers of measurable capacities within children, and by constructing endless sets of norms from this data, children could be assessed against their peers, their shortcomings documented, and the relevant forms of intervention set in motion. Students were no longer to be normalised on just their punctuality or their spelling. Instead a densely saturated *corrective* apparatus was put in place, an apparatus that normalises everything from speech to sports, from attitude to arithmetic. Thus, by individuating students, they can be differentiated, and by differentiating students, they can be normalised. And a normalised population is a manageable population.

## Managing time

Space was not the only thing to be subdivided into manageable units within a disciplinary society. Such disciplinary societies are, in part, also characterised by techniques for taking charge of the *time* of individual existences. This does not simply extend to the rigorous demarcation of the working day. Rather, it is comprised of a minute positioning in relation to the pervasive division of time – the organisation of time into successive or parallel segments; the arrangement of these segments into a graded, cumulative series of increasing complexity; and the connecting of these series into an overall developmental plan. The disciplinary management of time is especially evident within contemporary schooling:

> It is this disciplinary time that was gradually imposed upon pedagogic practice – specialising the time of training and detaching it from adult time, from the time of mastery, arranging different stages, separated from one another by graded examination; drawing up programmes, each of which must take place during a particular stage and which involves exercises of increasing difficulty; qualifying individuals according to the way they pass through these series. (Foucault 1977, 159)

## Society as a reflection of the school

Common sense would normally suggest that societies produce education systems that are a reflection of themselves, a small reproduction of the larger whole. The most self-evident features of a culture – its forms of organisation, its structures of authority, its mechanisms of socialisation – ought logically to find their way into the schools, just as they most likely find their way into all other forms of communal life.

Only in this instance, that isn't the way it happened; in fact, in many ways, it was quite the reverse. The features of the disciplinary societies that emerged in the great institutions of the nineteenth century proved to be so successful as techniques of population management, they spilled out of those institutions and into the wider society, where they started to shape a new way of governing the entire social body. We now take it for granted that we will be surveilled, that CCTV cameras will be placed at regular intervals throughout our cities, in police stations, in shopping malls, and in their basement car parks. We know that extensive records are kept about us detailing our health, our financial status, our purchasing habits, our educational achievements, and our automotive transgressions. We also know that we will be differentiated into virtually endless categories of existence: sexual categories, medical categories, professional categories, socioeconomic categories. Finally, we expect that we will be normalised, that if we are found to have shortcomings in some aspect of our lives – how we behave in public, how we treat our children, how we drive, how we interact with each other – we expect to be subject to various forms of targeted social intervention, and to have our conduct steered back towards what has been deemed normal. All of these familiar techniques of government had their origins within institutions such as the school.

# Conclusion

The central purpose of this chapter has been to show the essential role that mass schooling plays in the government of contemporary society. This role is not simply about giving everyone a good education, such that they can all behave relatively reasonably and get themselves a job, thereby maintaining the status quo. The role of mass schooling is far more fundamental than that. It constitutes probably the most important site for the shaping and managing the conduct of the population. Indeed, it was probably the most important sites for the notion of the population to emerge. Furthermore, with the decline of sovereign rule, the school provided a vital relay through which the new 'liberal' forms of governance could guide the shaping of the citizenry while still appearing to mind its own business. Finally, the school constitutes a 'disciplinary society', which, through continual surveillance, endless testing and category-production, acts as a vast normalisation machine.

Two further points are of note here. The first is that the various forms of the exercise of power raised here – sovereignty, discipline, governance – should not be regarded as mutually exclusive. The blunt instruments of sovereign rule, with its laws, decrees and regulations, did not simply disappear when discipline started to emerge in the seventeenth and eighteenth centuries, before really taking hold in the nineteenth century. Likewise governance, within its all-pervasive 'conduct of conduct', did not simply trump all that remained; or to put it another way, discipline did not replace sovereignty, only to be replaced itself by government. Rather, 'one has a triangle, sovereignty–discipline–government, which has as its primary target the population …' (Foucault 1991, 102).

The second point is that it is often assumed that governance and disciplinary management only occurs in obvious and visible ways. That is, the disciplinary technologies already discussed here – panopticons, timetables, specified seating arrangements, individual records, and so on – as most usually associated with the primary or secondary classroom. This leads to the assumption that other educational environments, for example the kindergarten or the playground, are somehow 'zones of freedom' where the notion of discipline takes a secondary position behind the 'real' life of children. This would be a mistake.

As previously mentioned, along with the pedagogic family (i.e. the *new* family, the family that willingly bore the burden of responsibility for producing good and healthy future citizens), mass schooling became one of the most important and convenient mechanisms for implementing specific forms of self-cultivation and distributing them to a mass population. However, these ends could not be satisfactorily realised solely through the mechanisms available at the beginning of the nineteenth century – that is, either the strict regimen of monitorialism or the pastoral care of the Sunday school. David Stow (1850), a nineteenth-century educational reformer, argued for a form of schooling which allowed a greater level of freedom than previously possible within the monitorial school, and yet which still permitted the subtle imposition of required social norms. This 'child-centred' pedagogy successfully combined the strategies of pastoral care with those of social administration. It also promoted a sympathetic relationship between teacher and pupil, in the form of the concerned teacher who observes and directs the moral development of children. However:

> The move to overcome 'mechanical' teaching and the remoteness of the classroom from 'life' through a new 'child-centred' pedagogy was, therefore, no fundamental opposition to the disciplinary normalisation of whole populations. Quite the reverse: it was the means by which the latter could be most successfully achieved (Hunter 1993, 25).

Even in educational sites like the playground, pastoral care is combined with social management. Within this remodelled school (which is still the dominant contemporary form of education), children move between the playground and the classroom, playing and discussing their play, beneath the benevolent, but all-seeing gaze of the teacher. Consequently, the 'freedom' of the playground and the 'discipline' of the classroom do not represent a 'fundamental opposition', but rather two tactics, which form part of a wider strategy aimed at the correct training of young people.

In support of this contention: the correct training of young people provides the focus for much of Debbie Tyler's (1993) work on the 1930s kindergarten – supposedly a site of self-expression and freedom. Tyler uses the example of the Lady Gowrie Centres, built during World War II and still a popular form of early childhood education. Within these institutions there operates a variety of subtle measurement and surveillance techniques. The measured organisation of bodies in space permits the teacher to assess each child against graded developmental norms at a glance, while a number of unseen observation posts are incorporated into the standardised design of the buildings themselves. Furthermore, careful records are kept of each child, detailing even the smallest elements of daily conduct, life and learning.

It is not, however, only the external actions of children which are now governed within the school, whether in the playground, the kindergarten or the classroom. Although the technologies and practices associated with the implementation of a disciplinary society effectively manage daily conduct – who does what, when and how – it has now become possible to administer an entirely new domain of life: that of the mind. As will be discussed at length in the next chapter of this book, the rise of psychology, with its ability to regulate the subjective experiences of citizens, has proven to be a crucial new tool within the field of social governance.

In summary, the central features of the modern school are so familiar to us that we often don't even notice them any more – timetables, academic records, rows of desks, playgrounds – of course they should be there; how could education possibly be otherwise? However, the evidence suggests that these features are neither inevitable, nor did not appear merely by chance. Instead, they are the most important components of a new type of institution altogether, one inexorably tied to the goals of government.

# Subjectivity

# Chapter 5

This chapter argues that our subjective experiences – how we experience the world, and understand ourselves within it – are just as closely governed as our objective conduct (discussed in the last chapter). Whether they realise it or not, contemporary teachers are expected to play a significant role in this form of regulation. After all, teachers are now not simply responsible for transmitting a given curriculum and keeping children in line, they are de facto psychologists, responsible for the mental health, regulation and development of their pupils.

## Myth #1 The sole purpose of psychology is to understand the nature of the human mind

*All societies have mentally ill people. Psychology began by explaining the workings of the normal human mind, and why some people were different. From there, the discipline eventually came to be used in schools.*

'Mental illness' is a relatively new way of understanding forms of conduct associated with 'unreason', and regardless of its function today, psychology originated not as an attempt to know the normal human mind, but rather as a system for finding and managing those unlikely to fit into the new, mass school.

## Myth #2 My conduct may be governed, but my mind remains free

*Disciplinary societies like the school certainly regulate our conduct, but they can't control our minds. That is, the power of the school may cover our bodies, but it doesn't extend inside our heads.*

Just as contemporary forms of governance have rendered our objective conduct amenable to regulation and normalisation, so too has the discipline of psychology made our subjective lives – our desires, motivations, intellectual capacities, perceptions, systems of thought – open to rigorously structured intervention and regulation.

## Myth #3 Psychology simply discovers new behaviour disorders; it plays no role in creating them

*Psychology reveals new facts about the human mind. It has recently found, existing in nature, a wide range of behaviour disorders affecting children's performance at school. It has also developed a range of treatments for these conditions.*

Just as other forms of governance operate by subdividing the population into manageable, bite-sized categories, each of which can be intervened upon differently, so too does psychology, and it is unrealistic to think that psychology had no part to play in the creation of these new pathologies. After all, when new ways of seeing are employed, new realities come into being. 'Behaviour disorders' are a perfect example of this.

# Introduction

It is important to make a particular point here, so important that it will be made again in the conclusion. This is not an anti-psychology chapter. Psychology is an interesting, useful and worthwhile discipline that contributes much to our understanding of what it is to be human. It is also a vital tool in the armoury of all teachers; indeed, you probably couldn't be much of a teacher without it. However, it is the role psychology plays in social governance that lies at the heart of this chapter, as it will be argued here that social governance is really what psychology is all about.

The first question that should now be asked is: why is this chapter titled 'Subjectivity', rather than 'Psychology', given that psychology seems to be its main focus? There are two main reasons for this. The first is that psychology is not the only discipline that deals with the governance of human subjectivity, rather it is just one of several, including psychiatry, psychoanalysis and psychometrics. As a group, these have often been referred to as the *psy-disciplines*. Certainly, in a text on mass education – and certainly within this chapter – psychology may well be the main player, but it is never quite alone.

The second reason is because this chapter sets out to examine the governance of subjective experience, the regulation of how we see the world, and how we go about seeing ourselves. While it examines in detail the role that psychology has played – and continues to play – in this process, the central focus here remains on the 'government of the self', the realisation that our inner selves are just as regulated within the schooling environment as is our behaviour.

## Understanding the human mind

On the surface, this whole topic area seems very straightforward. Psychology is one of the most important discipline areas within the field of education. Of course we should spend a significant amount of time and energy trying to better understand what goes on in our students' minds – how they subjectively relate to the world. After all, not only will this help us create more effective environments for them to be educated in, and organise the delivery of the curriculum in ways that make it easier to learn, it will also help us know what to do when those minds don't work quite in the way we'd like them to.

In many ways, this justification for the central role of the psy-disciplines – both within our education system and within our wider society – is premised upon a couple of important assumptions, assumptions that will form the basis of myth #1. The first is that there exists a relatively neat distinction between those minds that work as they should – that are normal, and that will function appropriately within the context of the school – and those that are not. Those that fall into this latter category are deemed to suffer from various forms of pathology – natural afflictions – whether full-blown mental illness, or simply any one of a large range of behavioural disorders. Like it or not, these pathologies exist as natural facts; ignoring them, or changing the paradigm by which they are understood, won't make them go away.

Having once accepted this foundational proposition, the second assumption is that we are lucky to have developed an unproblematic and objective way of explaining how the human mind works, and why sometimes it doesn't. The psy-disciplines themselves play no role in giving shape to the pathologies they uncover. They simply sit outside the problem, and make objective observations and assessments of what the issues are, and how they should be treated.

It will be contended here, when addressing myth #1, that the situation is much more complex than this, and that the medicalisation of mental differences should not necessarily be regarded as a logical *fait accompli*, but rather came about for very specific historical reasons. Also, the psy-disciplines did not develop as a way of mapping the human mind in a detached and objective way, rather they emerged primarily as forms of educational administration for dealing with those children who didn't fit the mould; it was a management tool for managing difference. As Foucault (1976, 74) states: 'It is not psychology that tells the truth of madness, because it is madness that holds the truth of psychology.' If this claim doesn't make much sense at the moment, hopefully it will by the end of the chapter.

## Schools, psychology and the management of difference

In the last chapter, it was shown how the very architecture of the school, along with its internal forms of organisation, was able to produce differences among pupils, which could then be effectively and acutely managed. Students learned to govern themselves; how they sat, when they talked, how and when they moved around the school. Individual differences were manufactured, and then utilised. It will be argued here – in myth #2 – that this was only half the process. That is, the notion of 'difference' doesn't only relate to the categories produced by the structure of the school – age groupings, subjects, classes, school blocks – it now permeates the children themselves, wherein it is just as tightly regulated, and arguably, this has been made possible thought the deployment of psychology.

In constructing a history of teaching, it would be a mistake to portray the job as having once consisted of simply covering the required curriculum and making sure the children kept quiet. As discussed in the conclusion to the previous chapter, the various tactics involved in trying to produce docile and industrious citizens were more complex and subtle than this. However, as those aspects of the system specifically involved in social administration found their voice, the notion of 'difference' has become increasingly important. Indeed, modern teachers are acutely aware of 'difference', as much of their job often seems to revolve around its effective management. Importantly, more often than not these differences are given voices within the discourses of psychology.

Arguably, it is the discipline of psychology that has provided the largest girders in a conceptual framework built around the humanist mantra that all pupils are individuals, each with individual needs, responses and abilities. This understanding of the teaching process regards the individual as the foundational unit of analysis. It is the primary point of departure, and the bedrock upon which everything else is built. Therefore, according to this logic, the fundamental task of educators is to variously accommodate, encourage and refine such differences so as to produce the whole and self-actualised individual – problems with this account of individuality aside (Mauss 1985; Hirst & Wooley 1985).

Therefore, when addressing myth #2 in this chapter, it will be argued not only that the school plays a huge role in the shaping of individual self-identity, but also that, far from leaving the subjective experiences of students to remain 'free', the school actively regulates and normalises student subjectivity, just as it seeks to manage and normalise their conduct. After all, they are not unconnected.

## Education and pathology

The rise of the inclusive school – that is, institutions where special needs students are to be given full access to, and involvement in, the daily life of the classroom – has now placed the teacher at the centre of diagnosis and treatment of a wide range of learning and conduct disorders. Teachers are now expected to be able to intervene upon a wide range of educational differences. These differences are no longer either below the threshold of intervention, i.e. regarded as relatively unimportant, or simply part of the human condition. Instead they are now deemed to constitute objective pathologies to be identified, categorised and normalised. It is this assertion that forms the substance of myth #3.

It is within the context of the inclusive school that the most significant differences between contemporary teachers and their historical predecessors can be seen. Modern teachers can now almost be regarded as de facto psychological therapists, and whereas once significant conduct or learning difficulties would be the trigger for either expulsion or removal to special schools, teachers now, with the guidance of experts, have been recruited into the ongoing management of 'problem' students (Lane 1990; Tyler 1993).

This management involves a number of elements: first, it requires a working knowledge of a lot of discipline areas, from pedagogy to psychology, from counselling to child welfare, and (increasingly) from paediatrics to pharmacology. Second, it necessitates a constant process of keeping up with developments and 'discoveries' within those discipline areas. It is not enough for teachers to know that certain forms of shyness have now been pathologised as Generalised Social Phobia (Turner,

Beidel & Townsley 1992), it also helps to be aware of some of its subdivisions – such as Selective Mutism (Cline & Baldwin 2004) or Avoidant Personality Disorder (Reich 2009) – as well as how to recognise them, what to do with them, and how to organise your classroom practices accordingly. Third, these developments and discoveries are normally manifest in terms of a burgeoning array of student differences, to the extent that education has become (curriculum transmission aside) the effective management of those differences.

The question here is: to what extent does psychology discover these disorders within the fabric of the natural world, and to what extent does it play a role in bringing them into existence? According to myth #3, phenomena such as Attention Deficit Hyperactivity Disorder (ADHD) have always existed, we were just unable to spot them, to realise that they were illnesses in their own right, in need of intervention and treatment. It was the rise of psychology that finally allowed us to see with sufficient clarity to produce a valid diagnosis. As with the first two myths, it will be argued here that there are other ways of interpreting the recent appearance of a swath of behaviour disorders, and that it has far more to do with the process of governing through the creation of categories of difference, than it does with triumphalist accounts of the steady march of scientific reasoning.

To summarise, the three myths to be dealt with in this chapter are:

**Myth #1** – The sole purpose of psychology is to understand the nature of the human mind

**Myth #2** – My conduct may be governed, but my mind remains free

**Myth #3** – Psychology simply discovers new behaviour disorders; it plays no role in creating them

# Myth #1 The sole purpose of psychology is to understand the nature of the human mind

We didn't really understand much about the human mind before psychology came along. There had always been mentally ill people, but it was only when psychology started to explain how the normal human mind worked that we could begin to figure out why some individuals were different. From there, psychology came be used in the school – always with the primary intention of helping individuals within the system.

There is a very familiar story concerning madness and the rise of psychology. It normally has two interrelated elements. The first is that mental illness is as old as humanity itself. There were people in ancient Greece who were mentally ill, just as now; there is no difference – after all, sick is sick. Examples of these mental illnesses can be seen throughout the ages, but it has only been with the rise of modern forms of assessment and treatment that we are finally able to do much about them, a gradual progress of learning what to do.

The second element of the story involves the birth of psychology. The history of dealing with these mental illnesses generally involves descriptions of a wide range of often bizarre forms of intervention and treatment. With the benefit of a perfect hindsight made possible through the rise of modern scientific reasoning, these interventions were little better than forms of guesswork based upon superstition and ignorance. Then along came psychology, and we were finally able to base our treatments upon a solid foundation of real knowledge. Born towards the end of the nineteenth century, psychology developed from a long line of attempts to understand the workings of the normal human mind. Fortunately, it was able to shed an equal amount of light on abnormal minds.

This myth can be addressed in two parallel ways. First, it will argued here that there is nothing natural and inevitable about the notion of 'mental illness'; the subject matter of the psy-disciplines is very much a social creation. The second point is that psychology has it own history, one not based in the pure, benevolent desire for knowledge about the human mind, but rather one based in the mundane imperative to manage school children who failed to measure up to expectations.

## The great confinement

Contrary to popular belief, those deemed to be mad have not always been regarded as 'sick'; citizens to be separated out from the rest of us, 'othered' (as discussed in Chapter 3), and made subject to all manner of interventions and cures. There is nothing natural and inevitable about this particular response to the various forms of conduct that we may find strange, or that does not meet our expectations. Rather, the best evidence suggests it came about as the end result of a series of social and administrative changes in Europe from the sixteenth century onwards. In the book *Madness and Civilisation*, Foucault (1965) charts the rise of contemporary ways of understanding and dealing with the mad. He begins by noting that during the Middle Ages, madness was largely an 'undifferentiated experience' (1965, ix), one where the mad formed part of the general fabric of society, cared for by their communities, or else wandering between towns. Foucault suggests the initial impetus for change from this model of madness to our own can be found in two historical events.

The first is the disappearance of leprosy across the Western world. The disease that had terrified Europe for over a thousand years all but died out by the fifteenth century. This left behind two things: a void where the great 'other' – the leper – used to be, the blighted space beyond the margins of society, and also nearly 19 000 leprosariums across Christendom with nobody left in them. The second impetus for change came in 1656. During a time of social upheaval and famine, it was decreed in Paris that all those incapable of contributing to the common good – the poor, the sick, the unemployed, the indolent, prostitutes, libertines, and of course, the mad – would be incarcerated, banished from society, held away from the rest of us, thereby purifying the social body. Within a few months, this 'Great Confinement' resulted in one in every hundred residents of Paris being locked away: the ultimate act of social othering. From there, this practice quickly spread across Europe, made all the easier by the availability of space left for them by the disappearance of the leper – not only in the metaphorical sense of a new group to loathe and fear, but also the physical sense of thousands of empty buildings with a new use. Indeed, the Great Confinement had begun in the Hospital General in Paris, itself in part an old leprosarium.

For the next 150 years, the mad were incarcerated within these great institutions (until they were 'discovered' by scientists such as Pinel and Tuke), innocents 'lost' among those otherwise deserving of their imprisonment. From 1800 onwards, the mad quickly became subjects of general scientific interest within what quickly became quasi-medical establishments, but always from within the perceptual framework that was the legacy of their initial forced confinement. That is, the mad were now to be regarded as fundamentally different to the rest of us, and as modern-day lepers, they were also to be feared.

## Why is this relevant?

Of the many arguments that Foucault makes in *Madness and Civilisation*, two are of interest here. The first is that there is nothing inevitable about the current understanding of madness; instead it is the product of history. That is, the notion that madness (and by extension, subgroupings such as behaviour disorders) has an objective reality, a timeless truth, defined in terms of 'sickness', is very much a product of the forms of knowledge that eventually took charge of it. If this had not happened the way it did, we would now understand mental difference very differently.

In spite of the relative success of the dominant medical model of madness, there has been no little dissatisfaction with elements of the labelling processes associated with 'mental illness'. Seminal work by Hollingshead and Redlich (1958) notes that an individual's chance of being committed to a mental institution varied in relation to their social class, a variable surely irrelevant to an 'objective' illness. Some writers, such as Szasz (1961, 1973), suggest that any understanding of 'insanity' as an objectively valid category needs to be abandoned. A number of 'objective' mental illnesses have already had this status questioned, such as split personality (Hacking 1986) and anorexia nervosa (Tait 1993). Furthermore, it is not just the more intangible regions of 'mental' illness that have had their self-evidency challenged. Just like mental illnesses, it has been argued that 'obvious' physical diseases, such as syphilis, asthma and tuberculosis, are not permanently fixed and labelled in nature, and hence have had their objective standing disputed (Fleck 1979; Gabbay 1982; Wright & Treacher 1982). This will be discussed in more detail when addressing myth #3.

Foucault's second point is that the medicalisation of madness isn't necessarily something that we should be celebrating. He suggests that there are significant moral implications associated allowing any form of truth-claim – scientific or otherwise – to decide who is sane enough to be considered normal and who isn't, and hence should be called sick.

> We have yet to write the history of that other form of madness, by which men, in an act of sovereign reason, confine their neighbours, and communicate and recognise each other through the merciless language of non-madness. (Foucault 1965, ix)

He is talking about psychology.

## Schools and psychometrics

Not all disciplines begin in the way in which most of their practitioners imagine. For example, modern physical education in schools did not spring, directly and fully formed, with the purity of purpose of the ancient Olympics and the romantic rigour of the playing fields of Eton. Physical education in schools developed largely as a set of disciplinary practices targeting the body; lines of pupils swinging their arms in time – individuated, differentiated and normalised – docile bodies to be governed for the national good (Kirk 1993).

The history of psychology is much the same. In his book *The Psychological Complex*, Rose (1985) suggests that psychology developed, in large part, not as a detached and unbiased attempt to understand the normal human mind, but as a set of governmental practices for dealing with the newfound problem of the 'feeble-minded', concerns largely driven by the logic of eugenics. The eugenic movement – based upon the belief that through selective breeding, based upon race and intelligence, the risk of 'degeneracy' could be reduced – was highly influential towards the end of the nineteenth century, remaining so for a further 50 years (see Chapter 3). Advocates of this reasoning perceived a threat to the wellbeing of the nation due to the excessive breeding habits of the genetically less-worthy (i.e. generally the poor). However, mass schooling had inadvertently revealed a new and unexpected menace to the gene pool.

## 'The feeble-minded'

Prior to this time, the subdivisions of mental abnormality had been relatively simply. 'Lunatics' were those for whom a cure was possible; 'idiots' and 'imbeciles' were those with congenital problems that doomed them to their condition. Unlike with lunatics, it was always deemed possible to spot idiots and imbeciles from their physical appearance:

> The idiot ... *was visible*. The mark of idiocy was impressed upon the surfaces of the body, in physical signs and external stigma. Idiots might pose a problem of economy, a problem of order, a problem of philanthropy, pedagogy or treatment, but they did not pose a problem of detection ... (Rose 1985, 97)

In the new mass schools, lunatics and the idiots could be excluded from the very start. Likewise, the deaf, blind and dumb were denied entry to the classroom, unable as they were to benefit from a 'normal' education. And so the problem was solved ... except that a proportion of the schooling population seemed unable to learn much at all. They had all their senses, and were clearly not physically marked out as idiots, so what on earth was going on?

A new category, halfway between the normal and the idiot, was speedily required, and the social and governmental obsession with feeble-mindedness began. Clearly new techniques of mental measurement were going to be needed if these feeble-minded people weren't going to be allowed to sneak through the net, mixed in among all the normal people, and breeding even more feeble-minded people. What a potential genetic disaster!

A very small, relatively insignificant group of loosely connected doctors and academics claimed the necessary testing expertise. The *psychometricians* began the process of IQ testing school children to see who should be excluded from the normal classroom. In doing so, they founded a new discipline, and began calling themselves psychologists. Interestingly, they quickly discovered that there were millions of children to be assessed, and hardly any of them (the psychometricians). Consequently they needed to recruit quasi-experts to help them with the mental testing, mini-psychologists who could collect the data, even begin any diagnostic processing needed, before passing the information on to fully trained psychologists when needed. These quasi-experts quickly became known as 'professional teachers'.

In summary then, psychology came to be the dominant discipline it is, not because it answered questions about 'normal' people like us, but because it provided strategies for dealing with people who weren't like us at all, and were causing disruption. Psychology was always, first and foremost, a form of social governance. This will become more apparent when addressing myth #2.

# Myth #2 My conduct may be governed, but my mind remains free

We may have our conduct closely regulated within a disciplinary society like the school – where we sit, how we are permitted to act, how our time is to be spent – but in spite of this social control, my thoughts remain as free as ever. The school may be able to surveil my body, but it can't surveil my mind. There are some basic limits to the reach of government; its authority does not extend into my head.

Following on from the last chapter, it is fairly undeniable that schools have a huge role to play within contemporary social governance. However, all the practices, techniques and forms of organisation discussed there are about our *objective* conduct; about how we appear to an external viewer. As discussed, they include where we sit, what we learn, how our bodies are physically regulated and how we are moved about in space and time. All this may be true, maybe our bodies are tightly managed, and our behaviour governed, but at least our minds remain zones of freedom. This is a democracy; surely we are free to think how we like. The evidence suggests otherwise.

## Psychology and governance

As discussed in the last section, psychometrics testing emerged as a way of ascertaining the existence of feeble-mindedness in circumstances where those mental deficiencies were not visibly written onto the surface of the body. The school became the perfect place for this form of evaluation; first, because it was a place all future citizens were compelled to attend; and second, because an entire new population of professionals – teachers – could be recruited into assisting with that testing. As a result of this, feeble-mindedness very quickly became established both as an objective condition, part of nature that had always been there, and also as an administrative category, a reason for excluding children from school. However, the implications of this testing went far, far deeper.

## The knowable individual

There were a number of other important social and governmental consequences of the rise of mental testing around the beginning of the twentieth century. Sutherland (1984) notes that the test did not stop at the boundaries of the abnormal. Psychologists such as Binet quickly noted its potential for assessing the far wider range of mental abilities than just the pathological – making what Rose (1990, 142) refers to as 'a device for creating a hierarchy of the normal'. This is a crucial leap, as psychological testing was now to be relevant for everyone, not just those who worried the eugenicists.

From there, the German psychologist Stern resolved to make the entire testing process more user-friendly and accessible to the lay audience (teachers, among others). He created a single scale, upon which everyone could be ranked, accomplished by dividing a person's mental age by their chronological age, and then multiplying by 100.

The resulting *Intelligence Quotient*, or IQ, quickly gained widespread acceptance, and helped cement the belief that there exists a singular measure of mental capacity – a highly contentious assertion, at best. The British psychologist Burt, and the American psychologist Terman then standardised the tests to permit their effective usage within schools. Furthermore, they organised the tests into written form (they had previously been oral), such that they could be administered and marked by the less highly trained (teachers again).

One of the most important implications of the new standardised measure of mental capacity – the IQ – is the easy comparison that could now be made between one child and another. What may have once been a vague, guiding teacher's intuition that one student was more capable than another, was now transformed into a rigid, quantifiable fact, a numerical value perfectly suited for ranking and streaming students. It became the ideal tool of governmental differentiation.

Of course, the IQ test was only the first of an array of forms of intellectual differentiation that arose from the new discipline, both formal and informal: these include various aptitude tests, subject tests, mental health tests, attitude analysis, as well as tests for adjustment, motivation, employability, morale, ethics and so on. Once again, each of these moved what would have previously been somewhat vague and insubstantial estimations, if they had been thinkable at all, into tangible, statistical realities. These are realities not only crucial to us all becoming more and more focused upon our own subjective experience, but also making the whole domain of individual difference more amenable to government. As Rose (1988, 187) notes:

> One fruitful way of thinking about the mode of functioning of the psychological sciences … might therefore be to understand them as *techniques for the disciplining of human difference*: individualising humans through classifying them, calibrating their capacities and conducts, inscribing and recording their attributes and deficiencies, managing and utilising their individuality and variability.

## The normal curve

There is no better demonstration of how a simple technique of governance can potentially reorganise the way in which we understand ourselves, and regulate our society, than the use of the normal curve. This is especially the case when addressing the rise of psychology. Rose (1990, 141) discusses how, in the latter half of the nineteenth century, Galton sought a way of making the rather abstract notion of human variability more thinkable, and hence more easy to act upon. As the concept of 'the population' was becoming more central to social management, the processes of differentiation occurring within institutions, such as the mass school, created more and more new categories and capacities. As such, the need to measure and calibrate these human variations became increasingly apparent; after all, what is the point of putting all that administrative effort into creating something like IQ, if you can't put it to any practical use?

Mathematically, the normal curve allows for a comparison of the respective amounts of an attribute possessed by members of a population. In simple terms, what it permits represents the Holy Grail of population management: the 'mathematicisation of difference'. Furthermore, the normal curve provided all the evidence that psychologists, as well as assorted educational administrators, needed that student variability is governed by natural statistical laws, and better still, that all this information could be reduced to a single graph that could be applied to anything. If a disciplinary society is based upon the threefold process whereby we individuate, so that we can differentiate, so that we can normalise, the normalising component of the process had found bedrock, and could now claim validation by nature. The brilliance of the normal curve – much like Stern's IQ – was the simple way it permitted an easy and accessible visualisation of the subject matter. They were both as much successful models of marketing, as they were scientific advances. It is probably fair to say, that at the bottom of almost every example of social governance you can think of, now lurks a normal curve.

## Developmental psychology

As can be seen, the rise of psychometric testing provided one of the cornerstones of the normalisation of childhood. Its widespread deployment of the normal curve meant that any capacity could be calibrated, and any given student measured, not only against their peers in a classroom, but also against some abstract notion of human nature itself. It provided a snapshot of any capacity, an instant judgement, and institutional administrators loved it.

But more was to come. Why settle for a snapshot when you can make a movie? Psychometrics compared students against normal curves that were fixed in time. This provided a very static way of understanding the distribution of capacities within a population, and an equally static way of ranking a student's abilities. It soon became apparent that the normal curve had a far greater potential than simple, one-off comparison. Why not make a series of sliding scales? Why just have a normal curve measuring, for example, a child's spatial awareness? Why not have an entire set of normal curves, based upon a child's age, against which their spatial awareness can be measured? It would then be possible not just to say whether a child was normal or abnormal when it came to this particular capacity – as with psychometrics – it would now be possible to say whether they were advanced or lagging; ahead of their age, or behind. This realisation represented a whole new dimension of governmental possibilities, justifying an encyclopaedia of new forms of intervention and normalisation. It also signalled the birth of a new sub-discipline: *developmental psychology*.

Importantly, as discussed in the last chapter, this form of governance – indeed, the entire discipline of developmental psychology – could not have come into being without the pre-existence of the new administrative and architectural arrangements of the modern school:

> Developmental psychology was made possible by the clinic and the nursery school. Such institutions had a vital role, for they enabled the observation of numbers of children of the same age, and of children of a number of different ages, by skilled psychological experts under controlled, experimental, almost laboratory conditions. They thus simultaneously allowed for standardisation and normalisation ... (Rose 1990, 145)

## Psychology, misconduct and risk

Rose (1990) goes on to make an interesting point about the types of education that are available to parents, a point that could well have been made in Chapter 1 of this book on the issue of social class. He suggests that two main models can be discerned:

one model of education for the wealthy, and a different one for the working class. Importantly, psychology is been able to play a foundational role in each, which has probably contributed to its ongoing success as a discipline.

For the wealthy, education seeks to produce the best possible adult, with all their capacities honed, and their potential capitalised upon. Parents are recruited into this process from birth, with each pedagogic choice scrutinised and justified, and each test result assessed and acted upon. Psychology has dovetailed neatly into this approach, permitting ever-greater scrutiny of students' abilities, and the promise of being able to inch those students up each and every normal curve throughout their educational career.

For the working class, the central issue has always been to minimise the threat they are deemed to pose to the social order. This has included a wide range of strategies, from the education of mothers in the 'correct' way of raising children, to the close policing of conduct in school, searching for signs of delinquency and its inevitable path to future dangers. Importantly, psychology quickly became especially good at this, and hence now underpins both the new disciplinary strategy of *behaviour management*, as well as the entire industry surrounding the notion of the '*at-risk' youth*.

## Behaviour management

The old models of intervening into unacceptable conduct – physical punishment, periods of confinement and repetition of tasks – have now long since been replaced by the far more subtle forms of intervention and guidance advocated by behaviour management. Uncooperative students are now identified, targeted and managed, recruited into their own self-reformation as part of a new tactic of governance, one founded in the individuating logic of psychology.

The suggestion here is not that this is necessarily a bad thing; the suggestion is solely that psychology has managed to place itself front and centre of the disciplinary life of the school. This has significant consequences for how problems within the school might be understood. Traditional structural explanations of misconduct – poverty, social disenfranchisement, hegemonic masculinity, lack of English as a first language, lack of parental education, lack of breakfast – are all far more likely to be considered irrelevant within a paradigm that locates the problem solely within the individual. You are messing up in class? Well it's not because the academic curriculum might be meaningless to you, or the teacher is boring, or the room has only one window, and you've been sitting in there all day, and you're starving. No, it's because you are naughty; the problem necessarily lies within you.

Behaviour management is an excellent way of organising and regulating the contemporary, individuated classroom. All teachers need it in their toolkit. However, it comes at a price in terms of who gets the blame.

## The 'at-risk' youth

The implications of psychological management now extend far beyond the boundaries of the school. Not only has the education system had its focus sharpened in recent years as an instrument for the production of employable citizens (Gee, Hull & Lankshear 1996), the school is now also widely regarded as one of the central sites for some of the most important aspects of ongoing social management. Children at risk of anything from unemployability to criminality are now targeted while still at school (McCallum 1993), and the central mechanism by which this future social programming occurs, is the production, identification, organisation and treatment of difference. Young people can now be measured against a graded and cumulative set of normal risks, both by their age category, and by the severity of the risk involved. Just as the disciplinary school has become characterised by the minute division of space and time, risk has also become an important indicator in the grid of governmental knowledge.

Once again, this all acts to significantly increase the scope of government. Whereas more traditional forms of surveillance require the spatial arrangement of the target population under a central, panoptic gaze, the new strategy of risk almost entirely avoids the need for such direct scrutiny. After all, the focus now falls not upon a given subject, but rather upon a set of abstract risk factors. For example, if a student has the personal demographics of a working-class background, just one parent, and English is their second language, as well as the psychological risk factors of low aptitude scores, poor adjustment, and a diagnosis of ADHD, alarm bells will be ringing all over the place. Castel (1991) argues that the deployment of risk in this manner permits a virtually limitless expansion of the possibilities of government, based primarily upon unlimited suspicion. Indeed Castel argues that:

> Prevention in effect promotes suspicion to the dignified scientific rank of a calculus of probability. To be suspected, it is no longer necessary to manifest symptoms of dangerousness or abnormality, it is enough to display whatever characteristics the specialists responsible for the definition of preventative policy have constituted as risk factors. (Castel 1991, 288)

For Ewald (1991, 199) 'anything can be a risk; it all depends upon how one analyses the danger, considers the event'. The reach of risk is now endless, and hence nothing remains beyond the reach of possible governmental intervention. Once again, it should be emphasised here that intervention is by no means necessarily a bad thing – far from it. The vast majority of governmental intervention is organised with the best of intentions, whether successful or otherwise, whether justified or otherwise. However, what this does illustrate is the depth of the role that psychology continues to play in the governance of populations.

# Myth #3 Psychology simply discovers new behaviour disorders; it plays no role in creating them

We are fortunate to have found a system of investigation – psychology – that has enabled us to discover otherwise-hidden truths about nature; more specifically, it has recently uncovered an ever-growing range of behaviour disorders that always existed, but that we were unable to see. Psychology is managing to peel away layers of ignorance, and shine an objective light into dark recesses of the developing human mind, finding more and more children with mental conditions, and helping them by pointing this out.

In the introduction to the book *The Problem of Medical Knowledge*, Wright and Treacher (1982) contend that scientific knowledge is always presented as objective, benevolent and teleological. The truths of the natural world are relentlessly uncovered, with the individual researchers merely perceptive observers to whom these truths are passed. They contend that this understanding, particularly of medical and psychological information, not only legitimates the pre-eminent status of these disciplines, but also acts to support the validity of their truth claim, and the categories they produce. However, they suggest medical and psychological categories don't really deserve this status. For example:

> Medical categories, we would contend, are social through and through; they are the outcome of a web of social practices and bear their imprint. When we speak of tuberculosis we are not reading the label on a discrete portion of nature, 'out there'; we are instead … employing a social meaning that has been generated by the activities of many different social groups, with diverse interests, working through many different forms of practice. (Wright & Treacher 1982, 10)

Exactly the same is true of psychological categories. While it is often reassuring to imagine that they exist as 'natural facts', timeless entities that we have merely uncovered, the evidence suggests otherwise. A brief review of our not-so-distant past reveals 'objective' categories of psychological difference that we now rightly regard as utterly ridiculous; clearly the product of the social views of the time. The 'hysterical woman' – a well-defined pathological category – was the product of an explanatory system that regarded women as innately weak and unstable. Female behaviour was generally understood as an extension of their reproductive capacities (hence, hysteria – *hysteros*, Greek for uterus). In practice, hysteria became a conveniently ambiguous term covering all forms of physical and mental stress, and which could be applied to anyone, as long as they were female and middle class.

Those psychologists invested in the possibility of objective categories of difference might simply say, 'Well yes, clearly that category was complete rubbish, but the ones we have now are true'. The real issue here is not whether categories are true or false (although clearly, some are utter junk), the issue is more about the realisation that *all* categories are the product of specific social, historical and intellectual forces. Attention Deficit Hyperactivity Disorder (ADHD) is a pretty good example.

## The rise and rise of ADHD

From its first appearance in 1987 – then as Attention Deficit Disorder (ADD) – the following quote is fairly typical of the way in which Attention Deficit Hyperactivity Disorder has been presented within the literature, and by those with an interest in its acceptance as a valid and objective category.

> ADD is an inherited neurobiological disorder which becomes evident in early childhood and usually continues throughout a person's life …There is no doubt in the scientific community that ADD is real … ADD is not a new phenomenon, it has always been with us but has not always been recognised. (Sosin & Sosin 1996, 6–7)

It is evident here that the disorder is understood as an objective condition, an indisputable fact of nature. In addition, it is deemed to have existed long before its identification by the clear-eyed and perceptive scientists who brought it to our attention, thereby dispelling the former erroneous explanations for the same conduct, and long before it became a familiar element within the schooling landscape. In contrast, superseded ways of understanding and healing are presented as superstitious, ignorant and/or barbaric. With the benefit of hindsight, psychologists argue, ADHD can now be delineated long before it was formally diagnosed. In fact, many texts point to the work of the paediatrician Still in 1902, who made some early observations on hyperactivity, and they often note that prior to the diagnosis, ADHD children were simply regarded as naughty and uneducable (Hurley & Eme 2004). Medical history is thereby presented in triumphalist terms: the heroic unmasking of the hidden realities of nature, the shedding of light into the mysteries of the human body and mind, and the identification and control of independent disease entities.

There is, however, significant literature that understands the process of producing medical and psychological classifications very differently. Arguably then, there are three basic problems associated with this approach to behaviour disorders, and more specifically, ADHD. First, there is far from universal support among psychologists regarding the validity of the diagnosis of ADHD. Indeed, a growing number of mental health professionals, not to mention teachers and parents, remain sceptical that a disorder that was rarely mentioned before 1980, could now exist in what is almost plague proportions (Cohen 2006). This concern aside, an even greater number of those professionals are uncomfortable with the use of amphetamines, such as Ritalin, as the central form of treatment.

Second, and from a more philosophical perspective, this approach is largely premised upon the unproblematic existence of objective, natural categories of difference, ones that endure irrespective of human opinion or belief. As previously discussed, this assumption rests upon the shakiest of philosophical ground. In addition, as Barthes (1972) has pointed out, positioning a problem within the realm of nature, removes that problem from social debate or social responsibility. Locating student misbehaviour within nature itself means that no further justification is required, and all those issues most frequently associated with student misbehaviour – social class, masculinity, school violence, educational failure, delinquency – can be considered irrelevant.

Finally, as has been contended throughout this chapter, the discovery of categories such as ADHD is driven, first and foremost, by the broader governmental practice of dividing the population up into ever-more manageable sub-units. Categories such as ADHD are a primary element within the fundamental functioning of a disciplinary society. By differentiating populations into smaller and smaller groupings, it becomes possible to target, with ever-increasing acuity, specific forms of governmental intervention into conduct. Not only does this permit ever more effective normalisation, but it also renders the population more knowable within the broader web of governmental intelligibility.

The issue here is not really ADHD, in and of itself. The issue is that ADHD is now just one of hundreds of categories of psychological difference, across which children (and increasingly adults) can be measured, assessed, found wanting, and normalised.

## Behaviour disorders by the hundred

As Tomlinson pointed out as early as 1982, this appears to be part of an ongoing and exponentially increasing process. After all, within the realm of educational difference/handicap, there were only two classifications prior to 1890: *idiot* and *imbecile,* quickly followed by *feeble-minded*, as discussed in the last section. This had swelled to eight by 1913 (including divisions such as *moral imbecile*, and *mental defective*), and on to twelve in 1945 (with *severely subnormal, maladjusted* and *delicate*) (Tomlinson 1982). Currently, the list of such differences is enormous – in excess of 300 – each with its own treatment, prognosis and educational implications (Tait 2010).

As previously mentioned, contemporary pupils are no longer simply too shy. They now have Social Phobia, or are Elective or Selective Mutes. Neither are they simply too lively, they were first to be reclassified as hyperactive, and now as suffering from ADHD, Oppositional Defiance Disorder (ODD) or Conduct Disorder (CD); and pupils are no longer simply unpopular or obnoxious, they are reclassified as Borderline Personality Disorder (BPD), or Antisocial Personality Disorder (APD). They aren't greedy, they have Binge Eating Disorder (BED); they aren't lazy, they have Motivation Deficit Disorder (MDD); and if they punch someone who happens to annoy them, they probably have Intermittent Explosive Disorder (IED).

Clearly, this process has a number of significant implications for how difference can be managed within schools. After all, the ever-increasing pathologisation of students exposes them to a vast new range of interventions, which in turn exponentially increases the effectiveness of the range of governmental strategies aimed at normalising young people. For example, identifying, organising and treating non-conforming children as ADHD and ODD sufferers serves a dual purpose: first, there are significant administrative benefits to be gained from keeping children in line by simply giving them a pill – ethical issues aside. Second, there is a greater social acceptability for a child to be suffering from a medical condition, than there is for one who might otherwise be regarded as wilfully naughty. As Meadmore (1998, 1) states: 'It is better for everyone for the child to be "sick" rather than "bad".'

The issue here is not to suggest the rejection of such pathological categories of difference outright. Instead, the point is that when new canons of judgement are employed, like psychology, new realities come into being. As a result of the rise of contemporary forms of governance, teachers are now confronted with a range of such new realities. Simply refusing to accept the veracity of disorders such as ADHD is ultimately of little use. The decision as to its 'truth' will be made in locations other than the school, and by knowledges other than those produced by educators. It should also be pointed out that it is not just new canons of judgement that produce new realities, so too do new forms of social administration. After all, medicine and psychology alone were not responsible for the production of ADHD, so too was the individuating/differentiating logic of the contemporary school itself.

That said, there is still perhaps a place for some healthy scepticism over the seemingly endless production of new categories of difference. As previously mentioned, it is part of the ongoing processes of government to keep finding new 'objective' classifications within which to normalise targeted sections of the population. Surely then, it is appropriate not to accept immediately, dutifully and uncritically every new personality and learning disorder that emerges. Perhaps longevity should be regarded as the primary test of veracity. Dyslexia has survived as a disease entity for in excess of 30 years, and still appears to operate well and validly within its definitional criteria, whereas the jury is still out on ADHD, and is likely to be so for some considerable time yet. However, questions are still to be asked over entities like ADHD because of the social and administrative *function* they appear to serve within the classroom. That is, suspicions will inevitably arise over the objectivity of such categories when their central purpose appears to be the maintenance of good order within a context as artificial and historically contingent as the modern classroom.

## Conclusion

This chapter has not set out to undermine the discipline of psychology. As stated at the very beginning of this chapter, psychology is an incredibly useful tool within the knapsack of all teachers, and offers one particular type of truth about the life-worlds of pupils in school: why some succeed and some don't; why some fit in and others don't; why some are happy and others not. However, it is also important to understand the role that psychology plays within contemporary governance; indeed, that is precisely where the discipline has its origins. Psychology has a huge role to play in regulating the subjectivities of the population, both at school and in the wider community. Our inner thoughts, desires, emotions, motivations and aspirations are now all open to assessment, intervention and normalisation – for better and for worse.

All that said, and in spite of emphasising the fact that this chapter is not simply a cheap swipe at psychology, most people with experience in the field would have discerned an ongoing tension between psychologists on the one hand, and philosophers/sociologists on the other. This is nothing new; academic and professional life is full of such disciplinary rivalries – the traditional enmity between mathematicians and physicists provides an even more vivid example. The important question is: why does this tension exist?

Bearing in mind that this book is written from a philosophical/sociological perspective, there are probably three reasons that are worth mentioning here. Addressing these in terms of increasing importance: first, there is disagreement over the romantic story told by psychology of its own foundation. As discussed here, the best evidence appears to suggest that the discipline emerged largely as an effective way of sifting out the feeble-minded from the normal population; i.e. it was simply a very effective form of social administration. Interestingly, this isn't really a damning indictment; the same sort of claim can probably be made about most social sciences.

The second point of tension generally revolves around psychology's claim to objective analysis (and the concomitant production of objective categories of difference). This really shouldn't come as a surprise. As science became the dominant mode of truth production within the era of modernity, its success was based upon its much-lauded status as a neutral observer, an impartial describer of the natural world. This was probably a practical necessity, given it was trying to set itself apart from previous ways of determining 'truth', ones largely based upon religious belief, sovereign command and half-baked opinion. As a science then, psychology has often understood itself in similar ways. For the sake of fairness, it should be pointed out that many modern scientists and psychologists do not unquestioningly share this understanding of their disciplines, or the 'reality' of the knowledges they produce. The problem lies with those that do.

Finally, and of by far the greatest importance, is the disciplinary disagreement over what constitutes the primary unit of analysis. Philosophers and sociologists tend to start with society, and then explain individuality, and individual circumstance, from there. Indeed, this entire section of the book is really an analysis of how modern understandings of individuality have been created by contemporary forms of governance and disciplinary management. Psychologists generally start from the other end, in that they begin with the individual and work out from there. The constant banter between the two camps is that psychology underestimates the importance of social influences – thereby coming uncomfortably close to the 'it's all up to the individual' line, critically discussed in Chapter 1 – while philosophy/sociology under-estimates the importance of the individual. The best answer to this issue is probably to reiterate that *how you look determines what you see*. Different disciplines produce different kinds of truth; decide for yourself which you find the most convincing.

Of course the flip side of this question is: having been given a philosopher's/sociologist's take on the issues, how would psychologists explain the tensions? There is obviously the same issue of what you take as your primary unit of analysis, the social or the individual, but other than that … you'd probably have to ask them.

# Chapter 6

# Pre-adulthood

This chapter argues that educators need to have a good grasp of all the various forms of pre-adulthood we take for granted, such as 'the child' and 'the youth'. These categories are the focus of a range of different disciplines, most of which found their explanatory models in nature itself. As such, the behaviour of children and youth may be deemed to require explanation, but not the very existence of the categories themselves. The issues raised in this chapter concern the degree to which childhood and youth are actually socially constructed categories, categories serving particular social functions. Of greatest interest here are the ways in which childhood and youth are both artefacts of, and vehicles for, social governance.

## Myth #1 'Childhood' and 'youth' are facts of nature

*We didn't invent children or youths; they have always been here. These aren't socially constructed categories. They exist in all cultures, and have existed in all eras.*

The evidence suggests that childhood and youth are both social inventions, childhood emerging from the fifteenth century onwards, and youth appearing in the early 1950s. It has also been suggested that childhood is now in the process of disappearing again, with youth expanding to fill its place.

## Myth #2 The categories of 'childhood' and 'youth' have nothing to do with governance

*Though not the product of nature, the notions of childhood and youth developed as they did for purely cultural reasons. These reasons have nothing to do with social governance.*

These categories of pre-adulthood are both the products of government, and the vehicles for its effective operation. They are shaped most thoroughly through the governmental sites of the mass school, and the pedagogic family.

## Myth #3 'Childhood' is characterised by its innocence, 'youth' by its natural resistance to authority

*Both childhood and youth have innate characteristics; young children are naturally innocent, and youth are naturally rebellious. Youth cultures are always oppositional in both content and purpose.*

Both childhood innocence and youthful rebellion are products of the way in which the categories developed and came to be conceptualised. The idea of childhood innocence arose from romanticism in the eighteenth century, and concerns over youthful resistance can be traced, in large part, to the theoretical framework employed to explain youth subcultures in the 1970s.

# Introduction

Within books of this type, categories like 'the child' are often taken for granted. They are the objects that social forces act upon, such as social class or gender, they are the targets of strategies of intervention, as with the law or disciplinary rules, and they are the focus of moral concern, discernable within analyses of the media and popular culture. What rarely happens is that the substance of these categories gets picked apart and discussed in their own right. That is the purpose of this chapter.

Teachers in particular have a large investment in pre-adulthood. Even in the era of lifelong learning, the notion of education is almost always associated with people who have yet to be granted the full status of adult. Whether these people are called infants, children, adolescents, teenagers, or youth, they have been made the focus of an entire profession, and whether the teacher is in early childhood, primary or secondary, they are each expected to know the 'nature' of their students, down to the smallest biological, psychological and intellectual detail.

However, it seems that these various categories of pre-adulthood don't represent a fixed target. How are teachers supposed to make the best of teaching 'youth' when the parameters of the group won't stay still long enough to allow any kind of consistent understanding? Arguably, the ways in which childhood was conceptualised, and in which children acted, even as late as the 1960s, bears only limited resemblance to current models of childhood. Children were dressed differently, even accounting for the vagaries of fashion, and occupied themselves differently, even accounting for the effects of technological advancement (Postman 1994). The question is: what are we to make of this? Or more specifically, how thoroughly do we need to theorise these categories to make sure we do the right thing by them?

The three myths addressed in this chapter try to address these questions, but not necessarily directly. The first myth examines the *ontological* status of notions like 'the child' and the 'youth' – that is, whether they exist as real beings, independently of how we think about them. The second myth addresses the role that governance plays in the shaping of these categories. Are they just subject to governance, or is the relationship more complex than that? The third myth looks at the qualities normally ascribed to children and youths, such as innocence in childhood, and resistance in youth. Are there grounds for thinking that these qualities are founded in anything but the historical circumstances of their formation?

## What are children? What are youths?

Sometimes, when we become so sure that the circumstances of our lives couldn't possibly be any other way, we ascribe those circumstances to nature. This gives them a certainty – a truth – and it means we no longer have to worry about justifying them. The best example of this has always been gender (see Chapter 2). We take something that *does* belong in nature (our sex, male or female) and wrongly conclude that the social formations roughly correlating with them (our gender, masculine or feminine) are also part of the natural order.

The issue here is whether popular understandings of concepts like 'childhood' are making the same error in logic. The inference we generally draw from our depiction of the young is that 'children' are simple facts of nature, and have been around for as long as we've been modern human beings; after all, even the Flintstones had a child (Pebbles). This reasoning suggests that you can't have adults without having children; they are a stage of life, one we mature out of on our way to becoming fully grown. The same is true for 'youth', who exist as a transitional stage between the total dependence of 'the child' and the finished product of 'the adult'.

The evidence suggests that the truth may be a little more complex than this. A number of writers have pointed out that artistic depictions of the very young in early medieval times appear to have fully mature faces, as if the young were just regarded as little adults. Other writers have noted that the term 'youth' doesn't appear anywhere describing a discreet stage of life before the early 1950s. Prior to this time, it was just an all-purpose word meaning 'young'. Surely, if these were timeless categories with historically fixed meanings, such confounding examples wouldn't exist?

## Is governance relevant to any of this?

Whether or not 'the child' is grounded in nature or otherwise, the historical evidence suggests that the new disciplinary apparatus of the mass school has certainly made children the focus of the widest imaginable array of management strategies: continual surveillance, rigorous location in space and time, extensive keeping of records, the production of categories of difference, normalising intervention. The same is the case for 'the youth' at the upper end of the secondary school; it is also individuated, differentiated and normalised. Furthermore, the school is not the only site wherein this 'government at a distance' occurs. The new *pedagogic family* plays a significant role in governance, particularly of 'the child'.

The issue here is whether the relationship between categories of pre-adulthood is more complex than this. That is, are these categories simply the target of governance, or are they more enmeshed in it than that? It could be argued that the various techniques, practices and forms of organisation associated with government constitute the very instruments that have produced 'childhood' and 'youth' in their current forms. This means that 'the child' is not simply the focus of governance; it is also an *artefact* of it. More than that, having produced such categories, as well as innumerable associated sub-categories, they then become the vehicles through which governance can occur more effectively.

## Shaping the capacities of pre-adulthood

Finally, the problem of understanding the dispositions of various categories of pre-adulthood needs to be addressed. Should teachers premise their pedagogy upon well-known natural elements of childhood, such as their innate innocence? After all, if this is a fixed and immutable element of 'the child's' makeup, then perhaps it could act as the solid foundation for all teaching practice, much as Descartes' *Cogito Ergo Sum* – 'I think therefore I am' – has acted as the foundation of rationalist philosophy for 500 years. But if this is not the case ... then what? How much of our understandings of childhood and youth, their 'natural' capacities and their pre-dispositions, are actually just social and historical inventions? If so, how liberating might this be for teachers?

To summarise, the three myths to be dealt with in this chapter are:

**Myth #1** – 'Childhood' and 'youth' are facts of nature

**Myth #2** – The categories of 'childhood' and 'youth' have nothing to do with governance

**Myth #3** – 'Childhood' is characterised by its innocence, 'youth' by its natural resistance to authority

# Myth #1 'Childhood' and 'youth' are facts of nature

Childhood is a fact of nature. We didn't invent children; they have always been here. Part of living is growing from childhood, through our youth, into full maturity, and from there, eventually, to old age and death. You can't avoid any of these stages now, any more than you could in ancient or medieval times. These aren't somehow socially constructed categories. They have existed in all cultures and in all eras.

There is something vaguely comforting about the notion of childhood. It is presented as a time of almost infinite potential, a time of innocence before the realities of the real world take hold; it is a stage of life that we all eventually outgrow, a smaller but purer version of ourselves; it is the colourful little caterpillar, before we turn into big ugly moths. The caterpillar analogy is a fair one, since it implies that somehow children are naturally different to ourselves; a separate type of being. Fair enough, unlike caterpillars and moths, children might look like tiny versions of us, but they are still somehow not the same. After all, the difference between a 10 year old and a 20 year old is not the same as the difference between a 50 year old and a 60 year old. Ten year olds occupy a different category of existence; they are children. This difference has always existed, and it will always exist.

Most writers in the field would disagree with both of these assertions. They suggest instead that childhood is a relatively recent cultural development; it is a new way of understanding the young, one grounded in neither nature nor necessity.

# The invention of childhood

## Aries – *Centuries of Childhood* (1962)

Aries (1962) advances the proposition that before the sixteenth century, the category of the child simply did not exist. Pre-adulthood consisted solely of being an infant – a category that lacked any real importance – and upon reaching the age of six or seven, they were immediately accorded the full status, rights and obligations of adults. Those too fragile to be considered adult simply did not count. From the sixteenth century onwards, he argues, the single status of adult started to fragment. Young people from the upper classes began to be represented distinctively in art, not just in the structure of their faces, but also in that they were clothed in a different manner from adults. Eventually, a separate status of child was demarcated from the broader status of adult.

Aries argues that the idea of *coddling* provided the focal point around which childhood was eventually to crystallise, in that children became a source of amusement and relaxation for the women who looked after them. While this occurred within the family circle, however, a parallel set of imperatives began to impinge upon the new space of childhood from outside the family, in that an assortment of churchmen and social moralists also began to take an interest in childhood. However, rather than lauding it for its simplicity and sweetness, they regarded the child to be in need of safeguarding and reformation. The family was deemed the appropriate place to provide protection and instruction for what were, indeed, future adults. Consequently, children were no longer to be dressed and treated as miniature adults; instead they were conceived of as a form of property to be admired, cared for, disciplined, and especially, protected.

## Postman – *The Disappearance of Childhood* (1994)

Aries has not been alone in arguing that a time existed when 'the child' did not. Postman (1994) argues that the ancient Greeks and Romans had some embryonic notions of childhood, and while they were by no means the same as ours, they did share some foundational ideas. The most important link can probably be traced through the centrality of education – and in particular, learning to read – to the concept of childhood, and when the Roman Empire fell and Europe entered the Dark Ages, education, literacy, and the notion of childhood, all fell with it.

Postman goes on to contend that childhood began the process of flickering back into life in the fifteenth century with the arrival of a seemingly unrelated invention: Guttenberg's printing press. In the medieval world, prior to the advent of print, everyone shared the same information, and hence the subordinate category of childhood was not required. However, alongside all the other social changes the printed word triggered, Postman suggests that this device came to create a different kind of adult, one that required new skills, aptitudes and forms of consciousness, largely based upon a new breadth and certainty of knowledge. These attributes quickly turned out to be a vital element of a new world, ones that could not exist in an almost entirely oral culture. Consequently:

> From print onwards, adulthood had to be earned. It became a symbolic, not a biological achievement. From print onwards, the young would have to *become* adults, and they would have to do it by learning to read, by entering the world of typography. And in order to accomplish that they would require education. Therefore, European civilisation reinvented schools. And in doing so, it made childhood a necessity. (Postman 1994, 36)

Two issues are of particular importance here. First, there began to develop specific indicators of childhood, symbolic markers that we now take for granted, but which came to delineate 'children' from 'adults'. For example, children started to develop their own games and forms of entertainment, whereas previously they had joined in with adult pastimes without reservation, such as gambling. They also came to be dressed differently, a fashion that reached its zenith during the Victorian era, where boys might be dressed in little sailor outfits, and girls as dolls. This stands in contrast with medieval times, where those over the age of seven would have worn the same attire as their parents.

The second issue involves the development of adult knowledge. As previously stated, prior to the rise of print, everyone shared the same information. There was no distinction drawn between what an adult knew, and what young children knew. Those children witnessed all the daily activities of life without censorship; the idea that there were certain kinds of knowledge to which the young should have no access, did not exist. Importantly, this included sexual knowledge. However, since only adults had access to print, a world separate from children, the idea soon developed that there were certain things that only adults should know, that were inappropriate for children to be exposed to. From there, it was only a short step to understanding the child as innocent, and in need of protection – a status the young had not previously been deemed to require. This will be discussed further in myth #3 in this chapter.

## Childhood comes, childhood goes

The second half of Postman's argument is as interesting as the first, and is even more relevant to those involved in education. He suggests that after its birth 500 years ago, and after half a millennia of development, the category of childhood has, over the last few decades, begun the process of fading away. He uses several examples to make his case, citing not only the 'adultification' of children, but also the 'childification' of adults, or to put it another way, the merging of these two categories. He notes that younger and younger children are being dressed in adult styles, and that the domain of children's games has all but disappeared, being replaced by quantified and bureaucratised mini versions of adult sports. While children still occasionally play

Bulldog, Red Rover and Brandy, the important space these games once occupied has been taken over by organised activities; children now join soccer leagues from the age of five, with uniforms, referees and play-offs. Postman also points to the reciprocal issues of adults playing computer games, and eating hamburgers, to show the process works both ways.

According to Postman, the reason the distinction between children and adults is breaking down revolves around the same issues that cause the split in the first place: access to knowledge. The suggestion here is that it has become increasingly difficult to maintain the distinction between those things that everyone should be allowed to know, and those that only adults should be privy to – and yes, we're largely talking about sex. To put it simply, children's increasing access to sexual knowledge is rendering the category of 'children' redundant.

## Critiques of these arguments

While these ideas have been very influential for those studying childhood, they have not been without their critics. It has been suggested that while Aries certainly makes a good point about the relative lack of 'child-like' faces in medieval art, according to some writers, they weren't missing altogether. Given the interpretation of art is always a subjective process, this is hardly damning evidence, but it does suggest that some degree of caution might be called for when claiming that each and every element of contemporary notions of childhood was utterly absent prior to the sixteenth century (Heywood 2001; Coster 2007).

Postman has also been subject to some criticism, but generally for a very different reason. One reading of Postman has been that he is bemoaning the disappearance of childhood, lost to a perceived rise of sexual permissiveness that is in the process of swallowing what was once the most innocent and beautiful stage of life (Prout 2005). If this is the case, the criticism is probably justified, since – whatever your opinion on the issue – this is a moral, rather than a historical, argument and hence should be made elsewhere. It also makes a number of unspoken assumptions about what is 'natural' for contemporary childhood, assumptions which hold little water given the descriptions of what was 'natural' for a seven year old from the fifteenth century. Still, if Postman's argument is taken in strictly historical terms, it is a fascinating one: once, we invented childhood, and now we are in the process of dis-inventing it.

## The gap between children and adults

There is perhaps one further problem with the general understanding of the Postman position. His work seems to suggest that as the boundary of childhood gets younger and younger, then so too does the lower limit of adulthood. This is clearly not the case, as there is now a third category in the equation, one that acts as an intermediary between the child and the adult.

## The youth

This third category is, of course, youth. After all, those young people who have reached an age where they no longer wish to be regarded as children, are not therefore aspiring to move directly into adulthood. There is the whole world of youth culture, and youth identities, waiting for them to explore.

Like childhood itself, there is nothing natural or innate about the category of youth. It also developed as a result of otherwise mundane social changes. Cashmore (1984) has argued that the notion of youth first emerged in the early 1950s as a consequence of the widespread demise of national military service, whereby entire cohorts of young people suddenly found themselves at a loose end, as well as the advent of hire-purchase, such that the relatively affluent young workers of the time (historically speaking) were able to acquire previously unattainable goods like fashionable suits and Dansette record players. This new purchasing power of the young was almost immediately translated into the development of a specific youth market, and the rest fell into place from there: youth fashions, youth music, youth culture, and a specific and identifiable, intermediary category of existence, independent of both childhood and adulthood.

Though youth itself had a traceable history of its initial appearance, as did childhood, it actually developed from a series of other categories of pre-adulthood, which childhood did not. In the nineteenth century, childhood arguably began to fragment into other functional sub-categories, such as the 'problem child' and the 'juvenile delinquent'. These in turn later went on to produce 'the adolescent' and 'the teenager', which were the direct precursors of 'youth'.

## The adolescent

Of these pre-youth groupings, adolescence was the most influential. Although some concerns had been expressed over adolescence during the latter part of the nineteenth century, these did not assume any coherent shape until the publication of G. Stanley Hall's massive study in 1904. Hall's adolescent was firmly rooted within the realm of biology; the book contained numerous chapters on subjects such as physical growth, instincts and (as a result of Hall's intellectual debt to Darwin) evolution. Furthermore, his emphasis on storm and stress came to form one of the central foundations of ensuing depictions of the adolescent persona.

> Dominant in all aspects of adolescence is the note of an equilibrium relatively less secure than what has preceded, of an old anchorage broken, of elements less harmonized, of coordinations yet incomplete, of adjustments to the environment less fine and less settled, of insecurity and ever-impending danger of mental or physical relapse, at the same time, of the promises and potencies of a slow but ever higher development. (Hall 1904, 49)

Unlike the notion of the 'innocent' child, the adolescent was also a personage to which the psy-disciplines attributed an active sexuality. Not surprisingly, Hall's adolescent reflected most of the dominant theoretical understandings of sexuality of the time. Male adolescents were seen to develop in terms of strength and aggression, while the development of female adolescents was interpreted predominantly in terms of preparation for maternity.

Despite the continuing pervasiveness of the category of adolescence within certain types of research (Roberts 2007), retrospect suggests that it was simply the product of the intellectual milieu of the time in the field of psychology, along with Hall's own eclectic background, rather than anything more concrete. Smith (1989) suggests that the adolescent was:

> an amalgam of neurological research, literary romanticism and nineteenth-century American child rearing advice – an amalgam which did not succeed in forming its constituent elements into a coherent object. With the somatic base of much of Hall's evidence discredited ... the adolescent became abstracted as merely a figure of storm and stress, without any determinate content upon which educational policy or technique could be formulated. (Smith 1989, 8–9)

In summary, categories such as childhood, adolescence and youth are not natural facts, inevitable stages of life existing in all cultures and at all times. This is not the case. All emerged at particular historical moments, and for particular historical reasons, and as we shall see, all have a huge role to play in contemporary social governance.

# Myth #2 The categories of 'childhood' and 'youth' have nothing to do with governance

The notions of childhood and youth may not have been given to us by nature – indeed, they may just be social categories that have developed over time – but they developed as they did for purely cultural reasons. Children may be the subject of governance, but childhood itself is not shaped by it. Governance occurs in schools; children just happen to be there.

## Yet more about governance

In Chapter 4, it has already been pointed out that the contemporary notion of individuality was made possible by the widespread use of various techniques of government, like the census; that the rise of liberalism led to government at a distance, through the medium of expertise; and that institutions like the mass school became disciplinary societies, effectively regulating space, time and conduct. On top of this, in Chapter 5, we've seen how psychology developed as an effective mechanism for managing those who appeared normal, but did not fit well into the environment of the modern classroom; how psychology permits our subjective experiences to be governed; and how this governance often occurs through the production of endless new categories of mental difference, such as behaviour disorders. Surely 'childhood' and 'youth' are just social descriptions of stages of our life, and they have nothing to do with governance. According to the reasoning that underlies all of Part 2 of this book, they most certainly do.

## Childhood and youth are fuzzy categories

Two issues need to be understood before unpacking this myth any further. The first is that these categories of pre-adulthood – 'the child' and 'the youth' – can't be understood as singular, coherent objects, unitary facts in themselves. As will be discussed shortly, the notion of 'the child' gets mobilised in a wide range of different sites, and by a plethora of diverse knowledges; likewise 'the youth'. 'The child' of criminal law – normally focused round *doli incapax*, the age of criminal responsibility (discussed in detail in Chapter 12) – is not 'the child' of physiology, based upon growth plates and hormone levels, which is not 'the child' of product marketing, based upon cultural tastes and parental spending power, and so on, almost *ad infinitum*. The same logic applies to 'the youth'. There is no single object at the heart of all these depictions. Rather, these notions are plural, fuzzy clusters of *family resemblances*, lacking an essential core, but still permitting a generalised conception to occur; they are threads, comprised of thousands of individual fibres (Wittgenstein 1952).

## Childhood and youth are both artefacts, and vehicles, of governance

Second, in stating that the categories of childhood and youth are all intimately tied to social governance, this occurs in two ways. First, these categories are the product of governance – artefacts – created by various systems of management and intervention, systems put in place to achieve specific ends within given contexts. For example, statistical analysis of the results of tens of thousands of psychometric tests, when plotted on a normal curve, produced a new artefact of governance: the 'gifted child'. This particular artefact illustrates the point made in the previous part quite well, since even within a fixed sub-category of child – such as 'the gifted' – precisely who gets to be called 'gifted' varies according to precisely who is making the assessment: psychologists (about 6% of the schooling population); parents (about 98% of their own children).

However, and second, as well as being artefacts of governance, upon creation such entities immediately become vehicles through which governance can occur. For example, as soon as the 'gifted child' is brought into administrative existence, it acts as a mechanism – a hook – upon which any number of governmental programs and forms of intervention can be hung. 'Giftedness' can now justify variations in budgetary allocation, implementation of curricula changes, new forms of specialised testing, re-evaluation of teaching techniques, strategies for social management, the formation of links with other centres of 'giftedness'; the list goes on.

Having set out these initial, underlying elements of the link between pre-adulthood and governance, it would now be useful to examine other, more specific, aspects of their working relationship, starting with 'childhood'.

## Childhood and governance

> Childhood is the most intensely governed sector of personal existence. In different ways, at different times, and by many different routes varying from one sector of society to another, the health, welfare, and destiny of children has been linked in thought and practice to the destiny of the nation and the responsibilities of the state. (Rose 1990, 123)

Throughout the ninteenth and into the twentieth century, 'the child' increasingly became a focus of legislation. Laws were enacted that attempted to reduce child abuse and suffering, to create better working conditions, and to improve the health of the young (see Chapter 12). These parliamentary instruments had some success, both in Great Britain and Australia, however it would be a mistake to think that such interventions were the only, or even the main, mechanisms by which the lives of children were to be managed. The difficulty arose because, as discussed in Chapter 4, the liberal State was now expected to keep its nose out of the business of childrearing. Therefore, if the State was going to have any control over the shaping of future citizens, it would have to do it by stealth – 'governing at a distance' – by subtly managing those sites where children were raised: that is, the school and the family.

## The school

We have already discussed how the school manages its pupils. Children are subdivided in space and time, they are continually surveilled, and their conduct is regulated and normalised, all crucial elements of a disciplinary society. The issue here is that children are not simply sat in classrooms with this disciplinary regime going on round them, they are actively shaped by it. Or, to put it another way, schools are in the business of producing particular types of children.

There isn't just one category to be dealt with here – the child – a single, self-evident stage of life; rather, there are countless. Some of these are familiar: the problem child, the gifted child, the disordered child; all of these are subject to intervention and management. Then there is the diligent child, the easily distracted child and the obedient child. In more specifically educational terms, there is the child who is good at sport, the female child who is good at maths, and the male child who is good at English. The whole point of this can be summed up in one sentence: the child is something you *make*.

Of course, this idea stands in opposition to the dominant model of childhood. The idea that the child arrives at the school in a natural state, innocent and yet fully formed, has provided the basis for a great deal of education research and that strand of philosophy that traces its origins to the philosophy of Rousseau. As A.S. Neill (1962, 114), the most well-known advocate of free schooling, states in the influential *Summerhill*: 'the whole idea of Summerhill is release: allowing the child to live out his natural interests'.

Tyler (1993) understands the role of the school somewhat differently. In an article titled 'Making Better Children', she discerns within child development literature an exhortation toward helping children achieve rationality, autonomy and self-regulation, and yet these qualities are simultaneously deemed part of the child's nature. That is, 'the child' is simultaneously a natural fact, a fixed entity, and yet also something that you have to work at making better.

The point here is that the school isn't just a holding pen for children. It plays the important role of producing particular kinds of future citizens. Those future citizens are shaped with very specific goals in mind, and those goals are best realised through the production not just of any old child, but the 'good' child. Once again, the 'good' child is not comprised of a single 'good' thread, but is rather made up of innumerable fibres formed throughout the entire schooling process.

## The family

In addition to the school, a number of historians have pointed to the modern family as being an equally important organ of governance. For example, Donzelot (1979) argues that a very specific creation – the *pedagogic family* – became a crucial component in 'governing at a distance'. This new type of family was to be regulated by a range of medical, educational and psychological experts, and these experts linked the inner workings of the family unit with the broadest objectives of government. By what Donzelot (1979, 169) refers to as 'the subtle regulation of images', it became possible to construct desirable and effective norms of family life, and these images recruited mothers into becoming 'good' mothers, a necessary prerequisite for the parallel production of 'good' children. In this manner, the family became crucial in establishing the capacities and aptitudes expected of the socially and pedagogically acceptable child.

Although Donzelot's analysis is concerned with French history, Counihan (1982) correctly indicates that these same arguments have wider application. In other contemporary Western societies, including Australia, the family is similarly enlisted as an effective mechanism through which to govern at a distance. For example, Reiger (1985) examines some of the changes that occurred in the structure of the Australian family between the 1880s and the 1930s, also noting that the family was enlisted in the production of 'good' children, and in particular that motherhood came to be depicted as a skill that required learning. No longer were women deemed to be innately possessed of the ability to raise children, rather maternal common sense became something that had to be taught.

> With the institutionalisation of the infant welfare movement, 'mothercraft' had emerged as a new domain of knowledge, now under professional control and ready for popular dissemination through the women's magazines and feature pages of the newspapers. The major theme was that of maternal ignorance and the need to educate parents and mothers in particular, because … they're 'on duty unremittingly night and day'. (Reiger, 1985, 128–9)

Women were deemed to need expert guidance in order to fulfil their maternal responsibilities, now deemed a vital element in shaping 'good' children. To repeat: 'good' children don't just develop by themselves; they have to be *made*.

## Youth and governance

Precisely the same arguments that have been made about the governmental construction of various types of child can also be made about youth. The category of youth is the product of innumerable forms of assessment, intervention and normalisation, as well as the vehicle for achieving a range of social and governmental objectives. In addition, youth is not a singular entity, but rather an entire range of sub-categories: the 'delinquent' youth, the 'subcultural' youth, the 'at-risk' youth.

This latter category is particularly relevant. If the entire classification of youth concerns the transition from childhood to adulthood, then the sub-group of 'at-risk' youth delineates those in danger of not making this transition successfully. The 'at-risk' youth itself is comprised of any number of other 'risk' categories, all the subject of research and management: youth 'at-risk of committing serious violence' (Loeber et al. 2005), youth 'at-risk of criminal behaviour' (Hine & Williams 2007), youth 'at-risk of social exclusion' (Squires & Stephen 2005), and so on.

Given the breadth of the category of youth, the 'at-risk' youth is also managed extensively through the existing governmental and disciplinary structures of the school. Indeed, from its inception in the mid 1980s, the notion of 'risk' has quickly become woven into the fabric of the school, and young people can now be measured against a graded and cumulative set of normal risks, both by their age category, and by the severity of the risk involved. So, just as the disciplinary school became characterised by the minute division of space and time, 'risk' has also become an important indicator in the grid of governmental knowledge. Importantly, it provides a versatile rationale for intervening in the conduct of those categorised as 'at-risk' youth, whenever it is deemed necessary.

While the 'at-risk' youth provides a useful example of the way in which youth is both an artefact and vehicle of government, the notion of youth is also more complex than just the label of a category; it is also an identity, and one that requires self-governance.

## Youth and self-governance

Young people are not just placed in administrative categories, and from there left to get on with their lives, subject to whatever management strategies are targeted at them. The categories are more pervasive than that, in that they become part of our identities, and this requires work. A good example of this is the array of governmental programs that have targeted the gendering of young people, programs that have attempted to construct 'appropriate' male and female youth. A great deal of effort has gone into the production of these particular categories: gender-specific curricula, codes of conduct within schools, rules for appropriate attire, and even single-sex schooling.

However, the important issue is that becoming a 'female youth' involves far more than being required to wear a skirt at school; it is an *identity*, one that requires ongoing and wide-ranging forms of self-governance. Two points are of importance here. The first is that young people are recruited into this self-management. In the same way that mothers are persuaded to become 'good' mothers, so the young are persuaded to do specific kinds of work on themselves, out of which 'appropriate' genders are shaped. That shaping is guided by far more than the resources available within the environment of school. Manuals of self-formation are to be found in a wide variety of places; one good example of this within the context of 'female' youth, are young women's magazines. These provide a vocabulary of ways for young girls and women to learn how to 'make' themselves; to regulate their identities.

The second point is that this regulation takes a number of forms, some of which might involve embracing particular styles of dress and musical tastes, adopting given attitudes, interests and ways of thinking, and acquiring specific bodily practices – all of which constitute a *habitus* (see Chapter 1). After all, there is much more to making yourself a female youth, than simply being 15 years old. These forms of self-governance have been called *practices of the self* (Foucault 1987).

The issue of acquiring specific bodily practices is an interesting one, particularly with regards to young women's magazines. Research has consistently shown that the successful acquisition of femininity is not a *fait accompli* for all teenagers; rather, becoming the kind of young woman that particular magazines consider appropriate requires hard work (McRobbie 1982; Tait 2003). Among other things, this hard work involves learning to use the body in certain ways, as *Cosmopolitan* points out in an article entitled 'The Walk That Drives Men Wild':

> Your head is up, shoulders are back, and you lead with your boobs. Your arms swing loosely back and forth while your hips swivel from side-to-side. Your weight is more in your heels. It may take practice to make it your go-to gait, so repeat this mantra to yourself when you walk: 'Shoulders, hips, heels ...'
> (Miller 2010)

In summary, the categories of 'the child' and 'the youth' are by no means unrelated to matters of governance. They are both given their general shape by various administrative practices of government, and yet at the same time, these new entities act as vehicles through which governance can occur. This happens most effectively within the sites of the mass school and the pedagogic family. Importantly, the governance of 'the child' and 'the youth' is not just about the imposition of assorted imperatives that somehow operate through the power of degree. Rather, different categories of young people are recruited into doing particular kinds of work upon themselves – practices of the self – that shape their identities in ways that correspond to the expectations of that group.

# Myth #3 'Childhood' is characterised by its innocence, 'youth' by its natural resistance to authority

Even though it is fairly clear that childhood and youth are not natural, timeless categories, they still have some innate characteristics that can be seen across all cultures. Young children are innocent, and youth are naturally rebellious. In fact, part of being a good secondary teacher is to be able to manage teenage children, who always seem to be testing the boundaries. When you think about it, youth culture is pretty much set up in opposition to accepted ways of doing things.

The first myth in this chapter addressed the notion that childhood and youth are somehow natural categories, and the best available research suggests that this is a mistake. No such timeless, trans-cultural classifications exist; instead they are social creations. However, just because childhood and youth aren't natural, doesn't mean that they can't possess some natural characteristics, common features that can be discerned within everyone of the right age. After all, don't we all know that young children are innocent? Don't we all know that teenagers are difficult and defiant, and that their cultural practices are primarily based upon their natural desire to thumb their noses at adults?

In spite of how broadly held these beliefs often are within Western societies, there are good reasons to think that they have limited grounding in reality. Rather, both viewpoints have historical starting points; we started to regard children as pure and innocent only with the rise of romanticism in the eighteenth century, and youth eventually became tied to inner turmoil and cultural resistance as a combined result of Hall's adolescent from the start of the twentieth century, and more recently, the success of youth subculture theory in the 1970s.

## Childhood as innocence

Christian belief had always painted a very particular picture of the nature of human-ity. The doctrine of original sin claims that we are all born into a state of sinfulness, a legacy of Adam and Eve's brush with the snake in the Garden of Eden. This belief had far greater reach than just religious canon, it also informed a range of philosophical thinkers, most notably Hobbes in the seventeenth century. Hobbes held that humans are naturally selfish, and that it is only the rules of society that hold our instincts in check. Without those rules, as he famously stated in *Leviathan*, life would be 'solitary, poor, nasty, brutish, and short' (1994, 12). This analysis of innate selfishness did not exclude children; they were just as bad as the rest of us.

One of the first – and certainly the most important – thinkers to reject this understanding of children was Rousseau (dealt with in greater depth in Chapter 10). One of the founders of romanticism in the eighteenth century, he took the opposite point of view. In the influential novel *Emile,* he set out the basis for this element of his philosophy, in that he concluded children were actually naturally innocent, and that it was society that eventually led them to a state of corruption (Rousseau 1956).

The question then became: how were we to best understand this innocence? Principally as a result of the central importance the Christian church had started to place upon sexual morality – curiously enough, prior to this time the focus had fallen mostly on the morality of diet (Tait, 1993) – the initial separation of the child from the adult came to be based largely round the notion of sexual innocence. That is, since sexually immoral people were now considered as being of the greatest concern, the innocence of children was therefore best conceptualised in terms of their total lack of sexual knowledge.

That children were naturally innocent, and needed to be protected, came to form a defining part of the relationship between childhood and sexuality, and this characterisation of the child reached its high point within the world of the middle-class family (Finch 1993, 70). Since children were now deemed to be intrinsically pure and innocent, by shielding them from the corruption of society (a corruption most normally characterised by the lifestyles of the working classes) for as long as possible, they could be equipped with the necessary moral faculties to cope by themselves (Weeks 1981, 49). Aries also contends that the idea of childhood innocence resulted in a particular approach towards childhood; that is, 'safeguarding it against pollution by life, and particularly by the "sexuality" tolerated if not approved of among adults' (Aries 1962, 116). This argument is supported by Donzelot (1979), who argues that many of the philanthropic crusades on behalf of children – such as the age of consent campaign – were focused around the themes of the corruption of innocence, and sexual corruption in particular.

The point of all this is that there is nothing natural and timeless about the depiction of children as inherently innocent – rather it came about as a result of the rise of romanticism, and increasing levels of concern over sexual morality. Even though more recent approaches to childhood have discerned in infants an active sexuality, and the same strengths and weaknesses of character as the rest of us (Freud 2005), the notion of innate innocence still haunts most discussions of children.

> … the discourse of innocence works in conjunction with the sacred status of the child, to produce childhood as a moral rhetoric. Children and childhood function to explain and legitimize any practice or opinion as right while removing the necessity to provide reasons: children are the reason. (Meyer 2007, 85)

# Youth as resistance

During the mid 1970s, youth briefly became *the* central topic within social analysis; more specifically, it was the spectacular youth subcultures that pricked the interest of researchers – Skinheads, Mods, Rockers, Punks, Teddy Boys and Goths – all seemed to demand some kind of immediate sociological explanation. That explanation came in the form of the highly influential subculture theory, whose effects are still being felt in terms of how youth is conceptualised.

The theoretical framework that underpins this position, arguably best represented by texts such as Hall and Jefferson's (1976) *Resistance through Rituals* and Hebdige's (1979) *Subculture,* positioned large numbers of young people within discrete categories, each with specific codes of behaviour and ways of relating to the outside world. The theory consists of three main components:

1 *Generational consciousness*: the belief that young people had started to perceive themselves to be intrinsically different from the parent generation.

2 *Style as discourse*: (discussed briefly in the last section) understanding fashion and self-shaping as a form of communication.

3 *Counter-hegemonic struggle*: the belief that young people attempt to resist the dominant social order, and create their own cultural space instead. It is this element of the theory that is relevant here.

# Counter-hegemonic struggle

As discussed in the brief introduction to this part of the book, arguments about governance have arisen, at least in part, as a rejection of the dominant understanding of power, an understanding where its exercise is necessarily coercive, where if one person has power, someone else necessarily lacks it. Subculture theory is an example of this type of reasoning.

Subcultural theory argues that the defeat of the labour movements of the 1920s led to the total domination of the working classes in the 1930s. However, after the watershed period of World War II and the ensuing social reconstruction, the 1950s saw the rise of popular ideologies centred around notions of increased affluence, consensus, and embourgeoisement. Unfortunately, by the late 1960s and 1970s, the promised affluence had failed to materialise, and the working classes were forced to recognise the relative permanence of their position at the bottom of the social hierarchy. As they lacked the means to effect any real change, the solution many working class young people chose was the 'magical' resolution of their problems within youth subcultures. In this manner, they conducted a struggle (albeit indirectly), against the dominant social order. That is, while the formation of youth subcultures posed no real threat to existing power relations, they constituted a form of symbolic resistance that enabled their members to win cultural space for themselves.

The relationship between social class, symbolic resistance, and the winning of cultural space, is exemplified in Jefferson's (1976) analysis of the Teddy Boy subculture of the 1950s. He argues that with its mock upper-class uniform of drape coats, crepe-soled shoes and bootlace ties, and its violent reputation, the Teddy Boy subculture (very similar to the Australian Bodgie) was a coded working-class response to declining status and encroachments upon its territory. This encroachment involved both that actual loss of land to postwar developers, and also the cultural encroachment of the loss of kinship networks and communal space. Thus, the Teddy Boy subculture was a form of symbolic resistance through which working-class male youth won back some of this lost cultural space. Very similar arguments were also made about the Skinhead subculture, and their symbolic resistance against the fragmenting of postwar working-class communities. For more on youth cultures, see Chapter 8.

The important point here is that just as the logic of subculture theory came to dominate youth research, so too did its underpinning reasoning come to dominate our perceptions of young people themselves. That is, even though there already existed the belief that there was something of a natural 'storm and stress' present within youth (courtesy of Hall's questionable version of adolescence), subculture theory then added to this the associated idea that youth are naturally predisposed to contest authority. This understanding of youth is by no means a global one, and to assume that our own models of growing up are shared by other cultures, that resistance to authority can be seen wherever you look at the cultures of young people – that this is 'natural' – is to make a serious conceptual error (Bucholtz 2002).

## Subcultures and governance

As discussed in the introduction to this part of the book, the coercive model of power isn't the only option available, and hence youth does not have to be understood in terms of resistance to authority. If a model is adopted wherein power is understood as productive, rather than coercive, youth subcultures begin to look very different, as does the whole category of youth.

To spell this out further: as discussed in myth #2 of this chapter, it can be argued that the category of youth has been formulated as an object of knowledge within a series of diverse disciplines that have posited youth as problem. For example, youth has been constructed and operationalised as a category through the different mechanisms and knowledges associated with law enforcement. Youth is defined as the object of expertise in areas ranging from psychology to orthopaedics, social work to sociology. Youth is the centre of a multitude of regulatory practices and techniques associated with pedagogy, and it is situated and interpreted in relation to the labour market by economists. Each of these knowledges plays a part in youth being positioned as the object of government

Understanding the manner in which the category of youth is produced, in part, as an artefact of government, allows for similar conclusions to be drawn about youth subcultures. Subcultures are not constructed as forms of resistance to the exercise of power; instead they can be best understood as the by-product of particular forms of government. Along with those already mentioned, these might include rationales and knowledges behind inner city planning; various demographics of immigration; the rise of particular types of reporting and styles of media coverage; and specific technologies of marketing. Hebdige takes this even further:

> The category 'youth' gets mobilised in official documentary discourse, in concerned or outraged editorials and features, or in the supposedly disinterested tracts emanating from the social sciences at those times when young people make their presence felt by going 'out of control', by resisting through rituals … When young people do these things … they get talked about, taken seriously, their grievances are acted upon. They get arrested, harassed, admonished, disciplined, incarcerated, applauded, vilified, emulated, listened to. They get defended by social workers and other concerned philanthropists. They get explained by sociologists … (1988, 17–18)

Of course, youth subcultures can also be partially located within the logic of a differentiating form of government. As has been discussed at length throughout the last three chapters, by classifying individuals into categories along an increasing number of axes, it becomes all the more possible to create a domain of government, enabling power to be exercised in a far more comprehensive and targeted manner. In our society, there tends to be a strong process of individualisation of those upon whom it is exercised; those who do not conform to accepted social norms are the subject of the greatest attention. That is, 'the child is more individuated than the adult, the patient more than the healthy man, the madman and the delinquent more than normal and non-delinquent' (Foucault, 1977, 193). It is through the construction and demarcation of pathologies – such as the 'juvenile delinquent' – that social, legal, psychological and medical norms can be reinforced. This process is especially evident when addressing the young: 'It is around pathological children – the troublesome, the recalcitrant, the delinquent – that conceptions of normality have taken shape … Normality is not an observation but a valuation' (Rose 1990, 131). As such, the focus on delinquent youth, and the categorisation of some of them into subcultures, is part of the broader processes of measurement and judgment against various sets of accepted social norms.

In summary, even though categories such as childhood, adolescence and youth cannot reasonably be considered facts of nature, it has been suggested instead that these groupings have 'natural' qualities to them: innocence in childhood, inner turmoil in adolescents, resistance in youth. Once again, the best evidence suggests that this is not the case. All of these beliefs have historical starting points, and as such they are neither fixed nor permanent. In the future, we may understand the 'nature' of these categories in different ways, or we may invent news ones altogether.

# Conclusion

This chapter has drawn three main conclusions about categories such as 'the child' and 'the youth': the first is that they are not natural, transcultural and transhistoric stages of life. The evidence suggests that they developed at specific historical moments, incidental by-products of social, technological and domestic changes. Writers like Aries and Postman paint a very historically contingent picture of the advent of childhood, and Postman goes on to suggest that, just as it once emerged out of the previously undifferentiated status of 'adult', it is currently in the process of disappearing again.

The second conclusion is that categories such as 'the child' and 'the youth' are both closely tied to imperatives of government. This social management occurs within both the mass school and the pedagogic family, where these categories of pre-adulthood are created as artefacts of governance, yet are also vehicles through which that governance occurs. Importantly, such imperatives don't work simply by putting a policy in place and then waiting for the expected changes to happen, rather they work by recruiting members of those categories into doing work on themselves. The case of 'the good mother' is a useful one here. This particular late-nineteenth century creation did not emerge as an effective entity simply by giving women instruction on preferred ways to raise children; it began to emerge when women actively sought to shape themselves in the likeness of the idealised images they were presented with. This is also the case, by way of example, with the creation of the many and varied sub-categories of 'youth'.

The third conclusion addresses the assertion that categories of pre-adulthood have 'natural' qualities to them, irrespective of whether they are essential categories themselves. These 'natural' qualities – innocence in childhood, inner turmoil in adolescents, resistance in youth – turn out to all have their own histories. The main implication of this is that our widely shared social conceptions of these categories are fluid, and therefore open to change.

So where do these arguments leave us? There are probably three issues to reflect upon here. The first is that, given the historically flexible nature of these categories, educators need to be aware of how these categories work, as reflected by equally flexible teaching practices. After all, many older secondary teachers, who once taught 14-year-old 'children', would now be teaching 14-year-old 'youths', with all the social differences that might entail. The second is that, given there is nothing 'natural' about the various categories of pre-adulthood, or the qualities that are attributed to them, we are free to either ascribe new qualities to existing categories – perhaps coming to regard adolescents as inherently vulnerable, or disorganised, or just plain annoying – or to create new categories altogether; the possibilities there are endless. The final issue is that abandoning the notion of 'natural' predispositions within children or youth, may well lead to more open and adaptable approaches to education practice for teachers. Surely questioning some of our ingrained ideas about what constitutes age-appropriate pedagogy wouldn't be a bad thing.

# Part 3

## Cultural Contexts of Contemporary Education

Having addressed some of the theoretical foundations of education, both from within the familiar modernist paradigm – though with some ground given to the logic of postmodernity – and also from within a Foucault-inspired governmental approach, the next part examines some of the cultural issues, concerns and contexts impacting upon contemporary education. While there is no direct, correlative link between the culture of a society, and the kind of schools it contains – where the latter is simply a function of the former – it would be a mistake to think that there are not important connections between the two. Indeed, a better approach might be to not consider them as discrete entities at all.

Chapter 7 *The media* addresses the relationship between education and the news media. It questions the assertions that 'media studies' is not a serious subject, and doesn't belong in the school curriculum; that media messages need an education to decode properly; and that the media is not responsible for whipping up moral panics, whether to further specific political ends, or to simply sell papers and gain viewers.

Chapter 8 *Popular culture* investigates recent concerns over the increasing presence of popular culture in the classroom. It questions the common view that all popular culture is rubbish, unlike 'high culture'; that teachers need to be popular culture experts if they are going to connect with their students; and that the classroom is no place for popular culture, as it has absolutely no educational value.

Chapter 9 *Technology* examines the rise of digital technologies and their implications for mass schooling. It questions the belief that these technologies represent the solution to many of education's enduring problems, such as limited access to information, particular kinds of social class disadvantage, and inconsistent standards of education; and that digital technology spells the end for traditional teaching, since learning resources can be accessed instantly from almost anywhere, and students now have access to virtually limitless information.

Two points are of particular note here: first, there is a significant overlap between the three chapters, not in terms of the content of this book, but rather in terms of the topics themselves. The subdivision of Part 3 into The media, Popular culture, and Technology is, in many important ways, an artifice. After all, digital devices such as the iPad and iPhone are significant cultural artefacts in and of themselves, irrespective of their digital properties, and they are also important mechanisms for the consumption of media. As such, they could legitimately have been discussed in all three chapters; actually, they aren't discussed anywhere, but the point is made.

Second, all three of these areas have already given significant ground to postmodernity, and it would be setting up something of a 'straw man' argument to suggest otherwise. It would be unlikely that you could read any contemporary book on any of these topics and find simplistic, modernist descriptions of how media messages are encoded – the 'truth' of the message – without parallel discussions of the plurality of ways they can then be decoded. Likewise, analyses of popular culture are no longer likely to be underpinned by the unspoken presupposition that most of the content is relatively worthless, and that we'd all be better off if everyone just switched their channels to the ABC, or started listening to classical music.

However, in spite of this, the evidence suggests that all three areas are often still asked to frame their conclusions in terms of modernist binaries, certainly when applied to broader educational debates. Is the media a positive or a negative force in the lives of children? Does popular culture belong in the school classroom, yes or no? Is digital technology a good or a bad thing for education? As will be seen, the answers are far too complex for either/or answers.

# Chapter 7

# The media

This chapter argues that the news media does not occupy a realm separate from the concerns of contemporary education; indeed it is important, for students and adults alike, to understand the pervasive, corporate, global and continually developing nature of our news media, and how this impacts upon education in a wide range of ways, both directly and indirectly.

## Myth #1 We do not need pointless subjects like 'media studies' in our already-crowded curriculum

*Children need to learn to read and write, and until they can do that properly, we can do without media studies; it doesn't add anything.*

On the contrary, understanding the media represents a new and important form of literacy for the twenty-first century. In addition to contributing to their critical thinking skills, it contributes to the production of active, global citizens, and it helps them understand the workings of one of our most important contemporary institutions.

## Myth #2 With the news media, you don't need to think, you just need to read and listen

*You don't need to 'decode' the news media; there's nothing mysterious or ambiguous about it. It tells us what's going on, nothing more, nothing less.*

The news media is not simply the objective and transparent communication of current events to a unitary audience. News gathering and selection is a subjective process, and those items selected generally have specific elements – negativity and conflict ranking high among them – and these stories can often support a given agenda, *The Australian*'s campaign against progressive education providing a good example.

## Myth #3 The media doesn't create moral panics, but even if it does, this doesn't affect education

*Even though the news media is under pressure to be entertaining, it isn't responsible for whipping up public hysteria when it happens.*

The evidence suggests that from time to time, the news media can create highly visible 'folk devils', not only to sell newspapers and garner viewers, but also to reinforce the boundaries between 'us' and 'them'. The treatment of 'illegal immigrants' in the Australian media has often taken this form, and this can have significant implications for how minorities are treated in our schools.

# Introduction

As discussed in the introduction to this part, there is significant overlap between all three chapters of Part 3. Indeed, each could probably be titled 'The media', depending upon the criteria used. 'The media' really is a very broad set of concepts, practices, agencies, technologies and forms of representation. For the specific purposes this chapter however, it will largely refer to the news media.

Within this more limited version of the term, there is still a wide range of possible issues to look at, all of which impact upon our understanding of mass education, both directly and indirectly. For example, one important topic might be the matter of ownership, and more particularly, the issue of media monopoly. In the era of News Corporation – i.e., when a huge percentage of our mainstream news media appears to be in the hands of a very limited number of owners – questions arise about the role of such organisations in presenting particular versions of the world for public consumption, versions which suit the political and economic interests of those owners (Herman & Chomsky 1994).

An associated issue might involve the specific subject matter of the news. Those topics deemed worthy of reporting are not chosen at random, and neither are the approaches taken to those topics, rather they generally reinforce dominant representations of, and structures within, Australian culture. It is perhaps not surprising then that, for example, women's sport make up only 9% of all sports coverage in Australian television news media (Lumby, Caple & Greenwood 2010). To put this figure in context, the sporting activities of horses receive greater media attention.

Another topic might concern the significant changes that the news media is currently undergoing. Traditional commercial newspapers are struggling under the twin onslaught of free newspapers, supported solely by advertising, and of the news available on the internet (Kuhn 2010). Likewise, traditional Australian television network news, such as channels Seven, Nine and Ten, have lost market share to their cable news equivalents. This is particularly the case in the United States, where News Corporation's ultra-conservative *Fox News* has gone some way to breaking the stranglehold of ABC, CBS and NBC, with all the political implications that flow from this.

All of these, and many more, are common enough topics within any analysis of the media, and it would appear that issues relating to 'News media and education' don't really get much of a look in. However, this would be incorrect, and for three main reasons.

## The importance of media education

First, there is considerable disagreement over the best way to introduce the media into the education curriculum. That is, education gets a look in because we appear to have trouble agreeing over the best way to educate *about* the media, or even whether we should educate about it at all. As will be discussed in myth #1, this debate has often been constructed as a modernist binary: i.e. the media isn't a problem, so we don't need to learn about it in the curriculum, vs the media is a problem, and children need to understand how it works. That is, more conservative commentators frequently bemoan the teaching of media studies, stating that this somehow represents the death rattle of traditional education.

Some schools abandon the more traditional academic subjects altogether and do not teach them at all … schools will have children take drama, PE, or media studies, abandoning history, physics or French to do so, and our so-called progressive thinkers rejoice … (Birbalsingh 2011)

Opponents of this position point to the importance of the media in giving students a window into the world, and in making active, informed citizens, citizens who can reason effectively, and who can participate in the shaping of our society in what is an increasingly global context.

## Educating about the media

Second, it is also suggested that it is important to teach students to 'decode' the media, to help them understand that the news is not impartial, and that the shaping of opinion through the media often comes with a range of different agendas. While the newspapers are full of domestic politics, world events, local issues, sports reports, cultural reviews, and adverts – likewise with television news coverage – at first glance, education doesn't seem to feature very often at all. However closer scrutiny not only reveals a fairly consistent stream of education-related topics in recent years – the school building program, funding levels for private schools, multicultural education, literacy standards and practices, postmodernism in the classroom, drugs and violence in schools – it also reveals a very particular set of stances on these topics.

It is not a huge leap to suggest that schools are often portrayed as hotbeds of drug abuse, violence and political sedition (Kemp & Vaughn 2009; Donnelly 2004), and that staff are depicted as being almost as illiterate as the children they teach (Bantick 2008). Myth #2 will address the manner in which one recent debate has been handled in the news media: the issue of student literacy. It will point to the importance of equipping students with the capacities necessary to understand that, to use the title of Burton's (2002) book, when it comes to what's going on in the media, there's *More than Meets the Eye*.

## The media and moral panics

Third, other than simply pushing certain agendas within the field of education, as will be discussed in myth #3, the media frequently plays a significant role in whipping up moral panics within our society, panics that have both direct and indirect consequences for education, and which feed back into public policy and determine our perceptions of what is going on in our schools.

Though the notion of a moral panic is most frequently associated with the activities of young people, it can apply to a wide range of issues and groups. It could be argued that the *Australian*'s campaign against progressive models of literacy education shared many of the characteristics of a moral panic – engendering widespread hostility towards teachers, a disproportionate response to the problems at hand, and so on – but a better example probably involves ongoing representations of 'illegal boat people' arriving in Australia. This has had repercussions that have spilled off the TV screen, directly into our classrooms.

To summarise, the three myths to be dealt with in this chapter are:

**Myth #1** – We do not need pointless subjects like 'media studies' in our already-crowded curriculum

**Myth #2** – With the news media, you don't need to think, you just need to read and listen

**Myth #3** – The media doesn't create moral panics, but even if it does, this doesn't affect education

# Myth #1 We do not need pointless subjects like 'media studies' in our already-crowded curriculum

How many times does the point have to be made? Schools aren't there as part of some ongoing experiment on our children's minds. The traditional curriculum survived for so long simply because it deals with precisely what's needed: the three Rs. We don't need each new, trendy social issue to be given space in the classroom. What are you going to take out, in order to find space for 'media studies'? Besides, kids watch enough TV as it is, without finding an excuse to watch it in school as well. Teach them maths; teach them to read and write; and if you want to teach them something trendy … teach them French.

One thing most certainly *is* true. There aren't an endless number of hours in the school day, such that everything we'd *like* to teach, we *can* teach. Anyone who has spent time in a school would know that constant battles are fought over various aspect of the curriculum: what gets taught, when, who has to teach it, which subjects get priority (either overtly or covertly), which subjects get more funding, which subjects become part of the school 'branding', which subjects become dumping grounds for underachieving students; and these are only school-level disputes. Wider debates are also fought out at state and federal levels about what should be taught in schools, and how.

Many subjects can make strong claims to a higher profile within Australian education. Given our obesity rates, advocates of daily physical education can mount a very strong case. Those who argue for compulsory second language education rightly point to the arrogant parochialism that can go with thinking you only ever need to be able to speak English. Part 4 of this very book, in addition to arguing that a knowledge of philosophy is essential for making sense of mass education, also attempts to make the case for its re-introduction into the school curriculum. Where does it end?

In spite of this competition for space, there are a number of arguments that support giving school children a better understanding of the media – and specifically the news media – as part of their formal education. These arguments vary in their approach, and their significance, but they all reach the same conclusion: the subject is far too important to ignore.

# 1  Finding space in the curriculum

The first question here is a purely practical one: do we have to kick out another subject in order to make room for media studies in the curriculum? The debate is often framed in such binary terms, and largely for reasons of rhetorical effectiveness; after all, who would really argue that we should abandon maths or history to do so? Nobody, except a straw man.

This generally leaves two options which, relatively unproblematically, represents the current situation within most Australian curricula (Burn & Durrant 2008). The first is to offer media studies as a stand-alone subject, although mostly at the level of junior high school, perhaps reflecting its continued lowly status as a subject. There have been various attempts to introduce it within the final years of schooling, with mixed success.

The second is to include the study of the media within a subject such as English. Given the flexibility of the contemporary curriculum to address a wide range of texts – while still examining issues of narrative, perspective, context, genre, and so on – it has become obvious that English doesn't always have to be about Shakespeare. 'Literacy' can take many forms, and there is plenty of evidence to suggest that media literacy has become just as important as the others (Hobbes 2007).

# 2  Critical thinking

Maths teachers would argue that maths isn't just of value because it teaches you to count; they would also contend that it teaches you to think in an orderly fashion, to organise your premises well in order to reach a valid conclusion, to reduce problems to their functioning elements, and to find some certainty in areas where there previously may have been none.

Those who see value in media education would make similar kinds of claims, suggesting that the conceptual skills required to better understand the media bring benefits beyond the boundaries of the discipline itself. Media studies as a discipline represents an ongoing exercise in critical thinking. That is, addressing the way news messages are assembled and disseminated, appreciating how audiences can receive and negotiate those messages, and thinking through the nature of the forces that give rise to those messages in the first place, all these processes of criticism and reflection result in the production of more intellectually competent, flexible and insightful citizens (Share 2002). This belief in the intrinsic value of media studies is supported by Hart (1991, 1), who states:

> When we are able to evaluate media messages with confidence and respond critically to them, we are much less likely to rely on the opinions of others and more likely to become autonomous rather than automatons. In learning how meaning is made in the media, we can gain more understanding of the world in which we live. We can be determined not to be determined.

## 3 Media literacy and active citizenship

Hart is making a good point here. Not only is a better understanding of the media good for intellectual ability and confidence, it also makes us more independent, questioning thinkers, which in turn has implications for the way in which we act as citizens who can effectively participate in our democracy. There is much more to a democracy than simply having the right to vote; citizens have to have access to accurate and appropriate public information, such that they can make informed choices – choices about candidates, parties, issues, and the future direction of their community.

Schirato et al. (2010) contend that the concepts of 'citizenship' and 'community' are not as straightforward as they might first appear, and that the media has always played a vital role in linking the two together. Citizenship concerns the rights and obligations we have as members of a community, but how do we form that community? After all, as Australians we have only met the tiniest fraction of the overall population, and that doesn't constitute a sufficient basis to form any kind of valid group identity. This is where the media is of importance, in that through the circulation of various forms of knowledge and information, *imagined political communities* can be established, allowing people to think about themselves, and their relationships to others. Without agencies such as the media then, the conceptual bonds that form the fabric of the community would quickly begin to dissolve.

The point here is that – ideally – citizenship is not a passive status. The public space, in which ideas are debated and opinions aired, only operates when citizens are both free to participate, and willing and capable of doing so. The media – the Fourth Estate (after the executive, legislative and judicial branches of government) – has the historical role of holding the government to account. Students in a democracy need to learn the importance of that process, and to participate in it, as soon as they can.

## 4 Global news, global citizenship

The implications of this now go far beyond the borders of Australia. We now live in a global economy, and no country is entirely immune from the financial difficulties that might beset any other – with the possible exception of North Korea, which shouldn't be a point of envy. This inter-reliance extends beyond the realm of the economic, into a broader convergence of ideas and identities. The notion of the 'global citizen' comes into its own here; the notion of global warming, with everyone equally at risk irrespective of nationality, provides a perfect example.

Significantly, it was writers on the media who were the first to foresee the rise of a global culture. McLuhan and Fiore (1967) noted that the advent of new forms of communication technology had overthrown the constraining factors of 'space' and 'time', and that as a consequence, we had begun to live in a *global village*. This famous term was coined over 40 years ago and clearly, by the second decade of the twenty-first century, the factors underlying this phenomenon have increased hyperbolically. While remaining aware of some of the criticisms of this position – that it is in danger of homogenising still-disparate cultures; that maybe not everyone can afford to live in this 'global village' (Branston & Stafford 2006) – they are still making a good point.

McLuhan and Fiore's claim is important for two reasons. First, it is no longer sufficient for students to know only about their immediate social and political environment here in Australia. As well as issues of global climate change, there is the matter of global terrorism, the global economic crisis, an ongoing global refugee crisis, risks of global pandemics, geopolitical issues ranging from the rise of China to the troubles in Europe, global repercussions of the Arab Spring, and the list goes on. All these issues impact upon Australia, directly and indirectly, and students now have to be both equipped to understand their implications and, as future global citizens, to begin to participate in the process of finding effective solutions.

The second reason involves the global nature of modern news organisations. Such news organisations are not new; agencies such as Reuters, AFP and AP have long gathered news internationally, which they then sold on to clients around the world. The more recent changes that have occurred involve the rise of media conglomerates like News Corporation, the blurring of the boundaries between national and global news agencies, and the boundaries between news, opinion, and entertainment, as is arguably the case with Fox News (Boyd-Barrett & Rantenen 2010).

## 5   Understanding one of our major social institutions

This latter point is important because it addresses the issue of the major institutions that organise the lives of all Australians, regardless of age. While we are aware of the civic importance of educating our children about our central legislative and judicial institutions – the House of Representatives, the Senate, the High Court, various state parliaments – as well as the functioning of major institutions such as the military, our education system, and the public service, this list generally excludes one of the biggest, and the most influential: the media.

Burton (2002) points to a number of associated reason as to why we should study the media, as a set of institutions. He suggests the extent of the media's power and influence enables it to shape our ideas about the world according to its own agendas. He suggests that its economic power gives it almost limitless reach to achieve its ends, and he also notes that the sheer scale of the media's operations mean that few are unaffected by its messages. Indeed, its diversity and concentration enables it to reach virtually any audience it chooses to target. Given the breadth of media forms, it now acts as one of our central mechanisms for gathering information, and can present, and re-present, that information in any number of credible and persuasive ways.

This is not to say that media institutions should then be understood in a simple, modernist, cause-and-effect manner, such that a singular thing – 'the media' – with a unified agenda and mode of operation, induces a predicable response within an equally unified audience. Rather, the entire equation is far more piecemeal, contingent and unpredictable than that. Media messages may be encoded with one idea in mind, but decoded by different audiences in entirely different ways. For example, just because the makers of news put together an item highlighting the dangers of train surfing, doesn't mean that some 18-year-old risk-taking youths won't read the very same news item as a 'how-to manual'. This notion of 'decoding the media' provides the final, and perhaps the most important reason for studying the subject.

## 6   Decoding the media

In suggesting that students need to be able to decode the media, this is not to jump headlong into what Share (2002, 8) calls the *protectionist approach* to the media, where we regard it as some kind of evil ogre from which citizens, young and old, need safeguarding; and that by educating against its manipulative tricks, we can avoid simply being passive victims of media indoctrination. The situation is far more complex and nuanced than that, but certainly there's a lot more going on than is apparent at first glance.

Rather than regarding the news media as a straightforward source of objective information, to be communicated and understood in a singular, unproblematic way, most media commentators would argue that the news we receive is neither neutral nor transparent. As Branston and Stafford (2006, 194) rightly note:

> News is a globally important media form … and modern democracies depend on accurate news to give adequate accounts of a complex world, even though this is far from always being the case. It matters greatly that news is understood as being 'made' and not 'natural' or 'given'. It matters what kind of news is made, under what conditions, what spaces and budgets it occupies, and the support or criticism it is given by its audiences.

Indeed, it matters so much, that the next two myths are devoted in their entirety to the need for citizens to be able to decode the news media; to realise that the newspapers they read, and the TV news programs they watch, often have agendas all of their own.

# Myth #2 With the news media, you don't need to think, you just need to read and listen

Reading a newspaper or listening to the news isn't an overly complex business. They simply tell you what's going on in the world around you; they don't just make stuff up – not the important stuff anyway – and if they don't make stuff up, what they are telling us must be true, so what's the problem? If it's true, you can't complain about not liking it. If the news tells us that kids in schools can't read like they used to, or that illegal immigrants in boats are swamping the country, well … facts are facts.

It would be nice and simple if there were only two options regarding the news: either the provision of Goebbels-like misinformation and propaganda, so easy to see through that a child wouldn't be fooled; or alternatively, utterly objective material, informing the audience with neither distortion nor omission. Unfortunately, this isn't the case, and for two main reasons.

First, as will be discussed in Chapter 12, the concept of 'truth' isn't a matter of black and white. Indeed, the belief that something can be unequivocally, eternally and objectively 'true' exists on very thin philosophical ice. This isn't to say that the falsehoods Goebbels constructed about the Jews can somehow be considered true – they can't – but it does mean that truth can be assembled in many different ways, depending upon what evidence is used, how the argument is constructed, the context that argument is placed in, and what conclusions are drawn. For example, if some children produce disappointing results in their literacy tests, can we conclude from this – as the *Australian* has continually suggested – that our schooling system is over-run with left-wing teachers bent on destroying traditional education? This particular truth-claim provides the focus for Snyder's (2008) *The Literacy Wars,* which will be discussed in greater detail shortly.

Second, as we shall see, there is no such thing as totally objective news. Burton (2002) rightly points out that news always comes in a particular form – a genre – and as such follows specific conventions in the way it is organised. The process of news gathering and selection is also necessarily subjective, and a function of perceived 'newsworthiness'. Furthermore, particular news values impact on whether an item in deemed newsworthy: Is the story negative? Is it simple to understand? Is there conflict involved? Also, language is often used in very particular ways, ways that relate to issues of authority and credibility. Underlying this, there are questions relating to the kinds of agendas that are operating: Is the item impartial, or are particular views of the world being pushed? Finally, is the media trying to whip up a panic over a given issue in order to further its own ends, and to sell more papers/gain more viewers? While these constitute only a fraction of the ways in which the news media can be decoded, they provide a good place to begin.

## 'The Literacy Wars'

In the second half of the last decade, a wave of articles appeared in Rupert Murdoch's the *Australian,* pointing to what they saw as the self-evident failure of contemporary education. Schools were infested with postmodern theory (Slattery 2005), traditional approaches to teaching were under attack from babbling left-wing ideologues (Donnelly 2005b), and children were being defrauded of a proper education (Kelly 2006). That is, unbeknownst to the vast majority of Australians, our schools had become the newest battleground in the ongoing war between the left and the right, and the *Australian* (and other associate New Corporation papers) felt it was their responsibility to point out how this battle was principally being fought – i.e. through the teaching of reading – and precisely what was at stake.

There is nothing new about concerns over student literacy (Dooley 2004), however in her book *The Literacy Wars*, Snyder (2008) details how the teaching of reading, an important but seemingly politically innocuous element of every primary teacher's professional responsibilities, somehow became transformed into something much, much more. That is, the conservative voice of the *Australian* championed the teaching of *phonics*, the traditional method of sounding out parts of words, as opposed to *whole-language* teaching, which involves memorising whole words, and which is associated with the broader educational philosophy of *constructivism*. Snyder suggests that by shaping this as a choice between two apparent polar opposites, and by associating whole-language teaching with loony left-wing faddism, it became possible to create a 'Literacy War' out of next to nothing.

At the risk of spoiling a good story, Snyder notes that good teachers actually appear to employ both methods in their classroom. She cites the research of Louden et al. (2005) who revealed that highly effective, highly regarded Australian teachers:

> … employed a wide repertoire of practices, some of which appeared decidedly whole language – process writing, reading groups and contextualised practice skills – and some of which appeared skills-orientated – explicit phonics lessons, sight word practice and comprehension instruction strategy (Snyder 2008, 67).

So the question arises, how was the *Australian* able to construct a 'war' out of thin air? Or to ask a different question; using the example of the Literacy Wars, what might a very basic framework for decoding media messages begin to look like?

## Decoding the news media

There are a number of entry points into an organised analysis of the news media. Below are just some from Burton's (2002) framework for media analysis, but they provide a good place to start.

## Genre

News comes in a variety of different forms, each with their own rules and features. News does not flow to us from the outside world, free and unimpeded; it is funnelled through particular types of media product. For example, television news is almost always organised in the same familiar way: two talking heads, both exuding gravity and trustworthiness, various reporters in the field, live feeds from trouble spots, little obvious editorialising other than by story selection, and a clear ranking of those stories, ending with sport and the weather.

Newspapers are no different; they follow familiar codes that we have come to recognise and expect. Broadsheets like the *Australian* follow somewhat different codes to tabloid newspapers, taking more seriously their role as civic guardians, and providing forums for debate. Editorialising is also generally accepted by the readership, with particular newspapers tilting to the left or the right in their coverage of issues. For example, the *Guardian* (UK) and the *New York Times* are both left-leaning newspapers. The UK's *Telegraph* and our own *Australian* tilt significantly to the right. That said, the right to a political perspective all too often spills over into blind partisanship and outright distortion.

The *Australian*'s campaign against progressive teaching can be read in terms of genre. The information is presented via editorials, opinion pieces and news articles, each with their own formats and conventions. The items are all composed of familiar elements that give the pieces their weight, authority and resonance. For example, stock characters (in this case, 'vulnerable children', 'left-wing fanatics' and 'right-minded Australians') are set within stock situations (yet one more defence of traditional Australian values), both of which are then continually repeated, and continually reinforced.

## News selection

For every news item chosen by a newspaper's editors for publication, a vast array is ignored. Likewise, for every bandwagon a newspaper decides to jump on, any number of other possible bandwagons are allowed to roll past. That is, decoding the news is as much about what has been left out of the selection process, as what has been put in.

> News, like any kind of media product, is the result of a process of selection and construction. Items are selected in or selected out. Newspapers or news programmes are artefacts that are put together. In effect, meaning is constructed into them … For example, the reporter or newsreader interprets events for us. As soon as they talk about 'confrontation', they are actually interpreting what has happened. They are asserting that there has been a confrontation, where someone else might have talked about 'disagreement' (Burton 2002, 182).

Interestingly, foregrounding the notion of 'confrontation' is clear in Donnelly's (2005a) piece on education in the *Australian,* not just with the title, 'Cannon Fodder in the Culture Wars', but also words and phrases from the piece itself, such as 'battle' and 'warrior'. There are alternative words that could have been chosen to describe the disagreements over the best way to teach literacy within schools: 'ongoing discussion', 'healthy professional disagreements', or 'debate' for instance, but of course, none of these are as effective when attempting to sell newspapers.

Unfortunately, the term 'debate' may not be an appropriate term within the context of the *Australian*'s coverage of the literacy issue, as it only seems interested in giving voice to the anti-progressive education side of the conversation, a fact which leads on to an associated issue: that of agenda. News content is not selected at random, nor solely in terms of how pertinent it might be considered by the readership. It is also selected because it fits within a given narrative; part of a political and cultural agenda pushed by the paper, in this instance, the conservative belief that everything was better in the good old days. This will be discussed again in the subsection on editorialising and bias.

## News values

In order for news items to be deemed newsworthy, it is widely preferred that they contain specific elements – values – and if they are not immediately present, an angle must be found where any trace of these elements can be expanded upon and foregrounded. After all, does anybody really want to read that Australian children are doing quite well in global literacy tables, and that teachers are hard-working professionals, who employ a range of diverse pedagogic strategies, in what is a very difficult task, within an ever-changing, multicultural society? No, you probably don't.

Generally speaking, items are far more likely to be selected – or once selected, regarded as effective pieces of news – if they exhibit most of the following criteria. In no particular order:

**Negativity**: bad news sells. The rosy picture painted above is regarded as far less interesting than the alternative notion that we are producing a nation of virtual illiterates; and worse, even the teachers can't read and write properly ...

**Simplicity**: good articles are ones that can spell the issue out easily. A complex picture of the nuanced and context-bound use of differing teaching strategies for literacy is nowhere near as journalistically desirable as the image of bad teachers using left-wing gobbledegook in the classrooms to the detriment of our children.

**Conflict**: this is an easy combination of negativity and simplicity. Why depict the subtle nuances of a debate between loose clusters of interest groups, theoretical positions, and practicing teachers, when you can construct the entire issue as a straightforward battle between good and evil? It seems far more exciting that way, and excitement sells newspapers.

**Human interest**: one of the most effective ways of driving home a story is to tie it to the lives of specific individuals, to the 'victims' of the conflict; pointing out generalised caricatures of the good guys and the bad guys only goes so far. A good news item then is likely to include the case of little Johnny the primary school child, who, after five years of being taught with whole-language methods was completely illiterate; now, after only one month with phonics, he has a reading age of 25.

## News and discourse

Language, and the manner and context of its use, is never neutral, and the news media is no exception. Just as using the terms 'war', 'battle', and 'cannon fodder' set a conceptual tone for the *Australian*'s coverage of the literacy debate, so too do other aspects of newspaper discourse. Through the presentation of news items in seemingly authoritative and credible ways (as opposed, perhaps, to more 'tabloid' newspapers), publications like the *Australian* are able to trade upon that credibility to add weight to their arguments within their opinion pieces and editorials. Consequently, when the *Australian* claims there is a crisis in education, people are more likely to believe it than if it was published in *Zoo Weekly* magazine.

In addition to the aura of authority and credibility emanating from broadsheet newspapers like the *Australian*, a further associated strategy involves the use of 'experts' to bolster their arguments. Allocating the status of 'expert' need not be based upon anything other than that they possess educational qualifications and agree with the newspaper's agenda, but it still adds weight to their overall argument. Interestingly, none of the 'experts' used by the *Australian* appear to be employed by faculties of education within Australian universities.

## Editorialising and bias

While there is an expectation (largely misplaced) that television news will remain politically impartial, and simply present the day's happenings in a neutral and objective manner, the same code of conduct does not necessarily apply to the print media. As discussed, many readers expect newspapers to have a gentle political slant – particularly the editorials – although if this is handled subtly enough, and it also aligns with the readers' own politics, then such a slant if often regarded as 'sensible, right-thinking', in contrast to other newspapers with which the reader doesn't agree politically, which can be dismissed as 'overtly biased'.

Two points are worth making here. First, it is important for all audiences to be aware that such biases exist; this forms a crucial component of media literacy. All newspapers have a slant, and sometimes just knowing who owns the title will be enough to let you know what that is (assuming it isn't self-evident). Second, understanding and accepting that there is a slant, is not the same as tolerating distortion, either as a one-off portrayal of a specific incident/issue, or as part of an ongoing campaign in support of a particular political position.

> The campaign was relentless – the populist press running anti-teacher and general education-decline themes day after day over periods of weeks during the whole year. Government ministers, the Right-wing press, the usual 'expert' pundits and the shock jocks – all mobilised and remaining firmly 'on message'. The education profession was demonised and Ministers and editorial writers were able to portray themselves as the saviours of the nation's schools (Sawyer 2006, 237–238).

In summary, the idea of 'totally objective news' is a myth. At one level, this is not a criticism; the very process of gathering and selecting news, the familiar categories into which it is shaped, the choice of aspects that are deemed to make something newsworthy, and the forms of discourse that become attached to the stories (indeed, the very notion of a 'story' itself) make the notion of 'objectivity' necessarily illusory. However, the ability to decode the effects of these elements is important, as is the ability to understand that other, less benign factors affect the objectivity of news. The ability to decode the media also includes, when such issues arise, the ability to recognise specific media agendas, to recognise overt and covert political bias, to recognise simplistic solutions to what are complex problems, and to recognise organised campaigns of disinformation.

# Myth #3 The media doesn't create moral panics, but even if it does, this doesn't affect education

> The media isn't in the business of whipping up public hysteria. It may use colourful language occasionally, and it may try to present news in exciting and engaging ways, but so what … it's a business after all. If your news isn't interesting, people will turn the TV over and find news that is. If the line is crossed every now and again, and the media lays it on a bit thick, this is only about things like bikie gangs, and a bit of a moral panic about them is probably justified. None of this has anything to do with education.

There seems little doubt that the media does exaggerate when it suits them, just as it engages in very selective representation, often with its own agenda, as was discussed in myth #2. Certainly, some parts of the media seem more responsible than others, almost as a matter of genre, and you often know what you're going to get before you even start reading or watching. For example, Channel Nine's *A Current Affair* and Channel Seven's *Today Tonight* seem much less concerned with journalistic accuracy, fairness and objectivity than does the *ABC News* or SBS's *World News*; likewise with tabloid newspapers, as opposed to broadsheets.

The question now is: what kind of implications can these less desirable forms of media conduct have? Is it just a matter of rolling our eyes – thanks to our newfound decoding skills – and accepting that all news media is, ultimately, part of the entertainment industry? Or are the social consequences of sensationalistic news reporting too far-reaching, pervasive and pernicious to be dismissed so lightly?

## Moral panics

In 1972, Cohen wrote the book *Folk Devils and Moral Panics*, a seminal text on the role played by the media in mobilising the public against perceived threats to the social order. Cohen analysed the spectacular fallout that occurred from a minor brawl in the small seaside town of Clacton in the UK in 1964. Two groups of bored youths, some in leather jackets, some wearing early-Beatles style clothing, engaged in ongoing scuffles throughout the course of a holiday afternoon. Some windows were broken, and a few elderly residents were frightened; injuries were slight, and a number of youths were picked up before being put on trains back home. Such an event would normally have barely warranted a mention in the national media, but this time it was different. The media picked up on the fracas, and ran with it. In line with the values of a good news story (negativity, simplicity, conflict) the protagonists soon became magically divided into two discrete warring camps, the Mods and the Rockers – modern-day *Folk Devils* – and a national moral panic began in earnest.

> The headlines are self-descriptive: 'Day of Terror by Scooter Groups' (*Daily Telegraph*), 'Youngsters Beat Up Town – 97 Leather Jacket Arrests' (*Daily Express*), 'Wild Ones Invade Seaside – 97 Arrests' (*Daily Mirror*) … editorials began to appear, together with reports that the home Secretary was being urged (it was not usually specified by *whom*) to take action … Feature articles then appeared highlighting interviews with Mods and Rockers. Straight reporting gave way to theories especially about motivation: the mob was described as 'exhilarated', 'drunk with notoriety', 'hell-bent for destruction' … (Cohen 1980, 30).

Having invented the phenomenon, the news media then salaciously reported the copycat riots that followed in other seaside towns; with equal glee, they then pointed out the terrible threat posed by the gangs of Mods and Rockers that had immediately established themselves within every town in the UK. Mods and Rockers were a threat to the nation's way of life; Mods and Rockers needed stamping out.

Cohen raised a number of interesting issues. The first, and the most obvious, is that the media is not simply a passive observer of news; rather it is instrumental in organising both its creation and its impact. He discussed how the media *exaggerated and distorted* the news, in terms of the significance of the events, the manner in which they were described, and the threats they posed. He examined the way in which the media used *prediction* as a vehicle for keeping the story alive: 'When will they strike next?', 'Who is in most danger?' They loudly anticipated riots with each new holiday, which quickly became self-fulfilling prophecies. He also addressed the symbolic role played by such media inventions. The terms 'Mod' and 'Rocker' became larger than themselves; they came to represent all that was wrong with the country. Even their clothes and their haircuts became endowed with particular new types of (negative) meaning. The Beatles' loveable mop-tops were no longer quite so loveable.

Now this is all very interesting, in a recent-history sort of a way, but what has this got to do with us? What does it have to do with Australia, in the twenty-first century, and what does it have to do with education? The point here is that, arguably, this synthetic process of *moral panic* creation, and the associated construction of *folk devils*, still happens on a relatively regular basis, and that it affects Australian education, both directly and indirectly.

It affects education directly, in that some moral panics are actually about education. The concern over literacy described in myth #2 most likely rises to the level of a moral panic – complete with its own associate folk devil: the radical left-wing teacher. Other moral panics directly relating to education might include drugs and violence in schools, with a similar folk devil to the Cohen studies: the out-of-control youth.

Importantly, moral panics also affect education indirectly. A good example within the Australian context involves the issue of 'illegal immigrants'. This can be examined through the framework set out within a more recent, but equally useful, approach to moral panics.

## The media and 'illegal immigrants'

As we all know, Australia is largely a nation of immigrants. With the notable exception of Indigenous Australians, the rest of the population are either immigrants themselves, or descendants of those who are. In spite of this fact, Australians have not always been generous to those who come here to start a new life, as they once did. Apart from some gentle ribbing directed at the English, the real venom has been saved, at various different times, for the Irish, the Chinese, Greeks and Italians, the Vietnamese, and currently, anyone who practices Islam.

A particularly vilified subset of this final category are those who have come here seeking asylum from troubles in their countries of origin, and especially, those who have arrived here by boat. Generally, and erroneously, referred to as 'illegal immigrants', they have been widely depicted in the news media as welfare bludgers, as queue jumpers, as potential terrorists, as disease carriers, and as liars. To put it another way, they are depicted as a threat, to us as individuals, and also to our prosperity and our Australian way of life. A discussion of news media depictions of asylum seekers could focus on any of these areas of characterisation, but 'welfare bludgers' seems as good as any. This has been the subject of no little discussion in the media, and appropriate examples can be found in news items from *Channel 9 News,* the *Courier Mail,* and Channel Seven's *Today Tonight*, as will be seen shortly.

These media depictions of asylum seekers, and the consequences of those depictions, can be understood through a variant on Cohen's model: the five-part moral panic framework as set out by Goode and Ben-Yehuda (2009).

## 1   Concern

There must first be increased levels of concern over the behaviour of a particular social group, as well as the consequences of that behaviour. This concern need not always be experienced in terms of fear, however, there must generally be a sense of threat, a threat that produces a widespread sense of anxiety. For example, media portrayals of the supposed conduct of Mods and Rockers produced levels of social unease that went right to the highest levels of government.

Concerns over 'illegal immigrants' have become widespread within the Australian popular consciousness, and the media has a huge role to play in this. With specific regard to the issue of the welfare cost to Australian society (that is, the unwarranted economic burden of their continued presence), there have been numerous items in the newspapers and on television that spell out the full price of our hospitality. Mention is rarely made of the fact that we are simply fulfilling our obligations under international law, and that the concerns continually articulated in the media – illegal immigrants are getting more than 'ordinary' Aussies, illegal immigrants are all playing the system – are largely false.

## 2   Hostility

After initial concern about the behaviour of the social group in question, comes increasing hostility towards that group, hostility stoked by the tenor of the news coverage they receive. As Goode and Ben-Yehuda (2009, 36) state:

> Members of this category are collectively designated as the enemy, or an enemy, of respectable society; their behaviour is seen as harmful or threatening to the values, the interests, possibly the very existence of the society; … a division is made between 'us' – good, decent, respectable folk – and 'them' or the 'other' – the deviants, bad guys, undesirables, outsiders …

In October 2011, Channel Seven's *Today Tonight* aired a report which claimed that refugees were being housed in a 'resort' where they lived in luxury, that they were given $400 per week living allowance, and that they were taken on regular expensive outings. They filmed an angry pensioner who talked about how unfair it was that 'boat people' got these benefits; precisely the kind of hostility referred to above by Goode and Ben-Yehuda.

The trouble is, none of it is true; they aren't housed in a resort, they don't receive $400 a week, the outings were a fiction, and as the angry pensioner later said: 'I wish I'd been told the truth'. The host of the ABC program *Media Watch,* Jonathon Holmes, stated when analysing *Today Tonight*'s report: 'I've spent four years in the *Media Watch* chair – and in all that time I have never seen a more mendacious, deceptive and inflammatory piece of "journalism"' (Holmes 2010). The key word here is 'inflammatory'.

## 3   Consensus

For the moral panic to take hold, and to generate significant social consequences, there must be widespread agreement that 'the problem' is worth worrying about. If concerns about 'boat people' were limited to *Today Tonight* viewers, this might not constitute much of an issue, but when it is echoed within other news media, on our radios and in our popular magazines, and even within the discourses of our parliament, then the necessary critical mass has been achieved. The Refugee Council of Australia (2009) notes that:

> Refugees, asylum seekers and the Australians who support them have had to endure countless media articles full of inaccuracies and stereotypes. But sometimes media organisations go one step further and publish information that is blatantly false.

The Refugee Council cites the example of the *Courier Mail*'s claim that the Australian Government intended to give dole payments to illegal immigrants, thereby fanning the flames of resentment even further against all those with whom they are often conflated: refugees, asylum seekers, and Muslims in general. Probably needless to say, the report was completely false, and yet the *Courier Mail* refused to either retract the claim, or issue an apology. Similar criticisms were also raised of *Channel 9 News'* coverage of the costs of Centrelink benefits for refugees.

## 4 Disproportion

An important part of the notion of a moral panic is that the threat is perceived as far greater than it actually is in reality, that is, in terms of an objective assessment of the risks posed by the 'folk devils' in question. In Cohen's study, Mods and Rockers were widely represented as a threat to the British way of life, a potent symbol of national decline. With hindsight, they were simply relatively innocuous subcultural fashion statements; in fact, they represented little more than two different types of musical taste, transportational preference, and choice in bad haircut.

The same is true of 'boat people'. How many people do we think 'flood' into Australia by boat each year, and are allowed to stay, thereby jumping the queue: 10,000? 20,000? 30,000? Given the levels of media publicity given to this problem, and the angst it seems to cause us as a nation, it must surely be a hell of a lot. According to *Media Watch* (2009):

> How many visas went last year to asylum-seekers arriving by boat? Precisely 206.

## 5 Volatility

An important issue with moral panics is that they are never permanent; they arrive, cause lots of trouble and anxiety, and then they fade away, to be replaced by some other social concern. Panics over Mods and Rockers were soon replaced by others involving football hooligans (Pearson 1983), Punks (Hebdige 1979), Goths (Tait 1999), and even latterly, children who underachieve at school (Miller 2008). Each serves the function of both selling newspapers and garnering viewers, but also legitimating the targeting of those groups for demonisation, and then punitive intervention.

The Australian moral panic concerning 'illegal immigrants/boat people' appears to be somewhat different to the norm. While it certainly appears to be volatile – in that the panic appears, gains momentum, occupies centre stage in the news cycle for a few months, and then fades away – it differs from other moral panics in that the story doesn't end there. The moral panic over 'illegal immigrants' then tends to reappear in one form or another, coincidentally every two to three years, normally just as Australia begins the process of heading into a general election. It seems that engendering a fear of 'the Muslim other' serves a very useful political purpose. You can draw your own conclusions here.

Having outlined the five elements of Goode and Ben-Yahuda's theory, it should be pointed out that moral panic theory is not without its critics. Given that all the chapters in this section detail concern over the modernist tendency to shape the debate into binary oppositions (the news media is good/bad, popular culture is good/bad, digital technology is good/bad), it doesn't necessarily help to employ a conceptual tool that appears to act as a master discourse (a single theoretical device that explains everything within its scope), which is a further foundational aspect of modernism. So, much as moral panic theory is a useful mechanism for conceptualising some of the ways in which the news media can shape and mobilise public opinion, often to the detriment of particular social groups, there is a tendency to homogenise the process somewhat. That is, the questions should always be asked: is the moral panic uniform throughout the social body? Is it actually unreasonable? Are there important differences within the 'folk devils'? Are there loud voices rejecting the substance of the moral panic altogether? In the case of the recurrent moral panic over 'boat people', let's hope so.

## The 'illegal immigrant' panic and education

There are three points to be made here. First, some facts about 'illegal immigrants': Australia does not 'take more than its fair share' of asylum seekers. When adjusted for GDP (a measure of the country's wealth), Australia is ranked in the bottom half of the world's nations (Crikey 2009). Also, a closer look at those here without the correct documentation paints a surprising picture. Our nation isn't overflowing with undocumented Iraqi refugees; they generally come from elsewhere, but in this particular instance, nobody seems to care. To quote part of an interview with a young Australian in the *Sydney Morning Herald*:

> 'The immaturity in political debate in Australia sometimes makes me sick,' Howes said. 'There are politicians in both the Liberal and Labor parties who are exploiting the issue of race to whip up fear in the community. Question time is dominated by 78 people on a boat. We have around 50,000 visa overstayers every year,' he said of people who arrive by plane rather than boat. 'Is anyone saying this is a national crisis? One reason there is no outrage is that these people are mainly white and speak English. Is anyone demanding we clean out the backpackers' hostels of Bondi and Surry Hills?' (Hartcher 2009).

Finally, 'boat people' has become a synonym for disease-carrying, bomb-carrying and queue-jumping. In 2001, the *Courier Mail* ran a story stating that nearly 1000 cases of infectious disease had been found in refugee centres, thereby implying that such people were a threat to the community. What the *Courier Mail* neglected to mention was that most were for inactive tuberculosis infections, common to one-third of the world's population, including one-third of the Australian population over the age of 50 (Mares 2002).

Likewise with the issue of terrorism: it has been suggested by various parliamentarians that arriving by boat would be a perfect way for 'people with bad intent' to hide among the Australian population. While these assertions have been ridiculed by counter-terrorism experts, who put the chances of this at 'infinitesimally small' (*Sydney Morning Herald* 2009) – why, after all, would you want to spend years in a detention camp, with no guarantee of entry, when you can simply fly into Sydney airport? – such absurd claims still have the effect of demonising both asylum seekers in particular, and the Muslim community in general.

As for queue jumping, this is the greatest misconception of all: *there is no queue*. Refugees by definition have left their country of origin, and have entered another country to seek asylum. Besides, as the Refugee Council of Australia (2012) notes, the UN resettlement system does not work like an orderly queue, such that if you join the end, you are guaranteed to reach the front if you wait long enough. Rather, it is more like a lottery, being based upon perceived need (which can change at any time, depending upon who arrives at the camp), and worse, many refugees actually lack access to the resettlement processes altogether. For many then, the only option is to set sail, and hope for the best.

Second, in spite of the facts about the asylum seekers who arrive by boat, the moral panic succeeds in producing its own types of 'truth', and those truths have consequences. A 2001 survey on public attitudes towards asylum seekers demonstrates the engendering of a frightening level of hostility. The following comments from the 2001 Port Augusta Survey on Asylum Seekers are cited in Dunn, Klocker and Salabay (2007, 581):

> '… the government should use real ammunition to gain respect and send the rag heads back home to their own country … The Navy should blow them out of the water. Sharks and sea lice would clean up.'
>
> 'Being close to the camp means that some will wander our streets so I will be able to spit on and abuse them … I can hardly wait.'

Third, and probably needless to say, these attitudes inevitably spill over into our schools. A recent study into the impact of racism on young people produced a range of significant results (Mansouri et al. 2009). Over 80% of students from non-Anglo-Australian backgrounds reported being subject to racist abuse. This has a couple of serious consequences: first, those students often felt as if they are not part of the schooling community. That is, they were 'othered' from the very beginning of the educational process; the boundaries are all neatly drawn, and they are placed on the outside. Second, they lose the desire to go to school at all. Given the language and learning difficulties often faced by migrant and refugee children, it can be hard enough to succeed in school without adding the issue of hating the place altogether for what happens to them there.

In summary, the media is more than capable of whipping up a public outcry when it considers it useful to do so, or when it sees a way to improve its bottom line; often both. Though moral panics are generally not about education directly – with the occasional exception – many of them impact upon education indirectly. Most commentators would agree that the conduct of some elements of the news media has been appalling in relation to its coverage of asylum seekers coming to Australia, and their ongoing vilification into 'folk devils'. This has implications not only for our education system, but also for our status as a civilised and decent nation.

# Conclusion

The news media plays a very important role within our society. Not only does it keep us informed of all the most important events within what is now a global community, as the Fourth Estate, it is also responsible for keeping our organs of government under close scrutiny. A healthy press is often a good sign of a healthy society.

That said, for the most part, the news media is now a business. This has two central implications. First, as a business, the news media is necessarily subject to market forces; or to put it another way, for all the history and idealism that underpins the news media, they now have to make money. As such, the line between news and entertainment no longer exists in the way it once did (or the way we thought it once did), and journalists have to compete for an audience. With this competition comes the temptation to pander to the worst aspects of our natures; bad news sells, conflict sells, simplicity sells … so perhaps it is not surprising that we get so many stories with simplistically drawn villains, in constant struggle with 'good' people like ourselves. So what if it's neither fair nor accurate?

The second implication is that *as* a big business, the news media is owned by powerful corporations, run by powerful individuals. Such individuals have their own agendas and political affiliations, and almost by definition, they have the means to influence public opinion in ways the rest of us can't. This takes the already tenuous notion of 'media objectivity' and makes it almost meaningless.

The truth is, there's not really very much that any of us can do about either of these issues; they reflect the nature of the society we live in. What we can do, however, is to educate ourselves, and our children, about the way the news media works. We can recognise its importance, but equally, understand its frailties, and identify those areas where it often fails to meet our expectations. Just as the media serves the function of holding many of our most important social institutions to account, it is equally important that we also learn the necessary skills to hold the media to account.

# Chapter 8

# Popular culture

This chapter argues that the relationship between popular culture and the classroom remains a contentious issue. Its presence has been used as a symbol of how much our culture has declined, and how educationally corrupted our schools have become, while its absence has been used to suggest our schools are out of touch with their primary constituency – young people. This is not a simple issue to address; even the notion of 'culture' itself is subject to considerable disagreement.

## Myth #1 Popular culture is rubbish – in terms of taste, it's awful; as an object of study, it's irrelevant

*Even though most of us consume various forms of popular culture on a daily basis, we still know it's the media equivalent of junk food; it's not really worth eating, and it's certainly not worth studying.*

The division between 'high' and 'low/popular' culture is largely a false binary, but still one that has significant implications for how we approach our most familiar cultural forms. It is fair to say that the label of 'high' culture is often more about its audience than its content, and that some popular culture can be of great value. Significantly, the academic study of popular culture can tell us much about ourselves as a society.

## Myth #2 Teachers need to be up to date with student cultures

*If you want to connect with students, you have to be able to communicate with them on their cultural terms. If you can't do that, then you won't be an effective teacher.*

This myth operates through the false binary of teacher culture and student culture as mutually exclusive entities. Both groups are consumers of popular culture, and there exist significant areas of overlap as audiences. That said, it is probably useful for teachers to be familiar with various elements of some student cultures, but without therefore having to be consumers of those elements themselves.

## Myth #3 Popular culture has no place in the classroom

*Students get enough of* The Simpsons *at home, so the last thing they need is yet more mindless tosh in the one place where they ought to be learning about the best our culture has to offer.*

This is the final false binary: i.e. either we stick with recognised classics in a traditional curriculum, or we just adopt every bit of popular culture that comes down the pipe. Arguably, popular culture has a place in the classroom if it is used deftly; it can be used to engage students, to develop general learning and reasoning skills, and to illustrate to students how aspects of their identities are often formed from within a vocabulary of choices set out within popular culture.

# Introduction

Snyder's book *The Literacy Wars* (2008), discussed in Chapter 7, addresses the circumstances in which a seemingly minor academic debate over the best way to teach reading to children, came to be represented as a battle for the very soul of Australian education. Largely played out in the Murdoch press, on one side were the noble conservative guardians of all that is good about traditional education, championing 'phonics', and on the other were the 'loony lefties', who advocate 'whole-language teaching'.

This debate is interesting for a number of reasons, but it is particularly important because it speaks to the wider theme of what constitutes, not only the *practice* of a 'good' education, but also the *substance*. Is a classical education, complete with an all-consuming focus on the three Rs, the only way to go, even in the twenty-first century? Do we still have far more to learn from the Elizabethan plays of Shakespeare, than we do from more contemporary forms of entertainment? Certainly, many have no doubt about the value of classical literature, and find it easy to caricature anything that deviates from the orthodoxy:

> Prime Minister John Howard describes some state English curricula as 'incomprehensible sludge' and asserted that 'we are robbing our children of their cultural heritage' because the teaching of English has been allowed to drift into a 'relativist wasteland', where Big Brother or a text message jostles with Shakespeare and classical literature for a place in the English curriculum … (Snyder 2008, 94)

In this manner, the issue is organised as a perfect modernist binary opposition: *either* we have a curriculum full of the classics, *or* we have the serious study of *Australia's Funniest Home Videos* as text – and this is by no means the only binary evident within the field of popular culture and education. Not only is there the explicit division between high and low culture, but also they are allocated the status of either good or bad, which leads to the contention that popular culture either has no place within modern education, or, since it represents the lived culture of the young, it should form the foundation of modern classroom practice.

One of the central problems here is, with all this concern over 'culture', we are often in complete disagreement as to what we mean by the term. There is probably no other concept within the social sciences that can be understood in as many different ways, and causes such discord – a response not limited to university lecturers; as the Nazi poet Johst (1933) once wrote: 'When I hear the word culture, I reach for my gun.'

## What do we mean by 'culture'?

The answer to this question is often based upon the specific discipline from within which it is asked. For example, the most general understanding can be found within anthropology, in which 'culture' is understood as the totality of a society's way of life.

Tyler (1871, 1) offered one of the first definitions, when he stated that culture was 'that complex whole which includes knowledge. Belief, art, morals, law, customs, and any other capabilities and habits acquired by man as a member of society.' To put it more simply, according to this approach, culture is virtually everything that is passed on from one generation to another that isn't biological.

A somewhat more specific usage is to be found within the discipline of sociology. In essence, culture refers to the systems of meaning that arise from within a society. That is, all societies have institutions relating to the family, the law, economics, politics, and so on: their *social structures*. How these structures are interpreted, and how patterns of meaning are organised, varies considerably; the specifics of these variations constitute the society's culture, and would include systems of belief, ethics, rituals and aesthetics (Lee & Newby 1983).

A further influential understanding of culture can be found within Marxism, and its intellectual successor, critical theory. According to these approaches, culture is given its shape by the economic structures and relations that form the foundation of any given society. Importantly, culture is not just a 'given' that emerges full-formed from this foundation, rather is it the product of struggle, in that the culture of the powerful is continually forced to reassert its domination over the cultures of the weak. Apple (1982, 41–2) makes this very point when addressing the role played by mass schools in social reproduction:

> They help maintain privilege in cultural ways by taking the form and content of the culture and knowledge of powerful groups and defining it as legitimate knowledge to be preserved and passed on … Schools, hence, are also agents in the creation and recreation of an effective dominant culture. They teach norms, values, dispositions, and culture that contribute to the ideological hegemony of dominant groups.

The final understanding of culture to be addressed here relates to the assemblage of practices, tastes, and forms of expression that carve out a relatively distinct realm – 'culture' – largely separated from the rest of social life. Williams (1981, 11–12) points to the '*informing spirit* of a whole way of life, which is … most evident in "specifically cultural" activities – a language, styles of art, kinds of intellectual work'. As such, he is clearly delineating this understanding of culture from the broader focus evidenced within other approaches, and it is this understanding of culture that will largely be used within this chapter.

## High and low culture

An important proviso needs to be added to this final understanding of culture. What is normally being referred to here is the notion of 'high culture'. Someone is generally regarded as cultured if they can play an instrument of status like the piano – not the piano accordion – and you also need to be able to play pieces on that instrument that are allocated cultural weight, pieces that reflect refinement and taste; it doesn't count if all you can play are drinking songs.

Underpinning this logic is the binary premise that some cultural forms have intrinsic 'quality', and others, the culture of the masses – popular culture – is shallow and vulgar. Myth #1 addresses the widespread belief that, whatever popular culture is, it isn't really worth worrying about too much. After all, there's Shakespeare and Beethoven, and then there's *Big Brother* and the Eurovision Song Contest.

This myth is extended into the realm of social analysis. After all, who would want to waste their time investigating popular culture? For example, what can we possibly learn from an analysis of the tripe that often passes for entertainment on our TV screens every day? Shouldn't we really be investigating issues of power, governance and identity? Perhaps we can do both.

## Youth culture

It would be a mistake to assume that just as culture can be divided into two opposite values, so too can audiences, with 'high' and 'low' cultures being consumed by 'cultured' and 'uncultured' audiences respectively. Other divisions also appear to mark out the field; one of the most important is the apparent split between the dominant culture and 'youth culture', which almost by definition, is deemed to form the central currency of the mass school.

Myth #2 addresses the belief that, as a result of the existence of this entirely separate and somewhat mysterious phenomenon of 'youth culture', teachers need to school themselves regularly in its ever-changing characteristics if they want to do their jobs effectively. If teachers aren't up to date with what kids are watching on TV, how can they find sufficient common cultural ground to establish an effective pedagogic relationship?

There are a number of assumptions built into these claims; that there is a clear boundary around youth culture; that schools are populated by two categories of person, the young and the old; that the best way to relate to pupils is through utilising elements of their external cultural life; that school children even *want* you to know about the TV they watch and the language they use. After all, is there anything worse than finding out your dad likes the same band you do?

## Popular culture and the school

This represents the final major binary associated with this area; the binary alluded to in the start of this introduction. Myth #3 asserts that low culture – popular culture – has no place within the school. Schools should be about coming to terms with the highlights of the Western canon, with the complexities of human nature as laid bare by the great writers and artists of the last 500 years. Students get enough popular culture outside the boundaries of the school. They don't need any more, and besides, there is absolutely nothing of value to be learned from *Twilight*.

Arguably, this is not an either/or situation, in spite of the way the debate is often presented in the media. Popular culture can find a place in the classroom, not necessarily at the expense of more familiar staples within the English curriculum, for example, but rather as an addition. Popular culture can be used to engage students where they otherwise may be uninterested; it may be used as part of the process of decoding what students see and hear, as discussed with the news media in Chapter 7; it may also be used as part of illustrating how contemporary identities, including the identities of the students themselves, are shaped by the various elements of the cultures they consume, and with which they interact (White & Walker 2008).

To summarise, the three myths to be dealt with in this chapter are:

**Myth #1** – Popular culture is rubbish – in terms of taste, it's awful; as an object of study, it's irrelevant

**Myth #2** – Teachers need to be up to date with student cultures

**Myth #3** – Popular culture has no place in the classroom

# Myth #1 Popular culture is rubbish – in terms of taste, it's awful; as an object of study, it's irrelevant

Even though most of us probably watch a fair bit of television, for the most part, we know it's generally depressingly lowbrow – after all, *South Park* isn't exactly Shakespeare. The same goes for the music we hear on the radio; it's formulaic rubbish; some of it may be catchy, but it's hardly going to stand the test of time. Besides, all you need to make it are three chords and a drum machine. And surely our university academics have better things to do with their time than investigate what is, for the most part, just faddish drivel.

We all know that there are some great novels out there: Joyce's *Ulysses* (1922), Proust's *Remembrance of Things Past* (1927), Tolstoy's *War and Peace* (1886). These are long, complex and nuanced works of art; most of us have never read any of them, but we know they represent something important. They are deemed to be part of a canon of literature, representing the best of Western culture.

Wildly popular though they are, Brown's *The Da Vinci Code* (2003) is not on this list, and neither is Collins' *The Hunger Games* (2008). They are considered to be something else. They are manifestations of a lower form of culture – popular yes, but lacking the beauty, depth and originality necessary for the novels to be considered works of art, to be considered genuine timeless classics.

We may take this division for granted, but who gets to make this assessment? Who gets to say that *Ulysses* is 'literature', and *The Da Vinci Code* isn't? Indeed, what does this division even represent, and where does it come from? Is it *real*, in any objective sense of the word?

# The invention of high culture

Nearly 2500 years ago, when Plato set out the subject matter for an appropriate education in *The Republic* (1974), he not only listed those areas crucial to a good education, such as astronomy, geometry and gymnastics, he also made it very clear as to what should be left out. There would be no place in Plato's idealised society for poets and painters, as their endeavours were not focused on the search for truth; rather, they were simply engaged in the act of imitation. That is, the emphasis on appearance lacks the philosophical weight of a genuine quest for truth, and hence they should be banned from the city. Weaver regards this as a vital moment in the development of contemporary understandings of culture:

> It is with Plato's quest to ban poets and painters from the Republic that marks the first attempt to demarcate between Culture and popular culture … For Plato, the poet offers nothing to elevate society, instead he will only pander to the lowly tastes and desires of the masses (2009, 3–4).

Weaver goes on to note that Plato is far from the only great philosopher who shares distaste for the cultural pursuits of 'the masses'. He cites Rousseau, Kant and Schiller, who, at various times, all expressed concern over the corrosive and stupefying effects of what then might have been called 'popular culture'. Kant (1979) was particularly pointed in his observations, regarding the masses as too ill-educated and base to be able to tell the difference between cultural forms with legitimate aesthetic and intellectual value, and those that, while entertaining, are ultimately worthless.

Probably the most influential text speaking to the divide between high and low culture is Arnold's *Culture and Anarchy* (1963). Written in England in 1869 at the height of the industrial revolution, Arnold was horrified by both the rise of a new type of society that seemed only interested in wealth and power, and by the most conspicuous leaders of this new social order, the newly rich merchants and mill owners, whom he regarded as 'barbarians'. Arnold wrote of about the civilising power of culture, by which he meant 'a pursuit of our total perfection by means of getting to know, on all the matters which most concern us, the best which has been thought and said in the world' (1963, 3). Thus, it would be through developing an appreciation for the classics of the liberal arts tradition that more complete individuals could be moulded, and hence a better society produced.

Arnold's ideas on the value of high culture have proven to be both durable and influential over the ensuing 150 years. Not only does it continue to lay the foundation for the emergence of texts such as Bloom's (1987) *The Closing of the American Mind* – a best-selling book which bemoans the abandonment of traditional high cultural forms by America's elite, and champions, in the style of Arnold, a list of 'great books' that must be read – it also continues to influence media discourse on the subject of popular culture and education here in Australia. As part of the *Australian*'s campaign for 'traditional education', Donnelly stressed the vital importance of the Western literary cannon: 'from Greek tragedy to Shakespeare, from Jane Austin to David Malouf' (2005a, 13).

Donnelly's complaint here appears to be twofold: first, that when classical literature is found in the school curriculum, it is no longer to be simply read and appreciated, as was once the case; it is now subject to the undignified, progressive process of postmodern 'deconstruction', wherein the text is interrogated for all manner of hidden elements. Second, other, less worthy texts are finding their way onto the curriculum, texts which can only be described as part of 'popular culture'.

## The arrival of popular culture

The notion of 'popular culture' is just as complex and as contested as its larger sibling, 'culture'. Whereas apprehension over the cultural shortcomings of the working classes has a very long history, as discussed above, the first theoretical concerns over 'the culture of the people' became manifest with a focus upon 'folk culture', an idealised version of quasi-rural life, focusing on the songs, stories and rituals of ordinary, non-elite life (Burke 1996). In many ways, this creation differs markedly from the notion of 'popular culture', 'folk culture' generally conjures up images of medieval dancing, traditional craftwork, and songs with phrases like 'Fie diddly oh' in them. These cultures are romantically regarded as having emerged organically from their host societies, passed down through generations – and centuries – and as such the cultures have specific meaning and resonance.

Arguably, 'popular culture' represents something else altogether. It is the product of new types of social organisation and technology. Though the rise of radio, movies, and eventually television, individual examples of particular cultural forms – songs, films, television programs – could be popularised almost immediately, and almost globally, in ways that were impossible at the beginning of the twentieth century. For example, within days of becoming popular in America, George Cohen's song 'Give my Regards to Broadway' could be hummed by people in Manchester, Sydney and Auckland, by people who didn't even have the faintest idea where Broadway was.

This leads on to another important point about poplar culture. It was no longer rooted within the host culture itself; rather it could increasingly trace its origins back to the United States. After all, not only were the most prolific examples of the new media forms based in the United States – Hollywood, most of the popular music industry, the most powerful television networks – but also American economic might acted as a co-partner in the exportation of American culture to the world, with the global familiarity of Coca-Cola, Levis jeans, and Marlboro (Schiller 1979). In many ways, the new creation of 'popular culture' bore, and continues to bear, an uncanny resemblance to American culture.

Of course, popular culture extends beyond *The Da Vinci Code* and rock'n'roll; it takes an incredibly wide range of forms, extending from the relatively obvious, to the subtle and the indirect. Popular culture extends beyond self-evident components such as fashion styling, television programming and the content of magazines. In a time where actions and ideas can be broadcast and popularised globally within a few hours, it is also evidenced through less tangible elements, such as in the choice of leisure activities (dance styles or beer selection), the embracing of particular types of belief (One Direction are the most attractive and talented human beings who ever lived), and the adoption of particular codes of speech ('Australian Questioning Intonation' – i.e. continually raising vocal pitch at the end of sentences – or saying 'like' instead of 'um'). Arguably, all of these are part of contemporary popular culture, or are directly constituted by it.

Having drawn some conclusions about the origins and parameters of popular culture, other questions begin to arise: how can we are conceptualise this relatively new phenomenon? What are the theoretical tools available to us? How can we place it in relation to other associated concepts, such as 'high culture', consumer society, social class and postmodernity?

## Some theories of popular culture

When addressing the question, 'So what is popular culture?', the most obvious answer is: those cultural forms which people like. Clearly, this doesn't really take us anywhere. More complex and satisfying answers have been proposed utilising a wide range of theories, from within an almost equally wide range of disciplinary starting points – cultural studies, sociology, philosophy, psychology, history, English – and all continue to have something to say about the subject. This section will address four of the most influential.

## Popular culture: the 'other' of high culture

The ideas of Arnold, discussed earlier, eventually spawned a coherent theoretical approach usually referred to as *Leavisism,* after its driving intellectual force, F.R. Leavis. In books such as *Mass Civilisation and Minority Culture* (1930), Leavis argues that the social elite – who had always dictated cultural tastes; indeed, they had regarded themselves as 'the guardians' of culture – were no longer venerated by their social inferiors, as had traditionally been the case. One of the consequences of this decline in respect for the ruling classes was a parallel decline in respect for the cultural forms they championed. Importantly, these forms of culture were regarded as 'better' than those enjoyed by the uneducated masses. As Leavis and Thompson (1977, 3) state:

> Upon the minority depends our power of profiting by the finest human experience of the past: they keep alive the subtlest and most perishable part of tradition. Upon them depend the implicit standards that order the finer living of an age …

Leavis believed it possible to discern objectively, for example, which literature meets the necessary criteria to be considered of value. All the others could then be grouped together as 'popular culture' – the mindless dross of the common people, pander-ing to the simplest of emotions – and the rise of which, according to Leavis, clearly represented a culture in intellectual and moral decline. It is the limited social access to 'high culture' that ties in with Bourdieu's notion of cultural capital, discussed in Chapter 1. That is, those who understand high cultural forms, who have the background to appreciate it and to use it, are able to translate this capacity into social and educational advantage.

Probably needless to say, the Leavisite position – 'high culture is better' – has been subject to considerable criticism; indeed, it acts as a counterpoint to almost all the approaches to popular culture. Many would argue that this theory is underpinned by a romantic nostalgia for a largely mythic past, and yet in spite of this fundamental flaw, it has constituted a remarkably persistent theoretical position, struggling only recently in the face of explanations emanating from cultural studies (Patterson 2008).

## Popular culture as mass culture

A second theoretical position on popular culture in some ways takes an almost diametrically opposite viewpoint from that of the theory above. The most logical way to disagree with Leavis surely would be to reject the notion that there exist objective criteria for assessing the worth of cultural forms. However, the advocates of the 'mass culture' position do not specifically disagree with the Leavisite contention that popular culture is mostly formulaic nonsense; their disagreement lies in their assessment of the implications of mass culture.

The Leavisites regarded popular culture as a threat to the power of the ruling classes. Popular culture was seen to represent a rejection of not only the high cultural forms of the ruling elites, it also represented a rejection of the authority that underpinned those forms. The 'mass culture' position argues the opposite. Writers like Adorno and Horkheimer (1979) suggest that the stultifying and conformist aspects of mass culture produce a desensitised, depoliticised, and easily manipulated population. These arguments are paraphrased by Storey (2003, 29):

> The function of the culture industry is, ultimately, to organise leisure time in the same way as industrialisation has organised work. Work under capitalism stunts the senses; the culture industry continues the process.

Thus the magazines, music and movies that constitute the bulk of popular culture are not designed to stimulate thought; they are there for passive consumption. Artistic and creative merit is all but irrelevant; the issue is conformity.

This understanding of popular culture constitutes a perfect example of a modernist approach to social analysis. There is a single truth to be uncovered, from within a single explanatory framework, a framework that can explain everything – a master discourse – and consequently this explanation has been criticised for all the reasons modernism has been criticised: it is reductionist, it is deterministic, and it is homogenising.

## Popular culture as resistance

The writers of the influential Centre for Contemporary Cultural Studies in Birmingham (CCCS) did not accept that the population were simply victims of some kind of 'popular culture conspiracy'. While they agreed that there was certainly a mass culture industry, they contended that different groups found space for themselves within these prevailing models, and by struggling against their *cultural hegemony* – their often-unspoken cultural dominance – they gained some measure of autonomy. It should be pointed out that they did not see popular culture as any kind of real threat to the social order, as did Leavis, and they certainly didn't think that high culture was somehow intrinsically better.

As discussed in Chapter 6, the CCCS focused mostly upon youth culture. It contended that youth subcultures were stylised responses to the dominant social order, and through the process of *bricolage*, such cultures could take bits and pieces from the dominant culture and endow them with new meaning: the Union Jack worn by Mods in the 1960s had little or nothing to do with patriotism. Consequently, popular culture is not 'the other' of high culture, and neither is it 'the opiate of the masses', rather it can be understood as offering the potential for a form of cultural independence, a place where non-elites can, in part, take material that appeal to them, and shape a culture of their own.

This approach does not escape all of the criticisms levelled at the mass culture model, however it moves some distance from the reductionist position of Adorno and Horkheimer. As was argued in Chapter 6, equating youth with resistance brings with it problems of its own, and suggesting that popular culture somehow necessarily contains the seeds of resistance, when taken outside the realm of youth subcultures, can be regarded as equally problematic.

## Popular culture and postmodernity

As has been discussed at various points throughout this book, postmodernity offers a viable alternative to the approaches taken by modernist sociologies, and the issue of popular culture is no exception. Rather than looking for the truth of popular culture, for an objective standard by which it can be measured, or for the key to understanding how its messages are to be interpreted, those studying popular culture from this perspective face a more difficult task.

Postmodern accounts of popular culture can be understood as having a number of features. First, there is no single explanation of popular culture to be had; postmodernism did not criticise the master discourses of modernity, only to then replace them with one of its own. Postmodern accounts are necessarily contingent, dynamic and partial, after all, arguably there is no fixed, stable and complete story to tell.

Second, postmodernism argues for the abandonment of the binary between high and popular culture:

> Perhaps the most significant thing about postmodernism for the student of popular culture is the dawning recognition that there is no absolute categorical difference between high and popular culture. This is not to say that one text or practice might not be 'better' (for what/for who, etc., must always be decided and made clear) than any other text or practice. But it is to say that there are no easy reference points … (Storey 2006, 146)

That is, not only are high and popular culture now relatively arbitrary categories, they can also lead to the questionable conclusion that high culture is somehow good, and popular culture is inevitably bad, and this is by no means the case. There are forms of popular culture that could arguably pass any kind of Leavisite test of inherent quality, whether this involves popular music (The Beatles, Stevie Wonder), Hollywood movies (*Casablanca, Pulp Fiction*), or television programs (*M.A.S.H., The Sopranos*). Insert you own favourites here.

Third, postmodern accounts of popular culture can be characterised by recognition that the process of decoding messages from cultural media is no less important than the initial process of encoding them; there is no 'correct' reading to be uncovered, just as there is no fixed and predictable idealised audience, who will interpret the messages as they were intended to be interpreted. Audiences are plural and fluid, and they create meaning for themselves – perhaps an extension of the process of *bricolage* mentioned above.

Finally, these postmodern interpretations arguably describe a thoroughly postmodern world, at least in the West. According to Baudrillard (1983), we now live in a society characterised by hyper-reality, a realm where, largely thanks to television, fact and fiction are no longer separate entities, where chains of signification refer to nothing but themselves, and where copies are made without the existence of an original (simulacra). For example, thanks primarily to the crime drama *CSI*, some juries are now asking for forensic evidence to be supplied in trials in order to reach a conviction, even where it is irrelevant – a phenomenon now referred to as the 'CSI effect' (Carpenter & Tait 2010). Likewise, Fettes College, one of the most prestigious schools in Scotland, now promotes itself as being like Hogwarts. The shortcomings of postmodern theory, and hence also of postmodern analyses of popular culture, are discussed in Chapter 10.

In summary, the assertion that popular culture is rubbish, and conceptually irrelevant, makes a lot of assumptions, most of which do not hold up to contemporary analysis. First, contending that popular culture is awful is normally premised upon a comparison with the supposed excellence of high culture, or to put it another way, is premised upon the modernist binary: high/good, popular/bad. Second, it is a gross generalisation to categorise all popular culture as worthless; certainly, some of it is formulaic and mindless, but in a similar vein, not all classical music is good, just because it's classical. Finally, the study of popular culture is far from irrelevant; over the last 50 years, cultural studies, and the study of popular culture in particular, has told us a lot about how our society works, and a lot about ourselves.

# Myth #2 Teachers need to be up to date with student cultures

One of the most important requirements for being a good teacher is to be able to relate to the students, and the only way that can be done is to speak the same cultural language as them. It's no use at all if a student talks about the things that interest them – their media interests, their musical tastes, their styles of dress, their specific ways of understanding the world – and the teacher can't contribute to the conversation, then the game is over before it's even really started.

There is no doubt that an important part of teaching involves the construction of a pedagogical relationship between the teacher and the pupil. Ideally, this relationship includes such features as mutual trust and respect, shared goals, good communication, enjoyment and positivity. The question here is: should it also necessarily involve shared frames of cultural reference? Should it involve teachers keeping up to date with youth cultures?

## From popular culture to youth culture

The arguments in the last section lead to the conclusion that there is no clear binary between high culture and popular culture, and that while social-class based patterns of consumption do still exist (Bennett et al. 2008), these are not exclusive divisions, with the ruling elites only listening to opera and visiting art galleries, while the common people only watch *Australian Idol* and hang velveteen prints of Elvis on their walls. Just as popular culture is not a discrete category, clearly demarcated from high culture, we can draw similar conclusions about a familiar sub-set of popular culture: that of 'youth culture'. But where did youth culture come from?

The concept of youth has been discussed at length in Chapter 6, however it would be productive at this point to remind ourselves of a number of arguments about how it came to take its present form. First, there is nothing natural about this category. Like childhood, it came into being as a consequence of quite ordinary and seemingly unrelated social changes. Whereas childhood emerged, in part, as a result of inventions such as the printing press (Postman 1994), youth appeared at the end of a long chain of previous categories of pre-adulthood, such as the child, the juvenile delinquent, the adolescent and the teenager. As noted earlier, according to Cashmore (1984) youth initially developed in the early 1950s, both as a result of the demise of national service, and also as a result of the purchasing power of a newly affluent section of the population – too old to be at school, readily employed and cashed up, too young and having too much fun to be married.

Second, and running in tandem with the appearance of this new 'stage of life' – and having significant feedback loops into it – was the parallel appearance of a culture to go along with the category. Indeed, perhaps the two are, in some ways, inseparable: it is the category that shapes the culture, which continually reshapes our understanding of the category. That is, the ability of the young to buy the objects and artefacts that interested them almost immediately spawned the category of youth, as well as a youth market, which in turn formed the foundations of a youth culture: music, fashion, identity.

Finally, it has been suggested that, to go along with this new category, there developed a 'generational consciousness', a consciousness of youth. This contention formed one of the central elements of the CCCS approach to culture discussed in the last section. The CCCS argued that from the 1950s onwards, youth as a group started to perceive itself as intrinsically different from the parent generation. So even though they shared the same fundamental material conditions as their parents, they experienced those conditions in a somewhat different manner. The writers of the CCCS suggest that the new consciousness of youth is best understood in relation to the life areas of education, work and leisure, with each of these areas having the tendency to reinforce notions of the relative autonomy of youth as a category.

It is important to note that before this time, young people – people who would later be categorised as youth – shared the same culture as their parents, be that some nebulous version of folk culture, popular culture, or even elite culture. Young people did not dress differently, listen to different music, seek to purchase different material goods, or develop a different habitus. The idea that of course young people must have their own culture is a relatively recent invention.

## A closer look at 'youth culture'

The myth driving this section of the chapter is that teachers need to be up to date with where their students are at; that teachers need to be plugged in to youth culture if they are going to be effective in their job. It is no longer acceptable just to be able to teach maths well; you have to be able to engage learners on their own terrain, and that terrain is cultural. However, this myth is based upon a number of faulty assumptions.

## A monolithic understanding of culture

The first premise is that there is a single, monolithic youth culture that teachers need to get to know. Imagining that there is a unitary set of practices, social references, forms of self-shaping, and cultural interests, is to ignore all the different groups, and varying degrees of affiliation to those groups, that exist within a school. Which one is *the* youth culture that teachers are supposed to get to know? There is no global, totalised entity that can be called youth culture, really any more than there is its singular mental equivalent – youth consciousness.

A more postmodern approach to youth involves not only recognising that youth is a plural category from the very beginning, but also that even if one culture were picked to represent all youth cultures – some kind of 'average' youth culture – this culture would not have clearly delineated boundaries that mark it out from all other cultures; neither would it have a fixed membership, that you were either part of, or were not; and nor would membership always mean the same thing to everyone. The idea doesn't really hold up to scrutiny.

## Binary #1 Either you know youth culture, or you don't

This myth is founded on the assumption that either you are up to date with youth culture, or you aren't; either you can function effectively within the knowledge-world of the young, or you can't. Premised upon the (erroneous) validity of the first assumption, this means that good teachers can understand and access youth culture, and bad teachers are excluded from it, and that is part of what makes them bad.

A more convincing argument would be to point out that knowledge does not work in this way. All social knowledge is partial, fluid and context-bound, and understanding that some young boys spend a lot of time playing *Call of Duty* or *World of Warcraft* on their computers – and can build a culture around this activity – does not mean that teachers have to play the game themselves, or even know how to play it, in order to know what the game is, and what it can mean to those involved. There are always going to be different levels of knowledge of 'youth culture'; this myth simply draws a line in the sand between knowledge and ignorance, and pretends it isn't arbitrary.

## Binary #2 Youth culture vs adult culture

The main faulty component of this myth is the distinction drawn between youth culture and broader, adult culture. These are presented as separate, autonomous domains, and knowledge of one has no relation to having any knowledge in the other; or more specifically, just because teachers are embedded in the wider popular culture, gives them no insight into the unrelated cultural universe of the young.

Except, these are not two entirely autonomous domains. Much of youth culture is drawn from the broader field of popular culture. Indeed, young people watch many of the same television programs and movies that adults watch. These are hybrid cultures, drawing their component parts, sometimes from the same pool, sometimes from different pools; sometimes extracting the same meanings, sometimes creating their own. Once again, the division is often arbitrary and contingent.

## Youth culture and inclusivity

The final problem with this myth involves the idea that young people unequivocally welcome the presence of adults within their cultural universe. Just because a teacher might know enough about some aspects of a given youth cultural form to warrant insider status, does not mean that the teacher will actually be allowed inside, or should go there even if they were.

According to the CCCS, youth subcultures are constructed, in part, as resistance to the dominant social order (Hall & Jefferson 1976). If we accept this proposition (and it does have its flaws), young people find space for themselves through the cultures they construct. Youths often regard themselves as excluded and powerless within the context of adult cultures – so they make their own. Arguably, allowing access to outsiders defeats the object of having the culture in the first place. Would it really be a 'youth culture' if lots of teachers were tramping around inside it?

## A worked example: The Goths

A good way to illustrate the arguments outlined above is through a specific youth subculture; an appropriate example is the Goths. Goths have been around as a subculture for over 30 years, and their appearance is instantly recognisable: 'They wear black: black clothes, long back-combed hair, black lipstick, eye make-up and nail varnish. Faces are as pale as possible' (Lees 1988, 7).

The very existence of the Goths rebuts the first faulty assumption of this myth: that there is a single youth culture that teachers need to get to know. Goths are just one of a plethora of youth subcultures, many of which are not even discernable from their physical appearance alone (what do *Call of Duty* players look like, other than the fact most are male?). Furthermore, the Goth subculture has itself been divided into a range of sub-subcultures, such as New Gothics and MiniGothics, a differentiation often based upon issues such as age, various specificities of dress, the length of time a person has been a Goth, and the perceived degree of affiliation to the subculture. So just as there is no single youth culture, there is not even a single Goth subculture. Unitary understandings and explanations of these categories simply don't work.

Likewise, the presumption is that teachers either know all about Goths, or they know nothing. Basic logic dictates that it is perfectly possible to know and recognise Goth-inspired dress codes, and to understand aspects of Goth identity formation and persona, without knowing the domain names for Goth websites, or having to listen to the Cure, the Sisters of Mercy, or Siouxsie and the Banshees. The binary of knowing/ not knowing breaks down before it even really gets started.

The second binary is the mutually exclusive distinction between adult and youth culture, or in this case, between dominant culture and Goth culture, and once again, the binary breaks down completely. After all, the notion of 'the Gothic' began in wider, adult culture, and only mutated into a youth subculture some 1000 years later. Leaving aside the Germanic peoples of antiquity who sacked Rome, the term originated as a disparaging, Renaissance way of describing non-classical architecture (Germann 1972). The Gothic revival of the eighteenth and ninteenth centuries was closely tied to the rise of the romantic movement, and extended beyond the architectural into the literary, with the 'Gothic Mood' informing poetry and the new literary form – the novel (Clark 1978). This mood emphasised a number of familiar motifs, such as the macabre, repressed desire, isolated settings, innocent young women, and a man with sinister secrets.

Interestingly, some of our greatest 'high culture' literature is, if not Gothic in its entirety, certainly informed by the Gothic Mood. Leaving aside Bram Stoker's *Dracula* (1897), and Edgar Allen Poe's *Fall of the House of Usher* (1839) as two obvious examples, other high culture classics might include Emily Brontë's *Wuthering Heights* (1846), Charlotte Brontë's *Jane Eyre* (1847) and Oscar Wilde's *The Picture of Dorian Gray* (1891). The point here is that contemporary Goth culture does not exist as a discrete entity, entirely removed from dominant adult culture; the two draw from the same well. In fact, not only are dominant models of popular culture quick to employ Gothic symbolism on a regular basis (the *Batman* movies – Gotham City anyone?), but so too are our exemplars of high culture.

Finally, there is the issue of the exclusivity of youth subcultures. Would the Goth subculture survive as part of the romantic fashioning of youthful identity, if a number of teachers started dressing all in black, with long black hair, and white pancake make-up? – assuming they would still have a job. There wouldn't be a single Goth left in school by the end of the first week.

In summary, every time there is a call for teachers to be more 'down with the culture of the kids', the questions should arise: Which kids? Which culture? Which parts of which culture? All teachers can do is to try and understand and recognise as many of the broad brush strokes of the cultures they find in their classroom, and manoeuvre their way through and around them as best they can; and within this context, structure the best pedagogic relationships they can.

# Myth #3 Popular culture has no place in the classroom

Have we really come to the point where texts that have stood the test of time, such as Shakespeare's *Romeo and Juliet* or *Macbeth*, have been replaced in the curriculum by whichever 'text' is currently in fashion? Surely some intrinsic underlying value has to be present in a book before it's worth presenting to our children. Nobody is going to be talking about *Twilight* in 10 years' time, not teenage girls, not cultural studies lecturers, nobody. So why teach about it now?

According to this myth, our schools have all but abandoned the literary classics, and we are now teaching, with a straight face, whatever happens to be the latest pulp novel at the top of the airport shelves. After all, when the Leavisite approach to culture was finally defeated in our universities, all notions of 'literary worth' went down with it. Consequently, we are as likely to study articles from women's magazines, as we are to study *Macbeth*. We are no longer supposed to enjoy reading books for the pleasure they may give us, we are supposed to 'interrogate' books for hidden meanings and power structures.

The trouble is, this just simply isn't the case. As discussed in Chapter 7, this straw man argument appears primarily designed to whip up a public support for a return to the good old days of a 1950s education. Apart from the claims made by a few articles in the *Australian,* the evidence suggests that the literary cannon is as much a part of the curriculum as ever. Also, as Snyder (2008, 90) states: 'In every English syllabus in every state, literature is studied not just for its social import but also for its aesthetic and ethical qualities and for the sheer pleasure of reading.'

Of course, this myth also implies that old literature is good, and that anything new finding a place in the school curriculum, must therefore be bad/pulp. Consequently, the literary canon can have the appearance of being 'frozen in time'. As discussed in myth #1, there are surely recent examples of literature that would pass the Leavisite test of quality; it would be a foolhardy traditionalist who considered Salman Rushdie's *Midnight's Children* (1981), or Gabrielle Garcia Marquez's *One Hundred Years of Solitude* (1970) as unworthy of inclusion.

So does this mean there is no debate to be had about popular culture in the classroom? And where does the notion of 'literary worth' fit into this debate? There are still a number of issues to be addressed regarding the link between literary worth and popular culture, and in truth, these have not always been restricted to the opinion pages of the Murdoch press. In *High Culture, Popular Culture*, Goodall (1995) suggests that the notion of 'literary worth' is a difficult one, and contends that just as the preoccupation with high culture accelerated the downfall of the traditional study of English, then so too might the refusal to engage with the issue of 'value' prove to be the undoing of cultural studies. That is, by refusing to rule on the worth of various examples of popular culture, by refusing to delineate its boundaries clearly, it is in danger of becoming everything and nothing. As Goodall (1995, 172–173) states:

> A 'Cultural' studies which feels it is able to ignore high art, Culture with a capital C … seems to me to be a fatally compromised project. While the notion of a study of texts, unworried and undifferentiated by any notions about quality, in their broad discursive contexts, has much to recommend it, one must point out at the same time, what is lost in the abandonment of the aesthetic dimension in the study of the text.

Goodall cites Eagleton (1983), one of the foremost advocates of the cultural studies position, who rightly notes that part of the problem lies in the fact that traditional literary criticism cannot justify restricting its scope to works of 'value', when it is part of the process by which they are allocated 'value' in the first place – a perfect example of a self-fulfilling prophesy. Eagleton has a point.

All this leads to one of several options when trying to conceptualise the high/popular culture divide, as it pertains to the curriculum. The first is to retreat into

Leavisism; it would certainly make the *Australian* happy. We can pretend that 30 years of postmodernity has never happened, and return to the modernist belief that there is an inherent truth to a text; that literary qualities are timeless and a-contextual; and that such qualities can be objectively assessed, ranked and passed on uncritically to yet another schooling generation.

Second, we can abandon the notion of 'value' altogether. It certainly is complex and, at times, seemingly completely arbitrary. Is it the place of teachers to tell children why one book is good, and another isn't? – as if the issue of personal taste doesn't exist – and why one cultural form is good, and another isn't? We were once told Elvis Presley's music wasn't just bad; it was evil. Whatever happened to that? The trouble with this position is that it falls relatively easily to a *reduction ad absurdum* argument: are we really ready to accept that *Hamlet* has no more intrinsic artistic value than some beer commercial – both are 'texts', after all. Is anyone *really* suggesting we go down this path? (That said, it can sometimes be quite instructional to study a good example of a bad example.)

Perhaps a third option is to begin by pointing out that the notion of 'value' is a difficult one. It is always constituted in terms of specific genre; it has currency at particular times and in particular places; it necessarily has its own history as a scale of assessment; and it is contingent upon who is making that assessment and why. Concluding that *Romeo and Juliet* belongs in the English curriculum and *The Da Vinci Code* doesn't, should perhaps be based upon making these sorts of judgements explicit; perhaps this is how the notion of 'value' can be salvaged. The funny thing is, it sounds very like the way the issue is currently dealt with in schools already.

## Three approaches to popular culture in the classroom

So having concluded that the binary between 'Popular culture is bad; we need the classics,' and 'The high/popular culture divide is an illusion, so anything goes,' is itself an illusion, how can we go about managing the relationship between popular culture and the classroom? White and Walker (2008) make three main suggestions.

## Education via popular culture

Most people would agree with the contention that education should be interesting and engaging; too many are likely to remember their own school days as exactly the opposite: boring, repetitive and irrelevant. Using popular culture in the classroom is one way teachers have attempted to make a connection with pupils who might otherwise remain disconnected, not only from the material normally utilised, but also from the entire schooling process. If students are at least listening, then surely they are part of the way to learning.

What may seem to be a no-brainer – using resources that engage with the students – is not without its critics. Needless to say, there are those traditionalists for whom the use of popular culture in the classroom is completely unacceptable, irrespective of its purpose; these opinions have already been addressed in some detail. Then there are those who regard education as an unwaveringly serious business, and as such, there can be no place for the triviality that comes with popular culture:

> A common sentiment among administrators and other school officials is that schools are for work and not for fun. The idea of barring fun from the school day seems to be gaining momentum, compelled by the 'north-bound high-stakes testing train'. It is common knowledge that it is easier to get on board that train than it is to stand in front of it …(White & Walker 2008, 16–17)

In spite of this, popular culture can be employed to teach everything from geography (Bell & Gropshover 2005) to business (Kneavel 2005). Indeed, the use of science fiction to engage students in the study of science has proven to be particularly successful (Gough 1993; Weaver, Anijar & Daspit 2004). Reworkings of classic texts, but modelled from within popular culture, are also effective within the teaching of English, whether directly, as in Baz Luhrmann's *Romeo + Juliet*, or indirectly, such as *Macbeth* via films like Brian De Palma's *Scarface*.

One further criticism raised regarding the use of popular media in the curriculum involves the possibility of rendering popular culture 'neutral' in the process of knowledge production. That is, by employing popular culture in an uncritical manner, simply to hold student attention, or to make other kinds of unrelated educational points, there runs the risk of reinforcing the belief that such messages have an inherent natural validity, and are therefore unworthy of scrutiny in their own right. This concern is precisely the issue for the second approach to popular culture in the classroom.

## Popular culture and social decoding

One of the most widely proffered reasons for addressing popular culture in the classroom relates to concerns over its effects on young people. As such, popular culture is not employed as a way of engaging students with the curriculum; it *is* the curriculum. The life-worlds of young people are shaped within the relentless contexts of popular culture – television, film, music, magazines, the internet, fashion – and it is important that they are able to make sense of the messages they receive.

This issue has already been addressed in Chapter 7, on the importance of possessing the skills to decode the media, and the arguments here are essentially the same. The issues of genre, selection, production, language choice, and bias are as relevant here as they are when listening to the news. For example, consumer culture (arguably inexorably intertwined with popular culture) largely provides the vocabulary through which young people assemble their identities. That is, by choosing one form of self-representation over another, by buying certain commodities, by reading particular magazines or listening to particular kinds of music, chosen identities are shaped and reshaped (Miller & Rose 1990, 25). Arguably, it is important for those engaged in this process – 'the artful assembly of a lifestyle put together though the world of goods' – to at least be taught about the rules of the game.

## Education, popular culture and complexity

This approach to popular culture seeks to address how the texts of popular culture can be interpreted in different ways; how we are positioned and shaped by its influence; and how our subjectivities are organised through complex relations of power. The issue here is not simply to present the skills to decode popular culture; it is about allowing students to participate more effectively in the fluid and reflexive processes of textual analysis, interpretation and, ultimately, enjoyment. This approach to understanding the relationship between education and popular culture is postmodern to its very core.

And it is this approach to the use of popular culture that seems to irritate the *Australian* so much. White and Walker contextualise this irritation by linking it back to an unapologetically modernist understanding of the function of education. This approach believes that schools should restrict their curricula to the basics – the three Rs, classic literature, and preparation for work. What constitutes real knowledge is virtually self-evident; there are not multiple readings of texts, there is the correct one, which students will be informed of by the teacher. Defoe's *Robinson Crusoe* can't be read as a metaphor about colonialism; it's simply an adventure story about a brave sailor and his uncivilised black friend.

Some of those who think that schools should play a more complex and challenging role have suggested that popular culture may have a useful role to play in this process. Furthermore, this more challenging view of education is not simply about reading texts from a wider range of sources, and with greater insight; it is also about expanding the ethical possibilities of schooling. As White and Walker (2008, 26) state:

> By learning to read texts from a variety of viewpoints, students can develop literacies that value difference, and can use the awareness of difference in creating a moral vision that a single perspective can never offer.

In summary, culture is a moveable feast, whatever label is placed upon it: high, popular, youth, folk. None of these are set in stone, and yet, when it comes to choice of material for our schools, it seems that some voices would have us do precisely that. It seems strange to limit ourselves to a choice of texts that no longer necessarily reflect who we now are as a community, or what we are interested in, or what we consider worthy. We do not have to abandon the notion of 'value', just because we may choose to step outside someone's idea of the literary canon. We do not have fall into a postmodern Neverland, just because we accept that texts may be understood in more than one way.

# Conclusion

This entire area, though thoroughly colonised by postmodern thought, still seems to find itself shoehorned into modernist binaries when it comes to wider fields of debate.

The list is quite impressive: high vs popular culture; adult culture vs youth culture; popular culture is good vs it's worthless; teachers need to know about youth culture vs no, they don't; finally, popular culture belongs in the classroom vs no, it doesn't.

Every time we see one of these reductionist and homogenising binaries, we should pause and reflect on the complexity of the issues we are dealing with. Part of the problem lies in the fact that the two different sides of these binaries represent competing views about the future of Australian education. One side represents a traditionalist view of what counts as a good education, the view that what constitutes an appropriate curriculum does not change with the seasons. The other represents the view that this type of education harks back to a romantic myth about our schools that only ever had limited purchase on reality; it also contends that we now live in a complex social and cultural world, and our education system needs to be able to prepare students for it.

Perhaps if we point to the artifice of these binaries for long enough, we can go some way towards removing them from the field of debate between competing models of education; and if so, perhaps we can find a role for popular culture within the classroom that can be valued by everyone.

# Chapter 9

# Technology

This chapter argues that the advent of contemporary information and communication technologies is normally presented as one of the great success stories of contemporary schooling, and while it has the potential to be a transformative force within education, the issues are complex and the outcomes far from certain. The field is often divided into those who grew up with such technologies – digital natives/students – and those who have come to these technologies at a later date – digital immigrants/ teachers. This binary articulates a central problem within a power relation where teachers are normally expected to know more than those they teach.

Furthermore, such new technologies do not simply represent mechanisms for accessing more information, more quickly, and in more interesting ways. By stepping outside the domain of traditional linear texts, traditional understandings of literacy start to lose their meaning. New digital technologies necessitate the adoption of the notion of 'multiliteracies', a plural understanding of literacy that encompasses a range of other modes of contemporary meaning-making – hypertext, audio, video, and so on – modes integral to the digital universe.

## Myth #1 Digital technology is the answer to all our education problems

*Computers don't know if you're rich or poor; or male or female; or even a refugee. Inequalities of educational access are a thing of the past. Just log in and learn.*

Digital technology does not guarantee an excellent learning experience; in fact, there are arguments to suggest quite the reverse. Furthermore, such technologies can exacerbate issues of educational inequity, regarding who has access, who has the necessary skills, who actually gets to use them, and who uses them in ways that prove to be educationally and economically productive.

## Myth #2 Technology signals the end of teaching

*We don't really need teachers anymore; we probably don't even need schools. Everything children need to learn is right there on their computer screens.*

Teachers have always dealt with new technologies, and information and communication technologies are ultimately no different. Teachers will not be rendered obsolete by such technologies; in fact, given the exponential rise in the amount of information available to students, teachers will be required more than ever to guide those students in appreciating the difference between the mere accessing of information, and the shaping of useful knowledge.

# Introduction

This book is full of contemporary debates and worries about education: from concerns over decreasing funding for state schools, to the difficulties in teaching for a multicultural society; from questions about the rise of Ritalin use among children, to arguments over teacher competence and responsibility levels; from moral panics over progressive models of education, to how best to manage truancy rates. All of these raise anxiety levels, not only among parents, but also among teachers, educational administrators and policy-makers – and probably even among the children themselves. Mass education is all too often understood as a site of contestation and disquiet, one where the news is almost always bad.

In contrast to all these worrisome educational reports, the domain of 'education and technology' has tended to shine like a beacon. Here is an area where the news almost always seems to be good: computers are spreading like wildfire, even in the most impoverished of schools; since children love computers, they are going to start to love the learning process; problems with access to information will become a thing of the past, even in the most remote of communities; access to knowledge will become more interesting and more structured; the division between work and play will start to disappear … the good news just keeps on coming. Sure, there is a wide range of concerns about the consequences of computer technology in the domestic realm – excessive Facebooking, internet predators, developing bad posture, pornography, cyber-bullying, violent games – but the use of computers in the school seems to be relatively immune from these types of criticism.

Is it that simple? Have new information and communications technologies (ICTs) heralded a brave new dawn of truly effective education, or is it all rather more complex than that? Certainly, the dominant discourses around technology and education have generally been positive. But does this actually reflect what is going on in our school? Boody (2001, 12–13) sceptically observes:

> Noted in an advertisement in a magazine for teachers was a quote from a principal in whose school a number of computers were installed: 'While I realise [major computer manufacturer in Silicon Valley] sells computers, I believe they really sell learning.' Really? I did not know that learning was available simply for money. I'd like to buy some myself.

Boody goes on to point out that while the desire for schools to 'keep up to date' is most likely laudable, the problem lies in the fact that this becomes translated as 'How do we get the best technology the quickest?', rather than the far more fundamental questions of, 'What kind of education do we want for our children, and what are the best ways of producing it?' That is, we are in danger of mistakenly assuming that we have already answered these questions, and the answer is the same – technology.

## Technophobes, digital immigrants, and digital natives

Early concerns over ICTs and education often centred upon the ability of the existing body of teachers to adapt to the new professional landscape. How were teachers in late middle age, many of whom couldn't even type, going to cope with the internet, with online curriculum packages, and with HTML? Indeed, how were they even going to cope with email? After all, nearly one-third of the population was deemed to suffer from technophobia: the fear of technology (Brosnan 1998). Such fears were not even limited to the techno-elderly; they encompassed women, ethnic minorities, the remote, in fact seemingly everybody other than young, white males

These concerns now almost seem quaint. While not suggesting that your average granny spends her evenings writing programming for software packages, many email, Skype, and surf the net with perfect competence. More significantly, teachers – whatever their age – are now expected to be able to use most of the technology that makes their schools operate on a daily basis, whether that be for administrative, pedagogic, pastoral or social purposes. The expected wave of teacher resignations, or redundancies, never materialised, and teachers now happily use their smart phones along with everyone else who can afford one.

Rather than technophobia then, the focus soon came to fall upon the distinction between those who have grown up with ICTs as a fundamental part of their life-world, often referred to as *digital natives*, and those who have come to them later in life, who consciously had to 'learn' about it, called *digital immigrants* (Prensky 2001, 2011). This division provided a useful way of articulating the division deemed to exist between students and teachers, and their respective relationships to digital technology.

> … the single biggest problem facing education today is that our Digital Immigrant instructors, who speak an outdated language (that of the pre-digital age), are struggling to teach a population that speaks an entirely new language. This is obvious to the Digital Natives – school often feels pretty much as if we've brought in a population of heavily accented, unintelligible foreigners to lecture them. They often can't understand what the Immigrants are saying. What does 'dial' a number mean, anyway? (Prensky 2001, 2)

Arguably, this is more significant than simply a 'failure to communicate'. As discussed in Chapter 6, according to Postman (1994), childhood became demarcated from adulthood on the basis of (a lack of) access to knowledge, as determined by knowledge of the written word. Childhood became a time of 'not knowing', particularly regarding issues of sexuality, and adults were those who *did* know. The relationship between teacher and pupil has been founded upon this principal: teachers know, students don't. The issue of student as digital natives versus teachers as digital immigrants has the potential to undercut this principal in the most fundamental of ways.

So what happens now? In order to retain their authority within the teacher/pupil hierarchy, will digital immigrant teachers be continually forced to try to know more than those digital natives who sit in front of them? Remember: teachers know, students don't. In the context of education and ICTs, this sounds rather like a fool's errand, and rather like a misunderstanding of the best use of technology in the classroom. First, good teachers can utilise the skills and capacities of their students without necessarily sacrificing their authority. This is a false binary; teachers don't know everything (nor should they), and those that pretend they do, are probably in for short and disappointing careers.

Second, it has been argued that the 'digital natives/digital immigrants' construct is itself a false binary. Bayne and Ross (2011) suggest that this depiction of the two relationships available to ICTs not only de-privileges the role of the teacher – important within the context of this book – it also sets up, 'not a peaceful co-existence of facing terms, but a violent hierarchy' (Derrida 1981, 41). It is a 'violent hierarchy' because the digital immigrant is necessarily inferior to the digital native, dominated by it, and subordinate to its knowledge. Implicit within this binary are a series of supporting sub-binaries – that is, native/immigrant equals student/teacher, fast/slow, young/old, future/past, playful/serious, and multi-tasking/sequential – binaries which run the risk of inappropriately organising the field of debate about education and technology, before the conversation really even commences.

## Multiliteracies

Irrespective of whether the digital immigrant/digital native binary is too much of an oversimplification, it is hard to disagree with the assertion that ICTs are reorganising how we go about accessing information, how we communicate with each other, and how we go about creating meaning. Traditional literacy has always focused solely upon the written word; students have generally been asked to read printed text, and then to write answers detailing their grasp of that text – basic reading comprehension (Cole & Pullen 2010). This is largely a singular, linear, sequential and stable process; meaning is regarded as inherent to the words used; and all students should progress through the text in the same way.

It has been argued that this is no longer the most appropriate way of understanding literacy. The New London Group (1996) coined the term *Multiliteracies,* and with this, they were pointing to two things: first, that in an era when national and cultural boundaries are breaking down, when we have both 'local diversity and global connectedness', and where English has become the dominant world language, English is fracturing into 'increasingly differentiated Englishes, marked by accent, national origin, subcultural style, and professional or technical communities' (Cope & Kalantzis 2000, 6). The idea of a single, standard version of our language, to which measures of 'literacy' can be attached, has now all but been abandoned.

Second – and central to the subject matter of this chapter – literacy no longer simply refers to the ability to access written texts. 'Multiliteracy' now involves both this initial, textual form of meaning making, as well as a range of other modes, such as the visual, the spatial, and the aural.

Digital texts – freed from the long-established rules of linear-based narrative construction – introduce dimensions that were unfeasible in traditional print-based texts. For example, an activity as indispensible as 'surfing the net' is no longer memory dependent, nor as dependent upon skills such as regimented eye movement or the decoding of alphabetic symbols. In contrast, web-based texts – via the combination of sound, movement, image and hyperlinks – introduce elements of fluidity that enable texts to be reconstructed in innumerable ways … (Burnett 2004b, 134–5)

When students access information from webpages, they are not necessarily reading the words in a traditional fashion, nor are they necessarily making meaning only from the words on the screen; there are sounds, videos, links in and out, hypertext, activities, pop-up boxes, other webpages open, all of which contribute to how meaning is shaped.

Given these variables, and the fact that no two students are likely to engage in this process in exactly the same way, it consequently makes little sense to regard literacy as the acquisition of a single set of skills, neatly bounded and forever useful in its current form. So unless we think we can simply ignore these changes – and pretend that the computer screen is just an ordinary page of a book, except one powered by electricity – then the rise of such technologies requires us to adopt the notion of *multiliteracies* if we are to get the best out of our students, and if we are to equip them properly for the digital age.

## Technology, better teaching, and educational equity

Regardless of these relatively unfamiliar aspects of digital texts, and the disquiet some 'digital immigrants' might feel towards the place of new technologies in the classroom, it has been widely claimed that ICTs have the potential to solve most of our current educational problems. In the realm of 'virtual schools', traditional stumbling blocks to success, such as whether your teacher is any good, what your first language is, how advanced your knowledge is, where you live, how time-rich or time-poor you are, how economically rich or poor you are, how you like to learn, how old you are, all start to melt away in the light of our technological advances (Berman & Tinker 2000).

Myth #1 in this chapter examines this technological fairyland, to see if the predictable structures of access and equity do not apply in the cyber-world. Perhaps not surprisingly, the usual suspects – social class, gender, race/ethnicity, age, geographical location, school type, social authority – all help shape who gets access to ICTs. As long as computers cost money, and some computers are better than others, then there will be differential access to those computers, as with any other educational resource.

But even if computers were free, and everyone was given one upon entering school (which is happening in some schools, though primarily in the private sector, hence they aren't really free), this would not guarantee an even take-up across the community. After all, access to a computer does not equal engagement with the possibilities made available via that computer. There remain social, cultural and practical obstacles in the way of computer learning, just as there are in the way of traditional, blackboard learning. There may exist a beautiful, virtual world of limitless learning, but students have to access it from our world, a world with a lot of problems and inequalities; one can't entirely compensate for the other.

## Classroom technology and the 'end of teaching'

Just because students now have access to limitless information, this does not somehow correlate with limitless knowledge. As will be discussed in myth #2, there is now the belief that teachers are in danger of becoming redundant. Every child with an internet connection has access to all the best libraries in the world; a virtually limitless storehouse of information, just waiting to be discovered. And while we're ridding ourselves of unnecessary burdens to the taxpayer, do we even need schools anymore? With the rise of 'virtual classrooms', and online interest groups, students can access such groups from anywhere on the planet, and once there, work through structured lessons in the company of other, like-minded students.

It will be contended here that these arguments are not particularly convincing. Schools are more than just buildings, and students get more from them than just information in a classroom. While not denigrating home schooling, education is a 360-degree activity, and the physical environment of the school plays a huge role in contemporary models of education. Likewise, information is not the same as knowledge, and increasingly it will be the task of the teacher to show children the difference. Consequently, if anything, the role of the teacher will likely become more important in the future, not less.

To summarise, the two myths to be dealt with in this chapter are:

**Myth #1** – Digital technology is the answer to all our education problems

**Myth #2** – Technology signals the end of teaching

# Myth #1 Digital technology is the answer to all our education problems

The digital revolution has drastically improved teaching. Teachers can now access virtually any resource they want, and school lessons are all the better for it. Rubbish teaching will be a thing of the past; so too will be bored schoolchildren. And what's more, education will become more equitable. Traditional models of schooling are almost inevitably unfair; some schools are rich, some schools are poor; some children can afford extra tuition, others can't; some children fit in, others don't. None of this applies to online education. All you need is a computer, and someone to point you in the right direction, and maybe not even that.

Arguably, mass schooling has had a number of false dawns; moments when the clouds appeared to part, and we thought we knew for certain that some existing educational problem was about to be put to rest. There was the advent of Comprehensive Education in the UK, where the elite grammar schools were abolished, and everyone had to muck in together; equity at last! Except it didn't really work as planned, as wealthy areas generated successful schools, and poorer areas didn't, which became self-perpetuating cycles of improvement and decay, respectively. Comprehensive education wasn't *all* bad news by any means, but it wasn't a magic bullet either. Likewise, there was the advent of Ritalin to deal with hyperactivity; no more troublesome children! Except, as discussed in Chapter 6, it now seems we are prepared to drug any child who manifests any kind of difference; and our schools seem the same as they ever were.

Digital education is the latest issue to be greeted with this kind of optimism, in that not only did it promise a revitalisation of stale old teaching practices, but it also held out the promise of finally eradicating some of our most ingrained forms of educational inequality. Improved teaching quality, within the context of improved equity – who wouldn't be enthusiastic about that? So is this the real deal, or is this Ritalin all over again?

## What's so great about digital teaching?

The advantages of contemporary teaching practices over their predecessors seem self-evident. A blackboard and some chalk seems pathetically inadequate in comparison with an entire world of information and resourcing available through a networked classroom projector. Teachers can now have access to interactive net resources, high-quality images and videos pertaining to their subject, pre-designed lesson plans, integrated PowerPoint presentations, instant online assessments, activities the teachers and the students can operate synchronously, and anything else that software designers can think up.

It certainly sounds better; perhaps it is better. It offers the potential of depth and variety, and it operates across familiar terrain for the students. Given the choice, you would be hard-pressed to find a teacher who would prefer the option of only chalk, to the option of everything technology has to offer. The issue here is that teaching with the benefit of ICTs is not necessarily better. There is the danger that technology-based teaching becomes an end in itself, and not a means to an end. To put it another way, it is quite easy to mistake a lesson comprised of lots of PowerPoint slides and video resources, for a lesson where important learning takes place; where students are encouraged to think critically, and with organised purpose. Teaching can become deceptively and monotonously easy.

In her book, *Digital Hemlock: internet education and the poisoning of teaching*, Brabazon (2002, 3) describes a scene familiar to most of us:

Settle down, people …

In keeping with our bullet-point culture, I will now dim the lights and attempt to activate my Power-Point presentation. Hopefully the projector will work. As I have not prepared a lecture, I will talk to the slides, filling in the space between the headings with banal comments and self-evident nonsense. You will, however, see some attractively coloured graphs …

Everything you need to complete the assignments is found in my Power-Point bullet points. Copying them down accurately will determine the calibre of your grade …

Brabazon suggests a number of problems with technology-driven learning. First, expanding on the point above, the ubiquitous nature of software such as PowerPoint can lead to formulaic, homogenised, short-cut teaching. This is not to say that having decided to utilise such a program, undesirable outcomes will inevitably follow, just that the structure of programs like PowerPoint are not neutral; they frame the presentation of knowledge according to certain rules, and within pre-defined boundaries. Furthermore, given the many professional pressures on lecturers, tutors and teachers, it is understandable why they may opt for the easiest option, pedagogically valid or otherwise.

Second, she argues that as a generation of students learn to organise their thinking in terms of bullet points, much of the subtlety and beauty of language is being lost. One of the principal ways of learning has always been to actually participate in the activity, and in an era of searchable databases and generic competencies, students no longer develop the skills of writing in the ways they once did. Knowledge is reduced to bite-sized chunks of information, with no necessary logical connection between them.

Third, she suggests that digital technologies, and online learning, are not generally conducive to critical reasoning. Various software packages may well be useful for activities such as drills and simulations, and for navigating oceans of information, but they are not so effective in the stimulation of autonomous thinking. There is still something rather either/or about the digital learning environment, and as she notes: 'If a definitive answer can be given, then the wrong question has been asked' (Brabazon 2002, 192).

Finally, and particularly within the context of the university, she suggests that it would be naïve to think that much of the drive towards augmented teaching technology was driven by anything other than cost. Generally speaking, with distance and online learning environments, more students can be dealt with, by far fewer staff. This is not pedagogy; it is economics.

Brabazon's position is not without its own problems, as she admits. There is more than a streak of nostalgic romanticism here, in harking back to the practices of a better era, back to a time when students actually read books, and weren't on Facebook during lectures. There is also something of a binary in operation: Socratic face-to-face education is good, versus online digital education is bad. That may be so, but as a polemic, her argument acts as an effective anecdote to utopian arguments that suggest digital technology is the answer to all our educational problems.

## The digital divide

Even if digital technology was as good as its proponents suggest in strictly practical terms, there is another problem that ought to limit our celebrations. All the various components of the digital universe – the internet, computer hardware, software, elements both real and virtual – do not blanket the earth evenly, like oxygen, where everyone gets an equal chance to do some breathing. As with every other resource you can think of, some people have ready access, some people have limited access, and some people have no access at all. The question is: who gets what?

There is an important proviso on this short section of the book. The conclusions to be drawn are only as good as the data they are based upon, and even though the majority of those conclusions here are probably fairly predictable, this is a rapidly changing field – more so than any other discussion in this book. Digital technology does appear to be spreading quite quickly, and some of the claims here may date equally quickly. That said, as will be discussed, having access to technology is not the same as knowing how to use it; and knowing how to use it is not the same as using it in ways which benefit education.

## Access to digital technology

In its broadest sense, our globe can be subdivided into zones of differing technological access. Not surprisingly, the G8 nations – the world's wealthiest and most advanced countries – appear to be in the strongest position; there are as many internet users in the G8 nations as the rest of the world put together, and there are eight times more internet users in the United States alone than in the whole of Africa. A nation as small as Denmark, population 5.5 million, has twice the bandwidth of the whole of central America and the Caribbean combined (United Nations 2005). In the realm of technology at least, the First World/Third World divide is alive and well.

This divide is not limited to comparisons between nations; it is also relevant *within* specific nations, and Australia mirrors the patterns of most industrialised countries. Chapters 1 to 3 of this book give a pretty good indicator of what those patterns might look like. After all, why should the inequalities of access to technology be any different to other zones of inequality?

> We had always known that the cross section of race, ethnicity, class, and gender defined the social structure of our society, and our goals were to diminish the ability of these socially constructed boxes to render individuals invisible and excluded. Access to ICTs not only crystallized these endemic problems but also added nuances and complicated our historical views. (Modarres 2011, 5)

Holley and Oliver (2011) take this a stage further and argue that the digital divide actually intensifies existing forms of privilege and exclusion. That is, lacking access to ICTs, perhaps due to socioeconomic disadvantage, acts to exacerbate that disadvantage; those digitally poor, due to poverty, get poorer. By way of a brief summary, the evidence suggests that access to ICTs is restricted in predictable ways according to social class (Argy 2006), gender (Cooper 2003), race/ethnicity (Samaras 2005), age (Milward 2003), and remoteness (ABS 2011).

At this point, it should be mentioned that the notion of a digital divide based solely upon access to digital technology was very much a product of the early days of analysing computer demographics; this is now regarded as something of an over-simplification. As more and more people gained access to computers – for example through schools, internet cafes, or libraries – this did not translate into individuals from otherwise socially and technologically marginalised groups suddenly gaining educational parity.

Fink and Kenny (2003) wrote one of the main papers discussing the complexity of the digital divide issue. They note that while access to information and communication technology is undoubtedly the starting point for understanding technological equity, there are three other aspects that also have impact. The first is knowing what to do with the technology once you have it; what kind of skills base do those with access actually have? The second, is actually using that technology; how often the ICTs are used, and for what purposes. The final issue relates to the impact of using that technology; what kind of returns does the technology give those who use it? While undoubtedly access and use are generally regarded as the most important, all are worth addressing, even if only briefly.

## Knowledge of digital technology

In a utopian world, ensuring all students own their own computer sounds like the perfect cure for the digital divide; unfortunately, it only addresses part of the problem. As everyone who has ever acquired a computer for their grandparents would know – in the hope of plugging them in to the twenty-first century – a computer is just a large box in the corner of the room unless someone also gives them the skills to make it work. They may now have access to ICTs, but so what?

The research suggests that those who have the skills to use ICTs, use them far more often. The possession of those skills is generally broken down according to the familiar patterns of advantage and disadvantage already discussed. Indeed, the evidence suggests that children whose parents who regularly use the internet at home, are almost twice as likely to use the internet themselves, as compared to children whose parents do not possess those skills. Likewise, children whose parents use the internet at work are nearly 50% more likely to use the internet (Cleary, Pierce & Trauth 2006). Since parents with ICT skills are more likely to be white and middle class, white middle-class children are therefore more likely to find themselves on the winning side of the 'knowledge and skills' digital divide.

## Use of digital technology

So, hypothetically, if there *was* equal access to ICTs, and an equal range of skills in using those ICTs, then what could possibly be left of the digital divide? Well just because technology *can* be used in particular ways, doesn't mean that it *will*. Modarres (2011) argues that different patterns of ICT usage have unforseen implications for those who use them. He uses the example of American research by Smith (2010) which finds that African Americans and Hispanics are more likely than the white population to access the internet on their mobile phones, with whites tending to use networked home computers. As a consequence of this difference, the former are more likely to be restricted to consuming information, as opposed to being in a position to create it.

> … it is much easier to fill out job applications and develop content for a Web site on a computer than on a cell phone. If we have presumably resolved the problem of the digital divide by increasing the number of cell phones among minorities and low-income populations, have we improved critical engagement with the content, including its creation? Or have we elevated the digital divide to the next level of content and differential usage pattern? (Modarres 2011, 6)

As the focus has largely shifted from a concern over equal access, to a focus on widening participation (Goodfellow 2006), the question needs to be asked: just what counts as participation? Clearly, some forms of participation have a far greater payoff in the non-virtual worlds of education, economics and social advantage than others.

## Outcomes from digital technology

Given these different patterns of ICT usage, it is not surprising that the outcomes are also different. Those who have access to ICTs, who have the skills to use them, and who use them in academically and professionally productive ways, will end up with a wide array of significant advantages in terms of outcomes, particularly concerning employment (Bynner et al. 2008). Those individuals are more likely to do well at school, more likely to gain entry to university, more likely to get more prestigious, higher paying jobs, and more likely to gain promotion within those jobs. This is the most important consequence of the 'digital divide'.

Even though the notion of the 'digital divide' is a useful construct for trying to understand who gets to benefit from ICT technology, as with many of the topics in this section of the book, there is more than a hint of a false binary here. In the real world, it is not a case of 'the haves' and the 'have-nots', with a clear distinction between what each group does, and does not, have access to or use; rather, there is a sliding scale of advantage and disadvantage. However, in spite of this, the term remains a convenient shorthand way of describing an important social and educational issue.

In summary, information and communication technologies may well have a great deal to offer education. However, they are not the answer to all our problems, and they come with a few problems of their own. They can lead to formulaic teaching, to bullet-point reasoning, and to impoverished writing. They do not offer a solution to existing patterns of educational inequality; currently, the best evidence suggests they tend to simply dovetail into them. Lockard and Pegrum (2006, 1) paint a salutary picture of the current state of affairs:

> The early, halcyon days of electronic education are gone. There is no longer a unifying belief, common during the Internet boom of the early 1990s, that this new medium provides a means for universal educational development. Many who embraced personal computers and the internet, and who devoted their work to creating new forms of electronic education have grown dissatisfied with the trend towards commodification and corporatization, a paucity of critical thought in e-learning, poor quality and inappropriate uses of distance learning, hierarchical organization, and the growing exploitation of teaching labour.

# Myth #2 Technology signals the end of teaching

> Do we need teachers anymore? After all, we don't really need schools, when students can just plug in their computer and join a virtual classroom; we could do something more useful with the buildings – bulldoze them for parks, sell them for real estate – and it would certainly stop the problem of children chatting at the back of the class. And with all this information available, who needs teachers to tell children where it is? You don't need a teacher to tell students how to click on the 'Go To Library' button on their computer; they can figure that out for themselves. With digital technology, we can just have online copies of the very best teachers talking about all the various topics on the curriculum. Who needs all those teachers at your local school? They probably aren't as good as that person on the video from America anyway.

Perhaps ICTs aren't the answer to every single equity problem that has ever beset mass education, and perhaps ICTs might lead to disjointed, bullet-point thinking, but we are still in a far better position than if they didn't exist; or maybe not. Myth #1 suggests that contemporary technology is in the process of improving education out of sight. Whether or not this is the case (most likely, not), this same rosy path to the future is not predicted for our teachers; their professional future is deemed to be bleak.

There are two parts to this miserable bit of soothsaying. The first is that teachers have never had to deal with a potential onslaught to their professional survival such as the one posed by technology. Teaching has always been based around the body of the teacher: their voice, their physical presence, their pure ability to communicate with their students. The suggestion here is that for the first time, technology is interposing itself into that equation.

The second argument is that teachers have always been needed to provide information for the students to learn. Apart from a few books that could be acquired from the school library, it was teachers who brought information into the classroom, and who set it out in ways their students could internalise. That professional function is no longer required. All the information in the world is only a computer screen away, and there are more than enough instructional programs on the internet to guide students through it.

## There's nothing new about technology

Part of the problem here lies in the term 'technology'. Within the context of education, the word now seems to be used almost exclusively to refer to ICTs. It suggests, at very least, a range of objects and devices in the classroom that have to be plugged in. More specifically, it implies some form of connection to computers, to complex software, and to the internet. Teachers have never had to deal with 'technology' before; what on earth will they do?

This, of course, is the first error in reasoning. 'Technologies' are far broader reaching than just the narrow association with ICTs. Arguably, it is the use of technologies that has made us what we are as human, that has marked us out from other species, and that has allowed us to build our societies and our cultures. At their most fundamental level, Rammert (1999) contends that technologies are comprised of four elements. The first is the materials from which the technology is made; the second is the specific shape it is formed into; the third is the end for which it is designed; and the fourth is the efficient action that results.

ICTs fit neatly into this model. For example, take a classroom computer. It is made from a complex array of materials; it is moulded, soldered, and screwed into an even more complex set of interrelated shapes; it is designed to process data at dizzying speeds; and it results in access to information in ways that were unthinkable before the technology was introduced – there are the four parts of the technology: material, shape, use, efficient action.

But ICTs are not the only things that fit this definition; so do some of our most primitive tools. A spear is largely made from wood; it is shaped to be long and thin, with a point at one end; it is designed to stick into things; and it allows us to kill animals more efficiently, and from a greater distance. As such, technologies are simply another word for tools.

This brings us to the second error in reasoning. Teachers have long dealt with new technologies in the classroom, without either giving up in befuddlement, or facing redundancy; take, for example, the blackboard – reputedly invented by Scottish teacher James Pillans in 1820. Following the four-part model: the original blackboard was made of slate; it was shaped into a large, flat sheet; it was used for writing on with chalk; and in terms of efficiency, it allowed teachers to write information out only once, rather than on the slate of every individual student. The same argument applies to the technology that largely replaced the blackboard – the overhead projector. This device, at its most popular in the 1980s and 1990s, allowed teachers to bring pre-prepared material to the classroom, and to write in a more comfortable, horizontal manner, rather that vertically.

The classroom is full of technologies, and always has been. ICTs are simply the latest tools to be deployed within the teaching space. Teaching has never been about a pure, unmediated relationship between teacher and pupil; technologies have always been in there somewhere, whether they be quills, parchment and canes, or uniforms, class bells and panopticons, or webcams, touchscreens and the internet. Teachers have generally greeted such changes with guarded optimism. After all, this is a dynamic profession, and teachers adapt.

## From information to knowledge

Having rejected the assertion that technology is something new, something that teachers have no experience in dealing with as a profession, the second part of the myth asserts that ICTs allow access to such huge amounts of information that teachers are now surplus to requirements. There is all the information that students could ever need, just at the click of a mouse. The argument here will be that this surfeit of information is precisely why we *need* teachers – at least in part – not need to do away with them

We live in a world now containing almost inconceivable amounts of digital information. According to Bohn and Short (2009), American households consumed 3.6 zettabytes of information in 2008 – a zettabyte is a 1 with 21 zeros after it, and that's rather a lot. This does not even include any of the information consumed in the workplace. In a similar vein, the CEO of Google, Eric Schmidt, stated that every two days, we now create as much information as we did from the dawn of civilisation, up until 2003 (Siegler 2010).

In addition to this, students don't just have their school library; they have access to literally thousands of libraries online. They can't just access books on history, maths, and English; they can access books on anything. They don't just have access to the voices of peer-reviewed authors; they have access to the voices of anyone and everyone in the blogosphere who wants to start talking – the wise, the weird and the witless.

The point here is that students aren't at school to gain information; they are at school to gain knowledge. This sounds like a matter of semantics, but the difference is an important one, one that teachers play a pivotal role in managing. A useful model for exploring the role teachers play in stepping beyond an information-based focus has been given by Ackoff (1989), and his 'Wisdom Hierarchy', also called the 'DIKUW Hierarchy'. DIKUW is an acronym referring to

Data–Information–Knowledge–Understanding–Wisdom, and the argument here is that you are only likely to get a short distance up this hierarchy without the help of a teacher. Taking these five concepts in turn:

**Data** is regarded as raw facts existing in the world, unconceptualised and without organisation. The world is full of an almost infinite amount of data, and it has no meaning until conceptual schema are applied to it. The room you are sitting in is full of such abstract data – the number of molecules in the air, the length of the walls, the varieties of bacteria on the cover of this book – but they remain abstract until recorded and organised.

**Information** is regarded as data that has been given meaning; information is organised data. The internet is full of information; indeed it is comprised of information – zettabytes and zettabytes of it. Children do not really need teachers to access information. All they have to do is turn on their computers, and information pours out at them.

**Knowledge** is a more difficult concept to define. It is largely regarded as applied information; it is not just an understanding of 'what', but also of 'how', and while knowledge certainly exists on the internet, it is often difficult to delineate from mere information.

Knowledge is a fluid mix of framed experience, values, contextual information, expert insight and grounded intuition that provides an environment and framework for evaluation and incorporating new experiences and information. It originates and is applied in the minds of knowers (Davenport & Prusack 1998, 5).

**Understanding** is the ability to take knowledge and to place it in wider contexts. If information is about *what* something is, and knowledge is about *how* that something operates, or came to be, then understanding is about *why*. There is a great deal of information available about the rise of mass education – dates, locations, curricula, instructional techniques – but knowledge requires linking these together to frame how the system came to take its current form, which represents a far more complex form of evaluation. Arguably, understanding is the ability to answer the question of why mass schooling developed – an even more complex process still.

**Wisdom** is the ability to take that understanding, and to project into the future. Wisdom involves the moral dimension of assessing what might be the right course of action to take. If we now understand why mass schooling developed in the way it did, wisdom denotes the ability to decide, as a society based upon principals of justice and democracy, where we need to take it next.

Having set out the main elements of the DIKUW hierarchy, we can return to the assertion that in the age of ICTs, tech-savvy children and online education, we no longer really need teachers. The most obvious reply to this claim is to suggest that if we were to limit our education to the bottom two elements of the hierarchy – the D, and the I – then that may well be correct. Students can download as much as they like from the web; facts galore, facts about everything. However, our concept of a good education is based upon significantly higher expectations than this. We expect our students to make it past the D and the I, to the K and the U, and for this they need teachers. In an era of almost limitless web-noise, arguably it will be one of the primary tasks of teachers in the future to help students understand the difference between this noise, useful information, and knowledge; and from there, to eventually mould that knowledge into understanding. As for the W – wisdom – all any of us can do is hope for a little of that.

In summary, for those prophesying the ICT-induced end of teaching as we know it; this is not a new phenomenon. The same claims were made about the advent of television when it first became popularised (*Seattle Times* 1962). Technologies change, and the circumstances of classroom life change, but if we want to continue working toward a 'wise' citizenry, then we need to accept that students will always learn more with a teacher than without, and learn in more profound and lasting ways.

# Conclusion

This chapter has sought to address the rise of ICTs within contemporary education. Some aspects of the education process have certainly had to change as a result; we now appear to be in the era of multiliteracies, and for a schooling system that intends to equip its graduates for life in the twenty-first century, it is no longer sufficient solely to work on the skills required for textual literacy. While the ability to read traditional linear texts is still crucially important, so is developing literacy skills across a diverse range of other forms.

The issues regarding ICTs are significantly more complex than simply expanding our notion of literacy. The first myth dealt with the assertion that ICTs are the answer to all our educational problems. This would remain just an interesting, if somewhat erroneous, view on the future of education, if it were not for the fact that such beliefs can have significant policy implications for where we place our priorities, and where we direct our funding. Useful though they are, ICTs do not inevitably equate with teaching excellence, and they are not the answer to all our ingrained problems of educational equity.

The second myth dealt with the belief that ICTs sound the death knell for traditional teaching; who needs teachers when we have instant access to all the wonderful resources of the internet? This assumption overestimates the value of the internet – at least without the guidance of someone who understands the difference between information and knowledge – and it underestimates the importance, and the resilience, of teachers. Technologies will come and go; teachers are here to stay.

The final point of this chapter is to note, once again – as with all the topics in this section – that there appears to be an abundance of binaries operating here. We have digital natives versus digital immigrants; we have the digital divide, which implies that you are either inside or outside the world of ICTs; and we have the dichotomous claim that we either will, or won't need teachers in the future. While such binaries can be useful in loosely highlighting specific issues, from that point onwards they tend to have the effect of reducing complex problems to catchphrases, and removing any subtlety and nuance from our policy solutions.

# Part 4

## Philosophy and Mass Education

In the previous three parts, the main tools of analysis have been primarily sociological and historical. Addressing issues of class, gender and race has always been the central prerogative of sociology; likewise, the chapters on the relationship between education and various elements of contemporary culture are also largely investigated through sociological reasoning. Alternatively, understanding the scope and impact of social governance, in all its forms, has principally been the result of detailed historical analysis. However, these are not the only options open to us; some of the most useful and far-reaching methods of inquiry belong to the discipline of philosophy.

If the intention is to look at mass education with a fresh pair of eyes, then philosophy can provide the necessary critical tools to do precisely that. As a discipline based upon clear thinking and cogent argument, philosophy is useful not only for the production of thoughtful future citizens, it is also a valuable skill set for anyone interested in studying our education system. Furthermore, mass education is also an ethically and legally complex domain, with important dilemmas continuing over issues such as positive discrimination, mandatory reporting of abuse, and levels of teacher responsibility – a fact that the philosophical study of ethics can help us address with clarity and fairness. Finally, if we are seeking the 'truth' of mass education, philosophy can help us at least understand what we might mean by that, as well as better understand the relationship between truth and the Australian curriculum.

Chapter 10 *Philosophy* examines the value of this discipline within education. It questions the assertion that we no longer need non-job producing subjects like philosophy in our school curriculum, the suggestion being that it's too abstract, too esoteric, and no longer relevant to the digital generation. It also questions the notion that education is fundamentally self-evident, and that by invoking the need for philosophy to study it, we are making it more complicated than it really is.

Chapter 11 *Ethics and the law* investigates the importance of the philosophical study of ethics, and its relation to the law within the context of mass education. It questions the common views that a good grasp of ethics is irrelevant to being a good teacher; that the law is one of the few areas where everyone agrees on what it is, and the objective moral purpose it serves; that our education system is non-discriminatory; and that mass education is now free of the ethical concerns and dilemmas that may have once characterised it.

Chapter 12 *Truth and postcolonialism* addresses the relationship between the notion of truth and Australia's postcolonial curriculum. It questions the belief that truth is the purest and most fundamental of all logical forms, a state that exists independently of human thought and action; and that the curriculum is full of nothing but unequivocal, universal truths – truths that would hold up to scrutiny irrespective of the social and cultural context of the school in which they are presented.

In many ways, chapters 11 and 12 are designed to act as case studies to illustrate the potential of philosophy, both as a discipline in general, and more specifically, as it relates to the particular ambitions of this book. Ethics and epistemology – the study of truth, or more specifically, of knowledge – are two of the most important branches of philosophy, and here they are applied to issues of the law and postcolonialism respectively. By the end, the intention is to demonstrate the utility of philosophy for making greater sense of mass schooling; it is also to show that these two important philosophical sub-disciplines can shed much light upon many of the laws that cross-cut our education system, and upon the educational legacy of our status as a former British colony.

# Chapter 10

# Philosophy

This chapter makes the case for the importance of philosophy, both as a discipline in its own right, and as a subject area vital to the better understanding of education. Philosophy is largely concerned with those areas of study and speculation beyond the reach of empirical analysis, addressing problems about how we construct knowledge, how we produce a just society, and how we determine 'right' from 'wrong'. Its central research methodology is simply to think with clarity. The significance of this discipline has not been limited to answering abstract questions about the human condition; philosophy has been instrumental both in making us into rational and reflexive citizens, and also in framing the ideas behind our entire system of mass schooling.

### Myth #1 Philosophy has no place in the twenty-first-century curriculum

*We don't have the space in the curriculum to teach philosophy. School children need to study subjects that will actually get them a job.*

The study of philosophy brings with it many benefits within mass schooling, benefits that extend far beyond the directly instrumental: the ability to think clearly and logically, an overall improvement in academic performance, and a greater sensitivity to social and ethical issues, not to mention the capacity to address essential questions about the human condition.

### Myth #2 'Education' is self-evident; we don't need philosophy to explain it

*We all know what education is. There isn't really any disagreement, or any confounding complexity – those with knowledge, pass it on to those without.*

Actually, there's a lot of disagreement over what education is, and how it ought to work in practice. By better understanding how philosophical approaches like idealism, realism, romanticism, pragmatism, Marxism, and postmodernism continue to shape our education system, we can better grasp the range of educational possibilities, as well as fashion our own teaching philosophies.

# Introduction

## What is philosophy?

Some subjects are easy to comprehend … not necessarily their subject matter, but certainly what they are about. Medicine is a good example. All the anatomy, biochemistry and physiology might be difficult, but the central idea is pretty straightforward: medicine is about making sick people better. The same applies to music. Nobody would pretend that playing the piano is simple, but we all know what music is. Philosophy isn't quite so obliging.

Partially as a result of some of the difficulties associated with defining philosophy, almost every book on the subject starts with its etymology: the word philosophy comes from the ancient Greek, and it means 'love of wisdom'. However, 'wisdom' is something of a broad field, and this bit of information doesn't really help delineate what philosophers should, and should not, be wise about. In truth, early philosophers didn't really care:

> For Plato and Aristotle there was no fumbling doubt about what they were professionally entitled to do, or the proper limits of philosophical inquiry. They were looking for answers to every conceivable question that could be raised, they were seeking to explain and understand the world in all its aspects (Barrow 1975, 15).

However, as the empirical sciences have grown, and marked out specific areas of knowledge for themselves, philosophy has tended towards addressing the more abstract and general questions of life; questions about ethics, knowledge, reason, and existence. This is not to say that philosophy has no role to play in other disciplines, far from it. It is an ill-equipped scientist who does not have a firm grounding in the philosophy of science, and many forms of knowledge are underpinned by a set of philosophical principles that give their discipline shape and rigor – medicine, for example.

Significantly, Western philosophy is not primarily about learning a body of knowledge, although there are texts within every field of philosophy that aspiring philosophers need to be acquainted with. Rather, first and foremost, philosophy is about learning how to reason clearly, or as Popper (1959, 15–16) puts it, 'stating one's problems clearly and of examining its various proposed solutions critically'. Emmet (1991) rightly concludes that while the empirical sciences are about 'going and seeing', philosophy is about 'sitting and thinking'. After all, as Hobbes states, 'Leisure is the mother of philosophy'. Perfect for university study then.

Importantly, philosophy isn't just about pointless speculation on ultimately irrelevant topics. Historically, it has had enormous impact on how we understand ourselves, and how we organise our world. For example, it was the philosopher Descartes' realisation, 'I think, therefore I am' – *cogito ergo sum* – that acted as one of the central triggers for the Enlightenment, in that it showed that the future of human knowledge belonged to *reason*, and not to superstition or blind tradition. Likewise, it was the ideas of political philosophers like Locke that laid the foundations of modern systems of social and political rights, given voice through the French and American revolutions. Finally, as discussed in Chapter 4, it was, in large part, the utilitarian ideas of Bentham and Mill that formed the regulatory framework for the disciplinary society we now all take for granted. These are just a few of the many, many examples of how philosophy has shaped, and continues to shape, how we think and what we do.

However, if the point of philosophy can to be summed up at all, it is with the most famous of quotes from the most famous of all philosophers – Socrates, as given voice through Plato (1989, 38a): 'The unexamined life is not worth living.' Unfortunately, if you see no merit in this contention, you might as well just skip to the next chapter.

## A brief history

Philosophy didn't just appear in the world, complete and fully formed; it has been through various stages, and organised itself in different ways, throughout the last 2500 years. The briefest of summaries of these stages might include the following: it all began, in Europe at least, with the *classical philosophy* of ancient Greece, and it has rightly been said that Plato wrestled with most of the philosophical problems we still wrestle with today. After Rome fell, and took philosophy down with it, the next 1000 years of arcane, religiously doctrinal *scholastic philosophy* produced next to nothing that lasted, and it was only with the rise of Descartes' *rationalism* – the belief that reason is the root of all knowledge – that the discipline came back to life. This was soon challenged by British *empiricism*, which claimed instead that the root of all knowledge is experience. Both these approaches were shown to have shortcomings, and after an early attempt by Rousseau's *romanticism* (which valued emotion over reason), it was Kant who made the most successful, though blindingly complex, effort at finding common ground between the two sides. From there, some of Plato's ideas had a rebirth through Hegel's *German idealism,* but philosophy eventually settled into a kind of loosely-based theoretical tribalism. German philosophers stuck with their idealism; Americans plumped for *pragmatism*, the assertion that all ideas must be founded upon how useful they are; the English focused upon *analytic philosophy,* with its concern over the truth and falsity of particular statements; and the French based their philosophy – in the forms of *phenomenology* and *existentialism* – around the issue of subjective experience. Finally, add some political philosophy through *Marxism,* and a little *neo-romanticism*, with the ideas of Kierkegaard and Nietzsche, and there you have it: the world's most over-simplified history of philosophy.

This is perhaps not that useful in itself, but it is a good list of places to start for those who are interested – and these are only the Western philosophies. There are other forms of knowledge, ones that don't necessarily have ancient Greece in their ancestry. Equally valid and long-lived forms of philosophy have emerged from China, India and the Middle East. However, these ideas never became part of the Western canon, and hence missed out on the global diaspora of classicism that came with European colonialism.

Importantly, philosophy isn't just a set of generalised speculations about life; it has always clustered into different areas of concern, some of which won't be dealt with here (such as justice and free will), and others that will (such as ethics and truth). The philosophy of education is one of the oldest, and most important, of all these areas. Socrates is important as a philosopher, not only because he had something important to say about education – 'Education is the kindling of the flame, not the filling of the vessel' – but also because he founded an entire technique of teaching: the *Socratic method*. This approach, still widely used, particularly at university level, involves asking a rolling set of questions that lead the respondent to re-assess the strengths and weaknesses of their position, and hence to consider the possibility of adopting another.

In general terms though, why is philosophy so important? Yes, it has an interesting history; yes, it has brought about some important social, intellectual and political changes; and yes, it deals with some important areas, but on a more specific basis, why still do philosophy? The question forms the basis for myth #1 of this chapter.

## The importance of philosophy

As discussed in the introduction to this part, even though philosophy has often struggled to find space within the twenty-first-century teacher-education syllabus – mostly due to short-term pressures favouring curriculum knowledge and instruction guidance subjects – few doubt its long-term intellectual value. As a general subject, philosophy has a lot to offer. It provides the tools for addressing some of the most important issues of life; fundamental questions of free will, truth and existence have still found their most convincing answers within this discipline. In addition, it provides the training to think with clarity and precision, to weigh evidence fairly and appropriately, and to construct valid arguments, as well as to recognise those that are not. It also provides the solid intellectual foundation for a range of other knowledges. In the final analysis, science, medicine, law – and education – all have philosophies that bind their discipline together.

Philosophy is particularly important to education. It has long been realised that education is a complex business; there has been 2500 years worth of disputes about exactly what it is, and how it ought to work. Philosophy succeeds in organising how these complexities might be understood, and in doing so, also gives us a better grasp of what kind of educational choices we have as a society. More importantly perhaps, it allows us to develop a personal philosophy of education. After all, if education is to be more than simple instruction, it requires significant reflection by all of us about precisely what kind of teachers we want to be.

Finally, philosophy has a lot to offer in the context of the school. It is not only adults that benefit from reflecting upon life; children also ask question that philosophy is best equipped to answer. Young children can also learn the basics of critical reasoning and organised thinking, with all the spinoff benefits that this brings, not only to their other studies, but also to their social interactions.

## Approaches to the philosophy of education

While no two philosophers would be likely to agree on precisely what content needs to be taught for a philosophy of education course, they would all agree that the course needs to be taught, in contrast to the belief that 'education' speaks for itself, as in myth #2. This content could equally well involve education's links to other philosophy sub-disciplines, such as social justice or knowledge production; it could involve the works of famous writers in the field, anyone from Aristotle to Montessori; or it could be based around fundamental approaches to the philosophy of education – the 'isms' – of which there are many.

It is this latter model that will be adopted here, bearing in mind that of those philosophers who agree with this strategy, many will still disagree with the list of specific approaches chosen, in this case idealism, realism, romanticism, pragmatism, Marxism and postmodernism. After all, remember the first law of philosophy: *For every philosopher, there is an equal and opposite philosopher.* (Second law: *They're both wrong*).

To summarise, the two myths to be dealt with in this chapter are:

**Myth #1** – Philosophy has no place in the twenty-first-century curriculum

**Myth #2** – 'Education' is self-evident; we don't need philosophy to explain it

# Myth #1 Philosophy has no place in the twenty-first-century curriculum

We don't have the luxury of adding a waffly subject like philosophy to our already crowded curriculum. School children need practical subjects that result in quantifiable outcomes. They need subjects that feed directly into the requirements of the employment market. Student teachers don't need philosophy either; they need instruction on how to get kids through exams, and how to keep classrooms quiet.

In some circles, philosophy is depicted as the best exemplar of a pointless education: impractical, self-indulgent, inconclusive, unproductive, and ultimately futile. It is suggested that we live in an era of severe financial pressure on our public institutions, and everything has to pay its way. There can be no passengers, either in terms of staffing or subject choices, and while we'd love for everyone to be able to spend leisurely hours doing art, music and philosophy, the state requires more of our schools than that. It requires the specific training of future workers.

This section of Chapter 10 will present a coherent counter argument to this instrumentalist position. It will suggest that just because the benefits of philosophy are often less tangible than the ability to do double-entry bookkeeping, they are no less real; in fact, philosophy is far broader in its reach, both in the practical sense of producing students who can reason clearly and effectively, but also because it has the potential to help us address some of the more important issues in life. So … much as double-entry bookkeeping is important, it is not as important as developing citizens who can understand what 'truth' is, or what 'justice' is, or how they might go about telling 'right' from 'wrong'.

## Why do philosophy?
## To answer important questions

Many questions can be answered simply by assessing the evidence: What kind of cell is that? Look through the microscope. Who murdered the vicar? Test the knife for fingerprints. How long does it take to boil an egg? Just boil some eggs and find out. Unfortunately, not all questions come with a ready blueprint as to how they should be answered, let alone convenient forms of verification. This is where philosophy comes in.

Hospers (1997) argues that after we have taken the empirically testable questions off the table – that is, questions that can be directly confirmed or falsified – what remains is the domain of philosophy; and that philosophy is the *study of justification* and the *analysis of concepts*. It is the study of justification in that it is concerned about how we justify the many assertions we make. For example, Descartes asked the question: '*If you say that something really happened, how do you know you did not simply dream it?*' Hume asked the question: '*You say we have free will, but how do you know?*' He also asked: '*If you say something is "wrong", where do you look for that "wrongness"?*' In each case, the philosophers are asking for people to explain and justify the claims they make.

In addition to the study of justification, philosophy is also the analysis of concepts. As Hospers (1997, 5) states: 'We speak of justice, but what is justice? We describe things as beautiful, but what is beauty? We speak of before and after, but what is time? We describe things as real, but what is reality?' These are some of the most important questions we can ask ourselves, particularly 'What is reality?', undoubtedly one of the most important questions in the history of philosophy. There is no microscope to peer through to draw definitive conclusions to these questions, no fingerprints to take. There is simply the possibility of 'sitting and thinking' until we arrive at viable answers. Some of those answers have been discussed since the time of Socrates, and we benefit from both the answers we have arrived at, and from the discussion itself.

## To think more clearly

We benefit from the discussion because philosophy sharpens our thinking; it looks for *clarity*. Within philosophy, it is not enough to bluff your way along, using dodgy premises, within badly reasoned arguments, which then get passed off as truth. Actually, that also happens in philosophy, but you're more likely to get caught. Here are two examples:

Lots of young boys have ADHD now, and hate sitting still.

Joe hates sitting still.

So, Joe must have ADHD.

At first glance, this argument seems perfectly valid – indeed, this argument currently gets used in Australian classrooms every day of the year. However, it is an example of a *logical fallacy* called 'affirming the consequent' (if A then B; B, therefore A). Just because Joe hates sitting still, does not logically mean he has ADHD, irrespective of the previous causal link between young boys with ADHD, and hating sitting still (let's given him Ritalin anyway, just to be on the safe side).

ADHD is fertile ground for logical fallacies. There is a fallacy called 'Petitio Principii' (Why A? Because of B. Why B? Because of A) – otherwise known as 'circular reasoning' – which covers the underlying logic of ADHD perfectly.

How do you know a child has Attention Deficit Disorder (ADHD)? Because he's impulsive and out of his seat. Why is he impulsive and out of his seat? Because he has ADHD. (Weist et al. 1999, 121)

Importantly, studying philosophy doesn't only enable you to spot logical fallacies, although this is a useful skill to acquire. In a far more general sense, it also fosters the ability to think critically. Rather than accepting every truth claim that we hear, like a sponge mopping up water, a solid grounding in philosophical thinking enables us to sort out the valid from the invalid, strong arguments from weak, and the plausible and the reasonable from the misleading. Philosophy equips us to distinguish between knowledge, and drivel masquerading as knowledge.

## To provide a solid foundation for other areas

Philosophy does not sit out on its own as a discrete discipline, calling out good advice from the sidelines. It has become a foundational component of many other disciplines. Science is probably the best, and most far-reaching, example here. Very few tertiary institutions would have sciences faculties that did not also offer units in the philosophy of science for its students. Science is in the business of making truth claims – the universe is expanding, the globe is warming, biodiversity is decreasing, and so on – and all good scientists understand that finding 'truth' is a far more complex business than simply having the equations add up (see Chapter 11, myth #1). Science is beset by the inherent problems within inductive logic; it is caught between competing understandings of reality (macro vs quantum); it is unable to free itself from the social elements of knowledge formation; it is uncertain of the limits of the relationship between causation and correlation; and it struggles with the gap between theories and laws.

All of these concerns have been shaped and bounded within the philosophy of science, and this hasn't even touched upon the topic of research ethics, upon how to decide what studies should, and should not, be done, and how they should be carried out. Deciding *whether* we should do embryonic stem cell research is an ethical issue, not a scientific one. Consequently, it is a question best addressed by someone with an expertise in ethics, not in cellular biology; it is a question best addressed by a philosopher. Of course, as we shall now see, philosophy also underpins the entire discipline of education.

## Why study philosophy of education?

## To gain a better understand of our education system

Education is neither a simple nor a straightforward concept. It has varied across time, and between cultures. For example, in ancient Athens children received a broadly based education – including music, literature and gymnastics – with the intention of producing 'rounded' citizens. Only a few hundred kilometres away in ancient Sparta, education existed solely as a preparation for war; learning was written into the contours of the body, and the fighting skills it came to possess, all shaped within a pedagogy of brutality and death. Perhaps fortunately, we have adopted a model of schooling far closer to the Athenian system ... with the possible exception of a couple of well-known rugby schools.

The point here is that all education systems are based upon underlying sets of beliefs, assumptions, and practices – whether we realise it or not (and often we're so close to our own schooling systems, we don't recognise that they could be organised otherwise). These sets of beliefs are called *educational philosophies*, and some of our most important will be addressed in myth #2 of this chapter. Clearly those that underpinned the education systems of Athens and Sparta were very different. Of course, unlike education, some disciplines don't require a philosophy at all; valuable though it is, you'd be hard-pressed to discern any philosophy underpinning electrical engineering.

Two issues are of note here. The first is that systems of education have underlying philosophies for a very simple reason: education is incredibly important to us; Socrates and Plato fretted over how best to educate the young, and nothing much has changed. Second, the best way to understand these educational philosophies is through the discipline of philosophy. There are two different uses of the word 'philosophy' here, but hopefully the thrust of the argument is clear: if you want to understand our education system, the discipline of philosophy is a good place to start.

## To gain a better understanding of our choices as a society

There is a close relationship between the kind of schools a society sets up – or more specifically, the kind of educational philosophy that underpins those schools – and the kind of society that its citizens are trying to produce. The Spartans didn't put their children through 14 years of relentlessly violent schooling, where they were turned into fearsome warriors, because they were a pacifist society who liked nothing better than a little bit of poetry. They educated their children that way because their society was a war machine.

However, not all the philosophies underpinning schooling systems are quite so obvious, instrumental, and easy to read as those of Sparta, and the discipline of philosophy not only enables us to understand the kinds of ideas and approaches that currently animate our schools, but also to plan for the kind of schools we'd *like* to have. After all, should education be about personal development? Should it be about preparing future citizens for their social and role? Should it be about learning a central core of timeless knowledge? Should it simply be about learning how to think? Should it be about producing citizens with a commitment to a just society? Each of these approaches has their strengths and weaknesses, and philosophy helps us determine what they are.

## To develop a personal philosophy

Philosophy is not just about acquiring a better understanding of the various possible approaches to education, or about which of these society ought to adopt, it is about organising a satisfactory personal relationship with the role of teacher. Arguably, this process has two interrelated components.

The first involves developing a personal judgement about what education – and more specifically, mass schooling – is all about. Do we find ourselves agreeing with Plato, that the important parts of schooling are those that teach us the deepest, most timeless forms of knowledge? Do we think that Aristotle's ideas have more to offer; with the belief that education's first responsibility is to be practical and useful? Or do we agree with Marx, that mass schooling is simply a clever device for legitimately funnelling working-class kids into working-class jobs? Philosophy helps us to figure out where we stand.

The second involves developing a personal philosophy of classroom practice, a philosophy of individual instruction. This might include deciding upon a style of teaching, whether this is based around Socratic dialogue, or Dewey's learning facilitation, or even Skinner's stimulus-response. It might involve deciding on a how the learning spaces should be organised, which might emphasise support and pastoral care, or hierarchy and structure, or fun and enjoyment. It might also concern the primary goal of that instruction, which could be directed towards generalised learning, or an enjoyment of the subject, or just the passing of exams.

## Why teach philosophy to children?

### For the same reasons as for adults

Children do not occupy an entirely separate conceptual space to adults, and if the case can be made that adults benefit from the study of philosophy, then the same argument surely applies to children. If adults can use philosophical reasoning to address some of life's more intangible questions, then why can't children? If adults can learn to reason more effectively, and hence think more clearly and critically, then why can't children? And the sooner the better.

In spite of the apparent value of philosophy to both life and learning, it has strug-gled to find a regular place in the contemporary curriculum, finding only a scattered presence within some, mostly primary, schools, and often in a variety of different forms. The case for the inclusion of philosophy in the National Curriculum was well made by Bini et al. (2009) in a submission to the Australian Curriculum, Assessment and Reporting Authority (ACARA). They rightly note:

> Almost every country in the world includes philosophy in its curriculum. Philosophy is recommended for inclusion in national curricula by the UN – and, in particular, by UNESCO – because of its importance in creating the conditions for a free and democratic society, and because of the role it plays in developing the general capabilities of citizens. (Bini et al. 2009, Part 3)

More specifically, they conclude that philosophy in schools brings both academic and social benefits. The following points summarise some of their arguments.

## For academic benefits

While philosophy can contribute positively to most general educational capacities, the evidence suggests that there are specific benefits that accrue from philosophical study in schools. As previously mentioned, the cluster of important mental activities that might be called *thinking skills* – developing, analysing and criticising arguments; problem-solving; decision-making; critical reasoning – are engendered by philosophy inquiry. Similarly, *creativity* is also significantly enhanced by philosophical studies. After all, the ability to be creative is fundamentally tied to intellectual flexibility, to the capacity to generate new ideas and new ways of seeing, and to the ability to be open-minded and adaptable. Importantly, the improvement in these two general capabilities is not just of a passing, theoretical interest. Research has shown that such improvements produce the most direct of educational benefits: better all-around aca-demic performance (Topping & Trickey 2007).

## For social benefits

One domain of philosophy is ethics, and it is important that students, as well as teachers, learn the ability to justify their ethical decisions, as will be discussed in Chapter 11. In the long term, citizens who are more able to think deeply about eth-ical issues are more likely to create a just society; after all, a complex problem often requires a complex solution, not a simple, unreflected knee-jerk response. In addition to fostering ethical behaviour, the study of philosophy in the form of 'communities of inquiry' also enhances teamwork and social competence. Debating issues, listening to opposing arguments and responding reasonably, agreeing with conclusions and new lines of discussion, all add to students' social skills and cooperative abilities. Finally, philosophy has a significant role to play in civics and citizenship, in that it helps to set out possible parameters of a 'good' society, as philosophy has tried to do since the time of Socrates. As is rightly noted, philosophy does not simply teach what 'democracy' is, or where it came from; by studying concepts such as justice, freedom, truth and rights, philosophy actually teaches students to *be* democratic (Bini et al. 2009, Part 2). Improving social capacities in these areas not only leads to better students, it also leads to a better society.

In summary, the reasons for studying philosophy are compelling. It is a subject that allows us to address some of life's more difficult questions, and to address them with clarity and perception. It allows educators to draw more informed conclusions about what mass schooling is, and about what kind of teachers we want to be. Finally, given the opportunity, it can be of great benefit to students: intellectually, academically and socially. All in all then, it's pretty useful.

# Myth #2 'Education' is self-evident; we don't need philosophy to explain it

Some things don't need any deep explanation, and education is one of them. It's all pretty simple: young people don't know very much, and if we want them to grow up to be useful, then someone has to teach them – someone who knows more than they do. You don't need a 'philosophical perspective'. You just need a classroom, a teacher, and a curriculum.

This myth is fairly easy to debunk. If education was as straightforward as is implied here, we most certainly wouldn't have spent 2500 years arguing about it, and it would be a six-week TAFE course, and not a four-year university degree. As it turns out, education has been one of the great topics of philosophical debate, one that has allowed the main theoretical approaches to do intellectual battle with each other.

## Addressing 'the content' of philosophy

At this stage, it might appear as if philosophy is mostly about learning to think clearly, and then using that clarity to address a range of somewhat-abstract questions, questions that the empirical sciences are largely unable to answer. While these are certainly an important part of the discipline, it only tells part of the story. There must also be something to think about – a body of knowledge, a range of 'stuff' to know. After all, it is surely important to gain knowledge of the arguments that have already been employed and assessed by previous thinkers, or we'll spend our time continually re-inventing the philosophical wheel.

There are a number of ways that this task could be managed when specifically addressing the philosophy of education. First, this could be approached by examining education through a series of topics – education and justice, education and language, education and governance, education and knowledge. In some ways, this entire book is structured in this manner, however it works less well when trying to understand, in the broadest possible terms, what 'education' is.

A second approach could be to address some of the most influential texts within educational philosophy – *The Nicomachean Ethics* (Aristotle 1980), *Some Thoughts Concerning Education* (Locke 1970), *Education as Initiation* (Peters 1964), *Culture and Anarchy* (Arnold 1963), *De-schooling Society* (Illich 1973); philosophers could argue over this list for years. However, the central purpose of unpacking each of these texts would be to try and understand the different ideas supporting each. Why not just go directly to those ideas and divide the field up accordingly?

The third approach does precisely that, and it is the strategy adopted here. This section of the chapter addresses a series of approaches to the philosophy of education, approaches that largely define the history of the ways in which education has been conceptualised. This is neither a definitive list of important approaches, nor is it a list that all philosophers would agree upon, by any means. However, it is a good enough place to start.

Each of the six philosophical approaches discussed here – idealism, realism, romanticism, pragmatism, Marxism, and postmodernism – will be approached in the same, four-part way: what the central ideas of the position are; how those ideas have been applied to education; how those ideas affect education today; and the ways in which those ideas have been criticised.

## Idealism

Idealism represents the first great Western philosophical system. It operates from the premise that, in the final analysis, reality is mental rather than physical (Winch & Gingell 2008). These ideas have their origins in the writings of Plato, who contended that life is primarily about the search for truth. However, given that truth is perfect and unchanging, it cannot lie in the material world, which is imperfect and ephemeral. Consequently, there must be another realm of existence – the ideal realm – of which our world is but an imperfect copy. Plato famously uses the 'allegory of the cave' to make his point. He described prisoners chained in a dark cave, staring at shadows cast on a wall. The prisoners took the shadows to be reality, when in fact reality was being played out behind them, and it was only when a prisoner managed to escape their chains and turn around, that they realised the truth.

Plato regarded education as a way of escaping our chains, of casting off the illusions of our material world, the 'false reality' of our cave, and slowly learning to access the realm of ideas, the realm of truth. In *The Republic* (1974), Plato even envisaged an education system that would produce an ideal, three-tier society. The society would consist of wise rulers, Guardians, schooled in philosophy; Auxiliaries, who protected the state; and Artisans, who produced the goods required for daily life. Education then, should be tailored to the tasks required of each citizen – an early version of streaming – with the brightest and the best given the intellectual skills to 'escape their chains', grasp the eternal truths present in the realm of ideas, and hence govern within justice.

Along with its influence on many later philosophers, such as Berkley, Kant and Hegel, the central legacy of idealism within modern education is the argument that the primary focus should be upon those things of lasting value; the great truths that animate our existence; the fundamental intellectual disciplines upon which all our knowledge is founded. According to this logic, schools should not be about the provision of mere skills, technical abilities that come and go. Such competences give no insights into truth, and they add nothing to our development as worthwhile and self-realised citizens. Schooling for the workplace is no schooling at all.

Idealism has been subject to a number of criticisms (Ozmon & Craver 2009). It has certainly struggled to find a place within an education system so heavily geared towards social and economic utility. Indeed, idealism could almost act as a metaphor for philosophy's wider struggle for inclusion in the contemporary curriculum: *Does it help with double-entry bookkeeping? No? Then, no thanks*. However, idealism's problems are as much theoretical as they are practical. In addition to the criticism that idealists have produced absolutely no evidence of the existence of a parallel ideal realm, it is also seen as an inherently conservative philosophical approach, in that it continually refers to 'timeless' and 'unchanging' ideals. More importantly perhaps, it has also been criticised as elitist; after all, arguably this kind of education is only relevant to future 'wise rulers'. Is it really relevant to someone who just wants to learn how to fix motors?

## Realism

Standing in fairly stark contrast to Plato's idealism, is the realism of his most famous pupil, Aristotle. Rather than regarding reality as being constituted within the world of ideas, Aristotle contended that we actually inhabit a material order of reality, one comprised of physical objects, and one that we can come to know and construct knowledge about (Harrison-Barbet 2001). To put it more simply, there isn't some special other place; this world is all we have, it exists independently of our thoughts; there is a physical reality we can come to understand.

Part of Aristotle's greatness lies in the ways that he translated his observations of our 'real' physical world into categories of knowledge, categories we now take for granted, and which are still an integral part of our curriculum. As a reflection of the realist belief in a logical and orderly universe, the realist curriculum has emphasised the practical study of the physical world, with a particular focus on mathematics and the various natural sciences. Furthermore, this information is to be transmitted from teacher to pupil in a systematic and standardised way. There is little room within this model for the Socratic method of teaching, relying as it does upon dialogue and mutual intellectual exploration. Rather, the realist teacher is required to know the content of each of the various subject areas, and to be able to pass that information on to students.

Arguably, the repeated calls for the 'three Rs' are part of the realist imperative within modern education; education has to be practical and useful to be deemed valid. By extension, the recent drive to vocational education can probably be traced to the same logic, although this is by no means what Aristotle had in mind:

> Aristotle was particularly derogatory about using education for any extrinsic or instrumental purposes and it is here that some of his aristocratic prejudices come out most clearly. Vocational education was fit only for the lower classes, for the Greek citizen it was the idea of education as making you a fuller and more cultured person that counted (Hobson 2001, 18–19).

Realism has had its fair share of critics. While initially standing in opposition to idealism, those disagreeing with this position also came from the ranks of romanticism, and then latterly postmodernism. The most obvious criticism of realism is that it has spawned a model of schooling that is too instrumental, and too focused upon ephemeral skills associated with the perceived needs of the employment market at any given moment, to the exclusion of more important and long-lasting types of knowledge. Also, postmodernists in particular have criticised realism for its belief that objective truth is out there, just waiting to be uncovered; the contrary position being that all knowledge is ultimately socially constructed. This debate will be discussed at length in Chapter 12.

## Romanticism

With its emphasis on reason and objectivity, the Enlightenment project of the eighteenth century was not without its critics. Leaving aside those who resented the rise of modern civil and political rights, a disparate group of artists, writers and thinkers also bemoaned what they saw as the destructive and homogenising effects of the growing obsession with reason. These 'Romantics' stressed the importance of emotion, creativity and intuition to the human spirit, rather than soulless predictability of the new scientific model. Romanticism valued subjectivity over objectivity, expression over analysis, and nature over society.

The first of the great romantics was Rousseau, who was instrumental in shaping the 'childhood as innocence' model discussed in Chapter 6. One of his most important books was *Emile*, and in this text he points to the corrupting influence of society: 'Everything is good as it comes from the hands of the Maker of the world but degenerates once it gets into the hands of man' (Rousseau 1956, 1). Rousseau's revolutionary idea was that children were to be best served, not by learning through oppressive and relentless regimentation, but by encouraging the full development of their natural, untainted spirit.

These ideas have been incredibly influential. In part, they were instrumental in the development of the free schooling movement, such as Neill's (1962) *Summerhill*. Such schools abandoned traditional notions of discipline and curriculum, and instead allowed children to follow their own intellectual paths. Far more significantly, Rousseau's ideas were pivotal to the rise of *progressivism* in education, a 'child-centred' model of learning, one that dominated the first half of the twentieth century (Darling & Nordenbo 2003), and one that could equally well have been given a section to itself.

Criticisms of educational romanticism are numerous. For example, given the greater contemporary understanding of the social construction of childhood, upon what is Rousseau's model of the natural, innocent child based, other than an historical fiction? Also, in an era that increasingly expects measurable outcomes from the schooling process, romantically inspired progressive education, where children are allowed to explore for exploration's sake, has – rightly or wrongly – come to be viewed as an unsupportable luxury.

## Pragmatism

Pragmatism is generally regarded as an American philosophy, and is normally associated with the late nineteenth-century work of James, and follows the logic that theorising is a pointless activity, in and of itself. The only relevance that theorising can have is when it is converted into the solution of concrete intellectual problems. A philosopher must ask, what is the practical worth of a particular idea? If the answer is 'nothing whatsoever', then the issue should be of no philosophical interest.

In relation to education, the main pragmatic philosopher is Dewey, probably the most influential of all twentieth-century writers in the field. His wide-ranging ideas are difficult to summarise, but – in contrast to Plato's idealism – he built his theories on the pragmatic belief that ideas are only of value in terms of their consequences for human existence. Many of Dewey's educational ideas were centred upon the notion of growth, and the belief that education is not simply preparation for life, but is part of life. Consequently, when deciding on the subject matter of education, student interests should be regarded as more important than a simple calculus of future social needs. Students must be shaped as active participants in their own education, in contrast to dominant, authoritarian models of teaching.

Just as Rousseau influenced progressivism, so too did Dewey, although in a different way. As Winch and Gingell (2008, 167–8) note:

> The Rousseau variant emphasises the importance of the individual in constructing his own cognitive world, while the Dewey variant stresses the role of the group in doing so. The former strand appeals to the work of Piaget while the latter appeals to the social constructivism that is (questionably) associated with the work of the psychologist Vygotsky. These tensions have practical effects on pedagogic strategies. While Rousseauian progressives emphasise individual learning at a pace chosen by the learner, Deweyans stress group and project work.

Criticisms of pragmatic approaches to education have largely centred upon the shortcomings of progressivism, an approach Dewey himself found fault with (e.g. classroom 'freedom' for its own sake). It has also been suggested that for Dewey's educational vision to be realised, the almost-utopian skill and knowledge sets required of teachers exceeds the reach of our current education system, particularly given the ongoing unwillingness of Western governments to fund education to the levels that would be required (Ozmon & Craver 2009).

## Marxism

As has been discussed in Chapter 1, Marxism has been highly influential within educational theory. In the final analysis, this philosophical approach is premised upon significant concerns over social and economic inequality. Marxism splits the social world into two opposing halves – those who have power, and those upon whom power is exercised – and it is this essential division that underlies all social structures, practices and forms of organisation. While Marxism eventually morphed into critical theory, a more subtle explanation of how society works, both are still principally concerned with issues of inequality.

Education is deemed by Marxists/critical theorists to play a crucial role in the ongoing success of the class system. Students aren't just educated; they are educated for particular social roles and outcomes, outcomes that are predetermined by social class. The system might look like a meritocracy, but this is an illusion: most of us end up in exactly the same social place as our parents. As such, schools aren't really about education; they are about social reproduction. That is, in practical terms, education isn't a vehicle for structural change, or personal social mobility. Schools are about subtly legitimating the contention that while you were given the opportunity to move up, you chose not to take it, or lacked the capacity to do so.

The effects of Marxism/critical theory can still be felt within contemporary education. Although a variety of philosophical approaches retain a commitment to social equity, it is generally critical theory that keeps this concern front and centre. Other writers influenced by Marxism also remain a potent voice within educational theory. For example, Freire (1970) in *Pedagogy of the Oppressed*, examines the way in which the lack of adequate education – and in particular, lack of basic literacy skills – has been used as a mechanism of social and political disempowerment for poor people. Although he was writing largely about South America, his arguments have wider application and significance.

In the past couple of decades, Marxist/critical theoretical approaches have been subject to considerable criticism. Indeed, much of Part 2 of this book can be seen in this light. Two central problems can be pointed to here. The first is that this approach necessarily regards the exercise of power as coercive; indeed the whole of our society and culture is regarded as a complex by-product of the rich exercising their power over the poor. Theoretical approaches based upon governance downplay the coercive aspects of power, focusing instead upon its productive potential. The second problem is that Marxism/critical theory is something of a master discourse, an explanatory model that tries to explain absolutely everything within a single framework. Postmodernism in particular has criticised this tendency as being reductionist; that is, it contends that the real world is far more complex than the one described by Marxism.

## Postmodernism

Towards the end of the eighteenth century, the Enlightenment, with its emphasis on human reason, had given birth to the era of *modernity*. For the next two hundred years, society was underpinned by the logic of modernism – truth, progress, objectivity – perhaps best exemplified by the rise of the scientific method. However, from the 1980s onwards, there was a growing belief that the Enlightenment project had failed in its goals, and that perhaps it was all rather more complicated than this. The resulting postmodern approach questioned the validity of singular, grand-narrative explanations of the world, the assumption that society was inevitably getting better, and the belief that socially neutral knowledge was possible (Lyotard 1984).

With regards to education, postmodernism shares many of critical theory's concerns over equity, but rejects the possibility of a single explanatory model, or even the possibility of agreement over what 'equity' might look like.

> No longer, for example, can the call: 'a free and equal education for all' provide a universal rallying point. Instead, we have a collection of quite separate and isolated groups often with conflicting or even mutually exclusive beliefs and goals … feminists, homosexuals, environmentalist, neo-Nazis, Christian and Islamic fundamentalists … It is very hard to mount a modernist universal call for justice and truth when so many cannot agree over what these things are or indeed over whether they exist at all (O'Farrell 1999, 13–14).

If postmodernism has manifested itself within contemporary education at all, it is by a fragmenting of some of the traditional certainties within the schooling system. There is no longer deemed to be a belief in a single, ideal curriculum, as with the old notion of the great liberal education, where the education of the best was the best education. Likewise, there has been a rejection of unitary models of truth and value; previously marginalised voices have started to be heard in subjects like history, literature and social science. Also, there are now multiple pathways through education, rather than just a linear filtering system that simply pushed the unworthy out at regular intervals.

Although the most recent of the philosophical approaches, postmodernism has not been immune from significant criticism. Postmodernism's refusal to give singular, simple explanations has been used against it, in that it is often characterised as overly complex, muddled and incoherent. Furthermore, following on from critical theory as it did, postmodernism has been accused of being apolitical, and lacking commitment to social and educational change. The argument here is that by refusing to stand for a particular version of freedom and equity, it is in danger of not standing for anything at all.

In summary, the six approaches addressed here – idealism, realism, romanticism, pragmatism, Marxism and postmodernism – are just some of the philosophies that continue to give shape to our understanding of education. There are others that could have legitimately claimed a place here. In addition to approaches such as progressivism and existentialism, there are a number of philosophies that deal explicitly with issues of gender, cultural diversity and indigeneity, as well as a wealth of non-Western philosophies that are often overlooked by Western universities (as will be discussed in Chapter 12). Needless to say, it is in the nature of the beast that some philosophers will be irritated by the absences here, let alone the depictions of those that have been included. Unfortunately, there is no 'perfect' selection.

Returning to the myth that began this section: we don't need philosophy to explain education. Rather than regarding mass schooling as some kind of self-evident, finished product, philosophy enables us to trace many of the ideas that have animated education over the last 2500 years. This begins with the initial idealist proposition that education should be directed towards uncovering the great truths that underwrite existence, to the subsequent realist emphasis of the more practical aspects of learning, manifest today in the calls for the three Rs. The eighteenth century gave birth to romantic notions of childhood innocence, and naturalistic ideas of education, which themselves formed part of later pragmatic approaches, with the positing of children as active participants in their own learning. By the twentieth century, more critical theories of mass schooling focused on the role of education in the reproduction of social inequality, concerns echoed by postmodern philosophers, but without any of the simple causal frameworks, or one-line solutions.

All of these philosophies – old and new – continue to play a role in shaping contemporary education; in shaping curriculum documents and informing classroom practice, in stimulating debates about policy and direction, and in providing the substance for irate editorials in our newspapers. By grasping how these philosophies work, and by understanding their strengths and weaknesses, we are all the more equipped to participate in this crucial process.

# Conclusion

If we are to make sense of mass schooling, the central purpose of this book, then a solid understanding of philosophy is just as important as a good grasp of history and social science. The study of philosophy offers us a lot. It provides us with the intellectual tools to answer some of the most important questions of life; furthermore, it allows us to address those questions in a clear and organised way. This clarity of thought is not then limited in its usefulness to the realm of esoteric inquiry. Such acquired skills spill over into daily life, and into the reasoned thinking required by all other intellectual disciplines, including education.

Philosophy also helps us plan for our educational future. Our system of mass schooling has, hidden within its fabric, significant traces of many of the various philosophies that have dominated education at different times, in different places, and for different reasons. This is of interest, not only for abstract, historical reasons, but also because understanding how these philosophies work, and which parts of them are still relevant to us, allows us to explore the possibilities of what schooling could be, and to work towards constructing a system based upon solid and viable conceptual foundations.

Finally, philosophy has a lot to offer anyone who takes an interest in it. Here are two final assertions regarding its relation to mass schooling: teaching is a profession that requires significant reflection, and philosophy helps to do that more systematically, and more productively, than any other discipline; also, philosophy has a lot to offer in the education of children, and more space should be found for it in the curriculum.

# Chapter 11

# Ethics and the law

This chapter address one of the most important areas of philosophy – ethics – and uses it to examine aspects of the role of the law within education. Of all the areas of philosophy, more has probably been written about ethics, and over a longer period, than any other. In addition, all cultures are structured around a fundamental ethical system: the law. However, irrespective of their importance, both subjects are currently notable for their lowly status within the teacher education curriculum.

## Myth #1 Understanding ethics doesn't help you to be a good teacher

*Knowing about ethics isn't a crucial part of being a good teacher. Teachers are there to teach a curriculum, not engage in complex ethical decision-making.*

Teaching is an ethically challenging profession. By having a solid grasp of the strengths and weaknesses of different ethical approaches, teachers are more able to make informed moral choices, and hence contribute to a more just schooling system.

## Myth #2 Unlike ethics, the law is straightforward, and everyone agrees upon what it is, and what it does

*The law is the clear expression of our most important rules. There is no serious dispute over its purpose, or its objectivity.*

On the contrary, the Australian system of law is complex, multilayered and highly contested. There is only limited agreement on how the law can be conceptualised, from being an extension of 'natural' rights and wrongs, to simply a political tool for the wealthy.

## Myth #3 We have an ethical education system; it does not discriminate

*We've come a long way from the days when racial and sexual discrimination were part of the system – discrimination is a thing of the past, particularly in schools.*

While its true that we have a range of laws protecting a wide range of categories of individuals from discrimination, they are far from perfect. Schools are still the site of more subtle forms of discrimination, especially regarding disability.

## Myth #4 There are no real ethical dilemmas left for education law to deal with

*Ethicists and lawyers have been scrutinising education for so long now, they've managed to sort out all the important problems. There's nothing left to worry about.*

On the contrary. For example there are significant ethical and legal debates occurring about mandatory reporting of suspected child abuse, or whether the law is stacked against teachers in negligence actions, or whether too much responsibility is placed on the shoulders of teachers. There's still a lot to reflect upon.

# Introduction

Having set out in Chapter 10 what philosophy is, what it can accomplish, and some of the main approaches that have been adopted within the discipline, this chapter will examine one particular area of philosophy – ethics – and then use it as a way of unpacking a second important area within contemporary education: the law. As will be seen in this chapter, these two sets of knowledges are both important in their own right, but are also closely and crucially related. Certainly, both of these are vital to the modern school, and it would be a foolhardy teacher indeed who regarded these topics as unrelated to their professional conduct or responsibilities. However, both appear to have a limited place within teacher education curricula, and the vast majority of teachers would be hard-pressed to explain the main elements of a philosophy of ethics, or demonstrate a working knowledge of those parts of the law that affect what they do every single day.

It is probably fair to say that people generally mean three different things when they talk about ethics. The first usage is synonymous with the term morals; the second is a set of principles, most often derived from moral values; the third is a body of academic knowledge, something you study at university. Interestingly, the vast majority of university study into ethics now concerns what is referred to as *meta ethics*: 'questions *about* morality, not *of* morality' (Cooper 1998, 3). To put it another way, whereas the philosophy of ethics has always been devoted to finding the best way to live a 'good' life, in recent years academic focus has fallen upon the nature of moral claims themselves. Just what is a moral claim? Are there objective moral facts? And why do we bother being moral at all?

## Ethics and teaching

Important though these questions are, they won't necessarily help us decide how we ought to act; how we can be ethical teachers. However, the other dominant type of ethics – *normative ethics* – may do just that. For most of its long history as a discipline, ethics has sought the means to determine right from wrong, with both validity and consistency. Myth #1 addresses the assertion that the relationship between teaching and ethics is a straightforward one, and one that needn't be worried about too much. Arguably, this is incorrect for two vital reasons. First, ethics itself is not a straightforward matter, in that it is not simple to define what we mean when we say something is wrong (i.e. is that just someone's opinion, or is it more than that?), and there is significant philosophical disagreement about how to structure any over-arching framework for ethical conduct. There are a number of different 'normative' ethical systems that attempt to give consistent answers about how we should act, and what kind of people we should be, and each guides our conduct as teachers in different ways.

Second, teaching is inherently an ethically complex discipline. Any profession that deals with the allocation of resources and the distribution of life chances, with the conduct of children and the organisation of punishment, with the valorisation of some identities and the marginalising of others, with normality and difference, with deciding whose history gets taught and whose culture gets to count, with deciding who deserves a second chance and who doesn't – and all on a daily basis – needs to be acutely aware of the mechanics of ethical decision-making.

## Ethics and the law

The link between these two areas is a fairly obvious one. It is often held that the law is simply right and wrong, set out in a legislative form; that our most important ethical principals are distilled into codified social rules, rules reinforced by social veneration and organised punishment. After all, surely we all know what the law is, and approximately how it works; there's no great mystery to the law. Myth #2 addresses these assertions.

First, our common law legal system is only one of several possibilities; other cultures and nations organise their mechanisms for the buttressing of right and wrong quite differently. In Australia, we have an intricate mix of statute and judge-made law, a hierarchy of courts, federal/state legal complexities, and a wide range of different legal areas. All of these impact directly on how the law operates, and more specifically, how schools work and how teachers do their jobs.

Second, there is considerable disagreement over exactly what the law is. Is it simply natural laws of right and wrong applied to humans? Or is it the mechanism by which those with power get to tell us what we can do and what we can't, based upon their own self-interest; for example, which acts deserve significant punishment (robbery), and which generally do not (tax evasion).

## Discrimination

One significant area of law that ties directly to ethics is that of discrimination. The question of whether it is right to treat someone differently on the basis of a given attribute is one that is of particular importance within education. Given that twenty-first-century schools are awash with laws, rules, regulations, policy documents, ethical guidelines and codes of conduct, myth #3 suggests that it is inconceivable they could be the site of anything as morally reprehensible as discrimination.

The evidence actually paints a far more complex picture of discrimination under Australian law. There is certainly a wide range of legislation, state and federal, coving a range of different areas. This legislation deals with both direct and indirect discrimination; that is, both with the kind of discrimination that involves directly denying rights to someone based upon some given attribute – 'You can't come to school here; you're disabled' – as well as indirectly denying those rights to someone by setting up a prerequisite condition with which they can't comply – 'Of course you can come to school here; as long as you can get your wheelchair up the stairs'. However, there is more to the legislation than this, as there also appears to be mechanisms within those very same laws that effectively permit discrimination to continue as before. As is often the case, the devil is in the detail, or more specifically, in the exemptions.

## Continuing areas of ethical and legal concern

Perhaps not surprisingly within a discipline as subject to legal constraint as education, many legal and ethical dilemmas are still seeking effective solutions. Myth #4 addresses a range of questions that require satisfactory resolution within the environment of the mass school. For example, should we have uniform mandatory reporting laws for teachers suspected of child abuse? Are our negligence laws currently stacked in favour of the plaintiff (i.e. those making the claim of negligent conduct) to the detriment of teachers? Is it fair to keep loading legal responsibilities onto schools, simply for the sake of convenience (Tait 2006)? All of these ethical and legal issues are a long way from being settled.

To summarise, the four myths to be dealt with in this chapter are:

**Myth #1** – Understanding ethics doesn't help you be a good teacher

**Myth #2** – Unlike ethics, the law is straightforward, and everyone agrees upon what it is, and what it does

**Myth #3** – We have an ethical education system; it does not discriminate

**Myth #4** – There are no real ethical dilemmas left for education law to deal with

# Myth #1 Understanding ethics doesn't help you to be a good teacher

Complex ethical decision-making isn't a necessary part of being a good teacher – after all, we're not philosophers. You just need to do your job, keep your head down, and stay away from anything controversial. We're not being asked whether or not we should have euthanasia, or the death penalty, or whether Australian troops should go to war. We are simply being asked to teach a curriculum.

Even educators with the most simplistic understanding of their own discipline would have trouble accepting this myth at face value. Teachers are acutely aware not only of the difficult ethical questions raised by our education system, but also of the complexity of the ethical choices they are personally asked to make. For example, our system of education raises a number of familiar macro ethical questions: is it appropriate that we allow parents who can afford it to buy a better education than those that can't? Should we have 'special schools' for those with physical or intellectual differences, or should they be in mainstream classes? On a more individual level, moral questions might include: should I spend part of my career teaching in an indigenous school, and contributing directly to indigenous education? To what extent will I allow my own understandings of appropriately gendered conduct to impinge upon my teaching? There are hundreds of questions, just like these, that teachers continually need to address. For the most part, we all bumble through the process as best we can, often without anything but the haziest of convictions that we're doing the right thing. The point here is that it is possible to equip educators to better understand the strengths and weakness of the various ethical choices made. This is the substance of normative ethics.

## Normative ethics

Whereas meta ethics is concerned with the very nature of ethics and moral decision-making, normative ethics is much more concerned with the content of moral behaviour. That is, normative ethics seeks to provide codes of conduct, or action guides, through which any given moral choice may be assessed and directed. Three dominant normative positions will be addressed here: virtue ethics, consequentialist ethics and deontological ethics.

## Virtue ethics

According to virtue ethics, in order to find 'goodness', the first place to look should be at a person's character. It is good character that best reflects and organises what we regard to be desirable, and this desirability is normally reflected in the virtues they possess, such as courage, temperance, wisdom and justice. These four are often regarded as the 'cardinal' moral virtues, however this list may also include generosity, benevolence, constancy and industry, although these are by no means fixed or agreed upon (Tannsjo 2002). The logic of virtue ethics is straightforward: if you have a moral dilemma, the correct course of action lies in what you know a good person would do.

Virtue ethics has its origins in the writings of Aristotle in the fourth century BC, principally in the *Nicomachean Ethics* (1980). In this text, he argues that 'the good' is the inherently worthwhile end point for all actions, and by working towards this, we are able to achieve happiness. This approach differs from its rivals – consequentialism and deontological ethics – in a number of significant ways, the most important way being the kind of ethical questions that need to be asked. Rather than inquiring 'What is the best way to live?', virtue ethics asks 'What kind of person should I be?' This is because the kind of person you are (e.g. a virtuous person) determines how your actions are to be interpreted (i.e. good). This reverses the logic of the other approaches that assess the nature of the person based upon a prior assessment of the specific action (e.g. stealing is wrong ... you stole ... *ergo*, you are bad).

Virtue ethics is generally regarded as the weakest of the three approaches. First: there is no necessary agreement as to which virtues should be considered important in the formation of a virtuous person. MacIntyre (1998) notes that virtues are relative to time and place, and that identifying core virtues can be a difficult proposition. Second, there appears to be circularity in parts of the reasoning. If a virtuous person does an act, the act is therefore good. But how do we determine that a person is virtuous? Mostly because of their good acts. Finally, if a good act is one done by a virtuous person, does this mean virtuous people are incapable of bad acts, and that bad people are incapable of good acts? Or, if both good and bad people do the same acts, are the acts to be interpreted differently?

## Consequentialist ethics

Consequentialism holds that moral evaluation between different courses of action should be made on the basis of a comparison of the consequences of those actions: that is, the action that brings about the best outcome is the right thing to do. The most important consequentialist position is *utilitarianism*. Harman (1977, 152) defines utilitarianism as, 'the theory that you ought always to act so as to maximise social utility, where "social utility" is simply another name for the general welfare'. The idea of utilitarianism was first developed in the eighteenth century by the British empiricist Hume, before being made fully explicit by Bentham (1988), and later in a more qualified way by Mill (1957). This theory has at its core the belief that an action is right if it is useful for increasing overall happiness, conversely an action is wrong if it decreases overall happiness.

Supposing you are confronted with a choice between two possible options; utilitarians would argue that the correct decision is one which, when considering all relevant factors, produces the larger balance of good over bad, pleasure over pain. In this manner, according to utilitarianism, you are freed from all ethical decision-making, other than the ability to sum the relevant components of the equation and thereby reach a conclusion. This strict form of utilitarianism – championed by Smart (1973) – is called 'act-utilitarianism'. A somewhat more sophisticated version of the theory is called 'rule-utilitarianism'. This latter approach stresses all the main points associated with act-utilitarianism, but proposes that choices are more often made on the basis of rules rather than by addressing individual consequences of specific actions. In this manner, the principle of utility is maintained, but not at the level of single judgements.

Both forms of utilitarianism have also been subject to significant criticism. Williams (1972, 1973) presents three main flaws within its logic. First, he argues that its fundamental axis – happiness – is problematic, suggesting that it is only viable if it is in some way a generalisable, cumulative concept, which it does not appear to be (Arrow's (1978) 'preference satisfaction' arguments aside). After all, a happy life may include a wide variety of moral values, all of which have little or nothing in common.

The second problem is the issue of negative responsibility. Williams uses the example of having to execute one innocent person to save 20, an unproblematic act within utilitarian thinking. He concludes that allowing a bad deed, in order to prevent a worse one, is symptomatic of utilitarians' inability to address issues such as social justice, individual fairness or personal integrity. His last criticism concerns the presumption that good can be simply defined in terms of the happiness of the greatest number. As Williams (1985, 86) states: 'If racist prejudice is directed towards a small minority by a majority that gets enough satisfaction from it, it could begin to be touch and go whether racism might not be justified.'

## Deontological ethics

Deontological ethics, otherwise called duty ethics or Kantian ethics, provides a coherent alternative to the utilitarian position. Supporters of this position argue that the consequences of an action should not enter into any judgement of whether that action is to be deemed right or wrong. Rightness or wrongness is inherent within the very nature of the act, and it should not matter what happens afterwards. Deontological ethics are almost always discussed in terms of the ideas of Kant, developed in the late eighteenth century. Kant's moral theories are complex and far-reaching, but three significant components are dealt with here.

The first addresses the centrality of the notion of duty. Kant believed that the pivotal element of morality is *motive*, and that acting in a particular manner simply because of a concern for the consequences is not to act morally. An act is only moral when an agent realises that they have a duty to act in a particular way, even to their own detriment. Therefore, what happens after an act is done – crucial to the utilitarian position – is completely irrelevant.

The second element of Kant's moral theory is his most well known. Kant sought to identify a moral absolute against which all actions could be measured, stating: 'act only in accordance with that maxim through which you can at the same time will that it become a universal law' (1998, 31). This is the famous *categorical imperative*. It is immoral for someone to lie, because by lying, they are asserting that it is acceptable for everyone to lie. As this is clearly unacceptable, we must therefore always tell the truth. After all, if we didn't follow this rule, the notion of telling the truth would become incoherent.

The final notable component of Kant's moral theory is sometimes referred to as the *practical imperative*. The operative principle here is that nobody should ever be thought of simply as a means to an end, rather they should always be regarded as ends in themselves. As an almost direct rebuttal of utilitarianism, this imperative precludes the possibility overriding the rights of the one in the name of the many. The point here appears to be that fundamental issues of equity and fairness cannot be traded away for some other 'greater' good.

Two main criticisms has been raised about deontological ethics. First, if you are asked to make choices on the basis of your duties, what happens when those duties are in conflict? Ethical decisions often involve more that one moral variable. If you promise to keep a secret, but are then asked to tell the truth about some matter contained in that secret, there are conflicting moral duties there, in terms of keeping a promise, and in terms of not lying. Second, Kant did not believe in making exceptions to his moral rules. After all, such rules would be fairly pointless if every time the circumstances proved difficult, it was possible to make an exception. Consequently, Kant would not accept that it was ever morally acceptable to lie, even if it meant preventing a much greater wrong. Certainly, there is little room in Kant's universe for sympathy or compassion.

At this point, having outlined the main elements of the three great systems of normative ethics, we can apply them to a given ethical problem to see how they stand up to closer scrutiny.

## The case of *L v Minister for Education*

In 1995, a seven-year-old girl – L – was suspended from her school in Brisbane. The girl had been diagnosed with 'global developmental delay, and teachers stated that they had difficulty managing her behaviour, as well as managing the education of the rest of the class. L's mother took her case to the Queensland Anti-Discrimination Tribunal, which found that although L had indeed been discriminated against, this discrimination was exempted under the *Anti-Discrimination Act 1991* (Qld) because 'unjustifiable hardship' would result for the school. In summary: L had to attend 'special' school.

The case of *L v Minister for Education* became the subject of much discussion in Queensland, not only among those involved in inclusive education, but also among mainstream classroom teachers (Butler 1995; Atkins 1996). Some of the issues raised are quite familiar: there was dispute between the experts called by the two sides of the case as to whether a mainstream education is the best choice for those children with disabilities (as well as benefiting the other children in the classroom, who learn vital life skills of flexibility, compassion, cooperation and respect for difference), or whether they are better off in specifically tailored surroundings. There were also concerns raised about the costs to other children of L's continued presence in the classroom, concerns which even merited an editorial in the *Courier Mail* (1996, 16):

> There is a place in the general education system for children with slight disability. As many of these youngsters as possible should be thus accommodated. But we must recognise that some cannot be: in their own interests as much as those of children whose schooling is disrupted by the unmeetable demands of a less fortunate classmate.

The issue of exactly whom a teacher ought to be reasonably expected to teach also caused a great deal of discussion and concern. This concern most frequently revolved around the question: 'What are the ethical responsibilities of a teacher, as they relate to disability?' Unfortunately, this is a question that does not lend itself to an easy answer.

## Normative ethics and the exclusion of L

The intention now is to use the three normative positions to gain a better purchase on the decision by L's teachers to seek her exclusion from the classroom. The intention here is neither to applaud nor to castigate those involved; they are simply being employed here as exemplars of a broader debate.

### Employing virtue ethics

This approach produces some ambiguous results. If the teachers are good people, and there is no reason to believe that they are not, then having L removed from the classroom was the right thing to do. It is possible that the decision reflected the presence of some of the 'cardinal' virtues of courage (in the face of a difficult decision), wisdom (for realising the decision needed to be made) and justice (in their concerns for the welfare of the other children). However, it could equally well reflect the absence of some of these virtues. It may well have been the lack of courage and sense of justice, as well as a lack of benevolence and industry, that resulted in L having to leave the classroom. Only the teachers involved can know, which admirably demonstrates one of the great weaknesses in virtue ethics: are these good acts by good people, or bad acts by bad people? Maybe neither.

### Employing consequentialist ethics

It is fairly clear that the central rationale behind the decision in *L v Minister for Education* is based upon utilitarian reasoning. As one of the teachers said at the tribunal, he could give L a good lesson, or he could give the remainder of the class a good lesson, but he could not do both (Butler, 1995). Under these circumstances, a utilitarian calculation was clearly made, and the maximum social good was deemed to lie with L's removal – although against her wishes and those of her mother. The judge in the tribunal makes the utilitarian nature of this calculation perfectly clear:

> ... it seems to me that other considerations, such as the stresses placed on teaching staff at Beta [the school] without specialist training and the disruption entailed to other children, are such as to outweigh to benefits to L and constitute unjustifiable hardship to the Department should it be compelled to accept L back into the Beta school. (*L v Minister for Education* [1996] QADT 2, 9)

This neat piece of mathematics demonstrates some of the flaws within utilitarianism. First, there appears to be little regard for issues of social justice and minority rights; if the majority of the class feel that they will benefit from L's removal, then L's right to stay is irrelevant. As previously mentioned, if the harmony of the classroom is disrupted because of the presence of someone with different colour skin, this logic may well also support their removal. Second, the calculations involved in utilitarianism are necessarily incomplete. When does the calculating stop? After all, the initial benefits of greater class discipline and order may need to be balanced against the acquisition of undesirable long-term beliefs that most difficulties can be solved by exclusion, that basic compassion is unnecessary, and that those with differences do not belong with the rest of us. It is not surprising that utilitarianism has struggled in the face of these criticisms.

## Employing deontological ethics

It seems fairly unequivocal that Kant would regard the decision to discriminate against L to be a wrong act. The fact that the Tribunal found that the *consequences* of L's inclusion in the classroom meant that the teachers were justified in excluding her is irrelevant within Kant's ethical universe. L is being treated as a means to an end – the 'better' welfare of others – contravening the practical imperative. Also, unless we have as a general rule that it is acceptable to discriminate against disabled children, the categorical imperative suggests that discrimination against L was wrong. This does appear to be a somewhat simplistic, harsh and inflexible model of ethical analysis.

## Compromise positions

While not exempt from criticism itself, Ross's (1930) theoretical adaptation of Kant offers one possible route out of this impasse. He points to seven prima facie duties – fidelity, reparation, gratitude, justice, beneficence, self-improvement and non-maleficence – which must to be adhered to before any other issues, such as consequences, can be taken into consideration. Using the example of L, the prima facie duties of justice, beneficence and non-maleficence probably apply to the teachers under these circumstances, in that they had a duty to prevent the improper distribution of good and bad, to help improve the conditions of others, and to prevent (emotional) injury. Teachers would then have to demonstrate that other serious reasons had caused them to resile from these duties, most likely by noting their duties to other children. Whether this argument is accepted would then be a matter of interpretation of the facts.

It is not only deontologists who have sought to find some common ground. Brandt (1978) argues that utilitarian conclusions need not be binding upon an individual; rather they may simply be used as a guide for action. Ross would only consider this proposal to be acceptable if utilitarian concerns were to be lightly overlaid on a solid deontological foundation, rather than the other way around. Arguably, this approach would probably be one of the most palatable within the discipline, given that most moral philosophers are now deontologists (Olen 1983).

In summary, it would appear that teachers are required to deal with ethical issues of great complexity. Understanding why being 'a good person' might not be enough to act as a foundation for an entire system of moral decision making, why the utilitarian notion of 'the greater good' might not be the answer to everything, and why the Kantian imperative to 'act as if it were to become a universal law' might struggle with issues of compassion, would allow teachers to weigh their choices with greater confidence, and help produce a more just education system.

# Myth #2 Unlike ethics, the law is straightforward, and everyone agrees upon what it is, and what it does

The law is our ultimate set of rules – clear, direct and unequivocal. If you follow the rules, you're fine; if you don't, those rules come with an equally clear set of punishments. Importantly though, the law is more than just rules; everyone knows the law represents the best of our culture's morality, translated into legislative form.

When we talk about breaking the law, we are generally taught to conceptualise this in a similar way as breaking school rules, or breaking one of the 10 commandments, in that the law is depicted as a clear list of things not to do. The law sets out our rights and obligations, delineates what we can do from what we can't, gives us certainty in our interactions and agreements, provides a mechanism for addressing wrongs, and prescribes appropriate punishments for those who fail to behave as they should. It's all very straightforward.

Unfortunately, it's a lot more complicated than that. First, the law is not a single and neatly bound set of rules. Australia inherited its legal system from the United Kingdom, and it is a complex mixture of statute and common law, shaped within different levels of government, assembled according to judicial precedence across a hierarchy of courts, divided into different branches and types, and loosely held together by a collection of constitutions. Furthermore, there is no real agreement on precisely what 'the law' is, or what it does. For example, does our law spring, virtually fully formed, from natural ideas about right and wrong? Or is it simply an objective set of historically determined rules that have little or nothing to do with justice? Or is it just a device through which the powerful make sure they stay that way? Or is it simply a piecemeal set of codes and subjective fictions that fail, under closer scrutiny, to bind into anything coherent at all?

## The basics

In stating that we do not have a legal system defined by given sets of rules and collections of codes, does not mean that such a system does not exist; the majority of the world's legal systems follow precisely this model – referred to as the *civil law* system – that initially developed from Roman law. With the exception of those countries following Islamic (Sharia) law, the main alternative is referred to as the *common law* system, so called because it was 'common' to all the people of England in the early Middle Ages, in contrast to the local rules that governed the customs in various different areas.

The common law system is a balance of statute law, and the unwritten law of judicial precedence, interpretation, expansion and modification: i.e. court-made law. In Australia, statute law is produced by both state and federal parliaments, with the latter taking precedence where any conflict occurs. The courts are set up in a hierarchy, with lower courts having to follow the legal precedents set by courts higher up the pyramid. State courts ascend from Magistrates Courts, through District Courts, to Supreme Courts. Federal Courts ascend from the Federal Magistrates Court, to the Family Court and the Federal Court. At the top of both of these judicial pyramids sits the Australian High Court. All of these bodies are responsible for the production, modification and implementation of Australian laws, including those that affect mass education.

The law is also not comprised of one enormous area of regulation; it is broken up into different fields and domains. These include the laws of contract, equity, tort and property, public law, administrative law, constitutional law, family law, international law and criminal law. Each of these impacts directly upon the way schools are organised and operated. The largest division within law is probably between criminal law and tort law, between those wrongs that have historically been deemed sufficiently important to be punished by the State – such as murder and theft – and those wrongs that are left up to the individual to pursue – such as negligence and trespass. Finally, all of this complex and interwoven body of law is underpinned by the Australian Constitution, and various state constitutions, setting out nebulous basic parameters of how and where the law may be applied.

The intention here is not to advocate the 'simple' civil law system over our common law – far from it. Common law countries are justifiably proud of their legal systems, and while these systems have many advantages over their civil law equivalents (such as flexibility, consistency and expediency), simplicity is probably not one of them. Rather, the intention is to note that the mass school, and its inhabitants, are subject to an incredibly wide variety of laws, both in terms of statute and precedent, from a range of disparate legal areas, spawning an equally wide range of policies, rules and guidelines, supported by a myriad of interventions, disciplinary procedures, professional penalties and criminal sanctions. There is absolutely nothing simple and straightforward about our law.

## So what is the law?

While not underestimating the importance of discipline and governance within contemporary education, as discussed in Chapter 4, we can see here that the mass school is also organised within complex networks of legislation that provide a generalised framework for organising the functioning of the institution. However, the question remains: Just what is the law?

> How does the law differ from and how is it related to orders backed by threats? How does legal obligation differ from, and how is it related to, moral obligation? What are rules and to what extent is law an affair of rules? To dispel doubt and perplexity on these three issues has been the chief aim of most speculation about the 'nature' of law (Hart 1961, 13).

Arguably, the answer to the question has produced a wide range of answers, the four most important of which will be addressed here: natural law, legal positivism, critical legal studies and postmodern jurisprudence. It will be argued that each of these answers leads to a different understanding of the role of law within education.

## Natural law

This understanding of the substance of law has a very long tradition. Cicero located the source of law within nature when he said 'True law is right reason in agreement with nature; it is of universal application, unchanging and everlasting' (1995, Book 3, Ch. 22). This idea was later taken up by religious scholars, such as St Thomas Aquinas, who contended that human laws should always be measured against the absolute values given to us by God, deduced through our understanding of the natural world. Natural law asserts that whatever naturally is, ought to be – thereby drawing a direct link between law and morality.

The connection between schooling and law is also founded within nature. Following Plato, the law is employed to organise an education system best able to shape a society, based around the most important of all natural forms: 'the good'. As such, morality is placed front and centre, and the role of legislation is to make manifest the laws we need to produce the schools we 'ought' to have.

Natural law has been heavily criticised, most frequently from the viewpoint that it is based upon nothing more than metaphysical speculation, given that no-one is capable of determining what the empirical substance of natural law actually is. The most damning criticism of natural law was set out by Bentham, the utilitarian, who regarded the entire position as 'nonsense on stilts', contending that claims to some transcendental point of origin renders the project empty of real substance.

## Legal positivism

This approach to law is not based upon an understanding of the law as 'positive', but rather refers to the law as 'posited', or written. That is, this model supports the belief that the law is a set of judicial norms established by the State, one that excludes any appeal to a higher transcendental authority, such as nature. The founder of legal positivism, Austin (2000), summed up the positivist critique of natural law when he stated 'the existence of law is one thing: its merit or demerit is another'. The debate between Hart and Fuller best exemplifies the tension between the two positions. Following the war crimes trials in postwar Germany, Hart – a positivist – insisted that the law is the law, irrespective of whether it meets external moral criteria, and that any potential moral abhorrence is a separate issue altogether. Fuller (1958) countered by arguing that minimum moral requirements are necessary for a law to be validly counted *as* a law.

A legal positivist understanding of schooling and the law would not seek to go beyond the text of the law concerned. Removing 'ought' from the equation suggests that debates over, for example, the relative ease by which schools can sidestep anti-discrimination legislation, as in the case of *L v Minister for Education* discussed in myth #1, have no useful correlation within positivist jurisprudence. The law is the law, and the rest should be debated elsewhere.

Needless to say, legal positivism has garnered a significant amount of criticism, not least because it largely regards as irrelevant the purpose behind legislation. Just as it developed out of dissatisfaction with the metaphysics of natural law, so too did legal positivism itself trigger new conceptual models, ones emphasising the social and political context within which laws are made. The first of these was legal realism, but this paradigm eventually evolved into critical legal studies.

## Critical legal studies

Closely tied to critical theory, as discussed in Chapter 1, critical legal studies emphasises the relations of power underpinning the law. Indeed, far from being a reflection of some idealised natural order, or a neutral collection of rules and procedures, the law in real life is deemed to be partial, fluid, inconsistent, often inequitable, and inevitably political. The law is not the ultimate objective arbiter of disputes; it is an object to be fought over by the powerful, who then use it in their own interests. Hutchinson and Monahan (1984, 206) note that: 'Law is simply politics dressed up in a different garb; it neither operates in a historical vacuum nor does it exist independently of ideological struggles in society.'

As critical legal studies understands the law primarily through the lens of social and political domination, the law as it specifically relates to schools is no different. It regards the law as providing primary support for an education system committed to social reproduction. Children are compelled to go to school, thereby ensuring a plentiful and docile workforce; the law sets up different schools for different classes, as well as for the normal and for the disabled. The law was even used to ensure that married women were forced to leave the teaching profession altogether. Critical legal scholars would argue that all of these forms of legislation dovetail neatly with existing social ideologies, reinforcing their claim that law is simply politics by another name.

The criticisms of this position mirror those pertaining to critical theory outlined in Chapter 1, most significantly, that this is a reductionist and homogenising understanding of the law, one which has struggled to maintain its intellectual authority in the face of its postmodern successors.

## Postmodern jurisprudence

Although critical legal studies dealt a severe blow to legal positivism, the coup de grâce came in the form of postmodern jurisprudence, an intellectual movement that eventually killed off critical legal studies as well, or at least, forced its mutation into new, and more specific, forms of criticism. One important point raised by postmodern jurisprudence involves the notion of legal objectivity. The notion of 'the reasonable man' occupies a central place within Western canons of law, and this pervasive legal fiction constitutes the abstract rational actor who forms the core of legal objectivity. However, many recent writers have noted that this 'reasonable man', supposedly the rational subject of the Enlightenment, is actually a pseudonym for a white, upper-middle class, educated, Western male. Such writers, whether discussing gender (Bottomley 1996), cultural difference (West-Newman 2001), or the effects of postcolonialism (Lenta 2004), all contend that such an assumption marginalises all other voices and experiences within the legal system. A postmodern understanding of the law presupposes no such singular objective position, no singular truth that animates the system, and no single knowledge base that deserves pre-eminence over all others.

Viewed through this lens, education law moves a long way from the positivist depiction of a neutral, disembodied set of rules and regulations that merely give the structure an effective framework. Such an approach regards the laws involved as a moveable pastiche of sometimes contradictory imperatives and rationalities, one that both lacks a singular set of animating principles, and fails to cohere within a singular logic. When freed of the false objectivity of the 'reasonable man' fiction, such an approach also has a far easier time explaining the French ban on headscarfs in schools, or laws that prevent equal access for girls to specific school sports – subjects upon which critical legal studies would also have much to say, though for different reasons. Not surprisingly though, this postmodern rejection of the possibility of any sort of objectivity, legal or otherwise, constitutes a primary component of most criticisms of the position, as can be seen in Chapter 10.

In summary, teachers inhabit a complex legal environment. Not only is modern schooling cross-cut by a complex web of federal and state statutes, case law, regulations and policies, but also the system from which this law emerges is inherently complex. Indeed, there is even only limited agreement on what the law actually is, and certainly we can't just point to it and say 'Here is the ultimate neutral umpire. You have a difficult problem within education? Stop worrying and let the law sort it out.' If only it were that simple.

# Myth #3 We have an ethical education system; it does not discriminate

We've come a long way from the era when black people weren't allowed in schools, women weren't allowed in university, and disabled people were made to go to their own 'special' places. Everyone has to be treated the same now – we've even got laws to make sure this happens. Discrimination is pretty much a thing of the past, most certainly in schools.

This myth is partly correct. We *have* come a long way since the era when it was perfectly acceptable – ethically and legally – to discriminate on the basis of any one of a wide range of attributes, from religion to disability, from race to marital status. That said, it was not that long ago when female teachers had to resign from their positions if they decided to marry, a policy that never applied to men; or to put it another way, social concerns over discrimination are, for the most part, relatively new. Importantly however, the problem of discrimination has not gone away, and the solutions we have put in place appear far from perfect.

## Discrimination and the law

The issue of discrimination has been dealt with at length in Chapter 3. It has been defined as *the process whereby members of particular groups are denied equal treatment, based solely upon their membership of that group.* Issues of overt and covert discrimination, as well as individual, institutional and cultural discrimination have also been discussed. The focus here will fall specifically upon attempts by the law to address the problem of discrimination. It should be noted from the outset that this is not intended in any way as a functional analysis of the legislation. For that purpose, texts such as Butler and Mathews' excellent *Schools and the Law* (2007) is a good place to start. Rather, it is simply meant as the briefest sketch of the important sections common to all the anti-discrimination Acts.

Anti-discrimination legislation has been enacted at both federal and state level. The federal Acts are the *Racial Discrimination Act 1975* (Cth), the *Sex Discrimination Act 1984* (Cth), the *Disability Discrimination Act 1992* (Cth), and the *Age Discrimination Act 2004* (Cth). Each state has enacted its own anti-discrimination legislation, such as the *Anti-Discrimination Act 1977* (NSW), the *Anti-Discrimination Act 1991* (Qld), and the *Equal Opportunity Act 1995* (Vic.). The state acts, rather than dealing with a given issue, cover a wide range of different forms of discrimination. The general structures however are basically the same.

## Elements of the legislation

The provisions in these Acts do not cover every aspect of life in Australia; that is not all forms of selection, are also discrimination. There may be many moments when we may feel we have been discriminated against, which would not rise to the necessary standard to be covered by the legislation. For example, you may once have been left on the bench for an entire game by the coach of your local under 10 soccer team – on the grounds that you were complete rubbish. This may have been cruel, but the question here is: have you been discriminated against, as understood and addressed by the relevant legislation?

## Activity

The first criterion to be satisfied is the nature of the activity; not all activities are included. The primary thrust of the legislation is to cover public life, and while all aspects of schooling are protected by the various Acts, it is less likely to be deemed applicable the further a complaint gets away from issues such as education and employment. Sporting clubs should still be covered by the legislation.

## Grounds

The second criterion involves the grounds by which the discrimination occurred. Whereas the federal legislation addresses a single, specific attribute – race, sex, disability and age – the state legislation contains a list of attributes, one of which must be applicable in that instance. 'Lack of ability' is not a functioning attribute in any of the state legislation; unfortunately then, with regards to the match you spent on the sidelines, you have no remedy under anti-discrimination law. However, if you had been left on the sidelines because of your religion, one of the attributes on the list, you may have had a case. The situation is more complicated with regards to physical disability, more on which shortly.

## Types of discrimination

The third issue involves the form that the discrimination has taken, in that there are two main legal types. The first is *direct discrimination*. This is where a person is treated less favourably on the basis of a particular attribute. This is the more straightforward type of discrimination: you can't have the job because you are black, or because you are a Mormon, or because you are a woman, or because you are gay. Most of these are covered by most of the state anti-discrimination legislation, although there are some local variations.

The other type is *indirect discrimination*. This is where a person is unreasonably required to comply with a particular requirement, and being unable to do so to the same degree as everyone else, they are treated less favourably. As Butler and Mathews note:

> Indirect discrimination arises where policies or practices which may appear fair in form and intention are discriminatory in impact and outcome. Accordingly policies or practices are judged by their effect rather than the employer's intention or motivation (2007, 183).

Back to the hypothetical soccer game: if the coach left you on the bench because he doesn't like Mormons, this would be direct discrimination. If the coach leaves you on the bench because you won't join with the rest of the team in having Gatorade at half time, because it might contain caffeine – which many Mormons won't drink – this may well amount to indirect discrimination. So even though the coach states that your omission has nothing to do with your religion, and that it's solely about the Gatorade, under anti-discrimination legislation, this amounts to the same thing.

A more plausible example of indirect discrimination involves the case of *Kemp v Minister for Education*. At the end of the 1980s, Australian state schools adopted a specific promotion policy that rewarded length of service and seniority. While there was no deliberate intention to exclude women from promotion opportunities – this would have constituted direct discrimination – because many women took time out of their professional lives to have a family before later returning to teaching, this new policy was found by the courts to have indirectly discriminated against women. That is, female teachers were required to comply with a particular requirement – a long period of professional service – and being unable to do so to the same degree as male teachers, were treated less favourably by being denied promotion.

## Exemption

The fourth issue involves mechanisms for softening the effects of the anti-discrimination legislation, most frequently in terms of taking into account the 'unjustifiable hardship' it might cause to the discriminating party were it forced to comply with a court order. There would be no hardship for either the coach of the soccer team, or the Australian Government, if they were forced, respectively, to choose players who refused to drink half-time Gatorade, or to put in place a more flexible promotion policy. This is not always the case. If a school refused entry to a wheelchair-bound student, ostensibly because they lacked the means to build ramps to a sufficient number of classrooms, the court may well find that the school had discriminated against that student, but also that it was allowed to do so, given that the cost of building the ramps would have constituted an unjustifiable hardship. Such a decision would always be a matter of degree.

Interestingly, if the coach had refused to pick you at soccer because you had a physical disability, while this would be a clear example of direct discrimination under both federal and state anti-discrimination legislation, this action may yet be permissible under most of that same legislation as a 'sporting exemption', on the basis that you were not reasonably capable of performing the tasks required of you. Once again, the decision would be a matter of degree.

## An example of disability discrimination

It would probably be useful now briefly to work through an example of the discrimination process, and what better case to choose than *L v Minister for Education*, as discussed in myth #1.

L's mother was unhappy with the decision to remove her daughter from mainstream education, and decided to seek a legal remedy through the available anti-discrimination legislation. At this point, two options were open to her. The first was to go through the federal system using the *Disability Discrimination Act 1992* (Cth). The second was to go through the state system using, in this instance, the *Anti-Discrimination Act 1991* (Qld). Most likely for a combination of practical and strategic reasons, she chose the latter, and her case was heard by the Queensland Anti-Discrimination Tribunal. Working through the Act:

## Activity

Education is an activity covered by this statute. More specifically, under Part 4, Division 3 of the Act, (Section 39c), 'an education authority must not discriminate by excluding a student'.

## Grounds

'Impairment' is one of the 13 named attributes covered by the statute, under Section 7(1)(h).

## Discrimination

L was removed from the mainstream classroom because of her disability. As such, she was treated less favourably than an ordinary child would be treated under the same circumstances. This is an example of direct discrimination, and contravenes section 10(1) of the Act. So far, so good.

## Exemptions

The exemptions specifically relating to education are set out in Part 4, Division 3, Sub-division B of the Act. In section 44(1) it states that it is not unlawful to discriminate on the basis of impairment against a person if they require special services or facilities, and supplying these special services or facilities would impose *unjustifiable hardship* on the educational authority. And this is where L's case to the Tribunal failed. It was determined that her presence would have been an unjustifiable hardship on the education authority – a decision largely based upon the consequentialist ethical reasoning discussed in myth #1.

Once again, the intention here is not to re-try the case nearly two decades later in print, or to suggest a different result might have been fairer. It is solely to make the point that just because an individual has been discriminated against, this does not mean that there is a remedy under anti-discrimination legislation; and even if there is found to have been discrimination under one of the Acts, this does not mean that such discrimination may not be exempted under those very same Acts. Perhaps adding weight to the jurisprudential position that 'the law is simply politics dressed up in a different garb' (Hutchinson & Monahan, 1984), it is interesting to note that power-ful, all-male clubs are permitted 'reasonable sex discrimination' by an exemption set out in section 98 of the same state legislation – although how this accords with the general purpose of law addressing discrimination is difficult to fathom

In summary, discrimination is still with us. We have enacted laws, at all levels of government, to address the problem. These laws address many different forms of discrimination, across most areas of public life, and they address both direct and indirect discrimination, in that discrimination does not always have to be intentional to be covered by the legislation. However, the legislation also contains a significant number of exemptions for each activity. Within the Queensland legislation discussed above, exemptions apply on a number of different grounds, and it is in this domain that more rigorous ethical analysis may still need to be done.

# Myth #4 There are no real ethical dilemmas left for education law to deal with

One of the reasons that we don't really need to educate teachers in either ethics or the law is because all the major problems have been sorted out. We're not in the dark ages anymore; we no longer allow corporal punishment, we have a far more democratic and inclusive curriculum, and both teachers and pupils have rights. What's left?

Quite a lot, actually. There are any number of dilemmas remaining regarding the intersection between ethics and the law within the field of education. After all, soci-ety should not be regarded as some kind of fixed object, a static entity that can, with sufficient care and attention, have all it problems sorted out, once and for all. Rather, society is a dynamic and fluid entity, and the forms of conduct that are acceptable today may not be tolerated tomorrow. Our ideas of right and wrong change, and our laws change as a consequence (although our laws also change as part of fine-tuning the social machine, adapting to demographic and cultural changes, and responding to economic and political pressures).

Any number of ethical and legal dilemmas remain within Australian education, dilemmas often based upon tensions between the consequentialist and Kantian eth-ics discussed in myth #1. For example, should we enact laws restricting individuals' rights to wear religious symbols in school, such as the hijab? Should schools be allowed to deny same-sex couples the right to attend end-of-year formals? Should schools be given greater powers of exclusion over troublesome students? In addition to these, there are other areas of debate.

## Mandatory reporting

There exists a range of legislation mandating that various professions are required to report incidents of child abuse and neglect when they occur, or their suspicions of incidents of child abuse and neglect. Not surprisingly, teaching is one of these professions. This doesn't seem to be much of an ethical or legal dilemma; surely we want our teachers to be looking out for the welfare of their students, and initiating an intervention process wherever necessary. Pastoral care has always been part of what we do.

Unfortunately, it's a much more complicated issue than it initially appears. Of the eight Australian states and territories, none have the same mandatory reporting requirements. At one extreme is New South Wales, which has an unqualified duty to report sexual and physical abuse, and a qualified duty to report emotional abuse and neglect, and at the other is Western Australia, which has no legal duty to report anything (Butler & Mathews 2007, 138–9). There are also differences in what constitutes abuse, in the extent of the harm that must be reported, in the age of the child involved, whether the suspected abuse has already happened or whether it is likely to occur, and even *who* is suspected of committing the abuse (in Queensland, teachers are only required to report suspected sexual abuse by school employees). In addition to these inconsistent legal obligations, there are equally inconsistent policy requirements that operate in different ways across different jurisdictions (Mathews et al. 2006).

Why is there such confusion? Surely abuse should be reported wherever it is suspected? Once again, the issue requires a more nuanced response than that. Is the average teacher sufficiently trained to spot, and differentiate between, the various types of abuse? Do we want teachers – trained or otherwise – casting accusations around in a domain where the consequence is professional and personal ruin, usually for the innocent as well as the guilty? Is the price to innocent teachers worth paying for the sake of all the children who might be saved by instituting a zealous reporting environment? – a familiar consequentialism vs Kantianism ethical dilemma. Mind you, is there any evidence that those jurisdictions with comprehensive reporting requirements produce better outcomes for children than those without? Indeed, do most teachers even know what their legal reporting requirements are? Or what Education Department policy reporting requirements are? Or even what the process for reporting suspected abuse is?

Recent research (Mathews et al. 2009) demonstrates that gaps exist in teachers' knowledge of their responsibilities regarding reporting abuse, both in terms of policy and the law, gaps that vary according to state/territory. Also, teachers do not always report their suspicions of abuse, although most would if they knew it was mandatory. The research also suggests that for mandatory reporting to be effective:

> Teachers' child protection training must begin in the preservice years... This training should promote positive attitudes towards reporting child sexual abuse, and emphasise that this is not simply a

bureaucratic imposition of policy, but a part of a teacher's professional and ethical role ... (Mathews et al. 2009, 811)

The evidence suggests that the area of mandatory reporting not only requires greater research to be conducted, it also requires a consistent and thorough analysis of the many issues involved. A second ethical and legal dilemma involves the issue of negligence; more specifically, whether teachers should be held accountable for almost every accident that occurs within the school.

## Negligence and foreseeability

Under Australian law, all actions in negligence are comprised of three elements: the existence of a *duty of care*, the *breach* of that duty, and resulting *damage*. The first of these three elements is unproblematic: both schools and teachers have an established, non-delegable duty of care towards their students. Likewise, the legal debate is not usually over the issue of damage – whether or not the pupil was injured – as this is generally self-evident. The element most frequently in dispute in a negligence action tends to be whether there has been a breach in the duty of care by the teacher, and therefore the school.

Breach of duty is comprised of two foundational components: the standard of care required in the circumstances, and whether or not this standard has indeed been breached. Most focus has recently fallen upon the latter issue, and in particular, the level of risk that teachers are required to guard against. That is, how does the law determine what could be considered as a 'reasonably foreseeable' risk? The common law has required all risk to be accounted for unless those risks are deemed to be 'far-fetched or fanciful'. Does this mean that teachers should foresee all possible risks except for injuries caused by falling space junk? Not surprisingly, it has often been argued that this level of foreseeability has been far too generous to the plaintiff, resulting in the situation where if an accident happened, it was foreseeable, and hence the defendant – the teacher – was almost certainly liable.

Chief Justice Underwood of Tasmania contends that the fear of being sued by pupils, one of the foremost concerns among teachers, has now reached debilitating levels:

> I have found that there is a widespread belief that if a claim is made it will follow that the courts will find that the teacher has breached the duty of care owed to the child and the teacher will be found to have been negligent ... I think that there was some justification for these fears ... It has been said that in order to avoid being found negligent you had to carry out your duties as a teacher with the cautionary habits of a maiden aunt, the reflexes of Michael Schumacher, and the skills of a heart surgeon and all the while, maintain 20/20 hindsight vision (Underwood, 2006, 5).

However, he also goes on to argue that some recent legal changes may have re-organised the field for the better, resulting in a tightening of the requirements regarding foreseeability, the intention being to attack 'the culture of blame' and to increase personal responsibility. With the exception of the Northern Territory, all

Australian jurisdictions have now introduced legislation to replace 'far-fetched or fanciful' with 'not insignificant', a slightly more defensible position for a teacher charged with negligence. The central issue here is whether this change in foreseeability provides a magic bullet for negligence actions in schooling contexts, or whether our teachers are still particularly vulnerable. In spite of this change, most teachers would contend that 'not insignificant' only represents a very small improvement on the previous 'far-fetched or fanciful', and that the bar is still set very high.

Optimistically perhaps, Chief Justice Underwood has a somewhat different viewpoint. While not decrying the legislative changes, he argues that this change was probably not strictly necessary, since 'the courts were already facing the proposition that the standard of care that had been imposed in the past was far too high and the wheel started to turn the other way'. He cites the case of *St Anthony's Primary School v Hadba* (2005), where a child was injured when another child grabbed her legs while she was playing on a flying fox. The court held that there was no breach of a teacher's duty of care for failing to provide constant supervision in this instance. It was noted in this judgement that it is not reasonable to supervise pupils at all times, as this would remove any element of trust between the two groups, a crucial component in the effective development of children. The ethical and legal debate continues.

## Levels of teacher responsibility

The final ethical and legal dilemma to be dealt with here is probably the most important: addressing changes to the nature and scope of the teaching profession. While it would be naïve to think that teaching has ever been solely about working through a curriculum, it could reasonably be argued that this still forms the core of the job. Of course, layered on top of this principle task has been the expectation of a certain degree of pastoral care; teaching is a responsible profession, and teachers have always been charged with the job of turning out the next generation of citizens – educated, healthy in mind and healthy in body.

The question is: how far should this responsibility extend? Just what should schools be responsible for? Obviously teachers should be responsible for the fundamentals of learning, but should they be held accountable for what the children eat, or how they choose to behave, or for every single risk, direct or indirect, that could conceivably occur within the school grounds? For example, a number of states have introduced laws limiting the kinds of food that can be sold on school grounds. Junk foods, such as hamburgers, pizza, chips and soft drink are banned, and replaced by healthier alternatives, all under the threat of legal sanction from the State. That is, rather than use the traditional liberal strategy of governing at a distance discussed in Chapter 4 – managing the population through the subtle regulation of images, such as 'the good mother', and 'the healthy child' – the government has decided to employ the blunt instrument of the law to enforce this particular social agenda.

The issue here is not the strategy of producing healthier and better-fed children. Obviously, this is a laudable goal, and perhaps schools *should* be part of a greater set of social programs aimed at improving the diet of children. However, the question needs to be asked: is the law the appropriate mechanism for this kind of social management? If so, should this not be part of a much greater set of legislative imperatives that include a few more targeted sites of intervention, by way of sharing the new levels of responsibility around a little more? After all, a number of other sites are available for governmental intervention, sites that are all but ignored: snack food companies, fast food companies, advertisers, and even parents themselves. It could be argued that educational institutions are targeted in this manner because they do not present the political difficulties associated with trying to compel businesses and parents to improve their practices.

Bit by bit, almost imperceptibly, new forms of responsibility are being added to the site of the school and, more specifically, to the professional life of the teacher. The issue here is not necessarily to challenge any of these diverse changes, but rather to question both the ability of schools and teachers to do their primary jobs effectively in the face of these increased responsibilities, as well as the ethics of asking them to do so. Two particular examples can be employed here.

## Risk management

One of the most common features of the modern school is the constant injunction to manage risk, in all its forms, as previously mentioned when addressing the issue of negligence. Indeed, the notion of risk is now one of the most fundamental tools for the effective governance of the population at large. Castel (1991) contends that, first, preventative policies associated with risk are constituted in terms of factors rather than specific individuals. That is, given dangers are now to be found, not hiding within the pupil themselves, but rather within constellations of relevant risk factors.

Second, risk legitimates increased governmental intervention. More traditional forms of surveillance, such as those associated with the school, have generally required the panopticon. This new strategy shifts the emphasis from such direct scrutiny, to a focus upon correlations between sets of often-abstract factors. The deployment of risk in this manner permits a virtually limitless increase in the possibilities of government.

Third, and most importantly, with each new possibility of governance comes an increased responsibility to administer the outcomes of that governance. Since, under the right circumstances, virtually anything can now be regarded as a risk, it now falls to teachers not only to be aware of gigantic numbers of these newly found risks, but also to have strategies in place for dealing with their hypothetical consequences. That is, it places teachers in the position of potentially being legally responsible for anything and everything.

### Managing the pathological student

As has been discussed at length in Chapter 5, the teacher has now been placed at the centre of diagnosis and treatment of a growing range learning and conduct disorders. Teachers are now expected to be able to intervene upon any number of educational differences, differences that are no longer below the threshold of intervention, or simply part of the human condition, but instead are now objective pathologies to be identified, categorised and normalised. Once again, it is the teacher who is liable for the outcomes of this categorisation, both socially and academically.

The argument here is that teachers now have a very different job from their predecessors. They are now expected to be de facto therapists, a form of management that involves a number of elements: acquiring a working knowledge of a number of psy-based discipline areas; keeping up with developments and 'discoveries' within those discipline areas; recognising these new pathologies when they occur; and knowing what to do with them, and organising classroom/playing field practices accordingly. It has been argued that with each new behaviour disorder, children are held slightly less accountable for their conduct. However, since somebody has to be legally responsible for their behaviour, arguably it will be teachers who end up shouldering the burdens that others will not. This one another issue that requires further ethical and legal scrutiny.

# Conclusion

A greater understanding of the discipline of ethics helps us make clearer ethical decisions in daily life, or at least, it provides us with the tools to recognise what kind of moral reasoning we are employing, and what the shortcomings of that reasoning are likely to be. Education is an ethically complex domain, both in terms of how we choose to structure our schools, and also in terms of the ethical choices teachers make as they try and do their jobs as best they can – often under very challenging circumstances.

In addition to ethics, a greater understanding of the law is also useful for teachers; this is not only because it is intimately tied to ethics, in that it represents our broadest understanding of right and wrong made manifest in statutory form, but also because all aspects of education, and teachers' professional lives, are now subject to legal scrutiny. As Butler and Mathews (2007) state on the back cover of their book:

> The legal environment in which schools operate and teachers work is increasingly intrusive. There are more statutes, more cases, more regulations, more departmental policies. The law is more complex and compliance is more difficult. Breaches are more serious, more heavily penalised and noisily publicised.

So, just as teachers need to understand the strengths and weaknesses of the various ethical positions they take, they also need to know their many rights and obligations under our most visible and important of ethical systems – the law. These rights and obligations are neither self-evident nor timeless; instead they are organised within given social and historical contexts, and according to specific relations of authority.

# Chapter 12

# Truth and postcolonialism

This chapter argues that the issue of 'truth' has played a foundational role, not only within the discipline of philosophy, but also within many different aspects of our culture. However, there seems to be little agreement on what it really is, and while some philosophers contend that truth is a meaningless concept – a linguistic mirage – most would argue there's *something* of importance there, but what is it?

Even if we struggle to determine the real nature of truth – as we did with the real nature of right and wrong in Chapter 11 – at least we structure our culture, our knowledges, and our school curricula around stuff we know to be unequivocally true ... or do we? Arguably, many of the assumptions we make, often derived from five centuries of European colonialism, do not stand up to close scrutiny. They are often 'truths' that suit particular interests of the powerful, and subtly act to reinforce their world view.

## Myth #1 'Truth' is the most straightforward thing there is

*Truth is simple. Certain things about the world are 'facts'. If we report them accurately, we are telling the truth; if we don't, we aren't. That's all there is to it.*

Actually, no it isn't. Philosophers have been debating the notion of truth for over 2500 years, debates that have resulted in very different approaches to this issue, most frequently divided into realist and anti-realist models. These models in turn generate different kinds of truth tests, which can be applied to given problems and statements. All in all, ascertaining what is true, and what is not – in the curriculum, or elsewhere – remains a complex and contested process.

## Myth #2 The knowledge in our school curriculum is both true, and culturally neutral

*There is nothing untrue or biased about our school curriculum. You could teach it anywhere in the world and it would be appropriate.*

The evidence suggests that, like all countries that were once colonies, Australia continues to exhibit a significant European legacy, not only within its educational institutions – the structure of the school and the content of the curriculum – but also within the very fabric of the country itself, within the ongoing relations between former coloniser and colonised, and within the regimes of truth that still operate there.

# Introduction

So far, this final part of the book has presented an overview of philosophy, and given an explanation of why it is of such immense value to educators (Chapter 10), and it has also addressed one specific area of philosophy – ethics – and briefly applied this to the field of law and education, also of significant value to educators (Chapter 11). This final chapter of Part 4 will unpack arguably one of the most important areas of concern within the discipline of philosophy: the notion of truth. It will then employ any conclusions reached to better understand the claims made by those writers and researchers interested in the legacy of colonialism within countries such as Australia. These 'postcolonial' thinkers rightly contend that the concept of truth, and the knowledges that spring from it, are far more complex than they may initially appear.

Of all the areas of philosophy, the search for truth is often deemed to be the most important. There is probably no other word in the English language that carries with it as much symbolic and romantic baggage. Henkin (1966, 1) states: 'The word "truth", as well as such words as "beauty" and "justice", refer to concepts so broad, and so deeply stirring to the human spirit, that some have set them as the aim of life.' Indeed, truth has not only been described as providing the principal foundation of the aforementioned beauty (Keats 1951) and justice (Disraeli 1851), but also virtue (Holyoake 1902), knowledge (Russell 1983), subjectivity (Kierkegaard 2001), and even human nature itself (Bacon 1985). Indeed, answering the question, 'What is truth?', has been described not only as the central purpose of philosophy (Foucault 2000), it has even been described as its *sole* purpose (Bierce 1995).

## So what is 'truth'?

In spite of the apparent importance of truth to most of our conceptual frameworks, there is actually considerable disagreement about exactly what it is. After all, the nature of things like 'facts' – from which models of truth are assembled – seem to be given to us with cultural assumptions already built into them. As Lin Yutang, a Chinese writer, observes:

> Western philosophers have always gone on the assumption that fact is something cut and dried, precise, immobile, very convenient, and ready for examination. The Chinese deny this. The Chinese believe that a fact is something crawling and alive, a little furry and cool to the touch, that crawls down the back of your neck. (Yutang, cited in Christian, 1981, 62)

Recent research involving undergraduate education students reveals a similar lack of agreement of exactly what the concept of 'truth' entails, most specifically that most of us appear to think that there are no 'right' and 'wrong' answers, in philosophy or in life, thus anything can be true (Tait et al., 2012). In contrast to this position, most philosophers would argue that truth is far more elusive than that, if it exists at all. Some philosophers – called *deflationary* theorists – contend that the whole problem of truth is nothing more than a 'linguistic muddle' (Ramsay 1927). When the statement is made, 'It is true that this book is made of paper', a deflationary theorist such as Frege (1977) would argue that its content is identical with the statement 'This book is made of paper' and therefore ascribing the property of truth adds nothing at all. That is, truth stands for nothing within a sentence, other than purposes of assertion or negation, and is hence not a genuine concept (Ayer 1935). As Horwich (1990, 5) notes about truth: 'No wonder that its "underlying nature" has so stubbornly resisted philosophical elaboration; for there simply is no such thing.'

Perhaps not surprisingly, this approach – i.e. that truth is simply a linguistic illusion – leaves most philosophers feeling rather unhappy and they have consequently come up with a number of other approaches. The commonsense realist approach to truth, as exemplified by myth #1, often depicts truth as the most straightforward thing there is: the direct correspondence between a particular statement, and the reality it depicts. However, there are also convincing *anti-realist* alternatives to this model (such as *pragmatic theory* and *coherence theory*) which suggest instead that truth is far from being objective, unchanging, universal, and self-evident, and as we shall see, the implications of this position are vary far-reaching indeed.

## Postcolonialism, truth and the curriculum

If we accept that truth is never fixed or absolute, and there are good reasons why we should, this leaves truth, and the knowledges shaped from it, in a far more precarious position than might previously have been the case. After all, it is often comforting to think that all the things we have been told are true: science is unequivocally true, what we are taught on the school curriculum is unequivocally true, what we have been told about our culture and its place in the world is also unequivocally true. Unfortunately, the evidence suggests that this just isn't the case. 'Truth' is more complex than that, and while the opposite of a truth isn't necessarily a lie, it is most certainly a falsehood.

Most philosophers would argue that, in a perfect world, all our academic disciplines would be founded upon a more solid understanding of the limits of their own truth claims, and we would better realise the degree to which such disciplines are, in very important ways, the products of their own intellectual histories. As discussed in Chapter 3, the science of 'race' is a perfect example, in that its 'truth' was based upon the bogus historical belief that white people are somehow intrinsically different, and better, than black people. Postcolonial theory takes this realisation a stage further. It investigates the social, cultural and educational legacy of colonialism, and examines the many often-unspoken truths, world views, and forms of knowledge bequeathed to those who remained in the colonies, both as colonisers and colonised.

For example, it is indisputable that Australia, in spite of striking out on its own as a young, vibrant and independent country, continues to be shaped by a complex set of British inheritances, inheritances that influence both our relationships with ourselves, and others, and influence how we see the world. It is also not only the case that the colonisation of Australia has been experienced in very different ways by Indigenous Australians, as opposed to those who came here as colonists, but also that the world view of the latter continues to dominate our school curriculum. That is, as will be discussed in myth #2, far from teaching timeless, indisputable, culturally neutral truths, our schools bear the ready imprint of our colonial past in terms of the knowledges we learn, and the truths they tell – very often truths which air brush our past, and subtly predetermine who is most likely to prosper in our future.

To summarise then, the two myths to be dealt with in this chapter are:

**Myth #1** – 'Truth' is the most straightforward thing there is

**Myth #2** – The knowledge in our school curriculum is both true, and culturally neutral

# Myth #1 'Truth' is the most straightforward thing there is

Truth is simple. We go to school to learn the truth … the truth about numbers, the truth about history, the truth about biology; we set up our legal system so we can protect the truth … who is in the right, who is in the wrong, how we can ensure justice for all; we even invented an entire system of knowledge acquisition – science – for impartially uncovering the truth of the universe. The truth may try to hide, but after you strip away all the rubbish, all the camouflage, and all the mystery, there it is.

The commonsense understanding of truth is that it exists independently of us. After all, surely the truth doesn't change just because we want it to, or because we approach the problem from a different angle, or because someone else has conducted the tests, or because we elect a new government. What is there to debate? Actually, as we shall see, the notion of 'truth' is not a simple matter at all.

## Differing approaches to truth

Philosophers have struggled over the notion of truth since the ancient debate between Socrates and Protagoras, and this argument is yet to be resolved. Socrates, as given voice by Plato, believed in the existence of absolute standards, standards having a reality independent of human action or perception. This is not to say that feelings, attitudes, biases and preconceptions are irrelevant in the process of constructing truth, however, once these are stripped away – by the kind of critical reasoning espoused by Socrates himself – then it would be possible to know the truth (Plato 1956). This understanding of truth is most frequently labelled as a *realist* approach. James (1917, 233) summarises this view by pointing to its reliance upon the notion of a 'world complete in itself, to which thought comes as a passive mirror'. It certainly constitutes the most familiar and widely used understanding of the relationship between ourselves and the world in which we live, and as will be discussed in greater detail shortly, the vast majority of science also appears to be based upon this logic. This is not, however, the only version of truth available to us.

In addition to realism, there also exists an *anti-realist* approach that can boast an equally long history and a formidable theoretical foundation. Lined up against

Socrates in ancient Greece was a group of itinerant teachers called Sophists, the most eminent of whom was Protagoras, who famously stated that 'Man is the measure of all things' (Plato 1974, 160). Sophists believed that finding absolute and unequivocal truth was impossible, and hence man had to learn to live, and construct knowledge, in its absence. In more modern times, this position is most clearly articulated by Nietzsche (1954, 46), who asks: 'What then is truth? A mobile army of metaphors, metonyms, and anthropomorphisms – in short, a sum of human relations...' His point here is that truths are formed, shaped and deployed within social contexts. The truth is not 'out there', waiting to be discovered, but is rather something that is brought into existence by force of the human will (Nietzsche 1967).

Nietzsche's approach to truth forms a crucial component in the work of many subsequent thinkers, specifically in relation to the exercise of power. Like Nietzsche, Foucault also proposes that truth is something that cannot exist in absolute terms, contending instead that there are a variety of truths, constructed within definite contexts as the product of specific legitimated knowledges. Therefore, because truth is actually the product of legitimated knowledges, as those knowledges change, then so too will truth (Foucault 1980, 131). Different societies produce different *regimes of truth*, and the production of these regimes is internal to the exercise of power.

These two generalised positions outlined above – the realist and anti-realist – while representing the primary philosophical subdivision over the issue of truth, by no means provide a comprehensive analysis of the field. The two approaches spawn a number of other, more specific, theories concerning the nature of truth. That is, the realist approach is most frequently understood in terms of *correspondence theory,* and the anti-realist approach in terms of *pragmatic theory* and *coherence theory.*

## Realism and truth

In the book *Truth in Context,* Lynch (1998) describes realism about truth as being based upon how the world is, not upon what we think about that world. Thus, it should make no difference as to who conducts an investigation into the nature of the world, the truth will always be the same, regardless of how different the researchers may be, or how diverse their backgrounds. The statements made by those researchers are true when they correspond to the external reality; that is, something is true if it corresponds to the facts. This is called correspondence theory.

## Correspondence theory

The first formulation of what later became correspondence theory is normally attributed to Aristotle, who stated: 'A statement is true if, as it signifies, so it is.' Aristotle is thereby comparing what is said about reality, with reality itself, and if there is a match, the statement can be said to be true. If the statement is: 'This book has 1000 pages,' this statement can be compared with the final number at the bottom of the last page. Is it 1000? Nowhere near actually, and so the statement is not true. Simple.

The central appeal of correspondence theory is its self-evidence, in that it seems to support a basic human perception as to the nature of truth. Furthermore, since it rules out human interpretive agency from the process, it objectively delineates the true from the false, thereby further adding to its apparent clarity and utility. For those who take up this position, it becomes possible to argue that once the direct link to 'reality' is removed from the truth equation – as with anti-realism – then it becomes possible that anything might be true (a contention which will be discussed in greater detail later).

However, the fact that the rigor and validity of correspondence theory appears to be self-evident, does not necessarily make it so. One criticism of the theory is that having stripped away the rhetoric of 'obviousness' from this model, there appears to be little in the way of conceptual foundation. Horwich (1990, 1) makes precisely this point when he states: 'The common-sense notion that truth is a kind of "correspondence with the facts" has never been worked out to anyone's satisfaction. Even its advocates would concede that it remains little more than a vague, guiding intuition.' A second criticism concerns the problem of gaining knowledge about a mind-independent reality from our own sense data. As Christian (1981, 193–4) notes, correspondence theory:

> compares a concept with a set of sensations – the sensations we use when we go about inferring what exists in the real world. Therefore, we are checking a subjective concept with a subjective set of sensations. If they match to some tolerable degree, then we call the concept true; if they don't, we call it false. This is not really a happy condition to live with, but given our present knowledge of the cognitive processes, the predicament seems inescapable … we can never be certain of anything.

That said, correspondence theory is still the dominant paradigm, perhaps not within the discipline of philosophy, but certainly in terms of common usage, and also within almost the vast majority of scientific discourse. However, the mechanisms by which science has attempted to come to terms with the notion of truth, have resulted in the unearthing of a number of equally obstinate and seemingly intractable philosophical problems.

## Science and truth

The scientific method was first outlined in 1620 by Bacon in his book *Novum Organum* (1952). His theory is premised upon the belief that the general aim of science is to push back the boundary between what is known and what is not known. This process is begun by scientists, who observe and record many examples of an event during the course of an experiment, thereby adding to the stock of knowledge around a particular subject. Eventually, as each scientist adds information to the totality, general rules emerge. Theories are then advanced which explain the existing pattern of events and can be used to predict future happenings of the same event, and by combining these theories, global laws are constructed. Thus, a limited number of experimental results become extrapolated into 'laws of nature'. The central principle here, that of 'induction', suggests that assumptions can be made about all members of a class from examining a few members of the class.

Unfortunately, inductive reasoning has a major flaw, first pointed out by Hume in 1737 in his *Treatise of Human Nature* (1969). He argues that assumptions cannot be made about all members of a class from examining a few members of that class. No matter how many times a specific 'cause A' is followed by 'effect B', it does not logically follow that A will *always* cause B. As Russell (1983, 35) notes:

> The man who has fed a chicken every day throughout its life at last wrings its neck instead, showing that more refined views as to the uniformity of nature would have been useful to the chicken.

Popper (1963) argues that the consequences of this observation for science and truth are severe: it becomes impossible to prove anything as true, no matter how many times an event occurs. Therefore, science should give up its quest for truth by attempting to prove a phenomenon to be true, and scientists should rather try to falsify existing theories, thereby creating new theories that would, in their own turn, be disproved. Advancement in science thereby occurs not by proving something to be true, but being unable to prove it false.

According to this logic, truth no longer belongs in the realist domain. Rather, truth is necessarily transient, being surpassed in time by new truths, ones that can account for both the new data, as well as the information that spawned previous theories.

## Anti-realism and truth

In contrast to the realist position on truth – based upon the belief that there exist indisputable facts about a singular reality – the anti-realist position argues that facts themselves necessarily reflect particular points of view. The central animating assumption is that it is impossible to describe any fact in the absence of a conceptual framework. Lynch (1998, 23) characterises this position as being founded upon the postulation that, 'There is no scheme-neutral way of making a report about the world. It would be a mistake to search for the scheme that tells it like it "really" is – there is no such thing'. Putnam (1981) argues that in the absence of a 'God's Eye' point of view, which many would argue is the unspoken prerequisite of realism, all that can remain are various interpretations of how the world is. Reality does not come 'ready made and complete' as realists would have us believe, but rather is shaped by our own interpretations of it.

It should be pointed out here that accepting anti-realist accounts of truth does not necessitate a slide into *radical relativism*, where truth becomes so nebulous that it can be found anywhere. Admitting that the truth is intimately associated with experience is not the same as suggesting that, as a consequence, all truths are equally valid. As Putnam (1981, 54) wryly observes:

> If anyone believed that, and if they were foolish enough to pick a conceptual scheme that told them they could fly, and act upon it by jumping out the window, they would, if they were lucky enough to survive, see the weakness of the latter view at once.

Anti-realist approaches to truth generally come in two distinct forms: pragmatic theory and coherence theory.

## Pragmatic theory

Pragmatism is normally associated with the work of James (1911), and follows the logic that theorising – whether about truth, or anything else for that matter – is a pointless activity in and of itself. The only relevance that theorising can have is when it is converted into the solution of concrete intellectual problems. A philosopher must ask, what is the practical worth of any particular claim? That is, what difference would it make if a set of claims were believed to be either true or false? If the answer is 'none whatsoever', then the issue should be of no philosophical interest. If an explanation can be translated into a verifiable and predictable outcome – an observable effect – then that explanation is true, if not, then the explanation is either false, or irrelevant, or both.

> Pragmatism asks its usual question. 'Grant an idea or a belief to be true,' it says, 'what concrete difference will its being true make to anyone's actual life? … What, in short, is the truth's cash-value in experimental terms?' The moment pragmatism asks this question, it sees the answer: *True ideas are those that we can assimilate, validate, corroborate and verify*. False ideas are those we cannot … The truth of an idea is not a stagnant property inherent in it. Truth *happens* to an idea. It *becomes* true, is *made* true by events. (James 1975, ix)

Thus, James rejects the realist notion that truth is a property independent of human intentionality. Pragmatic theory avoids the requirement for a 'God's Eye' view for a final and complete understanding of truth. Rather, a statement is deemed true because it works as an explanation, not because it corresponds with an abstracted objective reality.

## Coherence theory

This theory evolved as an attempt to sidestep some of the problems of correspondence theory. Since we can never know whether a statement corresponds to external reality, all that can be said is that the statement coheres with a given set of already accepted beliefs. Generally, things we believe to be true form part of a huge, interrelated matrix. The truth of a statement is therefore assessed by how well it fits into that matrix – if it dovetails well with the ideas in the matrix, it is regarded as true; if not, it is regarded as false. For example, we readily accept the truth of the statement that 'dogs can't fly', because it coheres easily with everything we already know about dogs, birds, paws, wings and gravity.

Of course, the questions arise of 'What counts as coherence?' and 'Under what conditions?' The clearest answers to these questions are given by Putnam (1981), who argues that within an anti-realist understanding of truth, the coherence of any given truth-claim should be assessed by an 'ideally rational enquirer', which suggests that valid truths cannot be created by the deranged, the deluded, or the drunk, just because they really admire dogs. That is, the alleged coherence of any given truth-claims to a wider matrix of truths must still withstand significant scrutiny.

However, in stating that there are no external truths, no absolute facts that exist independent of human experience, it is equally false to identify truth with rational acceptability; the two are not synonymous. Putnam uses the example of the historically changing shape of the earth, pointing out that the earth has not actually changed from being flat to being a sphere over the last 500 years, only accepted truths have changed. Therefore, what remains is an understanding that 'truth is an idealisation of rational acceptability', a rational acceptability which is both tensed and relative (Putnam 1981, 51).

Anti-realist theories of truth, such as pragmatic theory and coherence theory, are not without their critics. For example, it has been argued that they are both unable to account for the possibility of there being a discrepancy between what we *believe* to be true, and what actually *is* true (Horwich 1990, 9). After all, simply believing something to be true, does not necessarily make it so. However, both anti-realist theories would regard this as an invalid criticism; pragmatism, because if it works as an explanation, what's the difference the anyway; and coherence, because of the role of the ideally rational inquirer.

## Truth tests

Importantly, these three theories are not simply abstract categories of interpretation; all are actually useful, in that they translate directly into truth tests. A truth test is a device for checking particular statements and assessing whether they are true or false. As will be shown, any statement making a fact-claim can have its veracity checked against one, or all, of the three tests. Indeed, when the truth of a particular claim or statement is being assessed, normally more than one truth test is applied.

### The correspondence truth test

This simply involves comparing a mental concept with an actual event, which can be done in a number of direct ways, such as by listening, by looking, by feeling, and so on. For example, if the statement is, 'It's a sunny day', this can easily be checked by walking outside and looking: if the sun is shining, if it is warm, and if there are not many clouds in the sky, then the statement will probably be accepted as true – although correspondence is always a matter of degree, and the more clouds there are in the sky, the less the correspondence, and the less likely the statement is to be categorised as true. Importantly, all forms of direct comparison between statement and event would come under this truth test.

### The pragmatic truth test

This involves testing whether a statement is true by checking if it works in a practical sense. This test of truth often involves the establishment of a working hypothesis by a process of elimination. For example, if a person's arms are pink and painful at the end of each day during summer, by a process of elimination, any number of possible causes can probably be ruled out – allergies, abrasion, dermatological issues, paint – especially if long sleeves and/or sun-block seem to solve the problem. That is, it is true that the pink and painful arms are actually sunburn because this works as an explanation.

## The coherence truth test

This involves comparing a mental concept against a set of concepts that are already taken as true. Once again, this can be done in a number of ways. For example, if the statement is, 'January is generally a hot month', then the process of determining the truth of the statement would begin by comparing it with any number of other sets of knowledges within a generalised matrix of accepted truths. These might include personal memories about January, meteorological inputs relating to temperatures, geographical knowledge about the hemispheres, even cultural data about what kinds of events happen in January. If the information in these sets of knowledges is taken to be true, and if the statement coheres with those knowledges, then the statement is deemed to be true.

It would be useful at this stage to work through an example taken specifically from education. Given Chapter 5 of this book deals with the governance of subjectivity and the rise of behaviour disorders, the issue of ADHD is probably the best place to start.

## ADHD and truth

Attention Deficit Hyperactivity Disorder (ADHD), which is primarily a theory concerning the misbehaviour of children, has yet to reach the status of 'established truth', in spite of what some of its more optimistic advocates may claim. Debates over the disorder continue, not only within the pages of learned journals, but also in the popular media, where various treatments and protocols of diagnosis are discussed, alongside the arguments of those who refuse to recognise the disorder at all. So, if truth is such a simple concept, perhaps we can use the three truth tests to determine, once and for all, whether the claim 'ADHD is an objective disorder that exists in nature', is true or false.

## Truth: ADHD exists in nature

First, employing the correspondence test to check the truth of ADHD presents a number of difficulties. ADHD is not a physical object that can be held up for scrutiny and compared to the subjective concept of the disorder. Rather it is an amalgam of various types of data – statistical, observational, behavioural, pharmacological, experiential, educational – which have been assembled to the point where their combined presence is deemed to correspond to the existence of an objective disorder. All in all then, the correspondence truth test isn't much help.

The pragmatic truth test is rather more useful. As has been discussed, the principal question regarding ADHD would normally be: 'Does this truth *work*?' Given that ADHD was originally formulated around the educational needs of a particular kind of at-risk student, there is little doubt that it aims to make a concrete contribution to the educational and emotional wellbeing of a specific category of child. Similarly, since the truth of ADHD is determined by whether the category works, it can be argued that the disorder provides a straightforward *workable* explanation as to why otherwise seemingly healthy and normal children are incapable of behaving well in class.

Finally, a coherence test of truth would also appear to work in ADHD's favour. The notion of ADHD meshes easily with any number of other sets of accepted beliefs within the truth matrix. For example, ADHD is based upon the premise that some kind of minor brain dysfunction results in unwelcome social behaviour, behaviour which had previously been categorised simply as naughtiness and inattentiveness. This re-appraisal coheres readily with a wide range of other accepted truths concerning the relationship between specific mental problems and undesirable forms of conduct. Also, ADHD involves the belief that, by uncovering more and more mental disorders, science is finally discovering the real workings of the human mind. ADHD thereby fits snugly into this understanding of the psychological sciences, and coheres with (and adds to) the validity of all the other new disorders.

It's decided then: 'ADHD is an objective disorder that exists in nature' is a true statement, since it appears to pass two of the three truth tests ... except for one tiny problem: a completely contradictory statement, 'ADHD is simply a by-product of the governance of subjectivity' also passes two of the three truth tests.

## Truth: ADHD is a social creation

Like the first statement, this second statement is also not particularly amenable to the correspondence truth test; social governance can no more be held up, examined, and compared to a mental concept, like a piece of brain tissue, than can ADHD.

The pragmatic truth test yields better results. A governmental understanding of ADHD works as an explanation of why there are so many new behaviour disorders, and why previously untapped areas of human conduct are now being pathologised; that is, *it allows for more effective normalisation*. This understanding of ADHD also works to explain why such disorders are discovered almost exclusively in areas where they pose a threat to effective social and educational management.

Likewise for the coherence truth test: a governmental understanding of ADHD coheres neatly with a truth matrix comprised of accepted historical theories and interpretations. It also dovetails into the widely accepted proposition that social governance is becoming more and more densely layered, as reflected in the fact that the number of accepted behaviour disorders continues to increase exponentially.

So what happens now? Both sides of the debate can make some solid claims to truth. Is ADHD a fact, 'cut and dried, precise, immobile, very convenient, and ready for examination', or is it something 'crawling and alive, a little furry …'? It would appear that 'truth' is not a simple matter. Some – realists – regard it as objectively ascertainable; it is 'out there' waiting to be uncovered. Others – anti-realists – regard it as inexorably tied to human conceptual frameworks, and that 'there are no eternal facts, as there are no absolute truths' (Nietzsche 1997, 12). If philosophical debate were a football match, then the anti-realists would currently be winning handsomely. That said, weigh the arguments and take your pick.

# Myth #2 The knowledge in our school curriculum is both true, and culturally neutral

We teach the truth in our schools. This isn't Nazi Germany, where the curriculum was used to indoctrinate children with utter falsehoods, such as that there is a race called the 'Aryans' who are somehow better than everyone else, and that the only reason the Germans lost World War I was because of the Jews. It's not like that in twenty-first-century Australia; our curriculum is made up of undeniable truths. You could teach our curriculum anywhere and it would still be regarded as true.

The argument here is that our curriculum is about knowledge, not ideology. Fair enough, we may be a former colony of Great Britain, but it's not as if our schools were set up to peddle their world view, and even if they were, that certainly isn't the case now. Australia is a young, vibrant and independent nation, and we are beholden to no-one; our school curricula reflect this fact.

## Colonialism and postcolonialism

While we may wish this were the case, there are strong arguments to suggest that the situation is considerably more complex. Certainly, Australian curriculum design-ers don't sit around chuckling, and mischievously thinking of ways of introducing falsehood into school lessons. However, the evidence indicates that at the core of our education system there beats a Eurocentric heart, and whether we realise it or not, the systems of knowledge and representation we valorise, and the truths we accept, have their origins there.

This should not really come as a surprise. For over 500 years, a number of European countries – primarily Great Britain, France, Spain, Portugal, Germany and Holland – extended their influence across the globe. Wave after wave of explora-tion across the Americas, Africa and Asia ultimately resulted in the foundation of global empires, empires largely built upon the resources they took from the lands they encountered. Importantly, this was not a one-way process. Though the minerals, spices, timber, and even the inhabitants, were shipped away by the Europeans, they left small versions of their homelands behind: hybrid adaptations of Spain in Central and South America, of France in North Africa, of Holland in South Africa, and of Great Britain in North America, India and Australasia.

These colonies were not just collections of towns and ports, clustered under the flag of a distant power. They introduced new languages, entirely different political and education systems, alternative forms of conduct, other ways of understanding the world – altogether new truths – as well as imported social, cultural and episte-mological hierarchies. This last point had particular significance for the lives of the colonised. As McLeod (2000, 19) states:

> Under colonialism, a colonised people are made subservient to ways of regarding the world which reflect and support colonialist values. A particular value-system is taught as the best, truest world-view. The cultural values of the colonised peoples are deemed as lacking in value, or even as being 'uncivilised', from which they must be rescued. To be blunt, the British Empire did not rule by military and physical force alone. It endured by getting *both colonising and colonised people* to see their world and themselves in a particular way, internalising the language of Empire as representing the natural, true order of life.

It is not as if when the British first arrived in Australia, Indigenous culture was under-stood as being of equal value, such that a 50–50 hybrid culture might somehow emerge; far from it. The beliefs and practices of the colonisers were assumed to be infinitely superior, with Indigenous Australians 'obviously' needing to be rescued from their cultural inferiority. Many would argue that even after 200 years, very little has changed.

Of course, European colonisation has not continued unchecked. First, there is really nothing left to colonise, no land left unclaimed or unconquered – even the Antarctic has been divided up like a giant cake – but if there were, the economic and ideological world superpower is now the United States, and the smart money would be on the United States to be the first to stake a claim (MacDonalds everyone?). More importantly though for our purposes, since the 1950s there has been a reversal of the colonising process. The world over, nations initially formed as colonies have gained independence from their colonial masters, either by negotiated political settlement, or by bloody struggle. However, this is far from the end of the matter.

## Postcolonial theory

It is not as if, upon gaining independence, the former colonies suddenly and magi-cally returned to their original state. Each postcolonial country has to deal with its own set of colonial legacies, and not just political and economic, but in terms of shap-ing viable identities, both at the scale of nationhood *and* of individual citizenship, former coloniser and former colonist. This is not an easy task, as the recent history of Australia amply demonstrates. The body of work that has attempted to address these difficulties is called *postcolonial theory*. It covers a wide range of areas, and the work of a plethora of writers. Four in particular will be dealt with here, specifically addressing how their work speaks to the notion of truth.

## Fanon: postcolonial identities

Fanon was a highly educated psychiatrist from Martinique, who struggled against the French colonisation of North Africa. Though most famous for his book on revolutionary decolonisation, *The Wretched of the Earth* (1961), he also wrote *Black Skin, White Masks* (1952). In this text he discusses how those with black skin always come to be defined as 'other' within colonial settings. This process of definition is not limited to whites – those who might consider themselves 'true' representatives of a national identity – but actually manages to co-opt blacks into the same reasoning. As such, those with black skin come to regard themselves as somehow 'less' than their white counterparts, never a colonial *subject,* but rather always an *object;* different and outside.

Once again, Australia provides a useful example of this argument. Bearing in mind the logic set out in Chapter 3 about white race privilege, it is unlikely that when an Anglo-Celtic Australian looks in the mirror that the colour of their skin plays any role in how they understand themselves. They are not a 'white Australian'; they are simply Australian. This cannot generally be said for the Indigenous. After 200 years of colonisation, they fully understand that they are necessarily 'the other', marked out not only by the colour of their skin, and their physical appearance, but also by elements of their hybrid identity, always excluding them for being 'true' Australians – an irony that needs no further comment.

## Said: misrepresenting 'the other'

One of the most influential texts within postcolonial theory is Said's *Orientalism* (1995). In this book, he discusses how 'the truth' of the Middle East – the Orient, as it was referred to in the late nineteenth and early twentieth centuries – was constructed with only limited reference to its subject matter. That is, Western experts ('Orientalists') came to shape our understanding of the Arab/Islamic world, not as a direct, objective reflection of the culture they were describing, but rather as an amalgam of the romanticised preconceptions, stereotypical prejudices, oversimplifications and ethnocentrisms that they brought with them in the first place.

> The Orient and Islam have a kind of extrareal, phenomenologically reduced status that puts them out of reach of everyone except the Western expert. From the beginning of Western speculation about the Orient, the one thing the Orient could not do was to represent itself. Evidence of the Orient was credible only after it had passed through and been made firm by the refining fire of the Orientalist's work (Said 1995, 283).

To put it another way, the truth of the Arab world only became *the truth* when it was authored by someone from the West, and importantly, this truth was necessarily a function of the colonial relationships of power from which it emerged: i.e. Arabs aren't like us; they are lazy, strange, exotic, dangerous; they are 'the other'. Once again, arguably very little has changed.

## Guha: the subaltern

Guha is one of the most important writers within the field of *subaltern studies*, a sub-branch of postcolonial theory. The term 'subaltern' refers to those of lower social status, those whose voice is not generally heard when it comes to the production of truth. While representations of nation and identity are generally shaped by the colonisers and not the colonised (the subaltern: after all, do we really think Indigenous world views carry the same weight and truth value as those associated with the West?), this is not to say that similar divisions don't also exist within the colonised themselves; between those whose voice is heard, and those who are silenced.

A good example of this silencing can be seen in Guha's essay 'On some aspects of the historiography of colonial India' (1988) in which he notes that the written history of the decolonisation of India has privileged the voices of the native elite, wherein they placed themselves, virtually alone, at the intellectual and political forefront of the struggle against British rule. Largely absent from these same histories are the activities and efforts of the many subaltern groups – those castes who generally lack the power to make themselves heard – and consequently, their efforts, and their truths, will ultimately vanish from the record.

## Connell: Eurocentric theory

Connell, probably Australia's greatest writer on education, has also contributed to debates around issues of colonialism. While there may be a temptation to think that while everything is slanted in favour of the West, in favour of the colonial powers that shaped the world in their own image, then at least the intellectual tools by which we conduct our analysis – the theories behind it all – are neutral in their application, and hence the truths produced by our social sciences are founded upon solid ground. This would be a mistake.

In *Southern Theory* (2007), Connell points to a number of ways that the social theories of the colonisers subtly marginalise the ideas of the colonised. There is the assumption of intellectual universality, for example in that the philosophy taught in Western universities remains valid across all cultural and intellectual contexts, whereas 'African philosophy' is a niche subject, with equally niche application. Likewise, there is a self-replicating process of selective exclusion, wherein Western ideas provide virtually all the content for books such as this, to the exclusion of equally valid work that simply made the mistake of being written by someone of non-European origin; unfortunately it's true … check the reference list at the back. Finally, she points to a 'grand erasure' for previous subaltern ideas and experiences from our analysis, as if our theories, and the worlds they describe, sprung from nowhere, pure and fully formed. As such, our truths become written on the spaces created by the erasure of other truths. Just as modern Australia was built on the myth of *terra nullius* – land belonging to nobody – so too are many of its ideas.

> *Terra nullius,* the coloniser's dream, is a sinister proposition for social science. It is invoked every time we try to theorise the formation of social institutions and systems from scratch, in a blank space. Whenever we see the words 'building block' in a treatise of social theory, we should be asking who used to occupy the land (Connell 2007, 47).

## Postcolonialism and education

While these are all important issues, in a general sense, there are also far more specific points that relate to particular postcolonial legacies and problems within education. It is not as if the aforementioned concerns over identity, the misrepresentation and stereotyping of other cultures and peoples, the marginalisation of subaltern voices, and a pervading Eurocentrism all stop at the gates of the school. Indeed, as with many ingrained social practices and assumptions, learning to take these things for granted, in a commonsensical and unquestioning manner, most often occurs within the school.

As Hickling-Hudson, Matthews and Woods (2004) note, our education system is full of colonial assumptions, knowledges and customs. As the great colonial powers spread out around the globe, they took with them specifically Western systems of education, and although the schools they established were often mere shadows of the institutions back in Great Britain, Spain and Holland, the logic was the same, their internal structures were the same, their world view was the same, and the truths they taught were the same. Poddar (1997, 62) makes the point that this did not occur by accident.

> ... western secular education was seen by the British establishment as the most convenient and effective means to establish 'the foundation for a stability that "even a political revolution will not destroy and upon which after many ages may rest a vast superstructure"' (from an 1826 Asiatic Journal, cited in Viswanathan 1989, 117).

Two particular elements of the colonial school are of particular importance here, both in terms of how education continues to operate in the postcolonial era, as well as addressing the implication of indigenous peoples – and in this instance, 'indigenous' refers not only to Australia's Indigenous, but to colonised peoples the world over. The first is the structure of the institution itself, and the second is the curriculum.

## The mass school

As was discussed at length in Chapter 4, the great institutions of the nineteenth century all developed according to the same logic (see Foucault, 1976). Whether they were prisons, factories, hospitals, asylums or schools, all were structured around the

minute subdivision of space and time, around continual surveillance, around hierarchical observation, around the examination, around uniforms; they were structured
around *discipline*. Schools based upon these principles became, not only the norm
for European education, but also to be regarded as the only viable model for schooling. It is hardly surprising then, that when colonial administrators sought to put in
place all the necessary elements of effective governance in the far-flung corners of
empire, they knew exactly what the schools ought to look like.

The implications of this are significant, both in terms of the enforcement of
European frames of reference, and the marginalisation of indigenous peoples. Three
familiar aspects of the mass school, almost chosen a random, can illustrate how this
occurs so easily.

## The subdivision of time

We often think that there is something self-evident about time, that in keeping with
the logic of the correspondence theory of truth, it exists independently of our perception of it. If this is correct, it is only so at a very simplistic level. Many cultures
understand time, and measure its passing, in completely different ways. Certainly,
very few other than ourselves have chopped it up into tiny, manageable pieces that
subdivide each day into 'specific places you have to be at any given moment'. By
imposing this regimen upon the structure of the school, native peoples generally not
only found schooling strange, they often struggled to meet this disciplinary requirement, a requirement that had no meaning or purpose within their cultural frames of
reference. The outcome of this was both the gradual marginalisation of other, non-
disciplinary ways of understanding time – other truths about how time should be
conceptualised – but also the development of potent stereotypes about indigenous
peoples being 'unreliable' and 'lazy'.

## The uniform

The notion that everyone should dress the same, and in a particularly Western
style, within the mass school also runs contrary to the practices of many cultures.
Furthermore, as is the case within non-colonial education settings, the unwillingness
or financial inability to wear the uniform appropriately is often translated as resistance to the education system in total. So when the issue is actually one of cultural
mismatch, or simply of poverty, indigenous pupils failing to meet the uniform requirements often have this conduct translated as 'lack of respect' – with all the associated
implications this has for their chances of success within the school.

## The examination

This important legacy of the colonial system continues to have very specific roles
to play within in the education system – and beyond. Not only does it reinforce the
Western notion that knowledge can be divided up into discrete little boxes, each
of which can be measured, assessed and normalised independently, it also acts as

an 'objective' tool through which the 'fair race' of the education system is run, and indigenous students are generally found wanting.

## The curriculum

In addition to the structure of the school, some important observations can be made about the curricula. In Australia, most would agree that until relatively recently, the curriculum remained recognisably British: British history, British sports, British literature. However, as the nation has grown in stature and confidence, and as migrants have arrived from a far greater variety of places and cultures, significant efforts have been made to de-colonialise the materials used in schools. The question is: how successful has this process been, and do we now have a genuinely postcolonial curriculum, or is it as British as it's ever been? This question can be addressed using a number of examples.

The evidence suggests that work still needs to be done in the area of teaching literature. Various writers have pointed to the problems associated with ongoing dominance of the European and American literary canon. Not only does this perpetuate the logic of Eurocentrism, now so out of place within postcolonial contexts, it also actively disengages many young students, who fail to recognise themselves, or their experiences, within any of the texts they are asked to read (Bean 2004). Similar observations have also been made about the teaching of art (Crouch, Chan & Kaye 2004). However, bearing these criticisms in mind, there is no suggestion here that a 'good curriculum' is therefore one somehow purged of Western influences.

> A postcolonial perspective does not seek to turn the tables and suppress the important legacies of European or 'Western' learning in order to promote Indigenous perspectives ... A postcolonial curriculum is a hybrid one, engaging with the elements of non-Western learning and experience which colonialism so determinedly cast aside (Hickling-Hudson & Ahlquist 2004, 43).

That said, if there has been one curriculum area wherein the struggle between the old and the new has been writ large, between colonial and postcolonial viewpoints, it is in the teaching of history. In what has been dubbed 'The History Wars', within the last decade defenders of more traditional 'white' histories of the colonisation of Australia, have responded critically to various attempts to give curriculum space to other perspectives, other truths, in this process – not all of them pretty (Parkes 2007). So who gets to write history then? Within postcolonial frames of reference, the obvious conclusion is that there's no singular truth to be told about the founding of Australia, and that many subaltern voices also have the right to be heard when it comes to telling the story of our past.

In summary, the evidence suggests that our schools bear the significant imprint of their colonial heritage. This does not simply include the structure of the school, its subdivision of space and time, its use of the examination and so on, but also the truths that are taught there; the knowledge that is imparted. This leads back to addressing Myth #2 directly: our curriculum is both true and culturally neutral.

Is the knowledge in our curriculum true? From what has gone before in this chapter, it can be seen that this is a complex question. What exactly do we mean by 'true'? If we mean *objectively* true in some realist sense, most philosophers would find this difficult to accept. If we mean 'true' in a more anti-realist sense – that we create various truths, and some of those are in our curriculum – then this sounds significantly more plausible.

Is the knowledge in our curriculum culturally neutral? The postcolonial theorists addressed here – Fanon, Said, Guha, Connell – along with work from a wide variety of educational writers, would suggest that it is not. This does not mean that the West should therefore take all its 'truths', and its education system, and just go away. While some postcolonial truths can certainly be seen to be fallacious, self-serving, and ultimately repressive, it is also important to note that other Western truths have proved invaluable to the cultures into which they were introduced, the notion of universal human rights providing a particularly vivid example.

# Conclusion

This chapter has sought to demonstrate that 'truth' is not a simple issue; it has provided the substance for philosophical debate for 2500 years, and to be honest, we are still arguing about many of the same things now. Does truth exist independently of human thought and action, as suggested by the realists? Or is truth simply a function of the social contexts within which it is formulated, as suggested by the anti-realists? These questions are important because, emerging from the wealth of truths we discover/accept, comes human knowledge, in all its forms – and surely, this is what schools are all about. If Protagorus is right, and 'Man is the measure of all things', does this mean that knowledge about the universe, and ultimately ourselves, can never be built upon completely solid ground? Most contemporary philosophers would say, 'probably not'.

This chapter has also sought to demonstrate that many of the truths we take for granted, particularly in a country like Australia, have been inherited as a result of our European colonial history. This is the case, irrespective of whether it relates to who we think we are, how we understand other peoples and cultures, or whose voices get to be heard. Importantly, the evidence suggests that our schools also continue to play a significant role in perpetuating these often-questionable Western truths. That is, there are many models for understanding the world, and we are often only presented with one.

Finally, while the three chapters comprising Part 4 of this book have set out to demonstrate the vital importance of the discipline of philosophy in gaining a better understanding of mass schooling, it is also important to note, particularly regarding the substance of this chapter, that all knowledge appears to be context-bound, and philosophy is no exception.

> One of the most robust and suspect theoretical moves of Western philosophy is to assume historical, temporal and spatial synchronicity – that indeed we might live in a 'universal' world where singular theoretical constructs and textual conceits might have generalisable explanatory and practical power. Yet the answers obviously depend upon where, to whom, by whom, when, with which available discourses and in which material conditions. (Luke 2004, 251)

# Conclusion

## The central aims of this book

This book set out with some very specific goals in mind, even if it has not necessarily achieved them all. The first is to address the issue of mass education in ways that have something to offer a range of different readers. This book is not aimed specifically at undergraduates, any more than it is at practising teachers, or university academics. Each chapter has been organised with a progressive layering of complexity and density, such that readers with differing levels of knowledge and expertise should still be able to get something out of it. This has not been written as a textbook, with bite-sized pieces tailor-made for tutorial digestion. The book was put together for a range of reasons: it is a summary of the current state of play within Australian (and global) theories of education; it is a resource book for those interesting in assessing the weight of different conceptual approaches to mass schooling; it is an analysis of various issues within contemporary society, as they relate to education; it is a (relatively) gentle critique of reductionist analyses of our schooling institutions and their outcomes; and it is a call for us not to forget the value of philosophy within the broader play of the social sciences.

Second, the intention has been to use a language that is as inclusive as possible. This has not been done with the intention, in any way, of dumbing down the content – far from it. Simple language, carefully used, can still convey all the nuance required from a text dealing with complex ideas. The goal was simply to write a book in a more conversational manner – in part because it is often more enjoyable to read, but also because it's certainly more enjoyable to write. This style has also not been adopted as a veiled criticism of books that maintain a rigorously academic voice throughout; both styles have their place. However, if a book is intended for a broad audience, it surely needs to be written in a broadly accessible manner.

Third, the book has been written with the intention of addressing a wide range of issues and ideas as they related to mass schooling, without descending into some sort of a scattergun approach, one giving five pages to every unit in the education faculty curriculum. It should be possible for anyone who wants to know more about the social, cultural and philosophical underpinnings of contemporary schooling to go to a book like this and find most of what they are looking for. This book covers the central axes of social inequality, in class, gender and race. It covers the rise of mass schooling as a disciplinary institution, including the governance of subjective experience, and the regulation of various categories of pre-adulthood. It examines various cultural influences on the field of education, from the news media, through popular cultural forms, to the rise of digital technologies. Finally, it addresses the influence of philosophical thought upon education, its relation to the law, and to the truth claims we make within a postcolonial societies such as Australia. As such, most of the main debates and topics within the contemporary sociology of education are covered here.

Finally, this text was written deliberately in a single voice. While there are many advantages in co-authoring books – workload, shared expertise, a greater communal safety net for errors, misstatements and misjudgements – the overall coherence of a book is not generally one of them. After all, conceptual disputes with oneself are not common, although succumbing to theoretical fence-sitting is (on second thoughts, perhaps conceptual disputes with oneself *are* common; perhaps that is the primary function of a book like this ... to engender such disputes). Likewise, edited collections can be uneven, contradictory and prone to containing large chunks of irrelevance. Hopefully, *Making Sense of Mass Education* has none of these shortcomings.

# The intended approach of this book

This book also set out with a very specific approach in mind. First, by utilising the idea of 'common myths', the intention has been to ground the book in some of the concrete, mundane ideas that appear to exist within public discourses about education, and then start working out from there. This is a very different proposition to the usual approach of outlining the parameters of a given theory, and then applying that theory to a range of different issues. In keeping with the general aim of accessibility, a criterion fundamental to this book, this seemed like a logical way to go.

Second, by grounding the book in the world of public discourse – i.e. starting with familiar meritocratic claims and questions, such as 'It's all up to the individual, isn't it?', rather than theoretical ones, such as 'Cultural capital is often misread as "ability"' – this book not only continues the theme of accessibility, it can also more readily act as an antidote to the multitude of simplistic discourses and aphorisms about education that those with knowledge in the area hear almost every day, generally coming from those without.

The third noteworthy aspect of the approach taken by this book is that it does not set out to champion a particular theoretical framework for the study of mass education. While Part 1 of this book does find significant shortcomings with traditional modernist approaches to the study of class, gender and race, it does not then seek to position its postmodern successor as the answer to all our theoretical problems. Neither does it suggest that governmental approaches to the study of mass schooling somehow trump everything that has gone before. Likewise, the final section on philosophy is not put there as a trans-disciplinary solution to the problem of theory; suggesting that in the final analysis, philosophy outdoes sociology. It would be a strange book indeed that ends with a chapter on the intangible nature of truth, and then claims to know the 'truth' of social theory. All theories have their strengths and weaknesses – some weaknesses more terminal than others – and understanding those theories, and what they say about mass schooling, isn't really a quest for the 'right' answer.

Finally, the four parts are not simply organised according to subject matter, whether this be the three main axes of social inequality in Part 1, or various manifestations of contemporary culture in Part 3. They are also organised according to a specific conceptual logic, a logic where each is built upon the reasoning of the last – or at least acts as a counterpoint to it – and each contributes to an effective lexicon of approaches for better understanding mass schooling. This book is not just a list of topics, with some associated guidelines for how to best address each one. Upon finishing the book, readers should have a sound grasp of how various theoretical positions work, how they relate to each other, and a knowledge of some the domains in which those ideas can be applied.

# Finally

Some concluding observations: first, while the dominant, modernist models of educational analysis have some demonstrable shortcomings, elements of these approaches still retain conceptual and practical utility. The suggestion here has not been to throw out the notions of class, gender and race altogether as no longer possessing any theoretical viability or merit. For whatever those terms now mean, when employed with a solid grasp of their limitations and weaknesses, they can still tell us a lot about how we are shaped as citizens, how our education system works, and who is most likely to win the race of life.

Second, a theoretical framework based around social governance, either alone or in tandem with aspects of the above, can offer an effective new lens through which to view education. By regarding power as fundamentally productive rather than coercive, the mass school can be seen, not as a giant engine for the replication of social inequalities, but rather as a crucial component of an otherwise piecemeal set of processes aimed at regulating the conduct and capacities of the population. That is, the mass school wasn't established with the intention of keeping the working classes in their place, or making sure women stayed in the kitchen (although it may have had a role to play in this occurring), rather it provided an efficient mechanism through which the population could be normalised.

Third, perhaps more than ever, the mass school needs to be understood as located within a complex mosaic of cultural practices, forces and innovations. This mosaic doesn't exist as an external distraction to formal learning, or as something that should, or should not, be incorporated into classroom practice. Education is not a separate domain, one that sought to remain somehow pure and unaffected by the distractions of culture. To paraphrase Dewey, we do not educate *for* life; education *is* life, and culture, in all its forms, is the context within which that life is shaped.

Finally, the working life of educators – whether in schools or universities – has become dauntingly complex, with the relentless focus on standards and testing, pressure to ensure equitable outcomes, managerialist working environments, ever-growing professional responsibilities and expectations, increasingly heterogeneous classrooms, and fairly relentless media criticism, to name only a few of the issues. The job requires continual self-reflection, a commitment to lifelong learning, and an ongoing dedication to the profession to remain viable at all. Making sense of it all – *Making Sense of Mass Education* – is not an easy task. Hopefully this book can help a little.

# References

Ackoff, R. 1989. From data to wisdom. *Journal of Applied Systems Analysis* 16: 3–9.

Adorno, T. and M. Horkheimer. 1979. *Dialectic of enlightenment*. London: Verso.

Althusser, L. 1971. *Lenin and philosophy, and other essays*. [London]: New Left Books.

Anderson, M. 2003. Whitewashing race: a critical perspective on whiteness. In *White out: the continuing significance of racism*, eds A.W. Doane and E. Bonilla-Silva. New York: Routledge, xii, 328.

Apple, M. 1982. *Education and power*. Boston: ARK.

Apple, M.W. 1979. *Ideology and curriculum*. London and Boston: Routledge & Kegan Paul.

Argy, F. 2006. *Equality of opportunity in Australia: myth and reality*, Discussion Paper 85: Asia Pacific School of Economics and Government, ANU.

Aries, P. 1962. *Centuries of childhood*. Harmondsworth: Penguin.

Aristotle. 1980. *Nicomachean ethics*. Oxford: Oxford University Press.

Arnold, M. 1963. *Culture and anarchy*. Cambridge: Cambridge University Press.

Arrow, K. 1978. *Social choice and individual values*. New Haven: Yale University Press.

Atkins, D. 1996. A learning process. *Courier Mail,* January 23, 11.

Austin, J. 2000 (1832). *The province of jurisprudence determined*. New York: Prometheus.

Australian Bureau of Statistics (ABS). 2011. Household use of information technology 8146.0.

—— 2010a. *Schools*. Vol. 4221.0.

—— 2010b. Where have all the male teachers gone? Vol. 1345.4 – SA Stats.

—— 2007. *Schools*. Vol. 4221.0.

—— 2006. *Schools*. Vol. Vol. 4221.0.

—— 1997. *Schools*. Vol. 4221.0.

Ayer, A. 1935. The criterion of truth. *Analysis* 3: 28–31.

Bacon, F. 1985 (1601). *On Truth. The Essays*. Harmondsworth: Penguin.

—— 1952 (1620). The new organon (Novum Organon). In *Great books of the Western World: volume 30, the works of Francis Bacon*, ed. R. Hutchins. Chicago: Encyclopaedia Britannica, Inc.

Bantick, C. 2008. Literacy taught by illiterates. *Australian*. February 27. http://www.theaustralian.com.au/news/opinion/literacy-taught-by-illiterates/story-e6frg6zo-1111115652926.

Banton, M. 1998. *Racial theories*. 2nd edn. Cambridge: Cambridge University Press.

Barrow, R. 1975. *Moral philosophy for education*. London: George, Allen and Unwin.

Barthes, R. 1972. *Mythologies*. London: Paladin.

Baudrillard, J. 1993. *Symbolic exchange and death*. London: Sage.

—— 1983. *Simulations*. New York: Semiotext(e).

Bayne, S. and S. Ross. 2011. 'Digital native' and 'digital immigrant' discourses: a critique. In *Digital difference: perspectives on online learning*, eds R. Land and S. Bayne. Rotterdam: Sense, 159–70.

Bean, T. 2004. The role of multicultural literature as a counter-force to the literary canon. In *Disrupting preconceptions: postcolonialism and education*, eds A. Hickling-Hudson, J. Matthews and A. Woods. Flaxton: Post-Pressed, 57–76.

Beauvoir, S. de. 1960. *The second sex*. London: Landsborough Publications.

Bell, T. and M. Gropshover. 2005. Pop goes the geographer: synergies between geography and popular culture. In *Popular culture studies across the curriculum*, ed. R. Browne. Jefferson: McFarland and Co., 89–103.

Bennett, T., M. Savage, E. Silva, A. Warde, M. Gayo-Cal and D. Wright. 2008. *Culture, class, distinction*. London: Routledge.

Bentham, J. 1988 (1781). *An introduction to the principals of morals and legislation*. New York: Prometheus Books.

Berman, S. and R. Tinker. 2000. The world's the limit in the virtual high school. In *The Jossey-Bass reader on technology and learning*, ed. R. Pea. San Francisco: Jossey-Bass, 192–6.

Bernstein, B. 1990. *Class, codes and control*. London: Routledge.

Better Education. 2011. http://bettereducation.com.au/SchoolRanking.aspx (accessed 16/06/2011).

Bierce, A. 1995 (1911). *The Devil's dictionary*. London: Penguin.

Bini, M., G. Burgh, P. Cam, E. Goddard, C. Golding, S. Knight, S. Millett, G. Oppy, J. Poulton, T. Sprod, A. Tapper and A. Walsh. 2009. The case for inclusion of philosophy in the National Curriculum. In *Paper submitted to the Australian Curriculum, Assessment and Reporting Authority*.

Birbalsingh, K. 2011. Trendy teachers cheat the poor and lay the groundwork for riots. *Australian*. September 23.

Bishop, K. and D. Wahlsten. 1997. Sex differences in the human corpus callosum: myth or reality. *Neuroscience Biobehavioural Review* 21 (5): 581–601.

Blackmore, J., L. Hardcastle, E. Bamblett and J. Owens. 2003. *Effective use of information and communication technology (ICT) to enhance learning for disadvantaged school students*: Deakin Centre for Education and Change; Institute of Disability Studies, Deakin University and Institute of Koorie Education, Deakin University.

Bloom, A. 1987. *The closing of the American mind*. New York: Simon & Schuster.

Bohn, R. and J. Short. 2009. *How much information? Report on American consumers*. Global Information Industry Centre, University of California, San Diego.

Boody, R. 2001. On the relationship of education and technology. In *Education and technology: critical and reflective practices*, ed. R. Muffoletto. Cresskill, NJ: Hampton Press, 5–22.

Bottomley, A. 1996. *Feminist perspectives on the foundational subjects of law*. London: Cavendish.

Bourdieu, P. 1986. The forms of capital. In *Handbook of theory and research for the sociology of education*, ed. J. G. Richardson. New York: Greenwood Press, 241–58.

Bourdieu, P. and J. C. Passeron. 1990. *Reproduction in education, society and culture*. 2nd edn. London: Sage.

Bowles, S. and H. Gintis. 1976. *Schooling in capitalist America: educational reform and the contradictions of economic life*. New York: Basic Books.

Boyd-Barrett, O. and T. Rantenen. 2010. New Agencies. In *The media: an introduction*, eds D. Albertazzi and P. Cobley. London: Pearson, 233–45.

Brabazon, T. 2002. *Digital hemlock: internet education and the poisoning of teaching*. Sydney: University of New South Wales Press.

Brandt, R. 1978. Towards a credible form of utilitarianism. In *Contemporary utilitarianism*, ed. M. Bayles. Gloucester, MA: Anchor, 143–86.

Branston, G. and R. Stafford. 2006. *The media student's book*. 4th edn. Abingdon, Oxon: Routledge.

Brontë, C. 1847. *Jane Eyre*. London: Smith, Elder, and Co.

Brontë, E. 1846. *Wuthering Heights*. London: Thomas Cautley Newby.

Brosnan, M. 1998. *Technophobia: the psychological impact of information technology*. London: Routledge.

Brown, D. 2003. *The Da Vinci code*. New York: Doubleday.

Bryson, L. 1990. Challenges to male hegemony in sport. In *Sport, men and the gender order: critical feminist perspectives*, eds M. Messner and D. Sabo. Champaign, IL: Human Kinetics, 173–84.

Bucholtz, M. 2002. Youth and cultural practice. *Annual Review of Anthropology* 31: 525–52.

Burchell, G. 1993. Liberal government and techniques of the self. *Economy and Society* 22(3): 267–83.

Burke, P. 1996. *Popular culture in early modern Europe*. Aldershot: Scolar Press.

Burn, A. and C. Durrant. 2008. Media education: a background. In *Media teaching: language, audience and production*, eds A. Burn and C. Durrant. Kent Town, SA: Wakefield Press, 11–28.

Burnett, B. 2004a. How does 'othering' constitute cultural discrimination? In *New questions for contemporary teachers: taking a socio-cultural approach to education*, eds B. Burnett, D. Meadmore and G. Tait. Frenchs Forest, NSW: Pearson Education, 101–12.

—— 2004b. Technophobes or technophiles. In *New questions for contemporary teachers: taking a socio-cultural approach to education*, eds B. Burnett, D. Meadmore and G. Tait. Frenchs Forest, NSW: Pearson Education, 127–40.

Burton, G. 2002. *More than meets the eye*. 3rd edn. London: Arnold.

Butler, D. and B. Mathews. 2007. *Schools and the law*. Annandale, NSW: Federation.

Butler, G. 1995. Teacher in tears over girl. *Courier Mail*, 14 December, 5.

Bynner, J., S. Reder, S. Parsons and C. Strawn. 2008. *The digital divide: computer use, basic skills and employment*. London: National Research and Development Centre for adult literacy and numeracy.

Campbell, C. 2010. Class and competition. In *Education, change and society*, eds R. Connell, C. Campbell, M. Vickers, A. Welch, F. Dennis, N. Bagnall and D. Hayes. Melbourne: Oxford University Press, 93–129.

Carpenter, B. and G. Tait. 2010. The autopsy imperative: medicine, law, and the coronial system. *Journal of Medical Humanities* 31(3): 205–21.

Cashmore, E. 1984. *No Future: youth and society*. London: Heinemann.

Castel, R. 1991. From dangerousness to risk. In *The Foucault effect: studies in governmentality*, eds G. Burchell, C. Gordon and P. Miller. London: Harvester/Wheatsheaf, 281–98.

Central Intelligence Agency. 2011. World factbook. https://http://www.cia.gov/library/publications/the-world-factbook/rankorder/2172rank.html (accessed 15/06/2011).

Chilcott, T. and J. Tin. 2010. Queensland OP school grades breakdown busts gender myth. *Courier Mail*. 31 May. http://www.couriermail.com.au/news/queensland/queensland-op-school-grades-breakdown-busts-gender-myth/story-e6freoof-1225873734368.

Christian, J. 1981. *Philosophy: an introduction to the art of wondering*. New York: Holt, Rinehart and Winston.

Cicero. 1995. *De re publica: selections*. Ed. J. Zetzel. Cambridge: Cambridge University Press.

Clark, K. 1978. *The Gothic revival*. London: John Murray.

Clarke, E. 1873. *Sex in education: or, a fair chance for the girls*. Boston: Osgood.

Cleary, P., G. Pierce and E. Trauth. 2006. Closing the digital divide: understanding racial, ethnic, social class, gender and geographic disparities in Internet use among school age children in the United States. *Universal Access in the Information Society* 4(4): 354–73.

Cline, T. and S. Baldwin. 2004. *Selective mutism in children*. 2nd edn. London: Whurr.

Cohen, D. 2006. Critiques of the 'ADHD' enterprise. In *Critical new perspectives on ADHD*, eds G. Lloyd, J. Stead and D. Cohen. London: Routledge, 12–33.

Cohen, S. 1980. *Folk devils and moral panics: the creation of the Mods and the Rockers*. 2nd edn. Oxford: Robertson.

Cole, R. and D. Pullen. 2010. Introduction to multiliteracies in motion. In *Multiliteracies in motion: current theory and practice*, eds R. Cole and D. Pullen. New York: Routledge, 1–14.

Colic-Peisker, V. and F. Tilbury. 2007. *Refugees and employment: the effects of visible difference on discrimination*. Perth: Centre for Social and Community Research, Murdoch University.

Collins, S. 2008. *The hunger games*. New York: Scholastic.

Connell, R. 2007. *Southern theory*. Malden, MA: Polity Press.

—— 2005. *Masculinities*. 2nd edn. Berkeley, CA: University of California Press.

—— 1977. *Ruling class, ruling culture: studies of conflict, power and hegemony in Australian life*. Cambridge: Cambridge University Press.

Connell, R., D. Ashenden, S. Kessler and G. Dowsett. 1982. *Making the difference: schools, families and social division*. Sydney, London, Boston: Allen & Unwin.

Cooper, D. 1998. *Ethics: the classic readings*. Oxford: Blackwell

Cooper, J. 2006. The digital divide: the special case of gender. *Journal of Computer Assisted Learning* 22: 320–34.

—— 2003. *Gender and computers: understanding the digital divide*. Mahwah, NJ: Lawrence Erlbaum Associates.

Cope, B. and M. Kalantzis. 2000. Introduction: multiliteracies: the beginnings of an idea. In *Multiliteracies: literacy learning and the design of social futures*, eds B. Cope and M. Kalantzis. London: Routledge, 3–8.

Coster, W. 2007. Social constructions of childhood. In *Childhood and youth studies*, ed. P. Zwozdiak-Myers. Exeter: Learning Matters, 3–12.

Counihan, T. 1982. Minding the family: Donzelot and his critics. *Local Consumption* 2–3, August: 19–48.

*Courier Mail*. 2001. Typhoid found in refugee centres. 23 June, 1.

—— 1996. Editorial. 10 August, 16.

Crikey. 2009. When it comes to asylum seekers, Australia is no Malta, 19 October.

Crouch, C., D. Chan and N. Kaye. 2004. Transforming visual culture: postcolonial theory and the ethically reflexive student. In *Disrupting Preconceptions: postcolonialism and education*, eds A. Hickling-Hudson, J. Matthews and A. Woods. Flaxton: Post Pressed, 77–89.

Darling, J. and S. Nordenbo. 2003. Progressivism. In *The Blackwell guide to the philosophy of education*, eds N. Blake, P. Smeyers, R. Smith and P. Standish. Oxford: Blackwell, 288–308.

Davenport, T. and L. Prusack. 1998. *Working knowledge: how organizations manage what they know*. Boston: Harvard Business School Press.

Davies, J., S. Sandstrom, A. Shorrocks and E. Wolff. 2009. *The level and distribution of global household wealth*. Vol. 15508, *NBER Working Paper Series*. Cambridge, MA: National Bureau of Economic Research.

Derrida, J. 1981. *Positions*. Chicago: University of Chicago Press.

Disraeli, B. 1851. *February 11*. House of Commons.

Doane, W. 2003. Rethinking whiteness studies. In *White out: the continuing significance of racism*, eds A.W. Doane and E. Bonilla-Silva. New York: Routledge, xii, 328.

Donnelly, K. 2005a. Cannon fodder in the culture wars. *Australian*. 9 February, 13.

—— 2005b. Teach the simple joy of reading. *Australian*. 26 July, 13.

—— 2004. *Why our schools are failing*. Sydney: Duffy and Snellgrove.

Donzelot, J. 1979. *The policing of families*. New York: Pantheon.

Dooley, K. 2004. How and why did literacy become so prominent? In *New questions for contemporary teachers*, eds B. Burnett, D. Meadmore and G. Tait. Frenchs Forest, NSW: Pearson, 55–70.

Dunn, K., N. Klocker and T. Salabay. 2007. Contemporary racism and Islamophobia: radicalising religion. *Ethnicities* 7(14): 564–89.

Durkheim, E. 1964. *The division of labor in society*. New York and London: Free Press Collier Macmillan.

Eagleton, T. 1983. *Literary theory: an introduction*. Oxford: Blackwell.

Elder, B. 2003. *Blood on the wattle: massacres and maltreatment of Aboriginal Australians since 1788*. 3rd edn. Frenchs Forest, NSW: New Holland.

Emmet, E. 1991. *Learning to philosophise*. London: Penguin.

Equal Opportunity for Women in the Workplace Agency (EOWA). 2010. *EOWA Census 2010 Key Findings Report*. Macquarie University.

Ewald, F. 1991. Insurance and risk. In *The Foucault effect: studies in governmentality*, eds G. Burchell, C. Gordon and P. Miller. London: Harvester/Wheatsheaf, 197–210.

Exley, B. 2010. A dog of a QCAT: collateral effects of mandated English assessment in the Torres Strait. *Australian Journal of Indigenous Education*. 39: 1–10.

Faludi, S. 1992. *Backlash: the undeclared war against women*. London: Chatto and Windus.

Fanon, F. 1961. *The wretched of the Earth*. Trans. C. Farrington 1963. New York: Grove Weidenfeld.

—— 1952. *Black skin, white masks*. Trans. C. Markmann 1967. New York: Grove Press.

Fausto-Sterling, A. 2000. *Sexing the body*. New York: Basic Books.

Finch, L. 1993. *The Classing Gaze: sexuality, class, and surveillance*. Sydney: Allen and Unwin.

Fine, C. 2010. *Delusions of gender: how our minds, society and neurosexism create difference*. New York: Norton.

Fink, C. and J. Kenny. 2003. W(h)ither the digital divide? *The Journal of Policy, Regulation and Strategy for Telecommunications* 5(6): 15–24.

Finot, J. 1913. *Problems of the sexes*. New York: The Knickerbocker Press.

Fleck, L. 1979. *Genesis and development of scientific fact*. Chicago: University of Chicago Press.

Foster, L. 1981. *Australian education: a sociological perspective*. Sydney: Prentice Hall.

Foster, V., M.S. Kimmel and C. Skelton. 2001. What about the boys?: an overview of the debates. In *What about the boys?: issues of masculinity in schools*, eds W. Martino and B. Meyenn. Buckingham UK and Philadelphia: Open University Press, xiv, 242.

Foucault, M. 2000. Questions of method. In *Power*, ed. J. Faubion. New York: New Press.

—— 1991. Governmentality. In *The Foucault effect: studies in governmentality*, eds G. Burchell, C. Gordon and P. Miller. London: Harvester Wheatsheaf, 87–104.

—— 1987. *The history of sexuality: the uses of pleasure*. Vol. 2. Harmondsworth: Penguin.

—— 1984. The politics of health in the eighteenth century. In *The Foucault reader*, ed. P. Rabinow. London: Penguin, 273–90.

—— 1980. Truth and power. In *Power/Knowledge: selected interviews and other writings 1972–1977 by Michel Foucault*, ed. C. Gordon. Brighton: Harvester Press, 109–33.

—— 1977. *Discipline and punish: the birth of the prison*. London: Penguin.

—— 1976. *Mental illness and psychology*. New York: Harper Collins.

—— 1965. *Madness and civilisation*. London: Tavistock.

Frawley, T. 2005. Gender bias in the classroom: current controversies and implications for teachers. *Childhood Education* 81(4): 221–7.

Frege, G. 1977 (1918). *Logical investigations*. Oxford: Blackwell.

Freire, P. 1970. *Pedagogy of the oppressed*. New York: Seabury Press.

Freud, S. 2005. *Three contributions to the sexual theory*. Montana: Kessinger.

Friedan, B. 1963. *The feminine mystique*. London: Gollancz.

Fullarton, S. and J. Ainley. 2000. *Subject choice by students in year 12 in Australian secondary schools*. Melbourne: Australian Council for Educational Research.

Fuller, L. 1958. Positivism and fidelity to the law – a response to Professor Hart. *Harvard Law Review* 71: 630–57.

Gabbay, J. 1982. Asthma attacked? Tactics for the reconstruction of a disease concept. In *The problem of medical knowledge: examining the social construction of medicine*, eds P. Wright and A. Treacher. Edinburgh: Edinburgh University Press, 23–48.

Gee, J., G. Hull and C. Lankshear. 1996. *The new work order: behind the language of the new capitalism*. Sydney: Allen and Unwin.

Germann, G. 1972. *Gothic revival in Europe and Britain: sources, influences, and ideas*. London: Lund Humphries.

Giddens, A. 1991. *Modernity and self identity: self and society in the late modern age*. Cambridge: Polity Press.

—— 1990. *The consequences of modernity*. Cambridge: Polity Press in association with Basil Blackwell Oxford.

Gilbert, R. and P. Gilbert. 1998. *Masculinity goes to school*. Sydney: Allen & Unwin.

Giroux, H. A. and D. E. Purpel. 1983. *The Hidden curriculum and moral education: deception or discovery?* Berkeley, CA: McCutchan Pub. Corp.

Goodall, P. 1995. *High culture, popular culture: the long debate*. Sydney: Allen & Unwin.

Goode, E. and N. Ben-Yehuda. 2009. *Moral panics: the social construction of devience*. 2nd edn. Chichester: Wiley-Blackwell.

Goodfellow, R. 2006. From 'equal access' to 'widening participation': the discourse of equity in the age of e-learning. In *Brave new classrooms: democratic education and the internet*, eds J. Lockard and M. Pegrum. New York: Peter Lang, 55–74.

Gordon, C. 1991. Governmental rationality: an introduction. In *The Foucault effect: studies in governmentality*, eds C. Gordon and P. Miller. London: Harvester Wheatsheaf, 1–52.

Gore, J. 1998. Disciplining bodies: on the continuity of power relations in pedagogy. In *Foucault's challenge: discourse, knowledge, and power in education*, eds T. Popkewitz and M. Brennan. London: Falmer Press, 231–51.

Gorman, C. 1992. Sizing up the sexes. *Time* 139: 42–52.

Gough, N. 1993. *Laboratories in fiction: science education and popular media*. Geelong: Deakin University Press.

Gould, S.J. 1996. *The mismeasure of man*. Revised and expanded edn. New York: Norton.

Gramsci, A. 1971. *Selections from the prison notebooks of Antonio Gramsci*. Trans. Q. Hoare and G. Nowell Smith. London: Lawrence and Wishart.

Guha, R. 1988. On some aspects of the historiography of colonial India. In *Selected Subaltern Studies*, eds R. Guha and G. Spivak. Oxford: Oxford University Press.

Hacking, I. 1986. Making up people. In *Reconstructing individualism: autonomy, individuality and the self in western thought*, ed. T. Heller. California: Stanford University Press.

—— 1982. Bio-power and the avalanche of printed numbers. *Humanities and Society* 5: 279–95.

Hall, G. 1904. *Adolescence: its psychology, and its relation to physiology, anthropology, sociology, sex crimes, religion and education*. 2 vols. New York: Appleton and Co.

Hall, S. and T. Jefferson (eds). 1976. *Resistance through rituals*. London: Hutchinson.

Hardaker, M. 1882. Science and the woman question. *Popular Science Monthly*, vol. 20, March.

Harman, G. 1977. *The nature of morality*. New York: Oxford University Press.

Harrison-Barbet, A. 2001. *Mastering philosophy*. 2nd edn. New York: Palgrave.

Hart, A. 1991. *Understanding the media: a practical guide*. London: Routledge.

Hart, D. 2000. Discipline in schools. In *Routledge international encyclopedia of women: global women's issues and knowledge, volume 1 ability – education: globalization*, eds C. Kramarae and D. Spender. London: Routledge, 394–96.

Hart, H. 1961. *The concept of law*. Oxford: Oxford University Press.

Hartcher, P. 2009. At last, we have a real leader – pity that it's not Rudd. *Sydney Morning Herald*. http://www.smh.com.au/opinion/politics/at-last-we-have-a-real-leader--pity-that-its-not-rudd-20091028-hl00.html.

Headley, B., D. Warren and M. Wooden. 2008. *The structure and distribution of household wealth in Australia: cohort differences and retirement issues*. Melbourne Institute of Applied Economic and Social Research.

Hebdige, D. 1988. *Hiding in the light*. London: Routledge.

—— 1979. *Subculture: the meaning of style*. London: Methuen.

Henkin, L. 1966. Truth and probability: the voice of America forum series. *Philosophy of Science* 4(1): <page no>.

Henry, M. 2000. It's all up to the individual … isn't it? Meritocratic practices. In *Practising education: social and cultural perspectives*, eds D. Meadmore, B. Burnett and G. Tait. Frenchs Forest, NSW: Prentice Hall-Sprint Print, 47–58.

Henry, M., J. Knight, R. Lingard and S. Taylor. 1988. *Understanding schooling: an introduction to the sociology of Australian education*. London: Routledge.

Herman, E. and N. Chomsky. 1994. *Manufacturing consent: the political economy of the mass media*. London: Vintage.

Heywood, C. 2001. *A history of childhood*. Cambridge, MA: Blackwell.

Hickling-Hudson, A. and R. Ahlquist. 2004. The challenge to deculturisation: discourses of ethnicity in the schooling of Indigenous children in Australia and the USA. In *Disrupting preconceptions: postcolonialism and education*, eds A. Hickling-Hudson, J. Matthews and A. Woods. Flaxton: Post Pressed, 39–56.

Hickling-Hudson, A., J. Matthews and A. Woods (eds). 2004. *Disrupting Preconceptions: postcolonialism and education*. Flaxton: Post Pressed.

Hine, J. and B. Williams. 2007. *Youth crime and offending, DfES Youth Strategy Review*. Youth Affairs Unit, De Montford University.

Hirst, P. and P. Wooley. 1985. *Social relations and human attributes*. London: Tavistock.

Ho, C. 2011. 'My school' and others: segregation and white flight. *Australian Review of Public Affairs*. May. http://www.australianreview.net/digest/2011/05/ho.html.

Hobbes, R. 2007. *Reading the media: media literacy in high school English*. New York: Teachers College Press.

Hobbes, T. 1994 (1651). *Leviathan*. Ed. E. Curley. Indianapolis: Hackett Publishing Co.

# References

Hobson, P. 2001. Aristotle. In *Fifty major thinkers on education: from Confucius to Dewey*, ed. J. Palmer. New York: Routledge, 14–19.

Hochschild, J. and V. Weaver. 2007. *Remaking America: democracy and public policy in an age of inequality*. New York: Russell Sage Foundation.

Hoffman, J. 2009. Can a boy wear a skirt to school? *New York Times*. 6 November (accessed 3 July 2011). http://www.nytimes.com/2009/11/08/fashion/08cross.html.

Holley, D. and M. Oliver. 2011. Negotiating the digital divide: narratives from the have and the have-nots. In *Digital difference: perspectives on online learning*, eds R. Land and S. Bayne. Rotterdam: Sense, 101–14.

Hollingshead, A. and F. Redlich. 1958. *Social class and mental illness: a community study*. New York: Wiley.

Holmes, J. 2010. Today Tonight: refugees from journalistic decency. *The Drum*. http://www.abc.net.au/news/2011–10–27/holmes-shaming-today-tonight/3603986.

Holyoake, G. 1902. *Sixty years of an agitator's life*. London: Unwin.

Hopkins, S. 2002. *Girl heroes: the new force in popular culture*. Annandale, NSW: Pluto Press.

Horne, D. 1968. *The lucky country: Australia in the sixties*. 2nd rev. edn. Harmondsworth: Penguin.

Horwich, P. 1990. *Truth*. Oxford: Oxford University Press.

Hospers, J. 1997. *An introduction to philosophical analysis*. 4th edn. London: Routledge.

Hume, D. 1969 (1739–40). *A treatise of human nature*. London: Penguin.

Hunter, I. 1993. Culture, bureaucracy and the history of popular education. In *Child and citizen: genealogies of schooling and subjectivity*, eds D. Meredyth and D. Tyler. Brisbane: Institute for Cultural Policy Studies, Griffith University, 11–34.

Hurley, P. and R. Eme. 2004. *ADHD and the criminal justice system: spinning out of control*. LLC: Booksurge.

Hutchinson, A. and P. Monahan. 1984. Law, politics, and the critical legal scholars: The unfolding drama of American legal thought. *Stanford Law Review* 36: 199–245.

Hyde, J., S. Lindberg, M. Linn, A. Ellis and C. Williams. 2008. Gender similarities characterize math performance. *Science* 321 (5888): 494–5.

Illich, I. 1973. *Deschooling society*. Harmondsworth: Penguin Education.

Jackson, J.P. and N.M. Weidman. 2004. *Race, racism, and science: social impact and interaction. Science and society*. Santa Barbara, CA: ABC-CLIO.

James, W. 1975 (1911). *The meaning of truth*. Cambridge, MA: Harvard University Press.

—— 1917. *Selected papers on philosophy*. London: Dent and Sons.

—— 1911. Remarks at the peace banquet. Lecture 12. In *Memories and studies*. New York: Longman Green and Co.

Jefferson, S. 1976. Cultural responses of the Teds. In *Resistance through rituals*, eds S. Hall and T. Jefferson. London: Hutchinson.

Johst, H. 1933. *Schlageter*. Munich: Langen-Muller.

Joyce, J. 1922. *Ulysses*. Paris: Shakespeare and Company.

Kant, I. 1998. *Groundwork of the metaphysics of morals*. Cambridge: Cambridge University Press.

—— 1979. *The conflict of the faculties*. Ed. M.J. Gregor. New York: Abaris Books.

Kay-Shuttleworth, J. 1973. The moral and physical condition of the working class of Manchester in 1832. In *Four periods of public education*. ed. J. Kay-Shuttleworth, Sussex: Harvester Press.

Keats, J. 1951. Ode on a Grecian urn. In *The complete poetry and selected prose of John Keats*, ed. H. Briggs. New York: Modern Library.

Kelly, P. 2006. Condition critical. *Australian*. 27 September. http://www.theaustralian.com.au/news/opinion/condition-critical/story-e6frg74x-1111112271968

Kemp, M. and J. Vaughn. 2009. Shame of our violent schools revealed. *Advertiser*. June 26. http://www.adelaidenow.com.au/news/shame-of-our-violent-schools-revealed/story-e6freo8c-1225748790099.

Kendall, F. 2006. *Understanding white privilege: creating pathways to authentic relationships across race. The teaching/learning social justice series*. New York: Routledge.

Kierkegaard, S. 2001. Philosophical fragments. In *The Kierkegaard reader*, eds J. Chamberlain and J. Ree. Malden, MA: Blackwell, 151–72.

Kirk, D. 1993. *The body, schooling and culture*. Geelong: Deakin University.

Kneavel, A. 2005. Popular culture in a business curriculum. In *Popular culture studies across the curriculum*, ed. R. Browne. Jefferson: McFarland and Co, 116–21.

Kostanski, L. 2009. Toponymic books and the representation of Indigenous identities. In *Aboriginal Placenames Old and New*, eds F. Hodges and H. Koch. Canberra: Aboriginal Studies Press, 175–86.

Kuhn, R. 2010. Newspapers. In *The media: an introduction*, eds D. Albertazzi and P. Cobley. London: Pearson.

Ladwig, J. 1996. *Academic distinctions: theory and methodology in the sociology of school knowledge*. New York: Routledge.

Lampert, J. 2005. The teaching that matters: merging our personal beliefs with our professional practice in the classroom. In *Introductory Indigenous studies in education*, eds J. Phillips and J. Lampert. Frenchs Forest, NSW: Pearson Education, 83–100.

Lane, D. 1990. *The impossible child*. Stoke-on-Trent: Trentham Books.

Leavis, F. and D. Thompson. 1977. *Culture and environment*. Westport: Greenwood Press.

Leavis, F.R. 1930. *Mass civilisation & minority culture*. Folcroft, PA: Folcroft Press.

Lee, D. and H. Newby. 1983. *The problem of sociology*. London: Hutchinson.

Lees, C. 1988. Youth tribes of Australia. *Bulletin*. 14 June, 7–13.

Lenta, P. 2004. The Tikoloshe and the reasonable man: transgressing South African legal fictions. *Law and Literature* 16 (3): 353–79.

Lockard, J. and M. Pegrum. 2006. From counterdiscourses to counterpedagogies: an introduction. In *Brave New Classrooms: democratic education and the internet*, eds J. Lockard and M. Pegrum. New York: Peter Lang, 1–10.

Locke, J. 1970. *Some thoughts concerning education*. Menston: Scolar Press.

Loeber, R., D. Pardini, D. Homish, A. Crawford, D. Farrington, M. Stouthamer-Loeber, J. Creemers, S. Koehler and R. Rosenfeld. 2005. The prediction of violence and homicide in young men. *Journal of Consulting and Clinical Psychology* 73 (6): 1074–88.

Louden, W., M. Rohl, C. Barratt Pugh, C. Brown, T. Cairney, J. Elderfield, H. House, M. Meiers, J. Rivalland and K. Rowe. 2005. *In teachers' hands: effective literacy teaching practices in the early years of schooling*. Canberra: Department of Education, Science and Training.

Luke, A. 2004. On postcolonial education and beyond: an afterword. In *Disrupting preconceptions: postcolonialism and education*, eds A. Hickling-Hudson, J. Matthews and A. Woods. Flaxton: Post Pressed, 251–4.

Lumby, C., H. Caple and K. Greenwood. 2010. *Towards a level playing field: sport and gender in Australian media*. Australian Sport Commission, University of New South Wales Journalism and Media Research Centre, and Media Monitors.

Lynch, M. 1998. *Truth in context: an essay on truth and objectivity*. Cambridge: Bradford.

Lyotard, J. 1984. *The postmodern condition: a report on knowledge*. Manchester: Manchester University Press.

Macdougall, N. 2008. Getting to know you: the journey from African refugee to African-Australian. Unpublished PhD Thesis, Murdoch University, Perth.

MacIntyre, A. 1998. The nature of virtues. In *Ethics: the big questions*, ed. J. Sterba. Oxford: Blackwell, 277–90.

Mansouri, F., L. Jenkins, L. Morgan and M. Taouk. 2009. *The impact of racism upon the health and wellbeing of young Australians*. Foundation for Young Australians: The Institute for Citizenship and Globalisation, Deakin University.

Mares, P. 2002. Reporting Australia's asylum seeker 'crisis'. In *Regional Seminar on Media and Ethnic Conflicts*. Makati City, Philippines, 22–4 May.

Marjoribanks, K. 2005. Family background, adolescents' educational aspirations, and Australian young adults' educational attainment. *International Education Journal* 6 (1): 104–12.

Marquez, G. G. 1970. *One hundred years of solitude*. New York: Harper Collins.

Martino, W. 2000. The boys at the back: challenging masculinities and homophobia in the English classroom. *English in Australia* 127–128: 35–50.

Mathews, B., K. Walsh, D. Butler and A. Farrell. 2006. Mandatory reporting by Australian teachers of suspected child abuse and neglect; legislative requirements and questions for future direction. *Australian and New Zealand Journal of Law and Education* 11(2): 7–22.

Mathews, B., K. Walsh, M. Rassafiani, D. Butler and A. Farrell. 2009. Teacher reporting suspected child sexual abuse: results of a three-state study. *University of New South Wales Law Review* 32(3): 772–813.

Mauss, M. 1985. A category of human mind: the notion of the person; the notion of the self. In *The category of person: anthropology, philosophy, history*, eds M. Carrithers, S. Collins and S. Lukes. Cambridge: Cambridge University Press, 4–12.

—— 1973. Techniques of the body. *Economy and Society* 2(1): 70–87.

McArthur, G. and S. McMahon. 2011. It's Official! Boys lose in the battle of the sexes at school. *Herald Sun*. April 30. http://www.heraldsun.com.au/news/more-news/its-official-b oys-lose-in-battle-of-the-sexes-at-school/story-fn7x8me2–1226047198903.

McCabe, J., E. Fairchild, L. Grauerholtz, B. Pescosolido and D. Tope. 2011. Gender in twentieth-century children's books: patterns of disparity in titles and central characters. *Gender and Society* 25(2): 197–226.

McCallum, D. 1993. Problem children and familial relations. In *Child and citizen: genealogies of schooling and subjectivity*, eds D. Meredyth and D. Tyler. Griffith University: Institute for Cultural Policy Studies, 129–52.

McIntosh, P. 1997. White privilege and male privilege: a personal account of coming to see correspondences through work in women's studies. In *Critical white studies: looking behind the mirror*, eds R. Delgado and J. Stefancic. Philadelphia: Temple University Press, 291–9.

McKenzie, P., J. Kos, M. Walker and J. Hong. 2008. *Staff in Australia's schools 2007*. Department of Education, Employment and Workplace Relations.

McLeod, F. 2008. Glass ceiling still firmly in place. *Australian*. June 27. http://www. theaustralian.com.au/business/legal-affairs/glass-ceiling-still-firmly-in-place/ story-e6frg986–1111116745159.

McLeod, J. 2000. *Beginning postcolonialism*. Manchester: Manchester University Press.

McLuhan, M. and Q. Fiore. 1967. *War and peace in the global village*. New York: Bantam.

McRobbie, A. 1982. Jackie: an ideology of adolescent femininity. In *Popular culture: past and present*, eds B. Waites, T. Bennet and G. Martin. London: Croom Helm and Open University Press, 263–83.

Meadmore, D. 2004. The rise and rise of testing: how does this shape identity? In *New questions for contemporary teachers: taking a socio-cultural approach to education*, eds B. Burnett, D. Meadmore and G. Tait. Frenchs Forest, NSW: Pearson Education, 25–38.

—— 1998. Re-thinking the ADD/ADHD epidemic. *Perspectives on Educational Leadership* 8(4): 1–2.

*Media Watch*. 2009. http://www.abc.net.au/mediawatch/transcripts/s2724620.htm.

Meyer, A. 2007. The moral rhetoric of childhood. *Childhood* 14(1): 85–104.

Mill, J. S. 1957 (1861). *Utilitarianism*. New York: Bobbs-Merrill.

Miller, K. 2010. The walk that drives men wild. *Cosmopolitan*, October.

Miller, P. and N. Rose. 1990. Governing economic life. *Economy and Society* 19(1): 1–31.

Miller, T. 2008. 'Don't know much about history': a critical examination of moral panics over student ignorance. In *Moral panics over contemporary children and youth*, ed. C. Krinsky. Aldershot: Ashgate, 167–82.

Milward. 2003. The 'grey digital divide': perception, exclusion and barriers of access to the internet for older people. *First Monday* 8(7). http://firstmonday.org/htbin/cgiwrap/bin/ojs/index.php/fm/rt/printerFriendly/1066/986.

Modarres, A. 2011. Beyond the digital divide. *National Civic Review* 100(3): 4–7.

Montagu, A. 1974. *Man's most dangerous myth: the fallacy of race*. 5th, rev. and enl. edn. New York: Oxford University Press.

Mosedale, S. 1978. Science corrupted: Victorian biologists consider 'the woman question'. *Journal of the History of Biology* 11(1): 1–55.

National Assessment Program: Literacy and Numeracy (NAPLAN). 2008. Achievement in reading, writing, language conventions and numeracy. http://www.nap.edu.au/_Documents/National%20Report/2ndStageNationalReport_18Dec_v2.pdf

Neill, A. 1962. *Summerhill: a radical approach to education*. London: Gollancz.

New London Group. 1996. A pedagogy of multiliteracies: designing social futures. *Harvard Educational Review* 66(1): 60–92.

Nicholson, L. 1994. Interpreting gender. *Signs* 20: 79–105.

Nietzsche, F. 1997 (1878). *Human, all too human*. Stanford: Stanford University Press.

—— 1967 (1911). *The will to power*. New York: Random House.

—— 1954 (1873). On truth and lies in an extra-moral sense. In *The portable Nietzsche*, ed. W. Kaufmann. New York: Viking.

NILS Report. 2005. *National Indigenous languages report*. Australian Institute of Aboriginal and Torres Strait Islander Studies.

O'Brien, P. and N. Osbaldiston. 2010. ePortfolios and Preservice Teachers: governing at a distance through non-human actors. In *Interaction in communication technologies and virtual learning environments: human factors*, ed. A. Ragusa. New York: Information Science References, 170–92.

O'Farrell, C. 2005. *Michel Foucault*. London: Sage.

—— 1999. Postmodernism for the uninitiated. In *Understanding education: contexts and agendas for the new millennium*, eds D. Meadmore, B. Burnett and P. O'Brien. Sydney: Prentice Hall, 11–17.

Olen, J. 1983. *Persons and their world: an introduction to philosophy*. New York: McGraw-Hill.

Ozmon, H. and S. Craver. 2009. *Philosophical foundations of education*. 9th edn. Columbus: Pearson.

Parkes, R. 2007. Reading history curriculum as postcolonial text: toward a curricular response to the history wars in Australia and beyond. *Curriculum Inquiry* 37(4): 383–400.

Parsons, T. 1951. *The social system*. Glencoe: The Free Press.

Partington, G. 2001. When two worlds meet: ethnicity and education in Australia. In *Sociology of education: possibilities and practices*, ed. J. Allen. Melbourne: Social Science Press, 183–210.

Patterson, A. 2008. Teaching literature in Australia: examining and reviewing senior English. *Changing English: Studies in Culture and Education* 15(3): 311–22.

Pearson, J. 1983. *Hooligan: a history of respectable fears*. London: Macmillan.

Pease, A. and B. Pease. 1999. *Why men don't listen and women can't read maps*. Buderim: Pease Training International.

Peters, R.S. 1964. *Education as initiation: an inaugural lecture delivered at the University of London Institute of Education*, 9 December, 1963. London: Published for the University of London Institute of Education by Evans Bros.

Phillips, J. 2005. Indigenous knowledge: making space in the Australian centre. In *Introductory Indigenous studies in education*, eds J. Phillips and J. Lampert. Frenchs Forest, NSW: Pearson Education, 11–26.

Plato. 1989. Plato's Apology. In *Bryn Mawr Greek commentaries*, ed. G. Rose. Bryn Mawr, PA: Thomas Library, Bryn Mawr College.

—— 1974. *The republic*. Harmondsworth: Penguin.

—— 1956. *Protagorus and Meno*. Harmondsworth: Penguin.

Poddar, P. 1997. Buttered scones at 4 pm on Sundays: configuring English in colonial India. In *Teaching post-colonialism and post-colonial literatures*, eds A. Collett, L. Jensen and A. Rutherford. Aarhus: Aarhus University Press, 61–76.

Poe, E. A. 1839. The fall of the house of Usher. *Burton's Gentleman's Magazine*. September.

Poplin, D. 1978. *Social problems*. Glenview: Scott, Foresman and Co.

Popper, K. 1963. *Conjectures and refutations: the growth of scientific knowledge*. London: Routledge and Kegan Paul.

—— 1959. *The logic of scientific discovery*. London: Hutchinson.

Postman, N. 1994. *The disappearance of childhood*. 2nd edn. London: WH Allen.

Prensky, M. 2011. Digital wisdom and homo sapiens digital. In *Deconstructing digital natives*, ed. M. Thomas. New York: Routledge, 15–29.

—— 2001. Digital natives/digital immigrants. *On the Horizon* 9(5): 1–6.

Preston, B. 2007. *The social make-up of schools: family income, religion, indigenous status, and family type in government, Catholic, and other non-government schools*. Melbourne: Australian Education Union.

Proust, M. 1927. *Remembrance of things past*. Paris: Grasset and Gallimard.

Prout, A. 2005. *The future of childhood: towards the interdisciplinary study of children*. London: RoutledgeFalmer.

Putnam, H. 1981. *Reason, truth and history*. Cambridge: Cambridge University Press.

Rammert, W. 1999. Relations that constitute technology and media that make a difference: towards a social pragmatic theory of technicization. *Techne: Journal of the Society for Philosophy and Technology* 4(3). http://scholar.lib.vt.edu/ejournals/SPT/v4_n3pdf/RAMMERT.PDF.

Ramsay, F. 1927. Fact and propositions. *Proceedings of the Aristotelian Society* 7 (Supplementary): 153–70.

Refugee Council of Australia. 2012. Myths about refugees and asylum seekers. http://www.refugeecouncil.org.au/resources/myths.php – queue.

—— 2009. Asking the media to correct mistakes. http://www.refugeecouncil.org.au/current/mediablunders.html.

Reich, J. 2009. Avoidant personality disorder and its relationship to social phobia. *Current Psychiatry Reports* 11(1): 89–93.

Reiger, K. 1985. *The disenchantment of the home: modernizing the Australian family, 1880–1940*. Melbourne: Oxford University Press.

Reissman, L. 1973. Social stratification. In *Sociology: an introduction*, 2nd edn, ed. N. Smelser. New York: Wiley, 127–90.

Roberts, I. 2007. Adolescence. In *Childhood and youth studies*, ed. P. Zwozdiak-Myers. Exeter: Learningmatters, 85–95.

Roberts, L. 2010. Boys failed by education system says Eton headmaster. *Telegraph*. http://www.telegraph.co.uk/education/educationnews/7026774/Boys-failed-by-education-system-says-Eton-headmaster.html.

Robinson, K. 1992. Classroom discipline: power, resistance and gender. A look at teacher perspectives. *Gender and Education* 4(3): 273–87.

Rose, N. 1993. Government, authority and expertise in advanced liberalism. *Economy and Society* 22(3): 283–99.

—— 1990. *Governing the soul: the shaping of the private self*. London: Routledge.

—— 1988. Calculable minds and manageable individuals. *History of the Human Sciences* 1(2): 179–99.

—— 1985. *The psychological complex: psychology, politics and society in England 1869–1939*. London: Routledge and Kegan Paul.

Rose, N. and P. Miller. 1992. Political power beyond the state; problematics of government. *British Journal of Sociology* 43(2): 173–205.

Rosenberg, P. 2004. Colorblindness in teacher education. In *Off white: readings on power, privilege, and resistance*, eds M. Fine, L. Weis, L. Powell Pruit and A. Burns. New York: Routledge, x, 453.

Ross, W. 1930. *The right and the good*. Oxford: Clarendon Press.

Rousseau, J. 1956 (1762). *The Emile of Jean Jacques Rousseau*. Trans. W. Boyd. New York: Heinnemann.

Rushdie, S. 1981. *Midnight's children*. London: Vintage.

Russell, B. 1983 (1912). *The problems of philosophy*. Oxford: Oxford University Press.

Ryan, K. and J. Cooper. 2010. *Those who can, teach*. Boston: Wadsworth.

Sadker, D. 2002. An educator's primer on the gender wars. *Phi Delta Kappan* 84(3): 235–41.

—— 2000. Gender equity: still knocking at the classroom door. *Equity and Excellence in Education* 56(7): 22–7.

Said, E. 1995. *Orientalism*. 2nd ed. London: Penguin.

—— 1979. *Orientalism*. 1st Vintage Books ed. New York: Vintage Books.

Samaras, K. 2005. Indigenous Australians and the 'digital divide'. *Libri* 55: 84–95.

Sawyer, W. 2006. Just add 'progressivism' and stir: how we cook up literacy crises in Australia. *Only connect: English teaching, schooling and community*. Adelaide: Wakefield Press, 236–262.

Schiller, H. 1979. Trans-national media and national development. In *National sovereignty and international communication*, eds K. Nordenstreng and H. Schiller. Norwood: Ablex, 21–32.

Schirato, T., A. Buettner, T. Jutel and G. Stahl. 2010. *Understanding media studies*. Melbourne: Oxford University Press.

*Seattle Times*. 1962. Seattle World's Fair souvenir edition: space age frontiers. http://seattletimes.nwsource.com/html/worldsfairsouveniredition/2017454924_all_152_pages_from_souvenir_section_in_pdfs.html.

Sechrist, F. 1920. *Education and the general welfare: a textbook of school law, hygiene and management*. Michigan: Macmillan.

Share, J. 2002. *Media literacy is elementary: teaching youth to critically read and create media*. New York: Peter Lang.

Siegler, M. 2010. Eric Schmidt: every 2 days we create as much information as we did up to 2003. *Telecrunch*. http://telecrunch.com/2010/08/04/schmidt-data.

Slattery, L. 2005. Fading theory has no place in schools. *Weekend Australian*. 23–24 July, 10.

Slee, R. 2011. *The irregular school: exclusion, schooling, and inclusive education*. Foundations and futures of education. London and New York: Routledge.

Smart, J. 1973. Outline of a system of utilitarian ethics. In *Utilitarianism: for and against*, eds J. Smart and B. Williams. Cambridge: Cambridge University Press.

Smith, A. 1776. *Wealth of Nations*. London: Strahan and Cadell.

Smith, A. 2010. *Mobile Access 2010*. Washington, DC: Pew Research Centre.

Smith, B. 1989. *Discipline: from the classroom to the community, Occasional Paper*. Brisbane: Griffith University.

Snyder, I. 2008. *The literacy wars: why teaching children to read and write is a battleground in Australia*. Sydney: Allen & Unwin.

Sosin, D. and M. Sosin. 1996. *Attention deficit disorder*. Melbourne: Hawker Brownlow.

Spender, D. 1982. *Invisible women: the schooling scandal*. London: Writers and Readers Publishing Cooperative Society Ltd.

Squires, P. and D. Stephen. 2005. *Rougher justice: anti-social behaviour and young people*. Cullompton: Willan Publishing.

Stoker, B. 1897. *Dracula*. London: Archibald Constable and Co.

Storey, J. 2006. *Cultural theory and popular culture: an introduction*. 4th edn. Harlow: Pearson.

—— 2003. *Inventing popular culture*. Oxford: Blackwell.

Stow, D. 1850. *The training system of education*. London: Longman, Green, Longman and Roberts.

Sutherland, G. 1984. *Ability, merit and measurement: mental testing and English education 1880–1940*. Oxford: Oxford University Press.

*Sydney Morning Herald*. 2009. Rudd slams Tuckey's 'terrorist' asylum seeker comments. 22 October. http://www.smh.com.au/national/rudd-slams-tuckeys-terrorist-asylum-seeker-comments-20091022-hamt.html.

Symes, C. and N. Preston. 1997. *Schools and Classrooms: a cultural studies analysis of education*. Melbourne: Longman-Cheshire.

Synott, J. and C. Symes. 1995. The genealogy of the school: an iconography of badges and mottoes. *British Journal of Sociology of Education* 16(2): 139–52.

Szasz, T. 1973. *The manufacture of madness: a comparative study of the inquisition and the mental health movement*. London: Grenada.

—— 1961. *The myth of mental illness: foundations of a theory of personal conduct*. New York: Harper Row.

Tait, G. 2010. *Philosophy, behaviour disorders, and the school*. Rotterdam: Sense.

—— 2006. Setting limits to teacher responsibility. *ACHPER Matters* 1: 3–6.

—— 2003. The seven things all men love in bed: young women's magazines and the governance of femininity. In *Youth cultures: texts, images and identities*, eds K. Mallan and S. PearceWestport, Conn: Praeger Publishers, 81–92..

—— 1999. Rethinking youth cultures: the case of the 'Gothics'. *Social Alternatives* 18(2): 15–21.

—— 1993. 'Anorexia nervosa': asceticism, differentiation, government. *Australian and New Zealand Journal of Sociology* 29(2): 194–208.

Tait, G., S. Davey Chesters, C. O'Farrell, J. Brownlee, R Spooner-Lane and E. Curtis. 2012. Are there any right or wrong answers in teaching philosophy?: Ethics, epistemology, and the Philosophy in Schools program. *Teaching Philosophy* 35(3).

Tannsjo, T. 2002. *Understanding ethics: an introduction to moral theory*. Edinburgh: Edinburgh University Press.

Taylor, S. 2004. Gender equity and education: what are the issues now? In *New questions for contemporary teachers: taking a socio-cultural approach to education*, eds B. Burnett, D. Meadmore and G. Tait. Frenchs Forest, NSW: Pearson Education, 87–100.

*Today Tonight*. 2011. Welcome to Australia. Channel Seven. 10 October.

Tolstoy, L. 1886. *War and peace*. New York: William S. Gottsberger.

Tomlinson, S. 1982. *A sociology of special education*. London: Routledge and Kegan Paul.

Topping, K. and S. Maloney. 2005. *The RoutledgeFalmer reader in inclusive education*. Oxford: RoutledgeFalmer.

Topping, K. and S. Trickey. 2007. Collaborative philosophical inquiry for school children: cognitive gains at 2-year follow-up. *British Journal of Educational Psychology* 77: 787–96.

Turner, S., D. Beidel and R. Townsley. 1992. Social Phobia: a comparison of specific and generalised subtypes and avoidant personality disorder. *Journal of Abnormal Psychology* 102: 326–31.

Tyler, D. 1993. Making better children. In *Child and citizen: genealogies of schooling and subjectivity*, eds D. Meredyth and D. Tyler. Brisbane: Institute for Cultural Policy Studies, Griffith University, 35–60.

Tyler, E. 1871. *Primitive culture*. London: J Murray.

Uditsky, B. 1993. From integration to inclusion: the Canadian experience. In *Is there a desk with my name on it?: the politics of integration*, ed. R. Slee. London: Falmer Press, ix, 268.

Underwood, P. (Chief Justice). 2006. 'It's safe to go out in the playground now'. Speech delivered at the ANZELA Conference, Hobart, 2 October.

United Nations (UN). International Telecommunication Union. 2005. World Summit on the Information Society. http://www.itu.int/wsis/tunis/newsroom/stats/.

—— 1965. International Convention on the Elimination of all Forms of Racial Discrimination.

US Census Bureau. 2010. *Poverty: 2008 and 2009*. Ed. A. Bishaw and S. Macartney, *American Community Survey Briefs*.

Valencia, R. 1997. *The evolution of deficit thinking educational thought and practice*. London: Falmer.

Vick, M. 2001. More than just classroom teaching: teachers and teachers work in a changing society. In *Sociology of education: possibilities and practices*, ed. J. Allen. Katoomba, NSW: Social Science Press, 65–87.

Vickers, M. 2010. Gender. In *Education, change and society*, eds R. Connell, C. Campbell, M. Vickers, A. Welch, F. Dennis, N. Bagnall and D. Hayes. Melbourne: Oxford University Press, 205–34.

Vickers, M. and F. McCarthy. 2011. Crossing borders: into the future. In *Crossing borders: African refugees, teachers, and schools*, eds T. Ferfolja, M. Vickers, F. McCarthy, L. Naidoo and E. Brace. Melbourne: Common Ground Publishing, 105–14.

Viswanathan, G. 1989. *The masks of conquest: literary study and British rules in India*. London: Faber and Faber.

Wallace, J., S. Goodkind, C. Wallace and J. Bachman. 2008. Racial, ethnic, and gender differences in school discipline among US high school students: 1991–2005. *Negro Educational Review* 59(1–2): 47–62.

Weaver, J.A. 2009. *Popular culture*. New York: Peter Lang.

Weaver, J.A., K. Anijar and T. Daspit (eds). 2004. *Science fiction curriculum, cyborg teachers, and youth cultures*. New York: Peter Lang.

Weeks, J. 1981. *Sex, politics, and society: the regulation of sexuality since 1880*. London: Longman.

Weist, M., O. Acosta, N. Tashman, L. Nabom and K. Albus. 1999. Changing paradigms in child and adolescent psychiatry: towards expanded school mental health. *American Society for Adolescent Psychiatry* 24: 119–31.

Welch, A. 2010. Cultural difference and identity. In *Education, change and society* 2nd edn, eds. R. Connell, C. Campbell, M. Vickers, A. Welch, F. Dennis, N. Bagnall and D. Hayes. Melbourne: Oxford University Press, 155–87.

West-Newman, C. 2001. Reading hate speech from the bottom in Aotearoa. *Waikato Law Review* 9: 231–64.

White, C. and T. Walker. 2008. *Tooning in: essays on popular culture and education*. Plymouth: Rowman and Littlefield.

Wilde, O. 1891. *The picture of Dorian Gray*. London: Ward, Lock.

Williams, B. 1985. *Ethics and the limits of philosophy*. London: Fontana.

—— 1973. A critique of utilitarianism. In *Utilitarianism: for and against*, eds J. Smart and B. Williams Cambridge: Cambridge University Press, 82–118..

—— 1972. *Morality: an introduction*. New York: Harper and Row.

Williams, R. 1981. *Culture*. London: Fontana.

Winch, C. and J. Gingell. 2008. *Philosophy of education: the key concepts*. 2nd edn. London: Routledge.

Wittgenstein, L. 1952. *Philosophical investigations*, eds. G. Anscombe and R. Rhees. Oxford: Blackwell.

Wolf, N. 1991. *The beauty myth: how images of beauty are used against women*. New York: Morrow.

Wollstonecraft, M. 1967 (1792). *A vindication of the rights of woman: with strictures on political and moral subjects*. Norton library; N373. New York: Norton.

Wright, P. and A. Treacher. 1982. *The problem of medical knowledge: examining the social construction of medicine*. Edinburgh: Edinburgh University Press

Young, M. 1958. *The rise of the meritocracy: 1879–2033: an essay on education and equality*. London: Penguin.

## Cases

*Kemp v Minister for Education*. [1991] EOC 92–340.
*L v Minister for Education*. [1996] QADT 2.
*St Anthony's Primary School v Hadba* [2005] HCA 31.

## Statutes

*Age Discrimination Act 2004* (Cth)
*Anti-Discrimination Act 1977* (NSW)
*Anti-Discrimination Act 1991* (Qld)
*Disability Discrimination Act 1992* (Cth)
*Equal Opportunity Act 1995* (Vic.)
*Racial Discrimination Act 1975* (Cth)
*Sex Discrimination Act 1984* (Cth)

# Index